ISBN 978-1-330-60844-9
PIBN 10081879

1 MONTH OF
FREE
READING

at

www.ForgottenBooks.com

By purchasing this book you are eligible for one month membership to ForgottenBooks.com, giving you unlimited access to our entire collection of over 700,000 titles via our web site and mobile apps.

To claim your free month visit:

www.forgottenbooks.com/free81879

Similar Books Are Available from
www.forgottenbooks.com

A GRAMMAR OF
THE OLD TESTAMENT IN GREEK

CAMBRIDGE UNIVERSITY PRESS
London: FETTER LANE, E.C.
C. F. CLAY, Manager

Edinburgh: 100, PRINCES STREET
Berlin: A. ASHER AND CO.
Leipzig: F. A. BROCKHAUS
New York: G. P. PUTNAM'S SONS
Bombay and Calcutta: MACMILLAN AND CO., Ltd.

A GRAMMAR OF
THE OLD TESTAMENT
IN GREEK

ACCORDING TO THE SEPTUAGINT

BY

HENRY St JOHN THACKERAY, M.A.
SOMETIME SCHOLAR OF KING'S COLLEGE, CAMBRIDGE

VOL. I

INTRODUCTION, ORTHOGRAPHY AND ACCIDENCE

Cambridge :

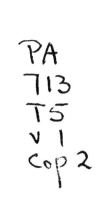
𝕮𝖆𝖒𝖇𝖗𝖎𝖉𝖌𝖊:

PRINTED BY JOHN CLAY M.A.

AT THE UNIVERSITY PRESS.

TO MY WIFE

Γυναῖκα ἀνδρείαν τίς εὑρήσει;
τιμιωτέρα δέ ἐστιν λίθων πολυτελῶν ἡ τοιαύτη.

PREFACE

THE Grammar, of which the first portion is here published, has during the last eight years been the occupation of the very limited leisure of a civil servant. It owes its origin to the suggestion of Dr Swete, who has throughout its preparation been the writer's kindly and encouraging ἐργοδιώκτης. It is due to his good offices that this portion now appears in the form of a separate volume, and it is needless to add that it is his edition of the text, together with the Concordance of the late Dr Redpath, which alone has rendered such a work possible.

It may be asked : What need is there for the work ? Why write a Grammar of a translation, in parts a servile translation, into a Greek which is far removed from the Attic standard, of an original which was often imperfectly understood ? A sufficient answer might be that the work forms part of a larger whole, the Grammar of Hellenistic Greek, the claims of which, as bridging the gulf between the ancient and the modern tongue, upon the attention of φιλέλληνες and philologists have in recent years begun to receive their due recognition from a growing company of scholars. The Septuagint, in view both of the period which it covers and the variety of its styles, ranging from the non-literary vernacular to the artificial Atticistic, affords the most promising ground for the investigation of the peculiarities of the Hellenistic or 'common' language. "La Septante est le grand monument de la Κοινή," says Psichari. But the Septuagint has, moreover, special claims of its own. Though of less paramount importance than the New Testament, the fact that it was the only form in which the older Scriptures were known to many generations of Jews and Christians and the deep influence which it exercised upon New Testament and Patristic writers justify a separate treatment of its language. Again, the fact that it is in the main a translation gives it a special character and raises the difficult question of the extent of Semitic influence upon the written and spoken Greek of a bilingual people.

The period covered by the books of the Septuagint was mentioned. This may conveniently be divided into three parts. (1) There is every reason to accept the very early tradition that the Greek Pentateuch, to which, it would seem, at least a partial translation of Joshua was soon appended, originated in the third century B.C. We are, then, in the Hexateuch taken back to the dawn of the Κοινή, to a period when certain forms and usages were in existence which had already become obsolete in New Testament times. Some of these are moribund survivals from classical Greek, others are experiments of the new language on their trial. (2) As to the remaining books, one result which clearly emerges is that the order in which they were translated was, roughly speaking, that of the Hebrew Canon. We may conjecture that the Prophets made their appearance in

a Greek dress in the second century B.C., Isaiah near
the beginning of it, the group consisting of Jeremiah,
Ezekiel and the Twelve (or large portions of this group)
nearer the close : the close of the century also probably
saw the appearance of 1 Kingdoms and portions of
2 and 3 Kingdoms. (3) The versions of most of the
"Writings." (Psalms perhaps excluded) and the composition of most of the apocryphal books seem, notwithstanding the oft-quoted statement in the Prologue
of Ben Sira, to belong to a period not earlier than
the first century B.C., while books like the Greek
Ecclesiastes and Theodotion's Daniel carry us as far
down as the second century of our era. To the third
period (at least if we may judge from the character of
the texts which have come down to us) we must also
probably assign the translations of some of the later
historical books, which the Hebrew Canon classed with
the Prophets, viz. the bulk of Judges and large portions
of 2—4 Kingdoms. Broadly speaking, we may say
that the Greek of the first period attains the higher
level exhibited by the papyri of the early Ptolemaic
age (the *Petrie* and *Hibeh* collections), while in that
of the second period we may see a reflection of the
more degenerate' style of the papyri of the end of the
second century B.C. (e.g. the *Tebtunis* collection). In
the third period two opposite influences are at work :
(i) the growing reverence for the letter of Scripture,
tending to the production of pedantically literal versions,
(ii) the influence of the Atticistic school, strongest, of
course, in free writings like 4 Maccabees, but which

I can claim no special equipment for my task other than a persistent interest in the subject, and am conscious of many imperfections in its execution. In arrange ment and treatment I have in general followed the guidance of the late Professor Blass in his *Grammar of New Testament Greek*, with which special associations have familiarized me. One subject there treated at length is missing in the present work. " "Word-formation," an outlying province of grammar, is, for the LXX, so vast a subject that any approach to an adequate treatment of it would have immoderately swelled this book, which already exceeds the prescribed limits. Possibly an opportunity may arise in the future for making good the omission. It may be thought that too much space has been allotted to Orthography and Accidence. I may plead in excuse that it is in these depart- ments that the papyri are specially helpful and afford some clear criteria as to dates, and it is hoped that the evidence here collected may be of service to the textual critic in the reconstruction of the original text of the LXX. Even the long series of references often have their message in showing the distribution of a usage, φωνέντα συνετοισιν.

A complete and independent Grammar of the LXX has until quite recently been wanting, and the student had to be content with such casual assistance as was given in the New Testament Grammars. The useful treatise of Thiersch, now nearly seventy years old, was

limited to the Pentateuch. In recent years the "Septua-
gintarian" (if the word may be allowed) has had the
advantage of a valuable chapter on the language in
Dr Swete's *Introduction*, while two Oxford scholars have
produced a very handy little volume of selections preceded by a concise but partial Grammar[1]. My ambition
to produce the first complete Grammar has, through
unavoidable delays, been frustrated, and Germany has
led the way. I have thought it best to work quite
independently of Dr Helbing's book[2], the first part of
which appeared just over a year ago: indeed most of
my book was written before the publication of the
German work. I append a list, not exhaustive, of works
which have been consulted. Psichari's admirable essay[3]
only came into my hands when the pages had been set
up. My slight incursions into modern Greek, with
which I hope to become more closely acquainted, have
convinced me of the truth of his statement that a
knowledge of the living language is indispensable for a
proper understanding of the κοινή διάλεκτος as represented by the LXX.

The pleasant duty remains of acknowledging assistance of a more personal and direct kind than that
obtainable from books. Of my indebtedness to Dr Swete,
the "onlie begetter" of this volume, I have already
spoken. I owe more than I can say to the counsel and
encouragement of Dr J. H. Moulton, Greenwood

[1] *Selections from the Septuagint*, F. C. Conybeare and St George Stock,
Ginn and Co., Boston, 1905.

[2] *Grammatik der Septuaginta, Laut- und Wortlehre*, R. Helbing,
Göttingen, 1907.

[3] *Essai sur le Grec de la Septante*, Paris, 1908.

Professor of Hellenistic Greek and Indo-European Philology in the Victoria University of Manchester. He has been good enough, amid his manifold duties, to read through the whole work in MS, and his generous and never-failing help has enriched its pages and removed many errors and imperfections. Through the *Prolegomena* to his brilliant Grammar of *New Testament Greek* and through private communications he has introduced me to much of the extensive literature bearing on the subject and held up a model of how a Grammar should be written. My thanks are also due to another Fellow of my own College, the Rev. A. E. Brooke, co-editor of the larger Cambridge Septuagint, who has kindly read the bulk of the proofs and offered useful suggestions. In the laborious work of verifying references much help has been rendered by Mr W. R. Taylor, sometime Scholar of St Catharine's College, Cambridge: he has also prepared the Index of quotations. Assistance of a kindred nature has been given by my sister, Mrs Loring, and by my wife. In conclusion, I must express my thanks to the Syndics of the University Press for their indulgence in consenting to the publication of this portion of the work as a separate volume and to all the officers, readers and workmen of the Press for their constant vigilance and well-known accuracy.

H. St J. T.

18 Royal Avenue, Chelsea,
31 January 1909.

CONTENTS

INTRODUCTION.

ORTHOGRAPHY AND PHONETICS.

ACCIDENCE.

PRINCIPAL AUTHORITIES QUOTED WITH ABBREVIATIONS

Anz H., *Subsidia ad cognoscendum Graecorum sermonem vulgarem e Pentateuchi versione Alexandrina repetita* (Dissert. Phil. Halenses vol. 12), 1894.

Archiv = Archiv für Papyrusforschung, ed. U. Wilcken, Leipzig, 1901 etc.

Aristeas (pseudo-), Letter of, in the Appendix to Swete's *Introduction to the Old Testament in Greek*, or in the edition of P. Wendland, Leipzig, 1900 : the §§ are those of Wendland which appear in Swete, edition 2.

Blass N.T. = Friedrich Blass, *Grammar of New Testament Greek*, English translation, ed. 2, 1905.

Brooke A. E. and McLean N., *The Old Testament in Greek*, vol. 1 The Octateuch, part 1 Genesis, Cambridge, 1906.

BDB = Brown, Driver and Briggs, *Hebrew and English Lexicon of the Old Testament*, Oxford, 1906.

CR = Classical Review.

Crönert = W. Crönert, *Memoria Graeca Herculanensis, cum titulorum Aegypti papyrorum codicum denique testimoniis* etc., Leipzig, 1903.

Deissmann *BS* = G. A. Deissmann, *Bible Studies*, Engl. trans. Edinburgh, 1901.

Dieterich K., *Untersuchungen zur Geschichte der griechischen Sprache (Byzantinisches Archiv*, Heft 1), Leipzig, 1898.

Dindorf W., *Poetae Scenici Graeci*, ed. 7, London, 1881.

Driver S. R., *A treatise on the use of the tenses in Hebrew*, ed. 3, Oxford, 1892 : *Notes on the Hebrew text of the Books of Samuel*, Oxford, 1890 : *The book of Daniel* in the *Cambridge Bible*, Cambridge, 1900.

Enc. Bibl. = *Encyclopaedia Biblica*, ed. Cheyne and Black, London, 1899 etc.

Field F., *Origenis Hexaplorum quae supersunt*, Oxford, 1875.

Gregory *Prol.* = *Novum Testamentum Graece*, C. Tischendorf, vol. 3 *Prolegomena*, scripsit C. R. Gregory, Leipzig, 1894.

Hastings *BD* = *Dictionary of the Bible*, ed. J. Hastings, Edinburgh, 1898 etc.

Hatch E. and Redpath H. A., *A Concordance to the Septuagint and the other Greek Versions of the O.T.*, Oxford, 1897–1906.

Hatch E., *Essays in Biblical Greek*, Oxford, 1889.

Hatzidakis G. N., *Einleitung in die neugriechische Grammatik*, Leipzig, 1892.

Herodiani Technici Reliquiae, ed. A. Lentz, Leipzig, 1867.

Herwerden H. van, *Lexicon Graecum suppletorium et dialecticum*, Leyden, 1902.

Indog. Forsch. = *Indogermanische Forschungen*.

Jannaris A. N., *An historical Greek Grammar chiefly of the Attic dialect as written and spoken from classical antiquity down to the present time*, London, 1897.

J. T. S. = *Journal of Theological Studies*, (London and) Oxford.

Kälker F., *Quaestiones de elocutione Polybiana* etc., *Separat-abdruck aus "Leipziger Studien zur classischen Philologie,"* Leipzig, N.D.

Kautzsch E., *Die Apokryphen und Pseudepigraphen des Alten Testaments übersetzt und herausgegeben*, Tübingen, 1900.

Kennedy H. A. A., *Sources of New Testament Greek or the influence of the Septuagint on the vocabulary of the New Testament*, Edinburgh, 1895.

Kühner-Blass or K.-Bl. = *Ausführliche Grammatik der griechischen Sprache* von R. Kühner, erster Teil, Elementar- und Formenlehre, dritte Auflage in zwei Bänden in neuer Bearbeitung, besorgt von F. Blass, Hannover, 1890–2.

Lagarde P. de, *Librorum Veteris Testamenti Canonicorum Pars prior Graece* (a reconstruction of the "Lucianic text" of the historical books of the LXX), Göttingen, 1883.

LS = Liddell and Scott, *A Greek-English Lexicon*, ed. 7, Oxford, 1883.

Mayser E., *Grammatik der griechischen Papyri aus der Ptolemäer-zeit* etc., *Laut- und Wortlehre*, Leipzig, 1906.

McNeile A. H., *An Introduction to Ecclesiastes with Notes and Appendices*, Cambridge, 1904.

Meisterhans = *Grammatik der Attischen Inschriften* von K. Meisterhans, dritte vermehrte und verbesserte Auflage, besorgt von E. Schwyzer, Berlin, 1900.

Moulton *Prol.* = J. H. Moulton, *A Grammar of New Testament Greek*, vol. 1 *Prolegomena*, 3rd edition, Edinburgh, 1908.

Moulton-Geden = W. F. Moulton and A. S. Geden, *A Concordance to the Greek Testament*, Edinburgh, 1899.

Mozley F. W., *The Psalter of the Church, the Septuagint Psalms compared with the Hebrew, with various notes*, Cambridge, 1905.

Nachmanson E., *Laute und Formen der Magnetischen Inschriften*, Uppsala, 1903.

Oracula Sibyllina, ed. A. Rzach, Vienna, 1891.

Ottley R. R., *The Book of Isaiah according to the Septuagint* (*Codex Alexandrinus*) translated and edited, 2 vols., Cambridge, 1904–6.

Reinhold H., *De graecitate Patrum Apostolicorum librorumque apocryphorum Novi Testamenti Quaestiones grammaticae* (Dissert. Philol. Halenses, vol. xiv, pars i), Halle, 1898.

Rutherford (W. G.) *NP* = *The New Phrynichus, being a revised text of the Ecloga of the grammarian Phrynichus*, London, 1881.

Schleusner J. F., *Novus Thesaurus philologico-criticus sive Lexicon in LXX et reliquos interpretes Graecos ac scriptores apocryphos Veteris Testamenti*, Leipzig, 1820.

Schmidt W., *De Flavii Josephi elocutione observationes criticae* Leipzig, 1893.

Schmiedel : see W.-S.

Schweizer *Perg.* = Schweizer (now Schwyzer) E., *Grammatik der Pergamenischen Inschriften, Beiträge zur Laut- und Flexions-lehre der gemeingriechischen Sprache*, Berlin, 1898.

Steindorff G., *Koptische Grammatik*, Berlin, 1894.

Sturz F. W., *De dialecto Macedonica et Alexandrina liber*, Leipzig, 1808.

Swete H. B., *The Old Testament in Greek according to the Septua-gint*, ed. 2, Cambridge, 1895–99 : *Introd.* = *An Introduction to the Old Testament in Greek*, ed. 2, Cambridge, 1902.

Test. XII. Patr. = *The Greek Versions of the Testaments of the Twelve Patriarchs* etc., ed. R. H. Charles, Oxford, 1908.

Thiersch H. W. J., *De Pentateuchi versione Alexandrina libri tres*, Erlangen, 1840.

Thumb A., *Asp.* = *Untersuchungen über den Spiritus Asper im griechischen*, Strassburg, 1888: *Handbuch* = *Handbuch der neu-griechischen Volkssprache, Grammatik, Texte, Glossar*, ib., 1895: *Hell.* = *Die griechische Sprache im Zeitalter des Hellenismus, Beiträge zur Geschichte und Beurteilung der* Κοινή, ib., 1901.

Veitch W., *Greek Verbs irregular and defective*, Oxford, 1866.

Wackernagel J., *Hellenistica*, Göttingen, 1907.

WH = Westcott B. F. and Hort F. J. A., *The New Testament in the Original Greek*, Cambridge, Text 1890, Introduction and Appendix (ed. 2), 1896.

W.-S. = *Winer's Grammatik des neutestamentlichen Sprachidioms, Achte Auflage, neubearbeitet* von P. W. Schmiedel, I Theil, *Einleitung und Formenlehre*, Göttingen, 1894.

Witkowski S., *Epistulae privatae Graecae quae in papyris aetatis Lagidarum servantur*, Leipzig, 1906–7. '

ZNTW = *Zeitschrift für die neutestamentliche Wissenschaft*, ed. E. Preuschen, Giessen.

The references to the above and other works are to pages, unless otherwise stated.

COLLECTIONS OF PAPYRI REFERRED TO IN THIS VOLUME

AP = *Amherst Papyri*, ed. Grenfell and Hunt, 1900–1.

BM i, ii etc. = *Greek Papyri in the British Museum*, ed. Kenyon, 1893– .

BU = *Aegyptische Urkunden aus den Koenigl. Museen zu Berlin, Griechische Urkunden*, ed. Wilcken etc., 1895–

CPR = *Corpus Papyrorum Raineri*, ed. C. Wessely, Vienna, 1895.

FP = *Fayum Towns and their Papyri*, ed. Grenfell and Hunt, 1900.

G = Grenfell, *An Alexandrian erotic fragment and other Greek Papyri, chiefly Ptolemaic*, 1896.

GH = Grenfell and Hunt, *Greek Papyri*, Series II, 1897.

GP = *Les Papyrus de Genève*, ed. J. Nicole, 1896–1900.

HP = *Hibeh Papyri*, Part I, ed. Grenfell and Hunt, 1906.

Leiden Pap. = *Papyri Graeci Musei...Lugduni Batavi*, ed. Leemans, 1843–85.

OP i, ii etc. = *Oxyrhynchus Papyri*, ed. Grenfell and Hunt, 1898– .

Par. = (Paris Papyri) *Notices et Extraits des MSS*, tom. xviii, ed. Brunet de Presle, Paris, 1858.

PP i, ii = *Flinders Petrie Papyri*, in *Proc. Royal Irish Academy, Cunningham Memoirs*, ed. J. P. Mahaffy, 1891–93.

Teb. = *Tebtunis Papyri*, ed. Grenfell, Hunt and Smyly, 1902.

TP = (Turin Papyri) *Papyri Graeci Regii Taurinensis Musei Aegyptii*, ed. Peyron, 1826.

ii/B.C. = 2nd century B.C., ii/A.D. = 2nd century A.D., ii/–iii/A.D. = a date falling about the end of ii/A.D. or the beginning of iii/A.D.

The abbreviations for the books of the O.T. for the most part explain themselves. Jd. = Judges, Jdth = Judith. For the signs used to denote the different strata in the last three Books of Reigns or Kingdoms (K. $\beta\beta$, K. $\beta\gamma$, K. $\gamma\gamma$, K. $\gamma\delta$, K. $\beta\delta$) see p. 10: for Jer. a, β and γ, Ez. a, β and $\beta\beta$, see p. 11 : for Parts I and II of Exodus, Leviticus and Psalms pp. 66 and 68. Job Θ indicates the passages in Job which are absent from the Sahidic version and are shown by their style to be later interpolations from Theodotion into the original partial Greek translation (see p. 4): other passages besides those so indicated may have been interpolated from the same source. Ψ tit. denotes the titles of the Psalms: some details in their vocabulary afford reason for thinking that they did not form part of the original Greek version. a' = Aquila, Θ = Theodotion. The text used is that of Dr Swete and, as this has by now well-nigh supplanted all others, it seemed needless to cumber the pages with the alternative numbers for the verses which he quotes in brackets.

CORRIGENDA AND ADDENDA

p. 10, 12 lines from end. *Read* "K. a has 151 examples" of the hist. pres.: my figures have been checked by Sir John Hawkins.

11, end of 2nd paragraph. *For* § 7, 44 *read* § 7, 46.

24, line 18. *For* Dan. Θ *read* Dan. O.

25, line 18. *For* "Tobit" *read* "the B text of Tobit."

38, line 16. *For* פַּה *read* פָּה.

50, last line. *For* ὀρᾳν *read* ὁρᾷν.

69, line 6. *For* εὐπρεπ(ε)ία etc. *read* εὐπρέπ(ε)ια, μεγαλοπρέπ.

79, line 12. *For* 4, 52 א *read* 4 א, 52 א.

80, note 6. *For* PP² *read* PP ii.

91, § 6, 32. *For* πρᾳύς *read* πραύς.

125, 3 (3) line 1. *For* ἴδου *read* ἰδού.

170, note 3, line 1. *For* Jos. xv. 60 *read* Jos. xv. 61.

172, note 1. *For* -ια *read* -ία.

238, line 10. *For* κατ- *read* κατα

---

p. 13. The severance of 2 Esdras from Chronicles LXX needs a word of justification. I believe Sir Henry Howorth to be right in his contention that 2 Esdras is the work of Theodotion: as regards Chron. LXX, certain Egyptian traits (p. 167 n., cf. *J. T. S.* VIII. 276 f.) and a rather greater freedom of style have made me hesitate in following Sir Henry to the natural conclusion that Θ is responsible for this translation also. A strong case has recently been made in support of this view, based mainly on the numerous transliterations in both portions, in a work to which Sir Henry drew my attention (*Old Testament and Semitic Studies in memory of W. R. Harper: Apparatus for the Textual Criticism of Chronicles-Ezra-Nehemiah:* by C. C. Torrey, Chicago, 1908). If these critics are right, it is necessary to suppose that Θ for Chron. made use of an earlier version, such as was not before him for Ezra-Nehemiah.

p. 33, lines 1, 2. To the renderings of שֵׁכָר should be added ζῦθος, the beer of Alexandria (Strabo 799), which the Isaiah translator appropriately introduces in "the vision of Egypt" (xix. 10).

p. 70. Ezekiel Part I, Part II: this indicates the main division of the Greek book into two parts: for further subdivision of Part II see p. 11—. The suggestion that the passage in 3 K. viii. 53 which is absent from M.T. may be a later gloss must be withdrawn: see on this very interesting section Swete *Introd.* 247 f.

p. 138, lines 3, 4. For further exx. of κἄν see p. 99, n. 2.

p. 146, § 10, 12. For 3rd decl. acc. in -αν see Psichari, *Essai sur le Grec de la Septante,* 164 ff.

p. 156, n. 3. But πάτραρχον Is. xxxvii. 28 and πάτρια viii. 21 are, as Prof. Burkitt reminds me, probably corruptions of an original παταχρά— Aram. פתכרא "a (false) god" or "idol," which must be added to the other Aramaisms in this book (γειώρας, σίκερα). See Field Hex. on viii. 21.

INTRODUCTION.

§ 1. GRAMMAR AND TEXTUAL CRITICISM.

Is it possible to write a grammar of the Septuagint? That is the question which must constantly arise in the mind of one who undertakes the task. The doubt arises not because the Greek, strange as it often is, is utterly defiant of the laws of grammar: the language in which the commonly received text is composed has some laws of its own which can be duly tabulated. The question rather is, "Where is the true 'Septuagint' text to be found?" We possess in the Cambridge Manual Edition the text of the Codex Vaticanus with a collation of the other principal uncials: in Holmes and Parsons we have a collation of the cursives and versions: and now in the Larger Cambridge Septuagint we have the first instalment of a thoroughly trustworthy collection of all the available evidence. But we are still far from the period when we shall have a text, analogous to the New Testament of Westcott and Hort, of which we can confidently state that it represents, approximately at least, the original work of the translators. Is it, then, premature to attempt to write a Grammar, where the text is so doubtful? Must the grammarian wait till the textual critic has completed his task?

It is true that no final grammar of the LXX can be written at present. But the grammarian cannot wait for the final verdict of textual criticism. Grammar and criticism must

T.

q̃ɔ

proceed concurrently, and in some ways the former may contribute towards a solution of the problems which the latter has to face.

The grammarian of the Greek Old Testament has, then, this distinct disadvantage as compared with the N.T. grammarian, that he has no Westcott-Hort text for his basis, and is compelled to enter into questions of textual criticism. Moreover the task of recovering the oldest text in the O.T. is, for two reasons at least, more complicated than in the N.T. In the first place, the oldest MS, containing practically a complete text, is the same for both Testaments, namely the Codex Vaticanus, but whereas in the one case the date of the MS is separated from the dates of the autographs by an interval (considerable indeed) of some three centuries, in the case of the O.T. the interval, at least for the earliest books, is nearly doubled. A yet more serious difficulty consists in the relative value of the text of this MS in the Old and in the New Testaments. The textual history of either portion of the Greek Bible has one crisis and turning-point, from which investigation must proceed. It is the point at which "mixture" of texts begins. In the N.T. this point is the "Syrian revision," which, although no actual record of it exists, must have taken place in or about the fourth century A.D. The corresponding crisis in the history of the LXX text is Origen's great work, the Hexapla, dating from the middle of the third century. This laborious work had, as Septuagint students are painfully aware, an effect which its compiler never contemplated, and he must be held responsible for the subsequent degeneration of the text. His practice of inserting in the Septuagint column fragments of the other versions, Theodotion's in particular, duly indicated by him as insertions by the asterisks which he prefixed, caused the multiplication of copies containing the insertions but wanting the necessary precautionary signs. This, together with the practice of scribes of writing in the margins (from which they were in later copies transferred to the text) the alternative renderings or transliteraticns contained in the other columns of the Hexapla, is the *fons et origo mali* as regards the Septuagint text. Now, whereas the Codex Vaticanus was written before the Syrian revision of the N. T., or at any rate contains a pre-Syrian text, it is posterior to the Hexapla, and contains a text of the O.T. which, though superior on the whole to that of Codex Alexandrinus, is yet not entirely free from Hexaplaric interpolations.

A few instances may be quoted showing the sort of mixture with which we have to deal.

(1) Take the A text of 3 Kingdoms at any of the passages where B has no rendering of the Massoretic text e.g. 3 K. ix. 15 ff. αὕτη ἡ πραγματία τῆς προνομῆς ἧς ἀνήνεγκεν ὁ βασιλεὺς Σαλωμὼν οἰκοδομῆσαι τὸν οἶκον κυ, καὶ τὸν οἶκον τοῦ βασιλέως καὶ σὺν τὴν Μελώ κ.τ.λ. We are at once struck by the occurrence of σύν preceding the accusative, which occurs in *vv.* 16, 24, 25, and is recognised as Aquila's rendering of את : other striking words are found to be either expressly stated to be Aquila's renderings in this passage or to be characteristic of his version and absent, or practically absent, from the record in the Concordance of LXX usage (e.g. καθόδους and ἀπήρτισεν in verse 25). Similar interpolations, presumably from Aquila, occur in the A text at 3 K. viii. 1, xi. 38 (N.B. κακουχήσω : the verb is frequent in Aquila, but occurs once only again in LXX viz. 3 K. ii. 26 where probably the text of both B and A has been interpolated), xiii. 26 (N.B. τῷ λέγειν = לאמר), 29 (with νεκρομαῖον cf. α' Dt. xiv. 8 νεκριμαῖον), xiv. 1—20, xxii. 47—50 : there are smaller insertions, apparently from the same source, in the A text of 4 K. e.g. xii. 4, xvi. 9 (Κυρήνηνδε), xvii. 14, xxv. 9.

From these passages we infer that in these two books (i) the shorter text of B is the older, (ii) that the passages which B omits were either absent from the Hebrew which the translators had before them or that the omission was intentional, the translation not aiming at completeness, (iii) that A has supplied the missing portions from Aquila, as Origen had probably previously done in the Hexapla, (iv) that B has remained comparatively, though probably not wholly, free from Hexaplaric interpolation.

(2) Or take the book of Job. A careful reading of the Greek and Hebrew will reveal the existence of two completely different styles, a free paraphrastic rendering in idiomatic

Greek, with every now and again passages of quite another character, containing Hebraisms, transliterations, etymological renderings of Divine names ('Ικανός = שׁדי, ὁ 'Ισχυρός = אל), in fact a rendering that aims at completeness and accuracy without much regard to style. Now we are told that the original version was much shorter than the received Hebrew text, and that Origen supplied the missing portions from Theodotion : and, by good fortune, the Sahidic version has preserved a pre-Origenic text, from which the Theodotion passages are absent[1]. We are thus enabled to mark off in Dr Swete's text, the Theodotion portions. But we cannot even then be quite certain that we have got back to the original text. Passages from Theodotion may have already, independently of the Hexapla, found their way into the Greek text on which the Sahidic version was based, or that text may have been affected by "mixture" of another kind. Still, a study of the vocabulary of the bracketed Theodotion passages will provide a criterion by means of which the critic will be better prepared to detect the influence of his style elsewhere. It will be noticed that in this book the text of B, and of all the uncials, is Hexaplaric.

(3) Or take the list in Jos. xxi. of the cities with their "suburbs" (מגרשׁים) which were given to the Levites, and note how in *vv.* 2—11 and again in *vv.* 34—42 the word for "suburbs" is rendered, 17 times in all[2] by (τὰ) περισπόρια (αὐτῆς), whereas in the intervening verses 13—32 it is rendered 35 times by (τὰ) ἀφωρισμένα (αὐτῇ)[3]. Now Aquila read περισπόρια in *v.* 15 (vide Field's Hexapla). It appears probable, then, that the original text had a shorter list of cities and suburbs =τὰ ἀφωρισμένα (cf. Lev. xxv. 34, Jos. xiv. 4), and that Aquila's version has again, as in the A text of 3 K., been drawn upon to complete the list[4]. Here again interpolation has affected the text of both B and A.

The elimination of Hexaplaric additions being, thus, the first task of the textual criticism of the LXX, a study of the style and vocabulary of the three later versions, more especially

---

[1] A list of the passages omitted in the Sahidic VS is given in Lagarde *Mittheilungen* 1884, p. 204. Cf. esp. Hatch *Essays in Bibl. Greek* 215 ff.

[2] Also by A in *v.* 19.

[3] Excluding τὴν (τὰς) ἀφωρισμ. in 27, 32, which render another word.

[4] In N. xxxv. 2—7 this word "suburbs" is rendered by four separate words, viz. προάστια, ἀφορίσματα, συνκυροῦντα, ὅμορα. Variety of rendering characterizes the Pentateuch, and it is not *necessary* to infer Hexaplaric influence here.

of Theodotion, is a necessary preliminary. The study of Theodotion's style is the more important for two reasons. (1) It was always a popular version, mainly, no doubt, because it steered a middle course between the idiomatic Greek, tending to paraphrase, of Symmachus, and the pedantic un-Greek literalism of Aquila : it combined accuracy with a certain amount of style. Theodotion's version of Daniel supplanted the older paraphrase in the Christian Bible, and it was to Theodotion that Origen usually had recourse to fill the gaps in the older version in the Septuagint column of the Hexapla. (2) Aquila's version betrays itself by certain well-known characteristics, whereas Theodotion fragments are not so easily detected. On the other hand we have in his version of Daniel (where it deviates from the Chisian text), and in the Θ portions of Job, a considerable body of material from which something may be learnt as to his characteristics. A complete vocabulary of the portions which can certainly be attributed to Theodotion is a desideratum.

In concluding these few observations on the text, it must be added that the present writer has practically confined himself to the text of the uncials collated for the Cambridge Manual edition. The first instalment of the larger Cambridge LXX has been consulted for all passages in Genesis where important grammatical points arise, though most of this portion of the Grammar was prepared before its appearance. Occasional use has also been made of Lagarde's edition of the Lucianic text, Field's Hexapla, and the great corpus of cursive evidence collected in the edition of Holmes and Parsons. A full use of the last-named work would not only have delayed the appearance of this work for perhaps many years, but would also have caused it to exceed the limits laid down for it, without (it is believed) a proportionate addition to any value which it may possess.

§ 2. GROUPING OF LXX BOOKS.

We have in the Septuagint a miscellaneous collection of Greek writings—some translations, others paraphrases, others of which the Greek is the original language—covering a period of upwards of three centuries, from the Pentateuch, the translation of which, there is no reason to doubt, goes back into the first half of the third century B.C., to the academical essay known as 4 Maccabees and the latter portion of Baruch, which must both be placed towards the close of the first century of our era. It is clearly desirable and should not be impossible, considering the length of this period, to find some means of classifying this motley collection. The first and obvious division is into translations and original Greek compositions. But the translations, though on a casual perusal they might appear to stand all on one level of mediocrity, on closer investigation are found to fall into certain distinct categories.

The object in view, and the method by which we seek to attain it, are not unlike the object and the method of the textual critic. The object, in this case, is not the grouping of MSS according to the character of the text which they contain, but the grouping of books or portions of books according to their style. The study of individual books from the linguistic point of view is followed by the study of groups. It would, of course, be unreasonable to expect undeviating uniformity of translation of the same Hebrew word in any one translator: if, however, it is found that a phrase is consistently rendered in one way in one portion of the Greek Bible, and in another way elsewhere, and if, as we proceed to extend our investigations to the renderings of other Hebrew phrases, the same divergence between two portions of the LXX is apparent, we gain an increasing assurance that we have to deal with two distinct groups of books, which are the production of different translators and possibly of different epochs. Each group may be the work of several translators, but, if so, they have all come under the same influences and belong, as it were, to a single school. The method upon which we proceed is not so much to trace the history of the meaning of a single Greek word through the LXX (though that method also may sometimes be fruitful in results) as to trace the rendering of a single Hebrew phrase in the different books. The Hebrew index in the final fasciculus of the Concordance of Hatch and Redpath facilitates this task. The difficulty is to discover Hebrew phrases which occur with sufficient frequency throughout the whole Bible to serve as "tests" and yet are not such every-day expressions that Greek translators of any class or period could not fail to render them in one and the same way. Vocabulary affords the easiest criterion to begin with : the results which it yields can then be tested by grammatical phenomena.

We proceed to take a few examples.

(1)   In the phrase "the servant of the Lord" (עבד יהוה) as applied to Moses the word "servant" is rendered in the following ways :

(i)   θεράπων in the Pentateuch (Ex. iv. 10, xiv. 31, N. xi. 11, xii. 7, 8, Dt. iii. 24), also in Jos. i. 2, ix. 4, 6 : cf. W. x. 16 (under the influence of Exodus) and 1 Ch. xvi. 40 (the words ἐν χειρὶ M. του θεράποντος τοῦ θεοῦ are unrepresented in M.T. and are probably a gloss). Cf. also ὁ θεράπων μου 'Ιώβ, Job *passim* (twice with v. l. παῖς).

(ii)   οἰκέτης Dt. xxxiv. 5.

(iii)   παῖς[1] constantly in Joshua (12 times) i. 7, etc., (in xiv. 7 A has δοῦλος), also in 1 Ch. vi. 49, 2 Ch. i. 3, xxiv. 9, 2 Es. xi. 7, 8, Bar. ii. 28 (cf. i. 20), Dan. O ix. 11.

(iv)   δοῦλος 3 K. viii. 53, 56, 4 K. xviii. 12, xxi. 8, 2 Es. xix. 14, xx. 29, ψ civ. 26, Mal. iv. 6, Dan. Θ ix. 11.

Extending the investigation to the rendering of the phrase when used of other servants of God (David, the prophets, etc.), we find that the versions fluctuate between (iii) and (iv). (iii) occurs throughout Isaiah (along with δοῦλος in the later chapters,

---

    [1] Used in the Pentateuch of Caleb, N. xiv. 24.

xlii. 19 etc.), in the latter part of Jeremiah (xxvi. 28, xxxiii. 5, xlii. 15, li. 4) and in Baruch (5 times). On the other hand the first half of Jeremiah (vii. 25, xxv. 4, xxvi. 27, cf. iii. 22)[1], Ezekiel (6 times) and the Minor Prophets (8 times) consistently use (iv).

Turning to the N. T. we find that the word θεράπων is confined to the O. T. quotation in Hebr. iii. 5 (= N. xii. 7), παῖς in metaphorical sense of a worshipper of God is limited to the O. T. quotation in Mt. xii. 18 (= Is. xlii. 1) and to the opening chapters in Luke's two writings, where it is used of Israel and David (Lc. i. 54, 69, Acts iv. 25) and of Christ (Acts iii. 13, 26, iv. 27, 30). On the other hand, the constant phrase in the mouth of Paul and other N. T. writers when speaking of themselves or of others is δοῦλος ('Ιησοῦ Χριστοῦ): note how the writer of the Apocalypse uses δοῦλος of Moses in xv. 3, though he has in mind Ex. xiv. 31 (θεράποντι).

We cannot fail to note in the LXX renderings a growing tendency to emphasize the distance between God and man. Θεράπων "the confidential attendant" is replaced by οἰκέτης[2] (which may include all members of the household and therefore implies close intimacy), then by the more colourless but still familiar παῖς, finally by δοῦλος the "bond-servant" without a will of his own.

(2) The same tendency as in the last instance is observable in the renderings of the *verb* עבד, viz. λατρεύειν and δουλεύειν[3]. The Pentateuch makes the distinction that λατρεύειν applies to the service of God (and the gods, Ex. xx. 5, xxiii. 24, L. xviii. 21, Dt. *passim*) whereas service rendered to man is expressed by δουλεύειν (by λατρεύειν only in Dt. xxviii. 48, see note 2 below). Joshua uses λατρεύειν similarly. Jd. (A and B texts) is inconsistent as regards the word used to express service of God and the gods, the A text having λατρεύειν 9 times, δουλεύειν twice, the B text having λατρεύειν 5 times (up to iii. 7) δουλεύειν 6 times. On the other hand 1 K. and the majority of the remaining books use δουλεύειν indiscriminately of service rendered to God or man, the only other examples of λατρεύειν occurring in 2 K. xv. 8, 4 K. (6 times), 2 Ch. (vii. 19). The grouping here is not quite the regular one, Jd. B, 2 K. (last part) and 4 K. usually siding with the latest group of LXX books.

(3) "The Lord (*or* God) of hosts": יהוה (אלהי) צבאות The renderings of this phrase show a fairly well-marked dis-

---

[1] Also as a v. l. in A in xlii. 15, li. 4.

[2] The last few chapters of Dt. seem to occupy a position by themselves in the Pentateuch.

[3] Θεραπεύειν only in Is. liv. 17.

tinction between the LXX books. The phrase, unfortunately, is absent from the Pentateuch as well as from Ezekiel, Job, etc.

(i) There is transliteration, (Κύριος) σαβαώθ, in 1 K. (i. 3, 11, 20, xv. 2, xvii. 45) and in Isaiah *passim* (about 57 times)[1]

(ii) There is paraphrase, (Κύριος) Παντοκράτωρ, in the first part of 2 K. (v. 10, vii. 8, 25 B, 26 A, 27), in 3 K. xix. 10, 14, 1 Ch. xi. 9, xvii. 7, 24 (xxix. 12, M. T. has no equivalent) and throughout Jeremiah and the Minor Prophets, Zechariah alone having some 60 examples of it.

(iii) There is translation, (Κύριος) τῶν δυνάμεων, throughout the Psalms, in 4 K. (iii. 14, xix. 20 [not in M. T.] 31) and sporadically elsewhere : (1 K. iv. 4 A), 2 K. vi. 18, 3 K. xvii. 1 (not in M.T.), xviii. 15, (Am. vi. 14 B), Zeph. ii. 9, Zech. (i. 3 B *bis*), vii. 4 (Jer. xl. 12, om. A*). (iii) is also Theodotion's rendering (Jer. xxxvi. 17) and from his version the *variae lectiones* in the passages last quoted have doubtless come. Aquila's rendering is Κύριος τῶν στρατιῶν : Symmachus has στρατιῶν, δυνάμεων and other words.

The limits of this work preclude further details of this kind. Pursuing these researches into vocabulary and grammar, we find that, considered from the point of view of style, the translated books (excluding the more paraphrastic renderings) fall into three main groups. At the head stands the Pentateuch, distinguished from the rest by a fairly high level of style (for κοινή Greek), combined with faithfulness to the original, rarely degenerating into literalism. At the other extreme stands a group, consisting mainly of some of the later historical books (Jd. + Ruth [B text], 2 K. xi. 2—3 K. ii. 11, 3 K. xxii. 1—4 K. end, 2 Es. : the Psalter has some affinity with it), in which we see the beginnings of the tendency towards pedantic literalism, which ended in the second century A.D. in the barbarous "version" of Aquila. Between these two extremes lie the remainder of the books, all falling behind the standard set up

---

[1] Also in Jos. vi. 17 B (τῶν δυνάμεων AF: M. T. merely ליהוה), Jer. xxvi. 10 AQ (om. σαβαώθ Bℵ), Zech. xiii. 2 BℵΓ (om. σαβ. AQ) : cf. 1 Es. ix. 46 A where it is prefixed to Παντοκράτορι.

by the Pentateuch, but approximating with varying degrees of success to that model.

We find also that diversities of style present themselves within a single book. These are not such diversities as can readily be accounted for by Hexaplaric influence : they are not cases (as in the Greek Job) where the gaps in an original partial version have been filled by extracts from Theodotion or from other sources. The break occurs at a definite point in the centre of a book, on either side of which the language has its own distinct characteristics. The evidence for this statement has been given by the present writer in the case of certain books, viz., (*a*) the books of Kingdoms, (*b*) Jeremiah and Ezekiel in the pages of the *Journal of Theological Studies*[1]. Further research may lead to the discovery of similar phenomena in other books.

The books of Kingdoms may be divided as follows ·

Earlier portions $\begin{cases} \text{K. } a \ (=\text{1 K.}), \\ \text{K. } \beta\beta \ (=\text{2 K. i. 1—xi. 1}), \\ \text{K. } \gamma\gamma \ (=\text{3 K. ii. 12—xxi. 43}). \end{cases}$

Later portions $\begin{cases} \text{K. } \beta\gamma \ (=\text{2 K. xi. 2—3 K. ii. 11}), \\ \text{K. } \gamma\delta \ (=\text{3 K. xxii. 1—4 K. end}). \end{cases}$

The portions K. $\beta\gamma$ and K. $\gamma\delta$ (referred to collectively as K. $\beta\delta$) are, it appears, the work of a single hand. They are distinguished from the remaining portions by their particles and prepositions (e.g. καί γε = ᴅꚗ, καὶ μάλα, ἡνίκα, ἀνθ' ὧν ὅτι, ἀπάνωθεν), by the almost complete absence of the historic present (K. a has 145 examples, $\beta\beta$ 28, $\gamma\gamma$ 47), by the use of ἐγώ εἰμι followed by a finite verb and by their vocabulary : they have much in common with Theodotion. The other portions are free from these peculiarities, though they do not rise much above K. $\beta\delta$ in point of style : the original version of K. $\gamma\gamma$, so far as it is possible to conjecture what it was like in the uncertain state of the text, seems to have been more paraphrastic and therefore more idiomatic than the rest. In the case of these books we are not without external support for the divisions to which we are led by considerations of style, nor is it difficult to conjecture why the books were divided as they appear to have been. The Lucianic text actually brings the second book

[1] Vol. IV. 245, 398, 578: vol. VIII. 262.

down to 3 K. ii. 11 (making the break at the death of David and the accession of Solomon, a much more natural point than that selected in the M. T.) ; 2 K. xi. 2 marks the beginning of David's downfall, and the Chronicler, like the translator of K. ββ, also cuts short his narrative at this point. It appears that the more disastrous portions in the narrative of the Monarchy were left on one side when the earlier translators of the נביאים ראשונים did their work.

The books of Jeremiah and Ezekiel are divided as follows ·

$$\begin{cases} \text{Jer. } a & = \text{i. 1—xxviii. 64 (li. 64 M. T.),} \\ \text{Jer. } \beta & = \text{xxix. 1—li. 35 (xlv. 5 M. T.),} \\ \text{Jer. } \gamma & = \text{lii.} \end{cases}$$
$$\begin{cases} \text{Ez. } a & = \text{i. 1—xxvii. 36 and xl. 1—xlviii. end,} \\ \text{Ez. } \beta & = \text{xxviii. 1—xxxix. 29 excluding} \\ \text{Ez. } \beta\beta & = \text{xxxvi. 24—38.} \end{cases}$$

The two styles in Jeremiah *a* and *β* are quite unmistakable, though, owing to a certain mixture of the two on either side of the juncture (in which the hand of a reviser may perhaps be traced), the exact point where the second hand begins cannot be certainly fixed to a verse : perhaps it should be placed a little lower down in chap. xxix. A clear test is afforded in this book by the phrase "Thus saith the Lord," which is consistently rendered in *a* by Τάδε λέγει Κύριος (about 60 times, down to xxix. 8), in *β* by Οὕτως εἶπεν Κύριος (about 70 times from xxx. 1), with a solitary example of a mixture of the two renderings at or near the juncture, τάδε εἶπεν Κύριος xxix. 13 B. Jer. *γ* is probably a later appendix to the Greek book : the occurrence of the form φυλάττειν (lii. 24 B, 31 A) suggests at least that this chapter has an independent history (see § 7, 44). *46.*

Equally unmistakable are the two styles in Ezekiel *a* and *β*. The two noticeable features here are (1) the cessation of the first style midway through the Book and its resumption after an interval of a dozen chapters, (2) the intervention in the second style which characterizes these twelve chapters of a passage, fifteen verses long (*ββ*), marked by yet a third style, closely resembling that of Theodotion. The passage in question (containing the promise of a new heart) has for many centuries been one of the lessons for Pentecost, and its use for that purpose appears to have been taken over from Judaism.

The problems awaiting solution in Jer. and Ez. are two, (1) Are the two main portions in either book the work of contemporaries and do they indicate a division by agreement of the labour of translating a book of considerable length, or was the first translation a partial one, subsequently completed? The former suggestion has in its favour the fact that the books appear to have been divided in the first place into two nearly equal portions (cf. § 5). (2) Is Ez. $\beta\beta$ earlier or later than the version of Ez. β which encloses it? In other words did the translator of Ez. β incorporate in his work a version which had already been made for lectionary use in the synagogues of Alexandria? Or, on the other hand, has a subsequent rendering, made for a Christian lectionary, ousted from all our MSS the original version, now lost, of these fifteen verses? The first suggestion would throw light on the *origines* of the Greek Bible : the second is, on the whole, more probable.

It should be added that the style of Ez. *a* and that of the Minor Prophets have much in common and the translators probably belong to the same period : Jer. *a* also has some kinship with this group.

The last sentence raises the question, Can we detect the reappearance of any translator in separate books of the LXX? Besides the possibility of the first hand in Ezekiel reappearing in the Minor Prophets, the strong probability, amounting almost to certainty, of identity of hands in the case of the latter part of 2 Kingdoms and 4 Kingdoms has already been mentioned. Again, the first half of Baruch is, beyond a doubt, the production of the translator of Jeremiah β[1]. Lastly the hand that has produced the partial and paraphrastic rendering of the story of the Return from the Exile (Esdras *a*) may, with confidence, be traced in the earlier chapters of the Chisian text of Daniel, a book which this paraphrast handled with just the same freedom as he had employed upon Chronicles—Ezra—Nehemiah[2]. In both cases it was subsequently found necessary to incorporate in the Greek Bible a more accurate version.

The following table is an attempt to classify the LXX books—translations, paraphrases and original Greek compositions—into groups from the point of view of style. The classification is, of course, a rough one. Isaiah, considered as a translation, would certainly not be placed in the first class. Class II is a large one, containing books of various styles.

[1] *J. T. S.* IV. 261 ff.
[2] See article "Esdras I" in Hastings *B. D.* I. 761 b.

Class III includes one production of Aquila and at least one book (2 Esdras) which may be the work of Theodotion. The question whether Tobit had a Hebrew original is an open one.

Translations.

1. Good κοινή Greek — Pentateuch. Joshua (part). Isaiah. 1 Maccabees.

2. Indifferent Greek — Jeremiah *a* (i.—xxviii.). Ezekiel (*a* and *β*) with Minor Prophets. 1 and 2 Chronicles (except the last few chaps. of 2 Ch.). K(ingdoms) *a*. K. *ββ* (2 K. i. 1—xi. 1). K. *γγ* (3 K. ii. 1—xxi. 43). Psalms. Sirach. Judith.

3. Literal or un-intelligent versions (style akin to that of Θ in many books) — Jeremiah *β* (xxix.—li.) with Baruch *a* (i. 1— iii. 8). Judges (B text) with Ruth. K. *βγ* with *γδ* (2 K. xi. 2—3 K. ii. 11 : 3 K. xxii. and 4 K.). Song of Solomon. Lamentations. (Daniel Θ). (2 Esdras)[1]. (Ecclesiastes)[2]

Paraphrases and free renderings.

4. Literary — 1 Esdras with Daniel O (part). Esther. Job. Proverbs.

Free Greek.

5. Literary and Atticistic — Wisdom. Ep. Jer. Baruch *β* (iii. 9—end). 2, 3 and 4 Maccabees.

6. Vernacular — Tobit[3] (both B and א texts).

A few notes are appended on some of the groups and in-dividual books in the above list.

Class I. The Greek Pentateuch should undoubtedly be regarded as a unit : the Aristeas story may so far be credited that the Law or the greater part of it was translated *en bloc*, as a single undertaking, in the 3rd century B.C. There are ren-derings, not found, or rarely found, elsewhere in the LXX, but represented in all five books of the Pentateuch (e.g. ἐπανα-

---

[1] Possibly the work of Theodotion (as has been suggested by Sir H. Howorth).

[2] The work of Aquila (see McNeile's edition).

[3] Should perhaps be placed under Paraphrases.

στρέφειν = שׁוּב) or in three or four of them (e.g. δέομαι [δεόμεθα]
κύριε = בִּי אֲדוֹנִי Gen. xliii. 20, xliv. 18, Ex. iv. 10, 13, N. xii. 11:
contrast ἐν ἐμοὶ κύριε Jd. vi. 13, 15, xiii. 8, 1 K. i. 26, 3 K. iii. 17,
26 : in Jos. vii. 8 the uncials omit the phrase, Syro-hex. ap.
Field has δέομαι κύριε ; cf. ἀποσκευή as the rendering of טַף
'little children' in Gen., Ex., N., Dt.). Yet there are not wanting
indications that even here there are different strata to be detected in the text of our uncials, notably in Ex. and Dt. The
vocabulary of the latter part of Ex. presents some contrasts
with that of the earlier part. In Dt. some new elements in the
vocabulary begin to make their appearance (e.g. ἐκκλησία as the
rendering of קָהָל = συναγωγή in the earlier books), particularly
in the closing chapters where the abundance of novel features
may be due to Hexaplaric influence. Joshua, as regards
phraseology, forms a kind of link between the Pentateuch and
the later historical books (cf. above p. 7 on θεράπων, παῖς) : we
may conjecture that the Greek version followed soon after that
of the Law.

Class III. Jeremiah β contains the most glaring instances
in the LXX of a translator who was ignorant of the meaning
of the Hebrew, having recourse to Greek words of similar
sound : αἶδε οἶδε = הֵידָד "shout" xxxi. (xlviii.) 33, xxxii. 16 (xxv.
30), κειράδας = קִיר חֶרֶשׂ xxxi. (xlviii.) 31, 36, τιμωρίαν = תַּמְרוּרִים
xxxviii. (xxxi.) 21, ἕως ᾅδου = הוֹי אָדוֹן "ah lord" xli. (xxxiv.) 5 !
This translator, moreover, has certain ἅπαξ λεγόμενα in vocabulary which place him in a class quite by himself.

The link which binds together the remaining members of this
group (excluding Eccl.) is the resemblance of their style to that
of Theodotion. Here we are met by a *crux* with regard to the
text. This resemblance, which runs through a large portion of
the later historical books, may be due to one of three causes.
(1) It may be the result of *interpolations* from Θ into an original
shorter text, affecting our oldest uncials, as in the book of Job.
(2) The books or portions of books, which are marked by this
resemblance, may be *wholly* the work of Θ, which has entirely
replaced the earlier version, if such ever existed. (3) The
original versions may have been written in a style afterwards
employed by Θ. Taking the books of Kingdoms as a criterion,
we find that the resemblances to Theodotion are confined
mainly to the latter part of 2 K. and to 4 K. and within these
limits they appear to extend over the whole narrative and not
to be restricted to short paragraphs : there is no marked distinction between two totally different styles as there is in the
Book of Job. In the Song and the Last Words of David
(2 K. xxii. 2—xxiii. 7) the similarity to the language of Θ is
specially marked, and quotations from Θ are for that section

absent from Field's Hexapla, and it may well be that these
two songs are taken directly from Θ. Elsewhere, however, we
have readings, differing from those of the LXX, attested as
Theodotion's, and the fact has to be faced that Josephus was
acquainted with these portions of the Greek Kingdoms in a
text resembling that of our oldest uncials. The phenomena
remind us of quotations from Daniel in the N.T. which agree
with Theodotion's second century version : critics have in that
case been forced to the conclusion that there must have been,
in addition to the loose Alexandrian paraphrase, a third version,
resembling that of Θ, but made before his time and in use in
Palestine in the first century B.C. In the case of Kingdoms βδ
a similar conclusion seems to be suggested, viz. that the bulk of
this portion of the Greek Bible, if the text of the uncials is at
all to be relied on, is a late production, falling between 100 B.C.
and 100 A.D., written at a time when a demand for literal versions had arisen and in the style which was afterwards adopted
by Theodotion.

Class IV. The most noticeable fact about the books in this
class is that they all belong to the third division of the Hebrew
Canon (the Kethubim). The prohibition to alter or add to or
subtract from Scripture[1] was not felt to be binding in the case
of writings which had not yet become canonized. To this cause
is due the appearance of these free renderings of extracts with
legendary additions at a time when the tendency was all in
the direction of stricter adherence in translation to the original
Hebrew. When the third portion of the Hebrew Canon was
finally closed at the end of the first century of our era, more
accurate and complete renderings were required. Thus we have
a free rendering of parts of Chronicles, Ezra and Nehemiah
grouped round a fable (1 Esdras) and by the same hand a similar
paraphrase of parts of Daniel, also with legendary additions :
Esther has been treated after the same fashion. The original
version of Job omitted large portions of the original. The
Greek Book of Proverbs includes maxims and illustrations
derived from extraneous sources, and metrical considerations[2]
sometimes outweigh in the translator's mind faithfulness to his
original. Even the Psalms, the most careful piece of work in
the Greek collection of "Writings," has an Appendix (ψ cli.).
Ben Sira may have specially had in mind some of these paraphrases when he wrote in his Prologue that αὐτὸς ὁ νόμος καὶ αἱ
προφητεῖαι καὶ τὰ λοιπὰ τῶν βιβλίων οὐ μικρὰν ἔχει τὴν διαφορὰν

---

[1] Dt. iv. 2, xii. 32 : cf. Aristeas, § 310 f. (p. 572 Swete *Introd.*).
[2] The number of fragments of hexameter and iambic verse in this book
cannot be accidental : possibly the first version or versions were wholly in
verse. Cf. the hexameter collection of maxims of pseudo-Phocylides.

ἐν ἑαυτοῖς λεγόμενα. Those words need not, of course, imply a *complete* collection of Greek versions of the prophecies and "writings" in 133 B.C., and in the case of Proverbs the consensus of the MSS as to the orthography of one word[1] suggests a date not much earlier than 100 B.C.

§ 3. The κοινή—the Basis of Septuagint Greek.

The Septuagint, considered as a whole, is the most extensive work which we possess written in the vernacular of the κοινή or Hellenistic language, and is therefore of primary importance for a study of later Greek, and the main function of a grammar of LXX Greek is to serve as a contribution to the larger subject, the grammar of the κοινή. That is the conclusion which, if not wholly new, has been strongly emphasized by the large increase in our knowledge of the κοινή brought about by the new-found Egyptian papyri. The LXX, being a translation, has naturally a Semitic colouring, but the occurrence in the papyri of many phrases which have hitherto been regarded as purely "Hebraisms" has compelled us to reconsider the extent of that influence. The isolated position which "Biblical Greek" has until recently occupied can no longer be maintained: "it has," as Dr J. H. Moulton says, "now been brought out into the full stream of progress[2]." The value of the LXX as a thesaurus of κοινή Greek has been proportionately increased.

The κοινὴ διάλεκτος is a term which has been used in different senses. We shall probably not be far wrong in adopting the definition of it given by the man who has done more than any other to promote a study of it and to point the way to its correct appreciation, namely Dr Thumb. He defines it as "the sum-total of the development of the Greek of common and commercial speech from the time of Alexander the Great to the close of ancient history[3]" The term, thus widely

---

[1] Οὐδείς (not οὐθείς) : see § 5.
[2] *Prol.* 2.   [3] *Hell.* 7.

defined, embraces both the vernacular κοινή and the literary
κοινή of Polybius, Josephus and other educated writers, which,
as Dr Thumb says, should be regarded as an offshoot of the
vernacular.   The translations contained in the LXX belong to
the vernacular class, but it includes also some specimens of
the literary κοινή (e.g. Wisdom).

The κοινή is the speech which replaced the old dialects of
the mother-land, when Greece lost her political independence
but bequeathed her language to the ancient world.   The main
cause of the dissemination of the Greek language and its estab-
lishment as the recognised language of intercourse was the
victorious march of Alexander.   But the Greek which was thus
diffused was not the Attic of Demosthenes.   Dialectical differences could not maintain their hold in the motley host of which
Alexander's army was composed.   But the fusion of the dialects
had begun even before then.   Aristotle, and still earlier
Xenophon, are precursors of the κοινή.   The mixture of clans
during the long marches across Asia under the latter's leader-
ship had on a small scale much the same effects of breaking
down the barriers which the mountains of Greece had erected
between tribe and tribe, and of diffusing an international
language, as were afterwards produced by Alexander's campaign.
Commerce had, even before Xenophon's time, brought about a
certain interchange of the Attic and Ionic dialects.   Out of this
fusion arose the κοινὴ διάλεκτος, in which the Attic dialect of
the people which had won its way to the front rank in politics,
literature and the arts naturally formed the main constituent.
But the Attic basis of the κοινή was not the Attic of the Greek
literary masterpieces.   The vulgar language, which had existed
beside the literary language, but had not gained an entrance
into it, except in Comedy, now forces its way to the front, and
makes itself felt in the diction of historians and philosophers.
Next to Attic in importance as a formative element in the κοινή
is Ionic, which provides a large part of its vocabulary and, in

particular, a considerable stock of words hitherto restricted to poetry. The other dialects appear to have played but a small part in the creation of the cosmopolitan language.

Now, one important fact to notice about the κοινή is that it appears for at least the first few centuries of its existence to have been a language practically without dialects. The old dialects lived on for a short time beside the new speech in some districts (Ionic on the sea-board of Asia Minor, Doric in Rhodes). But they soon had to give way before the levelling process which was at work. It seems to be an assured result of philological criticism that with a single exception (that of the old Laconic, which still held its own in the fastnesses of the Peloponnesus, and survives in the modern Zaconic) none of the old dialects survived in the competition with the κοινή, and that from it all the dialects of modern Greece, with the one exception mentioned, are descended. The κοινή was the resultant of a process of merging and amalgamation, and was the starting-point for a fresh dialectical differentiation. It was, of course, not entirely uniform ; there was a period during which there was a struggle for the survival of the fittest, and two forms were in existence side by side. Some forms, such as οὐθείς, were "transitional," having a life of a few centuries only, and then passing out of existence. In other cases the competition between two forms has continued down to modern times. On what grounds, it may be asked, is it held that the κοινή was a language without dialectic differences? The sources of our knowledge of the κοινή in order of importance are: (1) the papyri, (2) the inscriptions, (3) the Hellenistic writers such as Polybius, (4) modern Greek. The papyri are, unfortunately, with the exception of the Herculaneum collection, limited to Egypt, for which district we now have abundant materials, extending over a millennium (300 B.C.—700 A.D.), for a study of the language of every-day life as spoken by persons of all ranks in the social scale. But the inscriptions extend over the whole

Greek-speaking world, and through the industry of German
scholars we are now able to compare the κοινή as written in
some of the different districts. The inscriptions give us a
slightly higher order of Greek than the uneducated vernacular
found in the letters and other writings, intended for ephemeral
purposes only, which make up the papyri. But the results
obtained, speaking generally, from the study of inscriptions and
Hellenistic writings is that the same principles were at work
and the same forms employed, at least so far as orthography
and accidence are concerned[1], throughout the Greek-speaking
world during the first three centuries before our era.

The foregoing remarks might seem to be disproved by the
fact that two grammarians[2] in the time of Augustus wrote
treatises, now unfortunately lost, on "the dialect of the
Alexandrians." But when we find forms like ἐλήλυθαν cited by
ancient writers as Alexandrian, which we now know to have
had a much wider circulation within the κοινή, we have good
reason to question the accuracy of the titles which Irenaeus
(Minutius Pacatus) and Demetrius Ixion gave to their works.
The probability is that they took too limited a view: as
Dr Thumb says[3]: "they recognised the distinction between
the colloquial language with which they were familiar and the
literary dialects which they studied, but overlooked the fact
that the Alexandrian vernacular was only one branch of a
great linguistic development, and consequently failed to grasp
clearly the points of difference between the Alexandrian idiom
and the rest of the κοινή." It is certain that many forms of the
later language were specially *characteristic* of Alexandria, and
some (e.g. such forms as are common to Codices א and A
but absent from Cod. B) may have been rarely used outside

---

[1] These are the tests most easily applied: the tests of vocabulary and
syntax have not yet been worked out.

[2] Swete *Introd.* 289.

[3] *Hellenismus* 171.

Egypt. But we are not in a position to draw a hard and fast line between what was specially Alexandrian, or rather Egyptian, and what was not. Specifically Egyptian traits are probably to be looked for rather in the region of phonetics (in the mixture of τ and δ, κ and γ, the omission of intervocalic γ, and the interchange of certain vowels) than in accidence and syntax[1]. With regard to the phrase "the Alexandrian dialect," we must further remember the position which Alexandria occupied in the Hellenistic world, both as the centre of literary culture and (through the constant influx of persons of all nationalities) as the principal agent in the consolidation and dissemination of the cosmopolitan speech. Such a metropolis might not unnaturally give its name to a dialect which was spread over a far wider area.

A question closely connected with that of dialectical differences in the κοινή is the question how far it was influenced by the native languages of the countries which used it. The question is important, as bearing on the "Hebraisms" of the LXX. The foreign influence seems to have been extremely small. In the Ptolemaic papyri Mayser[2] finds no more than 23 words which are "probably Egyptian": 14 only of these are words which are unknown to the older literature. Only a single instance of Coptic syntactical influence has been discovered in the whole papyrus collection[3]. The contribution of the indigenous languages of Asia to the κοινή vocabulary appears to be equally negligible[4]. Latin alone brought a relatively large number of words into the common stock: but its influence on the grammar was quite slight. The general impression produced is that the resistance which Greek offered to the intru-

---

[1] Thumb *op. cit.* 133 ff.
[2] *Gramm. der Griechischen Papyri* 35—39.
[3] Ὄνος ὑπὸ οἴνου = "an ass laden with wine" and the like: Thumb, op. cit. 124. There are several examples of ὄνος ὑπὸ δένδρα in *BU.* 362 (215 A.D.).
[4] Thumb *op. cit.* 119.

sion of foreign elements was much the same in the Hellenistic period as in the age of Pericles[1]. The Greek language was at all times the giver rather than the receiver[2], and when it borrowed it usually clothed its loans in a dress of its own making.

The κοινή has often been unduly disparaged by comparison with the classical language. It has only in recent years come to be considered worthy of serious study, and its investigation on scientific lines is yet in its infancy. How much light may be thrown on its vocabulary and grammar by a study of modern Greek, which is its lineal descendant, has been shown by the researches of Thumb and others. The gulf between modern Greek and that, e.g., of the N.T. is in some respects not much wider than that which separates the latter from Attic. The κοινή is not estimated at its true worth when regarded merely as a debased and decadent Greek. Though it abandoned many of the niceties of the older language, it has some new laws of its own. It does not represent the last stages of the language, but a starting-point for fresh development. The resources which it shows in enriching the vocabulary are amazing. It evolves distinct meanings out of two different spellings of a single word. Simplification, uniformity, lucidity (together with a disregard of literary style[3])— these may be said to be the dominant characteristics of the κοινή vernacular. Analogy plays an important part in their production. "Lucidity," it is true, is not a conspicuous feature of many of the translations in the LXX: but that is due to the hampering fetters of the original[4].

---

[1] Thumb *op. cit.* 158.

[2] Witness the long list of Greek words found in Rabbinical writings, collected by Krauss *Griechische und Lat. Lehnwörter in Talmud Midrasch und Targum.*

[3] This of course does not apply, without considerable reservation, to the literary writers and the Atticists.

[4] Dr Swete speaks of "the success with which syntax is set aside [in the Apocalypse] without loss of perspicuity or even of literary power," *Apoc.* p. cxx.

The following are some of the principal features in the κοινή which may be illustrated from the LXX.

Orthography. Attic ττ is replaced by σσ, except in a few words (ἐλάττων, ἥττων, κρείττων, with derivatives) in which both forms are found, and in Atticistic writings (e.g. 4 Macc.). Οὐθείς (=οὐδ-h-είς) is the prevailing form down to about 100 B.C. Among the vowel-changes which begin to appear in the Ptolemaic period mention may be made of the tendency to weaken α to ε especially when in proximity with ρ (τεσσεράκοντα, μιερός, etc.). The shortening of -ιει- to -ει- (e.g. ταμεῖον), though strongly attested in the LXX MSS, appears from the papyri to be hardly older than the first century A.D. There is a tendency to drop the aspirate, while in a few cases, partly under the influence of false analogy, it is inserted where not required. The desire to keep individual words and the elements of words distinct appears to account on the one hand for the avoidance of elision, especially with proper names (ἀπὸ Αἰγύπτου, not ἀπ᾽ Αἰγ.), on the other for the want of assimilation within words (συνκόπτειν, not συγκ. etc.). The reverse process, the extension of assimilation to two separate words is, however, found in the early Ptolemaic papyri (ἐμμέσῳ, mainly in Cod. A, is almost the only LXX instance of this). The increasing tendency to insert variable final ν and ς (e.g. in ἐστίν, οὕτως) before consonants as well as vowels marks a loss of feeling for rhythm.

Accidence. The cases of nouns of the first declension in -ρᾰ are brought into line with other nouns in this declension (μαχαίρης not -ρας etc.). The "Attic" second declension is obsolescent : ναός replaces νεώς. In the third declension an assimilation to the first is seen in forms like νύκταν (in LXX almost confined, however, to אA, and their originality is doubtful). The most striking example of the casting off of luxuries is the disappearance of the dual, which not even the fact that analogous forms in the Hebrew had to be rendered could recall into life. Other words expressing duality are also on the way to extinction. Adjectives formerly taking two terminations are used with three : a form like αἰσχρότερος (Gen. xli. 19) is another instance of analogy at work. The same cause produces the declension πᾶν (for πάντα, on the model of μέγαν)—πᾶσαν —πᾶν. Πλήρης is commonly used indeclinably. Ἀσεβῆν etc. (mainly in אA) are the natural sequel to νύκταν etc. Δεκάδυο for δώδεκα appears to be due to a preference for placing the larger number first as when symbols are used (ιβ´) : similarly δεκατέσσαρες etc. are preferred to τεσσαρεσκαίδεκα etc. Ὃς ἐάν begins to oust ὃς ἄν in the last quarter of the first century B.C. and remains the predominant form for several centuries: its *raison*

d'être is not clear. In the verb the most salient innovations are
(1) the transference of -μι verbs, with certain reservations, to
the -ω class, (2) the formation of new presents, ἀποκτέννω,
ἀποχύ(ν)νω, -κρύβω, -λιμπάνω, and the like, (3) the tendency of
the "weak" aorist terminations to supplant the older "strong"
forms, εἶπα, ἦλθα, ἔπεσα etc. The same preference for the 1 aor.
termination is seen in forms like ἤλθοσαν (which are curiously
rare in Jd.—4 K., though frequent in the Hexateuch and other
parts of the LXX). The intrusion of the 1 aor. termination into
the 3rd plur. of the impf. (ἀνέβαιναν) and perf. (ἑώρακαν) was
apparently a later development and is rarely attested in LXX.
The syllabic augment is dropped in the pluperfect, and duplicated
in some verbs compounded with prepositions : the temporal
augment is also liable to omission (εὐλόγησα).

Syntax. In the breach of the rules of concord is seen the
widest deviation from classical orthodoxy. The evidence which
the LXX affords for a relaxation of the rigorous requirements
of Attic Greek in this respect is fully borne out by the contemporary papyri. Instances in LXX of "nominativus pendens"
and of what may be described as "drifting into the nominative
(or accusative)" in a long series of dependent words connected
by καί are frequent. The nom. (the name case) is the usual
case for proper names after καλεῖν (Gen. iii. 20 ἐκάλεσεν...τὸ ὄνομα
τῆς γυναικὸς Ζωή etc.). "Constructio ad sensum" plays a large
part, e.g. in the extended use of πᾶς, ἕκαστος etc. with a plural
verb. Λέγων, λέγοντες are used without construction in phrases
like ἀπηγγέλη λέγοντες, very much like our inverted commas or
the ὅτι which often introduces direct speech in Hellenistic (and
Attic) Greek. Neuter plurals may take either a singular or a
plural verb : this gives scope for some distinctions unknown to
classical Greek.

The extended use of the genitive of quality equivalent to an
adj., is partly but not altogether due to literal translation. (The
dative, which has disappeared in modern Greek, shows but little
sign of waning as yet.) As regards comparison of the adj., a
common substitute for the comparative is the positive followed
by παρά : though the Heb. מן גדול is partly answerable for this,
it is noticeable that the preposition ἀπό is hardly ever used in
the Greek, though in the modern language e.g. μεγαλύτερος ἀπό
has become the normal phrase[1]. The superlative is waning
(forms in -έστατος are almost confined to two or three literary
LXX books) and usually has *elative* sense (esp. μέγιστος,
πλεῖστος). The general Hellenistic rule that the comparative does
duty for both degrees of comparison is reversed in the case of

[1] Thumb *Handbuch der Neugr. Volkssprache* 52.

πρῶτος which in LXX, as elsewhere in the κοινή, stands for
πρότερος. As regards pronouns, the otiose insertion of the
oblique cases of αὐτός is shown by the papyri to be a Hellenistic
feature, though the frequency of the usage in LXX comes from
the Heb. Ἑαυτούς, -ῶν, -οῖς are used of all three persons of
the plural, supplanting ὑμᾶς (ἡμ.) αὐτούς : a transitional form
ὑμῖν ἑαυτοῖς occurs in the Hexateuch.

The use of intransitive verbs with a causative sense is remarkable : verbs in -εύειν and compounds of ἐκ afford most of
the examples (βασιλεύειν "to make king," ἐξαμαρτάνειν "to cause
to sin") : the limitation of the verbs affected indicates that the
influence of the Heb. hiphil is not the sole cause. The historic
present tends to be used with verbs of a certain class ; apart
from λέγει etc. it is specially used of verbs of seeing in the
Pentateuch, of verbs of motion (coming and going) in the later
historical books : its absence from K. βδ distinguishes the later
from the earlier portions of the Kingdom books. A few perfects
are used as aorists ; εἴληφα Dan. Θ iv. 30b, ἔσχηκα 3 Macc. v.
20 : papyri of the second and first centuries B.C. attest the
aoristic use of both words. The periphrastic conjugation is
widely extended, but only the strong vernacular of Tobit employs
such a future as ἔσομαι διδόναι (v. 15 B text). The optative
almost disappears from dependent clauses (its frequency in
4 Macc. is the most obvious of the Atticisms in that book) :
besides its primary use to express a wish there are several exx.,
principally in Dt., of its use in comparisons after ὡς εἰ (ὡς).
The infinitive (under the influence of the Heb. לְ)[1] has a very
wide range : the great extension of the inf. with τοῦ, alternating
with the anarthrous inf., is a prominent feature : a tendency is
observable in some portions to reserve the anarthrous inf. of
purpose to verbs of motion (coming, going, sending). The
substitution for the inf. of a clause with ἵνα is quite rare : the
Heb. had no corresponding use. (The use of the conjunctive
participle is yielding to the coordination of sentences with καί,
largely under Heb. influence : it is not clear whether the use
of the part. for a finite verb in descriptive clauses such as
Jd. iv. 16 καὶ Βαρὰκ διώκων…"and B. was pursuing" is wholly
"Hebraic.") The genitive absolute construction is freely used
where the noun or pronoun occurs in another case in the same
sentence.

The tendency, where a genitive is dependent on another
noun, to use the article with both or with neither on the
principle of "correlation" is exemplified outside "Biblical
Greek," but the consistent omission of the art. in such a phrase,
even where it forms the subject of the sentence, as in 1 K. (e.g.

[1] To the Heb. is due an enlarged use of the "epexegetic infinitive."

iv. 5 ἦλθεν κιβωτὸς Κυρίου, cf. v. 1 καὶ ἀλλόφυλοι ἔλαβον) appears to be wholly due to imitation, the Heb. art. being an impossibility with nouns in the construct state.

Under the head of prepositions the chief innovations are (1) the partial or total disuse of one of the cases after prepositions which in Classical Greek take more than a single case, (2) the supplementing of the old stock of prepositions proper by adverbs, adverbial phrases and prepositions: ἐναντίον ἐνώπιον etc. (for πρό), ἐπάνω (for ἐπί), ἐπάνωθεν ἀπάνωθεν ὑπεράνω (for ὑπέρ), ὑποκάτω (for ὑπό), ἀνὰ μέσον (for μεταξύ), κύκλῳ περικύκλῳ (for περί), ἐχόμενος etc. (for παρά). Modern Greek has several similar forms. Possibly it was thought necessary in this way to distinguish the old local sense of the prepositions from the metaphorical meanings which subsequently became attached to them. Among many new details the use of ὑπέρ for περί may be noticed. Ἐν and εἰς are on the whole still carefully discriminated: the use of ἐν for εἰς after verbs of motion is characteristic of the vernacular style of Tobit (i. 6, v. 5, vi. 6, ix. 2)β and of Jd.—4 K. (= ב): ultimately εἰς alone survived. Among particles mention may here be made of the prominence given to such a phrase as ἀνθ' ὧν = "because," owing to the Heb. having similar conjunctions formed with the relative אשר: in the latest translations this is extended to ἀνθ' ὧν ὅτι, ἀνθ' ὧν ὅσα etc.

The foregoing is a brief conspectus of some salient features of the κοινή which appear in the LXX: a more detailed investigation of these and kindred innovations will be made in the body of this work.

The vocabulary of the LXX would require, if fully discussed, a volume to itself. The reader must be referred to the useful work done in this department by Kennedy[1] and Anz[2] and to the lists of words given in Dr Swete's *Introduction*[3].

§ 4. The Semitic Element in LXX Greek.

The extent to which the Greek of the Old and New Testaments has been influenced by Hebrew and Aramaic has long been a subject of discussion among grammarians and

---

[1] *Sources of N.T. Greek* or *The Influence of the LXX on the vocabulary of the N.T.*, Edinburgh, 1895.

[2] *Subsidia ad cognoscendum Graecorum sermonem vulgarem e Pentateuchi versione Alex. repetita*, Halle, 1894.

[3] 302 ff., 310 ff.

theologians. The old controversy between the Hebraist School, who discovered Hebraisms in Greek colloquial expressions, and the Purists who endeavoured to bring every peculiarity under the strict rules of Attic grammar, has given way to a general recognition that the basis of the language of the Greek Bible is the vernacular employed throughout the whole Greek-speaking world since the time of Alexander the Great. The number of " Hebraisms " formerly so-called hás been reduced by phenomena in the papyri, the importance of which Deissmann was the first to recognise : his investigations, chiefly on the lexical side, have been followed up by Dr J. H. Moulton, who has carried his papyri researches into grammatical details, with the result that anything which has ever been termed a " Hebraism " at once arouses his suspicion. It is no doubt possible that further discoveries may lead to the detection in non-Jewish writings of parallels to other Hebrew modes of expression, and that the category of acknowledged " Hebraisms " (for which no parallel exists in the vernacular) will be still further depleted

But the emphasis which has been laid upon the occurrence of certain words and usages in the Egyptian papyri which are exactly equivalent to, or bear a fairly close resemblance to, phrases in the Greek Bible hitherto regarded as " Hebraic " is likely to create a false impression, especially as regards the nature of the Semitic' element in the LXX.

What results have actually been gained? It may be said, in the first place, that the papyri and the more scientific study of the κοινή, which has been promoted by their discovery, and the recognition of the fact that it was quickly adopted the whole world over, that it had little or no dialectic differentiation and was proof against the intrusion of foreign elements to any considerable extent, have given the death-blow to, or at any rate have rendered extremely improbable, the theory once held of the existence of a " Jewish-Greek " jargon, in use in the Ghettos of Alexandria and other centres where Jews congregated. The

Greek[1] papyri have little to tell us about the private life of the Jews of Egypt: they hardly figure among the correspondents whose letters have come down to us. The marshes of the Delta, less favourable than the sands of Upper Egypt, have not preserved for us the every-day writings of inhabitants of Alexandria, the chief centre of the Jewish colony and the birthplace of the oldest Greek version of the Scriptures. Yet we need have little hesitation in assuming that the conditions which applied to the Egyptians and Arabs, who wrote good κοινή Greek with little or no admixture of elements derived from their native speech, held good of the Jews as well. The "peculiar people" were not exempt from the influences at work elsewhere. The Greek of the LXX does not give a true picture of the language of ordinary intercourse between Jewish residents in the country. It is not, of course, denied that they had a certain stock of terms, such as ἀκροβυστία[2] and the like, which would only be intelligible within their own circle: but the extent of Semitic influence on the Greek language appears to have been limited to a small vocabulary of words expressing peculiarly Semitic ideas or institutions. The influence of Semitism on the syntax of the Jewish section of the Greek-speaking world was probably almost as inappreciable as its syntactical influence on the κοινή as a whole, an influence which may be rated at zero.

One of the strongest arguments which may be adduced to disprove the existence of "Jewish-Greek" as a separate dialectical entity is the striking contrast between the unfettered original Greek writings of Jewish authorship and the translations contained in the Greek Bible. Of primary importance is the difference in style noticeable when we pass from the preface of the son of Sirach to his version of his grandfather's work—a contrast which is analogous to that between Luke's preface

---

[1] As opposed to the new-found early Aramaic papyri from Assuan.

[2] Ἀνάθεμα 'curse' has been found in 'profane Greek': J. H. Moulton *Prol.* 46, note 3.

and his story of the Infancy. The same contrast is felt on passing from the paraphrases (e.g. 1 Esdras) or original writings (3 Macc.) of the LXX to the version of e.g. the Pentateuch, or from the allegories and expositions of Philo to the LXX text which he incorporates in his commentary. The fact that "Hebraisms" are practically a nonentity in the Greek translation of his *Jewish War* which Josephus made from the Aramaic original points to the same conclusion. Philo and Josephus present us, it is true, with the literary κοινή, but too sharp a line of demarcation should not be drawn between that species and the vernacular variety, and Jewish-Greek, if it existed, could hardly fail to have left some traces even in such literary writers as these. The book of Tobit (not e.g. 4 Kingdoms) is probably the best representative in the Greek Bible of the vernacular as spoken by Jews.

The Hellenization of Egypt appears to have been rapid and to have affected all classes of the community, at least in Lower Egypt: towards the South it made less headway. The majority of the Jewish residents probably had a greater knowledge of the κοινή Greek than of the original language of their sacred writings. It must be remembered, too, that so far as they employed a second language, that language was not Hebrew but Aramaic. The word used for a "proselyte" in the early versions of Exodus and Isaiah[1] (γειώρας from Aram. גִּיּוֹרָא, Heb. גֵּר) is significant. The mere fact that a Greek translation was called for at all, taken together with the large number of transliterations in some of the later historical books, indicates a want of familiarity, which increased as time went on, with the original Hebrew. The primary purpose which, in all probability, the translation was intended to serve was not to enrich the library of Ptolemy Philadelphus, nor to extend an acquaintance with the Scriptures to the non-Jewish world, but to supply a version that would be intelligible to the Greek-speaking Jew

---

[1] The later books use πάροικος or προσήλυτος.

when read in the ordinary services of the synagogue. That the desired intelligibility was not always successfully attained was due to the conflicting claims of a growing reverence for the letter of Scripture, which resulted in the production of literal versions of ever-increasing baldness.

Notwithstanding that certain so-called " Hebraisms " have been removed from that category or that their claim to the title has become open to question, it is impossible to deny the existence of a strong Semitic influence in the Greek of the LXX. The papyri have merely modified our ideas as to the extent and nature of that influence. Dr J. H. Moulton has been the first to familiarize us with the view, to which he frequently recurs[1], that the " Hebraism " of Biblical writings consists in the *over-working* of and the special prominence given to certain correct, though unidiomatic, modes of speech, because they happen to coincide with Hebrew idioms. His happy illustration of the overdoing of ἰδού in Biblical Greek by the " look you " which is always on the lips of the Welshman in Shakespeare's *Henry V* is very telling. This view appears to the present writer to be borne out to a great extent by the linguistic phenomena of the LXX, at least as regards the Pentateuch and some other of the earlier versions. The Hebraic character of these books consists in the *accumulation* of a number of just tolerable Greek phrases, which nearly correspond to what is normal and idiomatic in Hebrew. If we take these phrases individually, we can discover isolated parallels to them in the papyri, but in no document outside the Bible or writings directly dependent upon it do we find them in such profusion. The κοινή Greek was characterized by a striving after simplification. Greek was on the road to becoming rather an analytical than a synthetical language. The tendency was in the direction of the more primitive and child-like simplicity of Oriental speech. And so it happened that the translators of the

[1] *Prol.* 10 f., 72 etc.

Pentateuch found ready to their hand many phrases and modes of speech in the current vernacular which resembled the Hebrew phrases which they had to render. These phrases they adopted, and by so doing gave them a far wider currency and circulation than they had hitherto possessed : the later translators took the Greek Pentateuch for their model, and from the Greek Bible these "Hebraisms" passed into the pages of some N.T. writers (Luke in particular) who made a study of the LXX.

It is, however, only with considerable reservations that we can apply the theory of overworked vernacular Greek usages to some of the "Hebraisms" of the *later* LXX books. The distinction between the earlier and the later books is a real one ; the reason for the change is to be sought, it appears, rather in a growing reverence for the letter of the Hebrew than in ignorance of Greek. There are well-marked limits to the literalism of the Pentateuch translators. Seldom do they imitate a Hebrew locution without adapting and accommodating it in some way to the spirit of the Greek language, if they fail to find an exact equivalent in the vernacular. On the other hand, the translators of the Kingdom books (especially of the portion βδ) were prepared to sacrifice style and to introduce a considerable number of phrases, for which parallels never, probably, existed in the κοινή, if Greek did not furnish them with a close enough parallel to the Hebrew. The demand for strict accuracy increased as time went on, and the prohibition against any alteration of the words of Scripture[1] was taken by the translators as applying to the smallest minutiae in the Hebrew, until the tendency towards literalism culminated in the ἐγώ εἰμι ἔχω of Kingdoms (βδ) and the ἐν ἀρχῇ ἔκτισεν ὁ θεὸς σὺν τὸν οὐρανὸν καὶ σὺν τὴν γῆν of Aquila. In the later period the books whose right to a place in the Canon had not yet been finally determined came off best in the matter of

[1] See note 1 on p. 15.

style, because paraphrase was here possible and the hampering necessity of adhering to the original was not felt. Had Ecclesiastes been translated before the time of Christ, we should no doubt have had a translation very different from that which now stands in our Septuagint. The discussion which follows of some principal "Hebraisms" of the LXX will illustrate the contrast between the earlier and later periods.

Hebraisms in Vocabulary.

The influence of Hebrew on the vocabulary of the LXX, though considerable, is not so great as might at first sight be supposed. Apart from a small group of words expressing peculiarly Hebrew ideas or institutions (weights, measures, feasts etc.), the instances where the Hebrew word is merely transliterated in Greek letters are mainly confined to a single group, namely the later historical books (Jd.—2 Chron., 2 Esdras). Now this is a group in which we have frequent reason to suspect, in the text of our uncials, the influence of Theodotion, and at least one book in the group (2 Esdras) has with much probability been considered to be entirely his work. We know that Theodotion was, whether from ignorance of the Hebrew or in some cases from scrupulousness, specially addicted to transliteration[1], and many of the instances in the later historical books are probably derived from him. Where there are doublets (transliteration appearing side by side with translation) the latter is doubtless to be regarded as the original text : the former has probably crept in either from the second column of the Hexapla (the Heb. transliterated) or from the sixth (Theodotion). On the other hand, the earlier translators for the most part rendered every word in the original, going so far as to translate the names of places. Transliteration is rare in the Pentateuch, Isaiah, Jeremiah a and the Minor Prophets. It is

[1] See Swete's *Introduction* 46, with the list in Field's *Hexapla* I. p. xl f.

entirely absent from Ezekiel β, the Psalter (excepting the titles and the word ἀλληλουϊά), Proverbs, Job (excluding the Θ portions) and most of "the writings."

A distinction must be drawn between words which are merely transliterated and treated in their Greek form as indeclinables, and the smaller class of Hellenized Hebrew words. The majority of the latter words had gained an entrance into the Greek vocabulary before the time when the LXX was written. The transliterations may be divided into (*a*) ideas, institutions etc. peculiar to Judaism, for which Greek afforded no exact equivalent, (*b*) geographical terms, e.g. ἀραβά, ἀραβώθ, to which may be added cases where an appellative has been mistaken for a proper name, (*c*) words of the meaning of which the translators were ignorant, (*d*) doublets. Hellenized Hebrew words mainly come under class (*a*). The Pentateuch instances of transliteration and Hellenized words are mainly restricted to this class, which also comprises most of the words which are repeatedly used in different parts of the LXX.

The Pentateuch examples of transliteration are as follows, arranged under classes (*a*), (*b*) and (*d*): there are no certain examples of (*c*).

(*a*)[1] γόμορ (= עֹמֶר "an omer") Ex. xvi. 16 etc.: also used in Hos. iii. 2, Ez. xlv. 11 etc. of the different dry measure חֹמֶר "an homer" (which is rendered in Pent. and Ez. xlv. 13 by κόρος), and so apparently in 1 K. xvi. 20 (M. T. חֲמוֹר "an ass"), cf. xxv. 18 (M. T. מֵאָה): in 4 K v. 17 γόμος should apparently be read (cf. Ex. xxiii. 5), where the corruption γόμορ indicates familiarity with this transliteration—εἲν (ἲν)=הִין, a liquid measure, Ex. Lev. N. Ez.—μάν Ex. xvi. 31 ff. and μάννα N. Dt. Jos. 2 Es. Ψ =מָן—οἰφί (οἰφεί)=אֵיפָה, אֵפָה Lev. N. Jd. R. 1 K. Ez., once (1 K. xxv. 18) corresponding to another measure in the M. T., פֶּסַח—πάσχα, פֶּסַח, Hex. 4 K. 1 2 Es. Ez.: a different transliteration, φάσεκ or φάσεχ, occurs in 2 Ch. and Jer. xxxviii. 8—

---

[1] ἄχι (=Heb. אָחוּ Gen. xli. 2 etc.) is an Egyptianism rather than a Hebraism: it renders other Hebrew words in Isaiah and Sirach. See Sturz, p. 88, BDB Heb. Lexicon s.v.

σίκερα, שׁכר intoxicating drink, Lev. N. Dt. Jd. Is. (elsewhere שׁו rendered by μέθυσμα, μέθη)—χερούβ plur. χερουβ(ε)ίν (rarely שׁוּ -β(ε)ίμ) LXX *passim*.

(*b*) 'Αραβά, ἀραβώθ N. Dt. Jos. etc.—'Ασηδώθ (אשׁדת the "slopes" of Pisgah) Dt. Jos. Other exx. of appellatives being treated as proper names are Μάσεκ Gen. xv. 2, Οὐλαμμαύς ib. xxviii. 19 (=לוז אולם), so Jd. xviii. 29 B Οὐλαμαίς, τὸν 'Ιαμείν Gen. xxxvi. 24, Σίκιμα xlviii. 22, Μεισώρ ("plain") Dt. Jos., 'Εμεκαχώρ ("valley of Achor") Jos. vii. 24 etc.

(*d*) Of this class Genesis supplies one example in xxii. 13 (ἐν φυτῷ) σαβέκ: probably also the word χαβραθά in xxxv. 16, xlviii. 7 is a doublet (cf. 4 K. v. 19 δεβραθά). 'Ομμόθ in N. xxv. 15 (ἔθνους "Ομμοθ = אמות) may also belong to this class.

The following transliterations occur in more than one of the later books, the words being translated in the Pentateuch or elsewhere.

Γεδδούρ = גדוד "a troop" 1 K. 1 Ch. (elsewhere rendered by λῃστήριον, λῃστής, μονόζωνος etc.)—'Εφούδ ἐφώδ Jd. 1 K. (Pent. ἐπωμίς, 2 K. vi. 14, 1 Ch. xv. 27 στολή)--Θεραφείν θαραφείν θεραπείν (once Hellenized into θεραπείαν 1 K. xv. 23 B) Jd. 1 K. 4 K. 2 Ch. (elsewhere τὰ εἴδωλα Gen. xxxi. 19 etc., κενοτάφια 1 K. xix. 13, 16, τὰ γλυπτά Ez. xxi. 21, δῆλοι Hos. iii. 4)—Μαναά, μαανά, μανάχ, μάννα etc. = מנחה "a present" or "sacrifice," 4 K. 2 Ch. 2 Es. Ez. Dan. Θ (elsewhere constantly rendered by δῶρον or θυσία)—Ναγέβ = נגב Jos. Ob. Jer. β Ez. a (elsewhere translated ἔρημος, λίψ, μεσημβρία, νότος)—Νέβελ = נבל a "wine-skin" or "jar" (elsewhere ἀγγεῖον, ἀσκός)--Σαβαώθ 1 K. and Is. (elsewhere τῶν δυνάμεων or Παντοκράτωρ)—Σεφηλά (elsewhere ἡ πεδινή, γῆ πεδινή, τὰ ταπεινά).

It is needless to enumerate other transliterations which, as already stated, are very frequent in the later historical books, especially in 4 K., 2 Ch. and 2 Es.

The Hebrew definite article sometimes forms part of the transliteration, e.g. ἀβάκ 1 Ch. iv. 21, ἀβεδηρείν ib. 22 (הדברים), ἀμασενείθ xv. 21 (this of course is to be expected where the word is a doublet and probably taken from the second column of the Hexapla, e.g. 1 K. v. 4 ἀμαφέθ). Sometimes the Greek article is prefixed to the Hebrew article and noun: Jd. viii. 7 B ταῖς ἀβαρκηνείν, 2 Ch. xxv. 18 τὸν ἀχούχ. The Greek article occasionally stands in the singular with a plural noun: Jd. x. 10 B τῷ Βααλείμ, Ez. xxvii. 4 τῷ Βεελείμ, xl. 16 B τὸ θεείμ (contrast 12).

The following are examples of *Hellenized Semitic words* used in the LXX, i.e. the Greek form of the word is declinable. Some of them had been introduced into the Greek language before the time of the LXX and are ultimately derived from Phoenician.

’Αρραβών -ῶνος=עֵרָבוֹן, Gen. (already used by Isaeus and Aristot., also in Ptolemaic papyri, probably Phoenician).

Βακχούρια neut. pl. =בִּכּוּרִים "first-fruits" 2 Es. xxiii. 31 (elsewhere, including 2 Es. xx. 35, rendered πρωτογενήματα).

Βάρις, plur. βάρεις βάρεων, from בִּירָה "a palace," which as well as other words it renders in 2 Ch. 1 and 2 Es. Ψ Lam. Dan. Θ and in the later translators. Jerome states "verbum est ἐπιχώριον Palaestinae," and a Scholiast on Ψ cxxi. 7 (where the compound πυργόβαρις is used) makes a similar statement (see Schleusner s.v.). The Heb. is once transliterated, βειρά 2 Es. xvii. 2. (A word βᾶρις -ιδος meaning an Egyptian boat is found in Hdt. and Aesch., but is probably unconnected with the LXX word.) Cf. Sturz 89 f.

Βῖκος=בַּקְבֻּק "a wine-jar" Jer. xix. 1, 10 (first in Hdt. I. 194 βίκους φοινικηίους, Ptolemaic pap.).

Βύσσος, βύσσινος render בּוּץ, from which they are derived, and other words (the adj. in Hdt. and Aesch.).

Γαζαρηνός Dan. ΟΘ appears to be formed from the Aram. plur. גָּזְרִין "soothsayers."

Γ(ε)ιώρας=גֵּר "a sojourner" or "proselyte" Ex. (ii. 22 ap. Philo *de conf. ling.* 17. 82) xii. 19, Is. xiv. 1 is noticeable as an instance of a Hellenized word formed not from the Hebrew but from the Aramaic גִּיּוֹרָא. (The Heb. is elsewhere rendered by πάροικος or προσήλυτος.)

Θῖβις, acc. -βιν dat. -βει, =תֵּבָה "a chest," Ex. ii. 3, 5, 6: the form θῖβις (not θίβη or θήβη) is that attested by the papyri where the word occurs as early as iii/B.C. (Mayser 42.)

[1] Κάβος=קַב, a dry measure, 4 K. vi. 25.

Κασία=קְצִיעָה, a spice, Ψ xliv. 8: cf. Ez. xxvii. 17.

---

[1] כַּרְפַּס (rendered καρπασίνοις Est. i. 6) is a loan word from Sanskrit karpâsa (BDB Lexicon).

[The Semitic origin of κιβωτός (Aristoph. and earlier writers) is doubtful.]

Κιννάμωμον = קִנָּמוֹן "cinnamon" Ex. xxx. 23 etc., of Phoenician origin as Herodotus tells us, III. 111.

Κινύρα = כִּנּוֹר "a lyre" 1—3 K. 1—2 Ch. Sir. 1 M. (elsewhere rendered by κιθάρα, ὄργανον, ψαλτήριον).

Κόρος = כֹּר, a Hebrew measure equivalent to the homer, twice in the Pentateuch corresponding to חמר of M. T., in 3 K. etc. = M. T. כֹּר.

Κύμινον = כַּמֹּן "cummin" Is. xxviii. 25, 27 (already in classical Greek, of Phoenician origin).

Λίβανος = לְבֹנָה "frankincense" (in class. Greek).

[Μανδύας renders מָדוּ, מַד (a garment) in Jd. 1—2 K. 1 Ch. (elsewhere rendered once by χιτών L. vi. 10, twice by ἱμάτιον). The word occurs in a fragment of Aeschylus, where it is used of a Liburnian dress: it is said to be Persian.][1]

[The Semitic origin of μάρσιππος, μαρσίππιον is doubtful.]

Μνᾶ = מנה a weight (classical Greek, probably introduced into the language through the Phoenicians).

Νάβλα = נֶבֶל, נֵבֶל, a lute or other stringed instrument, 1—3 K. 1—2 Ch. 1 M. (in 1 K. x. 5 B νάβαλ): the Heb. is elsewhere rendered by ψαλτήριον Is. 2 Es. Ψ Sir., κιθάρα Ψ lxxx. 2, ὄργανον Am. Νάβλα occurs in a fragment of Sophocles (Dindorf 728) and seems to have come from Phoenicia. (The transliteration νέβελ is kept for נֵבֶל = a wine-jar, see above.)

Νάρδος = נרד (already in Theophrastus).

Νίτρον = נֶתֶר, carbonate of soda, used as soap, Jer. ii. 22. Herodotus and Attic writers use λίτρον in the same sense: νίτρον is used exclusively in the papyri and inscriptions from iii/B.C. onwards (Mayser 188 f.), and, if the Semitic origin is the true one, must have been the original form.

[Παλλακή = פִּלֶגֶשׁ LXX *passim*. The word occurs in classical Greek from Homer (in the form παλλακίς) onwards, and its Semitic origin is very doubtful.]

Σάββατον = שַׁבָּת (שַׁבָּתוֹן) the Sabbath, first found in LXX. In the Pentateuch (except Ex. xxxi. 15 A) and in some of the other books the plural τὰ σάββατα is used both for "the sabbath" and "the sabbaths": the sing. τὸ σάββατον appears in 4 K. 1—2 Ch. 2 Es. Is. lxvi. 23 Lam. 1—2 M. (and in Ψtit with the meaning "week"). Dat. plur. usually σαββάτοις, in 1 M. ii. 38 σάββασιν. Derivatives: σαββατίζειν, προσάββατον.

---

[1] Μανιάκης Dan. Θ 1 Es. is another word probably of Persian origin· it is taken over from the Greek in the Aramaic הַמְנִיכָא in Daniel, where other loan-words from the Greek occur (BDB Lexicon s.v.).

[Σάκκος = שַׂק LXX *passim*. Used in classical Greek, and probably derived from Phoenicia.]

Σαμβύκη (Dan. OΘ) = Aram. שַׂבְּכָא (סַבְּכָא) a stringed instrument, translated in the English Bible by "sackbut" (incorrectly, as the latter was a wind-instrument). Found already in Aristotle and in Polybius (= a siege-engine). Strabo (471) refers to the "barbarous" origin of this and other words for musical instruments: Driver (Dan.) accepts the Aramaic derivation, others consider the word to be "of Syrian or late Egyptian origin" (*Enc. Bibl.* s.v. Music 10).

Σάπφειρος = סַפִּיר, lapis lazuli. (Already used by Theophrastus and the adj. by Aristotle.)

Σίκλος (never σίγλος in LXX MSS) = שֶׁקֶל *passim*, usually of the weight, less often of the coin (the coin in the Hexateuch is generally rendered by δίδραχμον [? δραχμή Jos. vii. 21 B], as also in 2 Es.). Σίγλος is the form attested in Xen. and the Inscriptions (Herwerden Lex. s.v.).

[Σινδών renders סָדִין in Jd. xiv. 12, 13 A, Prov. xxix. 42, but the Semitic origin of the Greek word, which is classical, is doubtful.]

Σιρώνων (gen. pl.) read by certain MSS (see Field: σιώνων A) in Jd. viii. 26 appears to be a Hellenized form of שַׂהֲרֹנִים ("crescents," μηνίσκων B).

Συκάμινος (συκάμινον Am.) = שִׁקְמָה (Aristotle and Theophr.).

Χαυών = כַּוָּן "a sacrificial cake," in Jer. vii. 18, li. 19 (in the latter passage א* reads χαυβῶνας, Q χαυάνας).

[Χιτών, which constantly renders כְּתֹנֶת, is probably of Oriental origin, though the Hebrew is of course not its parent. In 2 Es. ii. 69 κοθωνοί B may be a corruption of κιθῶνες = (in the papyri) χιτῶνες.]

The influence of the Hebrew on the vocabulary of the LXX shows itself not only in transliterations and Hellenized Hebrew words but also in a tendency observable in books other than the Hexateuch to use *Greek words of similar sound to the Hebrew.* The translators in some few cases may have been influenced by a popular but doubtful etymology, e.g. in rendering מוּם by μῶμος: more often, doubt as to the exact meaning of the Hebrew has made them resort to this expedient. Some of the instances may be due to later scribes extracting a meaning out of what were originally transliterations, as when teraphim becomes θεραπείαν (1 K. xv. 23 B), but the most flagrant instances of this confession of ignorance, namely those in Jer. β, appear to go back to the original translator. (See on this tendency e.g. Driver on 1 Sam. x. 2, Deissmann *BS* 99, Mozley *Psalter of the Church* xx.)   The following examples may be quoted: the list is doubtless capable of extension.

(Χελιδών) ἀγροῦ = עָגוּר Jer. viii. 7 (no doubt a corruption of a translit. ἀγούρ, στρουθία being a doublet).   (᾽Αερίνην = וָחוּר "and white" Est. viii. 15 אc.a.)   Αἶδε, οἶδε = הֵידָד "a shout" Jer. xxxi. (xlviii.) 33, xxxii. 16 (xxv. 30).   ᾽Αλαλάζειν, ἀλαλαγμός, ὀλολύζειν, ὀλολυγμός = יָלַל hiph., יְלָלָה *passim* in the Prophets: both the Heb. and the Greek words are onomatopœic.   (῎Εως) ἅμα (τῷ ἡλίῳ) = (הַשֶּׁמֶשׁ) חֹם(עַד־) 2 Es. xvii. 3.   ῾Αρμονία = הָמוֹן Ez. xxiii. 42 (the Heb. may mean "sound" as well as "multitude").   ᾽Αρχι-εταῖρος Δαυίδ applied in 2 K. xv. 32 etc. to Hushai the Archite the friend of David (הארכי רעה דוד) is a curious instance: it might be a natural corruption of an earlier ᾽Αραχεὶ ἑταῖρος (cf. xvii. 5), but the rendering ὁ πρῶτος φίλος in 1 Ch. xxvii. 33 is clearly an adaptation of ἀρχιεταῖρος and is a witness to the early currency of this reading.   ῎Αφεσις = אָפִיק a channel or stream in 2 K. xxii. 16, Jl i. 20, iii. 18 must be partly due to the same cause, similarity of sound, but see Deissmann *BS* 98 ff. on this use and on ὕδωρ ἀφέσεως = מֵי אַפְסָיִם Ez. xlvii. 3.   Βάρβαρος = בָּעַר "brutish" Ez. xxi. 31 (36).   (Βδέλυγμα 4 K. xii. 8 B is probably a scribe's improvement upon the translit. βέδεκ, which A has in this verse and both MSS in the preceding *vv*.) Βόθρος = בוֹר in both parts of Ez. (xxvi. 20, xxxi. 14 etc., but Ez. β also employs the usual LXX rendering λάκκος)[1].   Καί γε = גַם (גַּם!) in some books of the LXX and in the later versions. (?) ᾽Εσχαρίτης "bread baked on the hearth" renders אֶשְׁפָּר (exact meaning doubtful) 2 K. vi. 19: the translators perhaps connected it with אֵשׁ "fire."   ῎Εως ᾅδου = הוֹי אָדוֹן "Ah! lord" (!) Jer. xli. (xxxiv.) 5: the words are correctly rendered in the first part of the book (xxii. 18 οἴμοι κύριε).   (The two exx. following are given by Driver.)   Θάλασσα = תְּעָלָה (a channel) 3 K. xviii. 32, 35, 38. ῾Ιερεῖς = עֶרֶשׂ (a couch) Am. iii. 12: Jerome (ap. Field) suggested

---

[1] ῎Ελαφος was the natural rendering of אַיָּל, which is carefully dis-tinguished by the translators from אַיִל = κριός.

that ἱερεῖς is a correction of an original transliteration. Similarity of sound partly accounts for ἵλεως[1]=חָלִיל (elsewhere rendered μηδαμῶς, μὴ γένοιτο, μὴ εἴη) in 2 K. xx. 20, xxiii. 17 = 1 Ch. xi. 19 (1 K. xiv. 45 A). Κειράδας ("shorn")=קִיר־חֶרֶשׂ Kir-heres Jer. xxxi. (xlviii.) 31, 36 may have arisen out of a transliteration. For χειμάρρους τῶν κέδρων = נחל קִדְרוֹן in 2 K. xv. 23 B, 3 K. xv. 13 see Lightfoot *Biblical Essays* 172 ff., on the readings in John xviii. 1. Κωλύειν (ἀποκωλ.) in several books renders כָּלָא. Λαγχάνειν = לָכַד "take" 1 K. xiv. 47. Λάμπας is the constant rendering of לַפִּיד. Μεγάλως = מֵעָלָי "from off me" Job xxx. 30 (not Θ). Μῶμος is the habitual and natural rendering of מוּם, מְאוּם. Ὀρμή = חֵמָה "fury" Ez. iii. 14, Dan. Θ viii. 6: ὅρμος = חוֹמָה "wall" Ez. xxvii. 11 (cf. ἁρμονία Ez. supra). Οὐαί = הוֹי אוֹי etc. (the Greek interjection appears first in the Alexandrian period). Παγίς (from πήγνυμι) frequently renders פַּח "a snare" (√=to spread), and the resemblance is made closer by the spelling πακίς. Ἡ ῥάχις in 1 K. v. 4 πλὴν ἡ ῥ. Δαγὼν ὑπελείφθη (רַק דָּגוֹן נִשְׁאָר) is a doublet, πλήν being doubtless the older rendering. Ῥοών "a pomegranate orchard" represents (Hadad)rimmon in Zech. xii. 11. Συκοφαντεῖν (-της -τία) renders √עשק "oppress," "defraud" in Ψ Prov. Job Θ Eccl., √שקר "lie," "deceive" in Lev. xix. 11. Τιμωρίαν = תַּמְרוּרִים "guide-posts" Jer. xxxviii. (xxxi.) 21 (possibly from a transliteration τιμρωρ(ε)ίν: Σειών ib. is another instance. Τόκος renders תֹּךְ "oppression" in Ψ liv. 12 RTא[c.a] (κόπος Bא*) lxxi. 14, Jer. ix. 6. Τοπάζιον is suggested by פַּז "refined gold" in Ψ cxviii. 127 (contrast λίθος τίμιος Ψ xviii. 11, xx. 4, Prov. viii. 19). Τύμπανον constantly renders תֹּף (the word should perhaps be included in the previous list as a loan-word). Φακός renders פַּךְ "a flask" (also צַפַּחַת "a cruse") in 1 and 4 K., but this meaning of the Greek word is classical. Φρουραί for Purim in Est. ix. 6 etc. is an illustration of the way in which a Hebrew word was twisted to yield an intelligible meaning to Greeks : the form, if not original, is at least as old as Josephus (*Ant.* xi. 6. 13 ἡμέρας…φρουραίας). Χελώνη Hos. xii. 11 appears to be suggested by the sound of גַּל "a heap," as χάος is suggested by גֵּי גִיא in Mic. i. 6, Zech. xiv. 4.

---

[1] Ἵλεώς σοι etc. were current phrases in the vernacular, J. H. Moulton, *Prol.* 240.

Semitic influence shown (1) *in new meanings and uses of words,* (2) *in syntax.*

Apart from transliterations and Hellenized words, the influence of the Hebrew shows itself in a considerable number of new uses of Greek words and in the coining of new phrases which correspond literally to the Hebrew. A list of new-coined words[1] and of words with a new connotation is given in Dr Swete's *Introduction* p. 307. Here it will merely be necessary to add a few remarks on some new uses to which a few common Greek words are put.

Διδόναι begins to supplant τιθέναι (which still retains its hold in some books), owing to the use of the Heb. נתן in both senses. The use is characteristic of the later historical books though not confined to them : Dt. xxviii. 1 δώσω σε ὑπεράνω, 2 K. xx. 3 ἔδωκεν αὐτὰς ἐν οἴκῳ φυλακῆς, cf. 3 K. vi. 18, 4 K. xvi. 17, Is. lx. 17 δώσω τοὺς ἄρχοντάς σου ἐν εἰρήνῃ, Jer. vi. 27 δοκιμαστὴν δέδωκά σε, Ob. i. 2 etc. (The use of the verb with inf. in the sense of "allow," Gen. xxxi. 7, N. xxi. 23, Jd. xv. 1 B – A ἀφῆκεν is classical.)

The use of ἀριθμῷ for "few" in N. ix. 20 ἡμέρας ἀριθμῷ (ימים מספר), Ez. xii. 16 ἄνδρας ἀριθμῷ (מ אנשי) is removed from the category of "Hebraisms" by a passage like Hdt. vi. 58 ἐπεὰν γὰρ ἀποθάνῃ βασιλεύς...δεῖ...ἀριθμῷ τῶν περιοίκων ἀναγκαστοὺς ἐς τὸ κῆδος ἰέναι "a certain number." The translators usually prefer to write ὀλίγοι (βραχεῖς, ὀλιγοστός) ἀριθμῷ : in Dt. xxxiii. 6 they have either misunderstood or intentionally perverted the meaning, ἔστω πολὺς ἐν ἀριθμῷ.

The Heb. ימים, when used of a year or other period of time, is literally rendered by ἡμέραι in phrases like ἀφ' (ἐξ) ἡμερῶν εἰς ἡμέρας Ex. xiii. 10, Jd. xi. 40, xxi. 19, 1 K. i. 3 etc., δύο ἔτη (ἐνιαυτὸς) ἡμερῶν Gen. xli. 1, 2 K. xiv. 28 (cf. xiii. 23 διετηρίδα ἡμερῶν), Jer. xxxv. 3, Lev. xxv. 29, μῆνα ἡμερῶν Gen. xxix. 14, N. xi. 20 f., Jdth iii. 10 (more classical Dt. xxi. 13

---

[1] Προσωπολημπτεῖν should be deleted (p. 44), and for ἀναθεματίζειν see p. 27 above.

κλαύσεται...μηνὸς ἡμέρας), ἑβδομὰς ἡμερῶν Dan. Θ x. 2 f. (Dan. O
omits "days" in 2 and inserts τῶν in 3), θυσία τῶν ἡμερῶν
(Heb. = "yearly sacrifice") 1 K. i. 21, xx. 6. The Heb. phrases
"year of days" etc. mean either "a year of time" (BDB.) or "a
full year" (R.V.) etc.: in the latter sense class. Greek writes
τέλεος ἐνιαυτός, τελέους ἑπτὰ μῆνας etc.

The use of ימים = "a year" has been misunderstood and the
word omitted in N. ix. 22 μηνὸς ἡμέρας (= M. T. "either two
days or a month or a year," lit. "or days"), cf. the omission of
ימים ו 1 K. xxvii. 7 : it is also misunderstood in 2 Ch. xxi. 19
(Heb. "at the end of two years") where the Gk apparently
means "when the time of the days amounted to two days."

Other examples of literalism in time-statements are ἀνὰ
μέσον τῶν ἑσπερινῶν Lev. xxiii. 5 (elsewhere in Pent. expressed
by (τὸ) πρὸς ἑσπέραν, τὸ δειλινόν, ὀψέ), ὡς ἅπαξ καὶ ἅπαξ
(= בפעם בפעם = as time after time) Jd. xvi. 20 B, xx. 30 f.,
1 K. iii. 10, xx. 25 (idiomatically rendered N. xxiv. 1 κατὰ τὸ
εἰωθός, Jd. xvi. 20 A καθὼς ἀεί).

Εἰρήνη takes over the meaning of the Heb. שלום in some
formulas of salutation, being used of the health or welfare of a
single individual, as well as of friendly relations between
nations. The Heb. phrase for "to greet" is שאל ל לשלום "to
ask someone about peace (welfare)." Hence in the later
historical books we find phrases like Jd. xviii. 15 B εἰσῆλθον εἰς
τὸν οἶκον...καὶ ἠρώτησαν αὐτὸν εἰς εἰρήνην (= A ἠσπάσαντο αὐτόν),
cf. 1 K. xvii. 22 A, xxv. 5 : we even find ἐπερωτᾶν...εἰς εἰρήνην
τοῦ πολέμου 2 K. xi. 7 for "to ask how the war progressed":
occasionally the neut. of the definite article is inserted, ἐρωτᾶν
τὰ εἰς εἰρήνην 1 K. x. 4, xxx. 21 B, 2 K. viii. 10 = 1 Ch. xviii. 10[1]
The same group of books uses εἰρήνη (σοι) "peace be to
thee," Ἡ εἰρήνη σοι; ἠ εἰρήνη τῷ ἀνδρί σου; κ.τ.λ. 4 K. iv. 26
"is it well with thee?" (class. χαῖρε, ὑγιαίνεις;): in 3 K. ii. 13

---

[1] In the N.T. Luke in xiv. 32, borrowing the LXX phrase, uses it of
a king negotiating for peace, thus keeping the classical meaning of εἰρήνη.

the noun takes the place of the adj., εἰρήνη ἡ εἴσοδός σου; Contrast with the later historical books the more classical phrases used in Genesis xliii. 27 ἠρώτησεν δὲ αὐτοὺς Πῶς ἔχετε; xxix. 6, xxxvii. 14, xliii. 27 f. ὑγιαίνει; etc., and the use of ἀσπάζεσθαι in Ex. xviii. 7, Jd. xviii. 15 A. The later books (including Tobit ℵ) further have πορεύεσθαι (βαδίζειν, δεῦρο) εἰς εἰρήνην (ἐν εἰρήνῃ): the Pent. also uses εἰρήνη in a similar way but with another preposition, μετ᾽ εἰρήνης ἀπέρχεσθαι (ἥκειν) Gen. xv. 15: elsewhere βαδίζειν ὑγιαίνων Ex. iv. 18, 2 K. xiv. 8.

ʿΡῆμα = דבר = *res* appears to be a Hebraism, but may have been so used in colloquial Greek: a similar use of λόγος has classical authority. Exx.: Gen. xv. 1 μετὰ δὲ τὰ ῥήματα ταῦτα, xxii. 1 etc., Gen. xxxviii. 10 πονηρὸν δὲ ἐφάνη τὸ ῥῆμα...ὅτι ἐποίησεν τοῦτο, Dt. ii. 7 οὐκ ἐπεδεήθης ῥήματος (= οὐδενός) etc. In the N. T. it is noticeable that the use is, apart from O. T. quotations, confined to the more Hebraic portions of Luke's writings. Exodus twice uses the adj. ῥητός in a similar way · ix. 4 οὐ τελευτήσει ἀπὸ πάντων τῶν τοῦ Ἰσραὴλ υἱῶν ῥητόν (= οὐδείς), xxii. 9 κατὰ πᾶν ῥητὸν ἀδίκημα "in any wrong doing whatsoever." The literal translation of על דברת "in the matter of," "to the end that" by περὶ λαλιᾶς, περὶ λόγου is a peculiarity of Aquila, Eccl. iii. 18, vii. 15, viii. 2: contrast Ex. viii 12 (8) περί = על דבר and the omission of דבר ib. xvi. 4 τὸ τῆς ἡμέρας εἰς ἡμέραν.

Υἱός is used to render some idiomatic phrases with בן, but this Hebraism is mainly confined to the literal group: the Hexateuch, Isaiah and Chronicles generally avoid it.

(a) Of age. Heb. says "a son of so many years" for "so many years old." Hence Gen. xi. 10 Σὴμ υἱὸς ἐτῶν ἑκατόν (the only example in the Hexateuch), cf. Jd. ii. 8 B, 1 K. iv. 15 2 K. iv. 4, v. 4, xix. 32, 35, 3 K. xii. 24 a, 24 h, xxii. 42, 4 K. *passim*, 2 Ch. xxvi. 3 BA, ib. (in A text only) xxviii. 1, xxxvi. 2, 9 (31 examples in all, of which 19 occur in K. βδ).

On the other hand the simple gen. of age or some other paraphrase is frequent in the Hexateuch (Gen. vii. 6, xii. 4 etc. : Ex. xxx. 14 ἀπὸ εἰκοσαετοῦς etc.: Ex. xii. 5 etc. ἐνιαύσιος), and Chronicles (1 Ch. ii. 21, 2 Ch. xxi. 5, 20, xxii. 2 etc.) and occurs occasionally elsewhere, 2 K. ii. 10, 2 Es. iii. 8, Is. lxv. 20, Jer. lii. 1, Dan. Θ v. 31. Παιδίον ὀκτὼ ἡμερῶν Gen. xvii. 12 is classical.

(*b*) Of characteristics, qualities etc. The same distinction in the books holds good. Jd.—4 K., 2 Es., Ψ, Ez. write e.g. υἱὸς ἀλλότριος, υἱὸς ἀλλογενής (an alien נכר בן), υἱὸς δυνάμεως, υἱὸς ἀδικίας e.g. 2 K. vii. 10 (= 1 Ch. xvii. 9 ‖ ἀδικία simply), υἱοὶ τῶν συμμίξεων "hostages," 4 K. xiv. 14 = 2 Ch. xxv. 24, υἱοὶ θανατώσεως or θανάτου 1 K. xxvi. 16, 2 K. xii. 5 (cf. Ψ lxxviii. 11, ci. 21, υἱοὶ τῶν τεθανατωμένων); on the other hand books like the Hexateuch and Isaiah omit υἱός or employ paraphrase, writing ἀλλογενής, ἀλλόφυλος Gen. xvii. 27, Ex. xii. 43 etc., Is. lx. 10, lxi. 5 (but υἱὸς ἀλλ. Gen. xvii. 12, Is. lxii. 8), ἐκ βοῶν etc. = בן בקר Ex. xxix. 1 etc. (contrast 1 K. xiv. 32 τέκνα βοῶν): further paraphrases occur in e.g. Dt. xxv. 2 ἄξιος ᾖ πληγῶν, Is. v. 1 ἐν τόπῳ πίονι, xiv. 12 ὁ πρωὶ ἀνατέλλων, xxi. 10 οἱ ὀδυνώμενοι.

Hebrew is fond of what may be called *physiognomical expressions*, that is to say phrases referring to parts of the human body, ear, eye, face, hand, mouth etc.: in particular, many prepositions are seldom found without some such adjunct. This accounts for a wide use of ὀφθαλμός, πρόσωπον, στόμα, χείρ etc., in the LXX: many of the LXX phrases are, however, passable, if unidiomatic, Greek expressions: the Hebrew has merely given them a wider circulation. A perfectly literal translation is avoided where the vernacular had some similar, but not identical, phrase. Thus ἐνώπιον, which is unknown to the classical language, but is found in papyri from ii/—i/ B.C. onwards[1], is a favourite rendering of לפני and בעיני.

---

[1] Deissmann *BS* 213 : Dr J. H. Moulton adds Teb. 14 (114 B.C.) and other examples of adjectival ἐνώπιος. The word is retained in modern Greek,

The following are some of the more striking instances of direct imitation of the Hebrew.

'Αποκαλύπτειν (ἀνοίγειν) τὸ οὖς (ὠτίον) τινος = "to reveal to someone" R. iv. 4, 1 K. ix. 15, xx. 2 etc., 2 K. vii. 27, 1 Ch. xvii. 25.

As regards the use of ὀφθαλμός in phrases like "to seem good" or "to find favour in the eyes (i.e. in the estimation) of someone" (בעיני) we find the same sort of distinction between the groups of books as elsewhere. The classical παρά τινι or other paraphrase is rarely found. As a rule the Pentateuch with some of the other books render בעיני by ἐναντίον (or the vernacular ἐνώπιον, ἔναντι), while the literal rendering ἐν ὀφθαλμοῖς is reserved for the later historical books[1].

Exx.: "To find (give) favour in someone's eyes" is rendered by (1) χάριν ἔχειν (εὑρίσκειν) παρά τινι in Ex. xxxiii. 12, 16, N. xi. 15 (cf. Est. ii. 15), (2) εὑρ. (διδόναι) χάριν ἐναντίον (ἐνώπ.) τινος some 24 times in the Pent., Gen. xxx. 27 etc., also in 3 K. xi. 19, Est. v. 8, vii. 3, (3) εὑρ. χάριν (ἔλεος) ἐν ὀφθαλμοῖς τινος in (Gen. xxxiii. 8 A: all other MSS ἐναντίον or ἐνώπ.) Jd. vi. 17, R. ii. 2, 10, 13, 1 K. i. 18, xvi. 22 etc., 2 K. xiv. 22, xv. 25, xvi. 4. The phrases "to seem good (evil etc.) in someone's eyes" are (1) paraphrased in Gen. xvi. 6 ἀρεστὸν ᾖ, Jos. ix. 31 ἀρέσκει, (2) rendered by ἀρέσκειν (ἀρεστόν, σκληρόν etc.) ἐναντίον (ἐνώπιον, ἔναντι) in the Pent., Gen. xvi. 4 f., xix. 14 etc., N. xxxvi. 6, Dt. xii. 8, 25, iv. 25, also in Jd. ii. 11, iii. 7, 2 K. x. 3, 1 Ch. xix. 3, (3) by ἀγαθὸν (εὐθές, πονηρὸν, εὐθύνεσθαι etc.) ἐν ὀφθαλμοῖς τινος *passim* in Jd., 1 K., 2 K. (from x. 12), 4 K. and in some of the later books. The adhesion of Wisdom (iii. 2, ix. 9) to the last group is noticeable.

Πρόσωπον (which is found in Polybius with the meaning "person") is kept in the rendering of נשא פנים "to accept the person" (to favour or be partial to anyone), but the verb is usually altered. Θαυμάζειν τὸ πρόσωπον is the rendering which met with general acceptance (Gen. xix. 21, Dt. x. 17, xxviii. 50,

Kennedy *Sources of N.T. Greek* 155. In N.T. its absence from Mt. and Mc. is striking: Lc. and Ap. make a large use of it.
[1] And is unexampled in the N.T.

4 K. v. 1, Prov. xviii. 5, Job xiii. 10 etc., Is. ix. 15). Another verb has been occasionally substituted, προσδέχεσθαι Gen. xxxii. 20, αἱρετίζειν 1 K. xxv. 35, ἐπαισχύνεσθαι Job xxxiv. 19. The literal version λαμβάνειν (τὸ) πρόσωπον occurs only in Lev. xix. 15 (necessitated by the use of θαυμάζειν in the same v.), Ψ lxxxi. 2, Job xlii. 8, Lam. iv. 16, Mal. i. 8 f., ii. 9. Later formations, unknown to the Alexandrian translators[1], and first appearing in the N.T., are προσωπολημπτεῖν, -λήμπτης, -λημψία. It is interesting to note the three stages through which the Hebrew idiom finds its way into Greek: first the possible but un-idiomatic version, then the baldly literal, then the new Greek words coined from the literal version. Ἀπὸ προσώπου, πρὸ προσώπου etc. (where the classical language would use the prep. alone) abound.

Hebraistic uses of **στόμα** may be illustrated by such phrases as ἐπερωτᾶν τὸ στόμα τινός Gen. xxiv. 57, ἐπὶ τῷ στόματί σου ὑπακούσεται πᾶς ὁ λαός Gen. xli. 40, ἐπὶ στόματος δύο μαρτύρων... στήσεται πᾶν ῥῆμα Dt. xix. 15. But the prepositional phrases עַל פִּי, בְּפִי, לְפִי "according to" are, in the Pentateuch at least, usually rendered by a simple prep., κατά c. acc. (Gen. xliii. 7, xlv. 21, N. vi. 21, Dt. xvii. 11), πρός c. acc. (L. xxv. 51 πρὸς ταῦτα) or ἐπί c. dat. (Dt. xvii. 6). The avoidance of anthropomorphism sometimes causes omission or paraphrase of "mouth" where God is spoken of: Jos. ix. 20 ἐπηρώτησαν, N. iii. 16 etc. διὰ φωνῆς Κυρίου.

The uses of **χείρ** in prepositional phrases (on the model of בְּיַד and kindred phrases) are innumerable: many of these, however, may be illustrated from the Hellenistic language. Ἐμπιμπλάναι (τελειοῦν, πληροῦν) τὰς χεῖρας Ex. xxviii. 37 etc., is the literal rendering of the Hebrew for "to consecrate." An example of literal reproduction of the Hebrew is 4 K. ix. 24 ἔπλησεν τὴν χεῖρα ἐν τῷ τόξῳ: in ἀποστέλλειν τὴν χεῖρα Ex. ix. 15

---

[1] Προσωπολημπτεῖν should be deleted from the list in Dr Swete's *Introduction* 307.

and similar phrases the Hebraism lies in the new meaning attached to the verb. (The meaning "handiwork" (Jer. x. 9) is known to secular Greek : possibly the translators attached the same meaning to Χεὶρ ᾿Αβεσσαλώμ, the name given to the "monument" (יד) of Absalom, 2 K. xviii. 18.)

Under the head of *pronouns* we notice an increased use of ἀνήρ (ἄνθρωπος), due to the influence of the Hebrew אִישׁ, where classical writers would have written ἕκαστος, τις or πᾶς τις, and of phrases like ἄνθρωπος πρὸς- τὸν πλησίον (ἀδελφὸν) αὐτοῦ for ἕτερος πρὸς τὸν ἕτερον. Though the imitation of the Hebrew is unmistakable, it is difficult to draw the line between what may be called "Hebraisms" and what is good vernacular or κοινή Greek. The use of ἀνήρ for τις can be illustrated from Aristophanes. The rarity of phrases like ἕτερος τὸν ἕτερον (still found in the Pentateuch, Isaiah and the early chapters of Ezekiel) is partly due to the tendency in the κοινή to abandon words expressive of duality. But it is noticeable that the use of ἀνήρ = ἕκαστος in phrases like δότε μοι ἀνὴρ ἐνώτιον Jd. viii. 24, λάβωμεν ἀνὴρ εἰς δοκὸν μίαν 4 K. vi. 2, is practically confined to one group of books viz. Jd., R., K. βγ (2 K. xiii. 29 B, xx. 1, 3 K. i. 49), K. γδ (3 K. xxii. 10, 4 K. iii. 23 etc.), 2 Es. (cf. Cant. iii. 8, Ez. xviii. 8, xxxiii. 26 A, 1 M. ii. 40) : in these books ἕκαστος, which is freely used in other parts of the LXX, is either wholly or nearly unrepresented[1]. Here, then, in view of the avoidance of the literal rendering in the majority of the books, we appear to be justified in speaking of a Hebraism. With a negative ἀνήρ replaces μηδείς or οὐδείς : 4 K. x. 19 ἀνὴρ μὴ ἐπισκεπήτω, x. 25, xxiii. 18. ᾿Ανήρ is occasionally used of inanimate things :

---

[1] The distinction between the portions of the Kingdom books should be noted. ῎Εκαστος = אִישׁ is freely used in K. a (19 times), K. ββ (5), K. γγ (13). On the other hand it is absent from K. βγ (excepting 2 K. xiii. 29 A) and occurs twice only in the B text of K. γδ (3 times in A text).

Job (probably Θ) xli. 8 (of the scales of leviathan).   The duplication ἄνθρωπος ἄνθρωπος, ἀνδρὶ ἀνδρί = "anyone" (Lev. xv. 2, xvii. 3 etc., Ez. xiv. 4, 7) is analogous to vernacular phrases (Moulton *Prol.* 97).

The pleonastic demonstrative pronoun appended to a relative pronoun or a relative adverb, e.g. ᾧ...αὐτῷ (= לו אשׁר), οὗ...ἐκεῖ (= שׁם אשׁר), is found in all parts of the LXX and undoubtedly owes its *frequency* to the Hebrew original.   But the fact that it is found in an original Greek work such as 2 Macc. (xii. 27 ἐν ᾗ...ἐν αὐτῇ) and a paraphrase such as 1 Esdras (iii. 5, 9, iv. 54, 63, vi. 32) is sufficient to warrant its presence in the κοινή[1].   In modern Greek the relative is expressed by the adverb ποῦ followed by the demonstrative in its proper case—a use which is strangely analogous to the Hebrew.   In the LXX the laws of concord are observed: the relative and demonstrative agree in gender, number and case, and if the demonstrative is preceded by a preposition the relative as a rule takes one as well (e.g. Gen. xxiv. 3 μεθ᾽ ὧν...μετ᾽ αὐτῶν : similarly ὅθεν ἐκεῖθεν Gen. x. 14 etc., not οὗ ἐκ.).   The fact that this phenomenon, which, as Dr J. H. Moulton remarks, is made familiar to Englishmen by the language of Mrs Gamp, should have grown up independently in the two languages is not surprising.

Under the head of *prepositions*, Hebrew is responsible for the *extensive* use of a large number of prepositional phrases in place of an accusative after a transitive verb.   The fact, however, that a phrase like φυλάσσεσθαι ἀπό τινος is found already in Xenophon makes us cautious in regarding all these as Hebraisms.   Several of them probably never found a place in the Greek language : the use of the preposition, which was allowable with one verb, was extended to others, where the Hebrew had an analogous use.   Besides the instance mentioned ἀπό (corresponding to מן) is used after αἰσχύνεσθαι, εὐλαβεῖσθαι, λανθάνειν, προσέχειν, τρέμειν, ὑπερηφανεύεσθαι, ὑπερ

---

[1] No instance of it seems, however, to have been found in the papyri: the example quoted by Kühner and Blass from Hdt. iv. 44 is rather different : Blass quotes ὧν...τούτων from Hypereides.   It would appear that it was not a very common use : in the N.T. it is quite uncommon, the Apocalypse alone using it with any frequency (7 times).

ὁρᾶν, φοβεῖσθαι. Similarly, ἐν (בְּ) is used instead of an accusative after αἱρετίζειν, εὐδοκεῖν, θέλειν, συνιέναι etc. In the same way, we find φείδεσθαι ἐπί (עַל) τινα, ἐξελέσθαι ἐπί τινα (Job Θ xxxvi. 21), συνιέναι ἐπί τινα (Job Θ xxxi. 1). The Theodotion portions of Job supply numerous examples of direct imitation of the Hebrew: ζητεῖν ὀπίσω τινός xxxix. 8, μέχρι (ἕως) ὑμῶν συνήσω (עַד) xxxii. 12, φῶς ἐγγὺς ἀπὸ προσώπου σκότους xvii. 12.

The frequent LXX use of ἐν of accompanying circumstances or instrument, as in St Paul's ἐν ῥάβδῳ ἔλθω...; (1 Cor. iv. 21) has been removed from the category of Hebraisms by the appearance of ἐν μαχαίρῃ, ἐν ὅπλοις 'armed with a sword' etc. in a little group of papyri of the end of ii/B.C. (Teb. 41. 4, *c.* 119 B.C., etc.).

A test-case for the length to which the translators were ready to carry their imitation of the Hebrew is afforded by their treatment of "the *infinitive absolute*" in phrases like מוֹת תָּמוּת "thou shalt surely die." (*a*) A solitary instance occurs of an attempt to render the Hebrew construction quite literally, Jos. xvii. 13 B ἐξολεθρεῦσαι δὲ αὐτοὺς οὐκ ἐξωλέθρευσαν (A ὀλεθρεύσει). (*b*) In a certain number of cases (mainly in the Pentateuch) the Hebrew inf. is simply omitted. (*c*) The practice of our English translators[1] of employing an adverb, particle or other form of paraphrase is occasionally resorted to: Gen. xxxii. 12 καλῶς εὖ σε ποιήσω (not a doublet), Ex. xv. 1 ἐνδόξως δεδόξασται, N. xxii. 17 ἐντίμως τιμήσω σε, 4 K. v. 11 πάντως ἐξελεύσεται, Prov. (in all three cases where the Hebrew construction appears[2]) xxiii. 1 νοητῶς νόει, xxiii. 24, xxvii. 23: Is. lvi. 3 ἀφοριεῖ με ἄρα: Job xiii. 10 οὐθὲν ἧττον, Gen. xlvi. 4 = Am. ix. 8 εἰς τέλος.

---

[1] E.g. Is. xxiv. 19, "The earth is *utterly* broken down, the earth is *clean* dissolved, the earth is moved *exceedingly*." The A.V. shows great versatility in its renderings. Elsewhere we have "*freely* eat," "*must needs* be circumcised," "*indeed* I was stolen away," "*in any wise* return."

[2] In Prov. xxiv. 22 a (not in M.T.) δεχόμενος ἐδέξατο.

But as a general rule the rendering takes one of two forms:
(*d*) finite verb with dat. of the cognate noun, e.g. βρώσει φάγῃ
Gen. ii. 16, (*e*) finite verb with participle of the same verb or
a verb of kindred meaning, e.g. Gen. iii. 16 πληθύνων πληθυνῶ.
The total number of occurrences of these two constructions
is about the same, approximately 200 of each : but there is a
marked diversity between the groups of books in the preference
shown for one mode of translation or the other. The Pentateuch prefers the construction of noun and verb, which is used
more than twice as often as part. and verb. The former
construction is always used in the Pentateuch where the verb
is in the passive, e.g. Gen. xvii. 13 περιτομῇ περιτμηθήσεται, xl. 15
κλοπῇ ἐκλάπην, Dt. xxi. 14 πράσει οὐ πραθήσεται. Where the
verb is active or middle either construction may be used: cf.
Gen. ii. 16 βρώσει φάγῃ with Lev. vii. 8 φαγὼν φάγῃ, Dt. xxiv.
13 ἀποδόσει ἀποδώσεις with xv. 10 διδοὺς δώσεις : but, generally
speaking, the Pentateuch translators prefer (*d*) wherever there
is a convenient noun available. Where the participial construction is used in the Pentateuch, it is often rendered more
idiomatic by varying the verb (e.g. Gen. xviii. 10 ἐπαναστρέφων
ἥξω, Ex. xxiii. 4 ἀποστρέψας ἀποδώσεις, Lev. xiii. 7 μεταβαλοῦσα
μεταπέσῃ, xiv. 48 παραγενόμενος εἰσέλθῃ) or by using the simple
and compound verb (as Herodotus uses φεύγων ἐκφεύγειν v. 95,
e.g. Gen. xliii. 7 ἐρωτῶν ἐπηρώτ., Lev. x. 16 ζητῶν ἐξεζήτησεν,
N. xii. 14, xxx. 15). Instances of the bald use of the pres.
part. and finite form of the same verb are not frequent till we
come to Deuteronomy, which has nine of them.

In the later historical books, on the other hand, the participial construction is used almost exclusively. The four
Kingdom books, apart from a single phrase[1] θανάτῳ ἀποθανεῖται
(θανατώσητε etc.: 1 K. xiv. 39, 44, xxii. 16, 2 K. xii. 14, xiv. 14,
3 K. ii. 37, 42, iii. 26 f., 4 K. i. 4, 6, 16, viii. 10, xi. 15) and its

---

[1] Its occurrence in the familiar story of the Fall (Gen. ii. 17, iii. 4)
probably accounts for its retention.

opposite ζωῇ ζήσῃ (4 K. viii. 10, 14), have only three examples of the verb with cognate noun, all in 2 Kingdoms, viz. i. 6 περιπτώματι περιέπεσαν, xviii. 3 φυγῇ φύγωμεν, xix. 42 βρώσει ἐφάγαμεν (βρῶσιν A). On the other hand in 1—4 K. there are 59 examples of the participial construction[1]. We note, further, that this construction is now used even where the main verb is passive, e.g. 1 K. ii. 27 ἀποκαλυφθεὶς ἀπεκαλύφθην, 2 K. vi. 20 ἀποκαλύπτεται ἀποκαλυφθείς, xx. 18 ἠρωτημένος ἠρωτήθην : the participle may stand after the finite verb, as in 2 K. vi. 20 : the use of different verbs or of simple and compound verb is abandoned (the nearest approach to this being 1 K. xx. 21 εἴπω λέγων, 3 K. xiii. 32 γινόμενον ἔσται, 4 K. xiv. 10 τύπτων ἐπάταξας). In the remaining books of the LXX the participial construction preponderates, except in Isaiah (eight examples of noun to three of part.), Ezekiel, Micah and the A texts of Joshua (two of noun to one of part.) and of Judges (ten of noun to eight of part.). The tense of the part. is present or aorist : a future is used in Jd. iv. 9 A πορευσομένη πορεύσομαι, Sir. xxviii. 1 διαστηριῶν διαστηρίσει, so Aquila in Ψ xlix. 21.

Neither construction appears to occur in the "Greek" (i.e. untranslated) books. Instances, however, are found of both forms where there is no inf. abs. in the M.T.: most of these are probably due to the translators having a different text from our Hebrew. In the N.T. there are no examples of the participial construction except in O.T. quotations (Blass § 74, 4). The other construction is employed by Luke in both his works (ἐπιθυμίᾳ ἐπεθύμ., ἀπειλῇ ἀπειλ., παραγγελίᾳ παρήγγ., ἀναθέματι ἀνεθεμ.), as also in Jo. iii. 29 χαρᾷ χαίρει, Ja. v. 17 προσευχῇ προσηύξατο (ibid. § 38, 3).

It appears, then, that the Pentateuch translators, in rendering this Hebrew idiom, had resort to one or other of two modes of translation, both of which had some authority in the

---

[1] For the Pentateuch the statistics are approximately noun and verb 108, part. and verb 49.

classical language, recalling, respectively, the phrases cited by
Blass and J. H. Moulton, viz. γάμῳ γαμεῖν ("in true wedlock"),
φυγῇ φεύγειν ("with all speed") and the φεύγων ἐκφεύγει
of Herodotus. Their successors confined themselves almost
entirely to the latter, probably considering the participle a
nearer approach to the Hebrew infinitive, but refrained from a
perfectly literal rendering which would have defied the laws of
Greek syntax. Even the participial construction seemed so
strange that it found no imitators in the N.T. writers.

Constructions with ἐγένετο. "When the Hebrew writers
have occasion in the course of their narrative to insert a clause
specifying the circumstances under which an action takes
place, instead of introducing it abruptly, they are in the habit
of (so to speak) preparing the way for it by the use of the
formula וַיְהִי '*and it was* or *came to pass*'" (Driver *Hebrew
Tenses*, ed. 3, p. 89). The sentence is usually, though not always,
resumed by a second ו. This construction is in the majority
of cases reproduced in the LXX. Of the three forms found
in the N.T. (almost entirely in Luke's writings), viz. (*a*) ἐγένετο
ἦλθε, (*b*) ἐγένετο καὶ ἦλθε, (*c*) ἐγένετο ἐλθεῖν, LXX, with a single
exception [1], uses the first two only. Luke in his Gospel writes
(*a*) twice as often as (*b*) and (*b*) twice as often as (*c*): in Acts
he abandons the first two altogether in favour of (*c*). (*c*), as
Moulton shows, can be closely paralleled from the papyri
which use γίνεται c. inf., and at a far earlier time γίγνεται εὑρεῖν
"it is possible to find" is attested in Theognis 639 (quoted by
LS). Xenophon, moreover, uses ἐγένετο ὥστε or ὡς "it happened that." (*c*) therefore had close analogies in the vernacular
and literary speech. (*a*) and (*b*), on the contrary, appear in

---

[1] 3 K. xi. 43 B καὶ ἐγενήθη ὡς ἤκουσεν Ἱεροβοὰμ...κατευθύνειν " he came
straight off" (the Heb. [xii. 2] is different). In 3 K. iv. 7 μῆνα ἐν τῷ ἐνιαυτῷ
ἐγίνετο ἐπὶ τὸν ἕνα χορηγεῖν the inf. is the subject of the verb, cf. 2 Ch. vi. 7.
In 2 M. iii. 16 (quoted by J. H. Moulton) ἦν δὲ...ὁρῶντα...τιτρώσκεσθαι,
21 V ἐλεεῖν δὲ ἦν, the verb seems rather the equivalent of ἔδει "it was
impossible not to," than of ἐγένετο: cf. ib. vi. 9 παρῆν οὖν ὁρᾶν.

Luke to be borrowed directly from the LXX, and for these constructions no illustration has yet been quoted from the κοινή. The statistics for the LXX are (if my count is right) as follows: passages where the readings vary (there are not many) have been included in both columns.

		(a) ἐγένετο ἦλθε	(b) ἐγένετο καὶ ἦλθε
Pentateuch { Gen. 34, Ex. 12, L.N.Dt. 4 }		50	{ Gen. 25, Ex. 5, L.N.Dt. 9 } 39
Jos.		7	9
Jd.—4 Kings		26	164
1 2 Ch.		1	19
1 Es. (A text)			—
2 Es.			11
Other "Writings"			4
{ Prophets, Min. Is. Jer. Lam. Ez. }		28	12
Daniel O		2	3
„ Θ		6	3
1 Macc.			5
	Total	145	269

The following results are to be noted. (1) The construction (b) predominates in the Greek as does its equivalent in the Hebrew. (2) But this preponderance is due to the support given to it by the later historical books, which generally follow the Heb. slavishly. (3) The first two books of the Pentateuch, on the other hand, and the prophetical books, prefer (a). A closer analysis shows that in Genesis the Heb. has a second ו in 30 out of the 34 cases where the Greek uses (a), as well as in all the cases of (b). 4 K. on the other hand, which reads (a) 12 times, (b) 26 times, only twice omits καί without warrant from the M.T. (v. 7, vi. 30). It appears that while both (a) and (b) were experiments of the translators, which must be classed as "Hebraisms," the apposition of the two verbs

---

[1] We may perhaps compare in the papyri καλῶς ποιήσεις γράψεις (πέμψεις) OP ii. 297. 3 (54 A.D.), ib. 299. 3 (late i/A.D) for the more usual γράψας.

without καί was rather more in the spirit of the later language, which preferred to say e.g. " It happened last week I was on a journey," rather than " It was a week ago and I was journeying." At all events the former mode of speech prevails in the earlier LXX books and in Luke's Gospel. (4) The free Greek books (2—4 Macc.) abjure both constructions, and the paraphrases make very little use of them. These two classes of books, on the other hand, retain the classical συνέβη with the inf.[1]

In Jd. xii. 5 A we appear to have a fourth construction καὶ ἐγενήθη ὅτι εἶπαν αὐτοῖς οἱ διασεσωσμένοι..., though ὅτι may be intended for "because" (Heb. כי = "when"): a similar doubt attaches to 2 K. xiv. 26, 4 K. xvii. 7, 2 Ch. v. 11 (Heb. כי = " because ").

The less frequent והיה (1) with the meaning "it shall come to pass" is rendered[2] by καὶ ἔσται, usually without a second copula, which is generally absent from the Heb., (2) in frequentative sense "it came to pass repeatedly" by the imperfect, Gen. xxxviii. 9 ἐγίνετο, ὅταν εἰσήρχετο..., ἐξέχεεν.

Next to ἐγένετο probably the most frequent Hebraism in the LXX is the *use of* προστιθέναι (προστίθεσθαι) = יסף *in place of* πάλιν or a similar adverb. Here again the construction takes three forms : (*a*) προσέθετο (προσέθηκεν) λαβεῖν (τοῦ λαβεῖν), (*b*) προσέθετο (προσέθηκεν) καὶ ἔλαβεν, (*c*) προσθεὶς (προσθέμενος) ἔλαβεν. (*c*), the only one of the three for which approximate classical parallels could be quoted, is limited to the following passages : Job xxvii. 1 ἔτι δὲ προσθεὶς...εἶπεν (so xxix. 1, xxxvi. 1), Est. viii. 3 καὶ προσθεῖσα ἐλάλησεν, Gen. xxv. 1 προσθέμενος δὲ Ἀβραὰμ ἔλαβεν γυναῖκα "took another wife" (the passage quoted in LS, Soph. *Trach.* 1224 ταύτην

[1] Also in Gen. xli. 13, xlii. 38.
[2] The Hexateuch sometimes omits the introductory verb: Gen. iv. 14, xlvi. 33, Ex. i. 10, iv. 8, xxxiii. 8 f., Dt. xviii. 19, Jos. vii. 15.

προσθοῦ γυναῖκα, "take to wife," is not really parallel), xxxviii. 5 καὶ προσθεῖσα ἔτι ἔτεκεν υἱόν. (*a*) and (*b*) are directly imitated from the Hebrew, (*a*) being far the commoner (109 exx. as against 9 of (*b*)).

The verb may be either active or middle, the instances of the two voices are nearly equal (60 : 58): προσθήσω and προσθήσομαι (προστεθήσομαι) alternate, but the mid. aor. προσεθέμην preponderates (προσέθηκα mainly in the later historical books, Gen. xviii. 29, Jd. viii. 28 B, xi. 14 B etc., 3 K. xvi. 33, 2 Ch. xxviii. 22, Dan. O x. 18). 1 K. only uses the mid. (προσέθετο with simple inf. 12 times): the Min. Proph. only the act. (προσθήσω or προσθῶ c. inf. with τοῦ 9 times).

There are also a few examples of an absolute use of the verb: Job ☉ xx. 9 ὀφθαλμὸς παρέβλεψεν καὶ οὐ προσθήσει, (? ☉) xxvii. 19, ☉ xxxiv. 32, Sir. xix. 13, xxi. 1. In the N.T. Luke again imitates the LXX, having three examples of (*a*), xx. 11 f. προσέθετο πέμψαι, Acts xii. 3 προσέθετο συλλαβεῖν and one of (*c*), xix. 11 προσθεὶς εἶπεν παραβολήν. The use of (*a*) is the only Hebraism which has been detected in Josephus[1]

An analogous use of ἐπιστρέφειν (= שׁוּב) followed by (*a*) inf. or (*b*) καί + finite verb is restricted to Theodotion, Aquila and portions of the LXX having affinities with the style of those translators: in some passages possibly the verb keeps its literal meaning: (*a*) Dt. xxx. 9 ἐπιστρέψει Κύριος...εὐφρανθῆναι, 2 Es. ix. 14 ἐπεστρέψαμεν διασκεδάσαι ἐντολάς σου, xix. 28, Eccl. i. 7, v. 14 ἐπιστρ. τοῦ πορευθῆναι, (*b*) 2 Ch. xxxiii. 3 ἐπέστρεψεν καὶ ᾠκοδόμησεν, cf. Mal. i. 4, Dan. ☉ ix. 25 ἐπιστρέψει καὶ οἰκοδομηθήσεται "shall be built again." Cf. a similar use of ἐπανέρχεσθαι c. inf. in Job (? ☉) vii. 7.

Elsewhere שׁוּב in this sense is rendered by πάλιν alone (Gen. xxvi. 18, xxx. 31 etc.) or with a verb, πάλιν πορεύεσθαι, βαδίζειν etc.

A few other verbs are similarly used with an articular inf. in place of an adverb: πληθύνειν 2 K. xiv. 11, 4 K. xxi. 6

[1] W. Schmidt *De Flav. Jos. elocutione* 516.

(the punctuation in Swete's text needs alteration), 2 Ch. xxxiii. 6, xxxvi. 14, 2 Es. x. 13, Ψ lxiv. 10, lxxvii. 38, Am. iv. 4 (once with a participle, on the model of λανθάνειν, 1 K. i. 12 ἐπλήθυνε προσευχομένη: contrast the rendering ἐπὶ πολύ Is. lv. 7): μεγαλύνειν Ψ cxxv. 2, Jl ii. 21: ἐθαυμαστώθη του βοηθηθῆναι 2 Ch. xxvi. 15 B "was marvellously helped": διεκλέπτετο...τοῦ εἰσελθεῖν 2 K. xix. 3 "came in stealthily" (contrast κρυβῇ ἀπέδρας Gen. xxxi. 26): ἐσκλήρυνας τοῦ αἰτή-σασθαι 4 K. ii. 10 "hast made thy request a hard one," cf. Ex. xiii. 15 ἐσκλήρυνεν Φ. ἐξαποστεῖλαι ἡμᾶς (but perhaps the meaning is rather "hardened himself [cf. vii. 22 B] against sending" than "hardly sent us"): cf. ταχύνειν τοῦ (ποιῆσαι) Gen. xviii. 7 etc.

The classical language had used verbs like λανθάνειν and φθάνειν with a participle in a similar way: in the later language the participle with (προ)φθάνειν was replaced by an inf.: the constructions given above may be regarded as a sort of extension of this use.

Other examples where the imitation of the Hebrew affects the structure of the sentence are the use of a question to express a wish, e.g. 2 K. xviii. 33 τίς δῴη τὸν θάνατόν μου ἀντὶ σοῦ; (R.V. "Would God I had died for thee"), and—more striking—the rendering of כִּי in adjurations = "(I say) that" by ὅτι, e.g. 1 K. xx. 3 ζῇ Κύριος καὶ ζῇ ἡ ψυχή σου, ὅτι καθὼς εἶπεν ἐμπέπλησται (contrast the rendering of כִּי by εἰ μήν, a form of adjuration attested by the papyri, in Gen. xxii. 17, xlii. 16, and its omission ib. xxii. 16). Similarly אִם, which in adjurations represents an emphatic negative, the imprecatory words being left to the imagination, is literally rendered, e.g. 1 K. xix. 6 Ζῇ Κύριος, εἰ ἀποθανεῖται.

Among cases where the usage of the Hebrew and the Greek vernacular coincide are the use of δύο δύο and the like in distributive sense, the use of εἷς as an indefinite article, and the coordination of sentences with καί. In other cases, as in the frequency of ἰδού, the influence of the Hebrew merely brought into prominence a word which held a subordinate position in the classical language.

One instance of a flagrant violation of Greek syntax stands by itself, namely the use of ἐγώ εἰμι *followed by a finite verb*, e.g. Jd. v. 3 B ᾄσομαι ἐγώ εἰμι τῷ κυρίῳ, vi. 18 ἐγώ εἰμι καθίσομαι. This use, however, is limited to a very small portion of the LXX, namely Jd. (B text five times, A text once) and Ruth (once), the βδ portions of the Kingdom Books (11 times), and Job Θ xxxiii. 31 (and perhaps Ez. xxxvi. 36 A). It also occurs in Aquila. The explanation of this strange use has been given elsewhere[1]. It is due to a desire to discriminate in the Greek between the two forms taken by the Hebrew pronoun of the first person, אנכי and אני. The observation of the fact that אנכי is the form usually employed to express "I am" led to the adoption of the rule, at a time when a demand for pedantically literal translation arose, that it must *always* be rendered by ἐγώ εἰμι, while ἐγώ alone represented אני. The rule reminds one of Aquila's use of σύν to express את the prefix to the accusative: the solecism is quite unlike the Hebraisms found elsewhere in the LXX, and the portions in which it occurs (if they are not entirely the work of Theodotion) may be regarded as among the latest additions to the Greek Bible.

§ 5. THE PAPYRI AND THE UNCIAL MSS OF THE LXX.

It is proposed in this section to consider how far the uncial MSS of the LXX, B in particular, can be trusted, in the light of the new evidence afforded by the papyri, in some matters of orthography and accidence. Have the MSS faithfully preserved the spelling and the forms of the autographs or at

[1] *J. T. S.* VIII. 272 f.

least of an age earlier than that in which they were written, or
have the scribes in these matters conformed to the practice of
their own age? The question has already been raised in the
case of the N.T. MSS by Dr J. H. Moulton, who points out that
"there are some suggestive signs that the great uncials, in this
respect as in others, are not far away from the autographs"
(*Prol.* 42). But this conclusion, if established in the case
of the N.T., does not *ipso facto* apply to the LXX, where the
autographs are much earlier, at least three centuries earlier in
the case of the Pentateuch, than the autographs of the N.T.
books.

The present writer, for the purpose of this work, has ana-
lysed and tabulated the evidence of numerous collections of
papyri which have been edited by their discoverers or custodians
in England or on the continent. The ground has already been
traversed by others, notably by Deissmann and J. H. Moulton:
but the principal object which those writers had in view was
the illustration of the N.T., and an independent investigation
for LXX purposes may not be useless, even if it merely serves
to corroborate the conclusions of earlier explorers in this field.
Moreover, fresh materials have accumulated even since the
appearance of Moulton's *Prolegomena*: the *Hibeh Papyri* have
largely increased the number of documents of the age when
the Greek Pentateuch came into being[1].

These papyri provide us with a collection of *dated* documents of a miscellaneous character, written by persons of all
ranks in the social scale, educated and uneducated, covering
a period of more than a millennium[2]. Documents of the

---

[1] All collections published before 1907 known to the present writer
have been investigated, except that the later volumes of the huge Berlin
collection have not been completely examined for the period i/ to iv/A.D.
The hundreds of documents for that period which have been consulted are,
however, sufficient to establish certain definite results. The recent (1907)
volumes of Tebtunis Papyri (Part II) and British Museum Papyri (Part III)
have not been used.

[2] HP 84 (*a*) is dated 301—300 B.C. The last will and testament of

Byzantine period are not very numerous, but for LXX purposes these may be neglected. Down to the fourth century of our era, the date of Codex Vaticanus, we have a nearly continuous string of documents exhibiting Greek as it was written and spelt by all classes of the community in Egypt during seven centuries. There is only one rather unfortunate gap. Papyri of i/B.C. and of the early part of i/A.D. are sadly scanty. The early part of ii/B.C. is also not very largely represented. On the other hand, iii/B.C. is now richly illustrated (by the Hibeh and Petrie Papyri, the Revenue Laws of Ptolemy Philadelphus etc.), as is also the period 133—100 B.C. (chiefly by the Tebtunis Papyri), and from about 50 A.D. onwards there is practically no missing link in the catena of evidence.

With this large mass of dated evidence covering such an extensive epoch in our hands, it ought to be possible to trace some clear indications of change and development, no less in matters of orthography and grammatical forms, than in formulae and modes of address[1], and to gain thereby some criterion whereby to test the trustworthiness in these respects of our oldest uncial MSS of the LXX. A few of the clearest instances of such development will here be considered together with their bearing on the LXX uncials. We begin with an instance which has not been noted by Moulton and which affords a more certain criterion than the one which he places in the forefront of his discussion (*Prol.* 42 f.). To Moulton's instance—the use of ὃς ἄν and ὃς ἐάν—we will revert later.

Abraham, bishop of Hermonthis (BM i. 77), is a specimen of writing in viii/A.D.

[1] E.g. the closing formula in correspondence, which, in the Ptolemaic age, according to the status of the person addressed, is ἔρρωσο (to an inferior or an equal) or εὐτύχει (to a superior). From i/A.D. διευτύχει usually replaces εὐτύχει. In iii/A.D. we have the more elaborate ἐρρῶσθαι (ἐρρ. σε) εὔχομαι, still further extended in iv/A.D. by the addition of πολλοῖς χρόνοις.

(1) Οὐθείς (μηθείς) *and* οὐδείς (μηδείς) [1].

The form οὐθείς (μηθείς) is one which we are in a position
to trace from its cradle to its grave.   First found in an inscription of 378 B.C., it is practically the only form in use throughout
the Greek-speaking world during iii/B.C. and the first half of
ii/B.C.   In 132 B.C. the δ forms begin again to reassert themselves, and the period from that date to about 100 B.C. appears
to have been one of transition, when the δ and θ forms are
found side by side in the same documents.   For i/B.C. we are
in the dark, but in i/A.D. we find that οὐδείς has completely
regained its ascendancy, and by the end of ii/A.D. οὐθείς, which
still lingers on in i/–ii/A.D., mainly in a single phrase ‘μηθὲν
ἧσσον, is extinct, never apparently to reappear, at all events not
within the period covered by the papyri.

Let us first take the evidence of the Attic inscriptions, as
given by Schwyzer-Meisterhans (ed. 3, 259).

	οὐθείς (μηθ.)	οὐδείς (μηδ.)
From 450 to 378 B.C.	o	12
„ 378 „ 300 „	23	34
„ 300 „ 60 „	28	o
Under the Roman Empire	5	18

The latest dates in the first column are two of ii/–iii/A.D.
The entire absence of οὐδείς from the inscriptions for over
250 years (300–60 B.C.) is most remarkable.

The evidence of the papyri is in general agreement with
this, but enables us to trace the use of the two forms rather
more closely between 300 and 100 B.C.

(Where there are several instances of a form in the same
document, the number of examples in that document have not
been counted : in these cases the figure is followed by + : where
there are several documents which repeatedly use the same
form, + + has been added.)

---

[1] Cf. Mayser 180 ff.

	οὐθείς (μηθ.)	οὐδείς (μηδ.)
iii/B.C. ⎫ from c. 301 B.C. ⎭	21 +	2[1]
ii/B.C.	51 + +	20 + +(all except one[2] after 132 B.C.)
i/B.C.	1[3]	4[4]
i/B.C.–i/A.D.	1[5]	1
i/A.D.	3[6]	29 + +
i/–ii/A.D.	o	4 + +
ii/A.D.	7[7] (of which 3 are μηθὲν ἧσσον)	68 + +
ii/–iii/A.D.	o	9 +
iii/A.D.		25 + +
iii/–iv/A.D.		1
iv/A.D.	8	26 + +

During the period of transition (132—100 B.C.), in which both forms are largely represented, we have the following examples of their occurrence in one and the same document: Act. I. col. 1 (131—130 B.C.) μηθέν but οὐδένα, Teb. 72 (114—113 B.C.) μηθέν μηδέν, Teb. 27 (113 B.C.) μηθέν *passim* but μηδένα, AP 31 (112 B.C.) μηθέν beside μηδέν οὐδένα οὐδενός, BU 998 (101—100 B.C.) μηθέν but, more than once, μηδένα. It appears that θ retained its hold more tenaciously in the neuter nom. and acc. than elsewhere.

The results which clearly emerge are that at the time when the Pentateuch and portions at least of the Prophets and the Kethubim were rendered into Greek οὐθείς was practically universal. Οὐδείς began to be rehabilitated somewhere about the time when the son of Sirach, who could refer[8] to Greek versions of "the law...and the prophecies and the rest of the

---

[1] PP ii. 20, col. 3 οὐδέν 252 B.C., ib. 44 μηδείς (undated, but apparently iii/B.C. like the rest of the collection).

[2] BM i. 42 μηδέν 172 B.C.

[3] GH 36 οὐθέν 95 B.C.

[4] BU 1001 μηδένα 56—55 B.C.: ib. 543 μηδέν 28—27 B.C.: ib. 1060 μηδένι 14 B.C.: BM ii. 354 μηδέν c. 10 B.C.

[5] BU 1058.

[6] BM ii. 256 (a) 11—15 A.D.: ib. 181, 64 A.D.: FP 91, 99 A.D. (the first and the third in the same phrase οὐθὲν ἐνκαλῶ).

[7] Μηθὲν ἧσσον OP iii. 492, 130 A.D., ib. 495, 181—189 A.D. (the latest date for θ), ib. 504, ii/A.D.: also ib. 497 μηθείς "early ii/A.D.," 504 and 530, ii/A.D.: BU 638, 143 A.D.

[8] Sir. prol.

books," settled in Egypt.   On the other hand, at the date
when Codex Vaticanus was written, οὐθείς was as obsolete as
to Englishmen of to-day is the spelling "peny," which only
recently disappeared from our Prayer-book.

We turn then to the LXX to test the uncials and obtain
the following statistics.

	(1) -θείς in all MSS	(2) -θείς -δείς v.ll.	(3) -δείς in all MSS
οὐ-	38	68	167
μη-	3	12	52
Total	41	80	219

- It is obvious that the later spelling largely preponderates,
and it is fairly certain that it must in many cases have replaced
an earlier οὐθείς.   Yet, even so, there remain 41 cases where
this archaism, as it was in the fourth century, has kept its place
in all the oldest uncials, that is in nearly 12½ per cent. of
all the passages where the words occur, while in 121 passages
out of a total of 340 it has left its trace in some of the MSS.
There is a strong probability that, where the readings vary
(i.e. in all passages included in column 2), οὐθείς is the older
form, as the natural tendency of the scribes was to replace it
by the spelling with which they were familiar.

It must further be remembered that some of the Greek
books (e.g. Ecclesiastes, Daniel Θ) were not written till after
the time of Christ, and in such books οὐδείς was no doubt
written in the autographs.   It is necessary, therefore, to
examine the LXX evidence in greater detail.   We obtain the
following results.

(1)   Οὐθείς is to some extent represented, with or without
a variant οὐδείς, in the majority of the books.

(2)   Three books alone, which use the pronoun more than

once, contain οὐδείς in all passages in all the uncials : these are Proverbs[1] (17 examples), Ecclesiastes (6), 4 Maccabees (15). In each of the following books the pronoun is used once only, and the uncials read οὐδείς : Judges (xiv. 6), K. βγ (2 K. xii. 3), Ezekiel (xliv. 2), Baruch (iv. 12).

(3)   Books where οὐθείς is found throughout in all MSS are 3 Kingdoms (iii. 18, xviii. 40, 43) and 2 Chronicles (ix. 20, xxxv. 3).

(4)   Books where οὐθείς has preponderant attestation are Genesis, Leviticus, Joshua, 1 Kingdoms, Jeremiah (both parts).

(5)   Οὐδείς preponderates in most of the other books, including Exodus, Numbers, Deuteronomy, Isaiah, and Minor Prophets ; in all of these, however, οὐθείς finds some attestation.

From the last sentence it seems fairly clear that the uncials cannot be altogether relied on : the Greek Pentateuch certainly goes back into iii/B.C., and the Greek Prophetical Books are probably not later than ii/B.C., and the autographs must almost certainly have contained οὐθείς : the three examples in the papyri of οὐδείς before 132 B.C. prevent us from speaking more positively.

The books mentioned under (2) above deserve notice as regards dates. The Greek Ecclesiastes is probably Aquila's work, a second century production, and 4 Maccabees is generally regarded as written in i/A.D.[2]   The δ forms are, therefore, what we should expect to find in the autographs. In the third book, Proverbs, the δ forms attested throughout by BℵA doubtless go back to the original translator. *This suggests a date* not earlier than 132 B.C., *probably not earlier than* 100 B.C., *as the date when Proverbs was translated.*

The Greek Sirach, we know from the statement in the prologue, was written in the period of transition (132—100 B.C.), and we are therefore not surprised to find the uncials uniting in support first of the one form, then of the other : the autograph

---

[1] But xxiv. 21 μηθετέρῳ Bℵ (μηδ. A).
[2] The last part of Baruch also belongs to the close of i/A.D.

probably contained both forms. The same fluctuation holds good in Wisdom (οὐδείς i. 8 B℟A ; οὐθείς ii. 4 B℟A ; οὐδείς ii. 5 B℟A ; οὐθέν iii. 17 B℟A etc.) ; and we are tempted to refer that book to the same epoch.

In the N.T. it is only what we should expect when we find that οὐθείς, which was expiring in i/A D., is limited in WH text to seven instances (5 in Luke's writings, 1 each in 1 and 2 Corinthians).

(2) Τεσσαράκοντα—τεσσεράκοντα.

Dr J. H. Moulton[1] has already called attention to the "dissonance between N.T. uncials and papyri" as regards these forms, and his statement applies with greater force to the LXX uncials. The substitution of ε for the first α in τεσσαράκοντα seems to have come into existence in some parts of the κοινή speech earlier than in others. Schweizer[2] quotes instances of τεσσεράκοντα, τέσσερες, etc., as early as iv/–iii/B.C. in Pergamene inscriptions, and he regards these forms, which are attested in Herodotus, when found in Asiatic territory, as survivals from the old Ionic dialect. On the other hand, in Egypt the form τεσσεράκοντα hardly appears before i/A.D. and does not become common till ii/A.D., from which date it is used concurrently with the classical form. Τεσσαράκοντα is universal in the Ptolemaic papyri. The earliest attested example of the ε form in Egypt, if it can be trusted, is on an inscription of *circa* 50 B.C., *Archiv* I. 209, δεκατέσ]σερα. Next comes τεσσεράκοστος BM ii. 262, 11 A.D., and τεσσεράκοντα once or twice in i/A.D. : on the other hand I have counted 15 examples of τεσσαράκοντα in papyri of i/A.D. From the beginning of ii/A.D. ε becomes more common. The ε in the second syllable of parts of τέσσαρες is much rarer. BU 133, 144–145 A.D., δεκατέσσε[ρα] is the earliest which I have noted, followed by GP 15 ("Byzantine") τεσσέρων.

---

[1] *Prol.* 46. Cf. *CR* xv. 33, xviii. 107 and Mayser 57, 224.
[2] *Gramm. d. Perg. Inschr.* 163 f.

Yet, though it is clear that the autographs in at least the majority of the LXX books must have contained τεσσαράκοντα, the form which is practically universal[1] in the uncials is τεσσεράκοντα. Here, then, we have an instance where the spelling of the uncials has been accommodated to that of a later date than the time of writing: the MS spelling may have come down from ancestors earlier than iv/A.D., but it is not likely to be older than i/A.D.

(3) Ταμεῖον and similar forms.

Moulton (*Prol.* 45) speaks of the coalescence of two successive *i* sounds as "a universal law of Hellenistic phonology" and states that "ταμεῖον, πεῖν and ὑγεία are overwhelmingly attested by the papyri." Perhaps it was owing to their chief interest lying in N.T. study, that neither he nor Deissmann (*BS* 182 f.) has noticed the contrast in this respect between papyri dated B.C. and those dated A.D. Mayser's list (92) shows that the longer forms ταμιεῖον, ὑγίεια, 'Αμμωνιεῖον etc. were those commonly written in the Ptolemaic age.

For ταμιεῖον—ταμεῖον (or Ταμ. as a street name in Arsinoe) the papyri give the following statistics:

	ταμιεῖον	ταμεῖον (-ῖον)
iii/B.C.	11[2]	0
ii/B.C.	1[3]	0
i/B.C.	0	0
i/A.D.	0	4[4]
ii/A.D.	1[5]	6 (or 8[6])

[1] The exceptions are Cod. E in Gen. v. 13, vii. 12 bis, xviii. 28 (σαράκοντα sic) bis: 2 Es. xv. 15 A, xvii. 67 ℵ, Ψ xciv. 10 RT, Cod. V four times in 2—3 Macc., once (3 M. vi. 38) being joined by A. [Cod. 87 has the α form in Dan. O iii. 47 and one of the correctors of B (usually B^b) generally alters the ε to α.] Against these examples must be set some 140 instances where τεσσεράκοντα is read by all the uncials.

[2] Add to Mayser's examples HP 31 c. 270 B.C. (six examples), PP i. 32 (1) 5 iii/B.C.

[3] AP 53, 114 B.C.

[4] The earliest is CPR 1, 83—84 A.D.

[5] BU 106, 199 A.D.

[6] Including OP iii. 533, ii/—iii/A.D., OP iv. 705, 200—202 A.D.

In iii/ and iv/A.D. only the shorter form is attested.

For ὑγίεια Mayser quotes five exx. from records dated ii/ and i/B.C., 99 B.C. being the latest date cited. Ὑγεία appears to begin in the papyri early in ii/A.D., e.g. OP iii. 496, 127 A.D., ib. 497 "early 2nd cent." Πεῖν also makes its appearance in the same century[1]. The same distinction between the early and later papyri holds good of the analogous forms from proper names, Σαραπιεῖον etc. (see Mayser, 92, 57). The longer forms are usual down to the early part of i/A.D. : Σαραπι(ε)ῖον OP iv. 736, i/A.D., OP ii. 267, 36 A.D. Σαραπεῖον makes its appearance in OP i. 110, ii/A.D. Mayser, however, has two examples from the end of ii/B.C. of Σουχ(ε)ίωι and cites one of 'Ασταρτεῖον from Mai (whose accuracy he questions) as early as 158 B.C.

Turning, now, to the three principal uncial MSS, we find the following statistics for the three words referred to above:

	ταμιεῖον	ταμεῖον	ταμῖον	Total
B	1[2]	19	18	38
ℵ	—	4	17	21
A	28	6	3	37
	ὑγίεια	ὑγεία	ὑγία	
B	2[3]	1	9	12
ℵ	—	3	6	9
A	6	—	8	14
	πιεῖν (κατα-)	πεῖν	πῖν	
B	33	12	—	45
ℵ	14	3	6	23
A	50	—	—	50

Only in the third word (as to the spelling of which papyrus evidence fails us) is there preponderant evidence in all the MSS

---

[1] Exx. from ii/A.D. are quoted in *CR* xv. 37, 434, xviii. 111, with two exx. of πεῖν from i/A.D. An early ex. of abbreviation (διασεῖν = -σείειν i/B.C.) is cited in Moulton's *Prol.* 45.

[2] Ez. xxviii. 16.   [3] Ez. xlvii. 12, Est. ix. 30.

for the longer form. In the other two words B and ℵ present forms which, in the light of the papyri, can hardly be regarded as original : in the first case A preserves the form which was probably in the autographs, but the general character of the A text leaves it doubtful whether this spelling has been handed down unaltered from those autographs or whether it is merely a literary correction (i.e. that the sequence was ταμιεῖον—ταμεῖον—ταμιεῖον). At all events in the Bℵ text we again have grave reason to doubt the antiquity of the MS orthography.

(4) If, however, we have seen reason in the last two examples to question the trustworthiness of the orthography of Codex B, there are, on the other hand, cases where the forms in use in the uncials carry us back to a period far earlier than the dates at which they were written and tell us something of a parent MS from which all the uncials, or a certain group of them, have descended. The phenomena to which attention will here be drawn point to a conclusion of considerable interest : they seem to indicate, beyond a doubt, the existence at a very early time, if not actually as early as the autographs themselves, of *a practice of dividing each book, for clerical purposes, into two nearly equal portions. Probably each book was written on two rolls*[1].

The clue to this discovery, in the case of two (or perhaps three) books of the Pentateuch, is afforded by the form which the particle takes in the indefinite relative ὃς ἄν (ὃς ἐάν) and kindred phrases, e.g. ἡνίκα ἄν (ἡνίκα ἐάν). If the reader will be at the pains to go through the examples of ὃς ἄν (ὃς ἐάν) etc. in the Books of Exodus and Leviticus in the Cambridge Manual Edition, he will obtain the following results. (The forms ὅπως ἄν, ὡς ἄν, ἕως ἄν, which in these books are invariably so written, are excluded from the investigation.)

[1] The subject has been dealt with more fully in an article by the writer in *J. T. S.* ix. 88 ff.

Exodus. Part I. (i. I—xxiii. 19)	ὃς ἄν etc.	ὃς ἐάν etc.	Total
B	7 exx.	14 exx.	21
A	11	10	21
F	7	8	15
Part II. (xxiii. 20—end)			
B	19	0	19
A	17	1 ⎫ 1	18
F	16	1 ⎭	17
Leviticus. Part I. (i. I—xv. 33)			
B	21	32	53
A	24	27	51
F	39	14	53
Part II. (xvi. I—end)			
B	48	7 ⎫	55.
A	44	8 ⎬ 2	52
F	45	9 ⎭	54

The noticeable point is that whereas, in the first half of either book, both forms are attested, ὃς ἐάν receiving rather the larger support, in the second part ὃς ἐάν entirely disappears in Exodus (excepting one passage in AF), while in Leviticus it is very sparsely represented. The examples, it should be said, are spread over the whole of the two books. The break in Exodus comes between xxiii. 16 (ὧν ἐὰν σπείρῃς BAF) and xxiii. 22 (ὅσα ἂν ἐντείλωμαι BF (ὅσα ἐντέλλομαι A)...ὅσα ἂν εἴπω BAF), and there can be little doubt that xxiii. 20 marks the beginning of Part II. In Leviticus the break comes towards the end of chap. xv., probably at the actual close of it, though, as BAF have ὃς ἄν in xv. 33, it might be placed at xv. 30.

The evidence indicates that all three MSS are descendants of a MS in which Exodus and Leviticus were both divided

---

[1] xxxiv. 24 ἡνίκα ἐάν AF (ἡνίκα ἄν B).

[2] Three examples occur in the last seven verses of the book (xxvii. 28 BAF, 29 BAF, 32 BAF). Excluding these the numbers are reduced to 4, 5, 6. Only in these closing verses do BAF unite in reading ὃς ἐάν.

into two nearly equal parts, which were transcribed by different scribes: the scribe of the second half of both books wrote ὃς ἄν, the scribe of the first half probably wrote both ὃς ἄν and ὃς ἐάν.

In Numbers something of the same kind may be traced in AF, which, after the Balaam episode, contain no examples of ὃς ἐάν : B* however has this form in both parts (though in Part II. it is twice corrected by Bᵃᵇ to ὃς ἄν, xxx. 9, xxxiii. 54). If the book be divided at the end of chap. xxiv., we obtain the following results :

	Part I. (i. 1—xxiv. 25)		Part II. (xxv. 1—end)	
	ὃς ἄν etc.	ὃς ἐάν etc.	ὃς ἄν etc.	ὃς ἐάν etc.
B	17	16	7	6
A	25	12	12	0
F	28	13	12	0

This change in orthography in these books of the Pentateuch does not appear to correspond to a change of translators. The evidence of the papyri makes it possible to suppose that the two spellings go right back to the autographs, although they show clearly that the forms ὃς ἐάν etc., did not become common till the end of ii/B.C. My statistics for the use in the papyri of the two forms (the materials have grown since Moulton's *Prolegomena*[1] appeared) are as follows :—

	ὃς ἄν etc.	ὃς ἐάν etc.
iii/B.C.	43 + +	(?) 4[2]
ii/B.C.	32 +	6[3]
i/B.C.	3	6 +
i/A.D.	5 +	39
ii/A.D.	13	79 + +
iii/A.D.	5	13 +
iv/A.D.	7	12 + +

[1] *Prol.* p. 42 f. Cf. *CR* xv. 32.

[2] HP 96. 10 and 28 ὧι ἐὰν ἐπέλθηι, 259–8 B.C. (N.B. ἐὰν ἐπέλθηι, hypothetical, occurs in the same context, line 9) : ib. 51. 3 ἅς [ἐ]ὰν, 245—244 B.C.: PP ii. 39 (g) ? iii/B.C.

[3] None earlier than 133 B.C., the earliest being BM ii. 220 col. 2, lines 6 and 8 (reading doubtful), followed by G 18. 27, 132 B.C.

῞Ος ἄν was, thus, the usual form in iii/–ii/B.C. down to
133 B.C., when ὃς ἐάν begins to come to the front, and from
i/B.C. onwards the latter is always the predominant form
the figures in both columns decrease in iii/–iv/A.D., when the
use of the indefinite relative in any form was going out of use[1].

Similar phenomena present themselves in quite another
part of the LXX, namely in the Psalter.   Here again we find
a distinction as regards orthography between the first and the
second half of the book.   The tests which have been found in
this book (three) are more numerous than in the Pentateuch : on
the other hand the only MS affected in all three instances is B ·
T keeps the same orthography throughout, while the evidence
for אA is not quite conclusive as to their derivation from a
parent MS which contained the two methods of spelling.   The
break appears to come at the end of Ψ 77, but there are at least
two Psalms in Part I. (20 and 76) where the spelling is that
ordinarily found in Part II.   The three tests are (1) the insertion
or omission of the temporal augment in εὐφραίνειν, (2) nouns
in -εία or -ία, (3) the interchange of αι and ε.

(1)   The evidence is as follows :

Part I.	Ψ xv. 9	ηὐφρ.	BAU	εὐφρ. א	⎫
	xxix. 2		B*ATU	„ א	⎬
	xxxiv. 15	„	BA	„ א	⎬
	xliv. 9	„	BאAT		⎬
	lxxii. 21	„	Bא*		⎬
	[lxxvi. 4	„	T	Bא]	⎭
Part II.	lxxxviii. 43		T	BאA	⎫
	lxxxix. 14	„	T	BאA*	⎬
	14	„	T		⎬
	xci. 5		T	BאA	⎬
	xciii. 19	„	A	T	⎬
	xcvi. 8	„	AT	Bא	⎬
	civ. 38			BאAT	⎬
	cvi. 30	„	AT	א	⎬
	cxxi. 1		„	אAT	⎭

[1] In Exodus a further distinction between Part I. and Part II. is seen in
the use of ἐναντίον in the former, ἔναντι in the latter.

(2) δυναστία xix. 7 B*, lxiv. 7 B*T, lxv. 7 B*ℵ, lxx. 16 B*, 18 B*ℵ, lxxiii. 13 ℵ*, lxxvii. 4 B*T, 26 B*ℵ as against δυναστεία [xx. 14 B*ℵAU] lxxix. 3 B, lxxxviii. 14 BA, lxxxix. 10 BℵA, cii. 22 B, and so B, sometimes joined by A, in cv. 2, 8, cxliv. 6 (with T), 11, 12, cxlvi. 10, cl. 2. There is a similar change in the case of εὐπρεπ(ε)ία, μεγαλοπρεπ(ε)ία : chap. xx. in its spelling of the last word again goes with Part II.

(3) Examples of αι for ε in the 2nd pers. plur. of verbs, in παιδίον (=πεδίον) and twice in μαι=με (xlii. 2 B*A, lviii. 2 B*ℵ) occur in B in xxiii. 7, 9, xxix. 5, xxx. 25, xxxi. 11 bis, xxxii. 1, 2, xxxiii. 9, xlii. 2, xlvii. 13, 14 bis, xlviii. 2, lvii. 3, lviii. 2, lxi. 4, 11, lxiv. 12, lxvii. 5, lxxv. 12, lxxvii. 12 (from xxix. 5 to xlviii. 2 B is joined by A)—examples of the reverse change in ix. 22 (with A), 23, 24, xiii. 3, xiv. 4 (with A), xliv. 8, liv. 22, lxxi. 7 (with T), lxxiv. 6 (with T). After chap. lxxvii. there appear to be no examples of this interchange in Cod. B.

Now, there is nothing to shew that the Greek Psalter is the work of more than a single translator: on the contrary the whole book is marked by a somewhat peculiar vocabulary. Here we have an instance of a division of clerical labour merely. But it is just possible that the two spellings go back to the autographs. The interchange of ε and αι begins in the papyri in ii/B.C.[1], when it is distinctly vulgar: it does not become common till ii/A.D. At all events the division of the Greek Psalter into two parts goes back at least to a MS of i/–ii/A.D.

The close resemblance existing between the cases which prove the existence of a practice of dividing the O.T. books into two parts, whether for purposes of translation (Jerem. Ezek.) or of transcription, is very remarkable. In at least five cases, representing all three divisions of the Hebrew Scriptures, this practice has been traced. In each case the division is made roughly at the half-way point without strict regard to subject-matter : in each case Part I. is slightly longer than Part II. and—what is specially noticeable—the excess of Part I. over Part II. in the Hebrew of the MT is practically a fixed quantity,

[1] The only example B.C. of αι for ε which I have noted is FP 12. c. 103 B.C. τραπαιζίτου (noted by the editors as "an early example"): the B.C. examples noted of ε for αι are ἀνύγετε Par. 50, 160 B.C., ὁρᾶτε ib. I. 386, ii/B.C. Mayser 107 adds a few more.

namely about one fifteenth of the whole book : that is to say, if each of these books were divided into fifteen equal sections, Parts I. and II. would be found to comprise about eight and seven sections respectively. The following statistics, in which the pages are those of an ordinary printed Hebrew Bible, and the books are arranged in order of length, will show what is meant.

		No. of pages.	Total.	Excess of Part I. over Part II.
Psalms	Part I.	$50\frac{1}{2}$	$93\frac{5}{6}$	$7\frac{1}{6}$
	Part II.	$43\frac{1}{3}$		
Jeremiah	Part I.	49	$92\frac{1}{2}$	$5\frac{1}{2}$
	Part II.[1]	$43\frac{1}{2}$		
Ezekiel	Part I.	$44\frac{1}{3}$	$83\frac{1}{3}$	$5\frac{1}{3}$
	Part II.	39		
Exodus	Part I.	$38\frac{1}{2}$	$72\frac{1}{4}$	$4\frac{3}{4}$
	Part II.	$33\frac{3}{4}$		
Leviticus	Part I.	27	$50\frac{1}{3}$	$3\frac{2}{3}$
	Part II.	$23\frac{1}{3}$		

A final instance may be quoted where B appears to preserve a spelling older than itself. In 3 Kingdoms B twice only writes οὐκ ἰδού (viii. 53, xvi. 28 c) as against ten examples of οὐχ ἰδού. The two passages, however, where the aspirate is not inserted are absent from the M.T. and are perhaps later glosses. B has preserved the differing spellings of the glossator and of the earlier text.

The preceding investigation will serve to show the use to which the papyri evidence, when duly tabulated, can be put, and how necessary it is, at each step in a work such as this, to take account of it. If we sometimes find that all MSS, including B, have been influenced by the later spelling, there are other instances which carry us back to a date not far removed from the autographs, if not to the autographs themselves.

[1] Excluding the last chapter which is a later addition in the Greek : cf. p. 11.

ORTHOGRAPHY AND PHONETICS.

1. Any attempt to determine the spelling adopted in the autographs of the LXX, as in those of the N.T., is beset with great difficulty, and, in the present state of our knowledge, finality is impossible, notwithstanding the assistance now afforded by the papyri. At the time when our oldest uncials were written (iv/–vi/ A.D.) and for centuries earlier there was no fixed orthography in existence. Changes had taken place in pronunciation which gradually made themselves felt in writing. In particular the diphthongs had ceased to be pronounced as such, and scribes now wrote indifferently αι or ε, ει or ι, οι or υ, having nothing to guide them in their choice but any acquaintance which they happened to possess with classical models. If we attempt to go behind the spellings which we find in the uncials, we are met by two unsolved problems. (1) No certain criteria have yet been reached for distinguishing dialectical and local differences, if such existed, within the κοινή. (2) The birthplaces of our uncials are still a matter of dispute.

These gaps in our knowledge are rather less serious to a student of the LXX than to the N.T. investigator, because in the Greek Old Testament we have no reason to doubt that we are concerned with writings which emanate with few, if any, exceptions from a single country, namely Egypt: and for that country the papyri supply us with evidence covering the whole period from the time of writing to the dates of the uncials.

Moreover, the palaeography of Codices ℵ and A (which, as Mr W. E. Crum points out, is closely akin to that of many of the older Coptic hands), as well as the appearance in these two MSS of certain orthographical phenomena—particularly as regards the interchange of consonants (§ 7. 2)—which have been traced to peculiarities of Egyptian pronunciation, make the Egyptian *provenance* of these two MSS extremely probable. On the other hand, the birthplace of B is more doubtful. Egypt, Rome, South Italy and Caesarea are rival claimants to the honour of producing it: the last-named place is that which has recently found most favour. Yet, if Tischendorf's identification of one of the hands of ℵ with that of the scribe of B may be trusted, the two MSS must apparently have emanated from the same country.

The probability of the Egyptian extraction of A and ℵ should, one would suppose, lend their evidence a peculiar interest. Yet the generalisation suggested by the available data is that B is on the whole nearer to the originals in orthography as well as in text. Cod. A contains much that we can recognize as characteristic of, if not peculiar to, Egypt, sometimes even modes of writing which are characteristic of the earlier Ptolemaic age (e.g. ἐμ μέσῳ, ἐγ γαστρί). More often, however, it is the case that the spellings found in A and in ℵ are shown by the papyri to have come into fashion in Egypt only in the Imperial age and may therefore be confidently attributed to later copyists. In orthography and grammar, no less than in text, A is generally found to occupy a secondary position in comparison with B. ℵ is marked by a multitude of vulgarisms which have obviously not descended from the autographs and deprive this MS of any weight in orthographical matters which its apparently Egyptian origin might seem to lend to it.

In addition to the changes in spelling due to altered pronunciation there are others which have a psychological basis
(influence of analogy, etc.). The latter are the more important, but even the 'itacisms' so-called have their interest
and may throw light on the history and character of the MSS,
when tried by the standard of documents, of which the date
and country are known.

2. Interchange of vowels.

Ă > E. The weakening of ă to ε[1] frequently takes place
where the vowel is followed by one of the liquids (ρ, λ),
especially ρ. In the first two instances to be mentioned the
change takes place only under certain conditions.

We have already examined the forms τέσσερα, τεσσεράκοντα,
etc. in the light of the papyri and seen reason to doubt their
existence in the LXX autographs (§ 5, p. 62 f.) : a few words must
however be added here as to the origin of these widely-attested
forms. Long before the Hellenistic age Ionic Greek had
adopted the forms with ε in the second syllable, τέσσερες, τέσσερας, τέσσερα, τεσσέρων, τέσσερσι, also τεσσεράκοντα. The LXX
MSS on the other hand keep the α in τέσσαρες, τεσσάρων,
τέσσαρσι, while commonly writing τέσσερα[2], τεσσεράκοντα. This
is not a case of Hellenistic Greek directly taking over Ionic
forms : some other principle must be found to account for
the discrimination. The masc. acc. in the LXX is either
τέσσαρας[2] or τέσσαρες (= nom.) : the latter is the constant form
of the acc. in the B text of the Octateuch and occurs sporadically elsewhere in B as well as in A and (twice) in א.—The
origin of τέσσαρες = acc.[3] is doubtless mainly due to assimi-

---

[1] Perhaps due to Coptic (Egyptian) influence : Thumb *Hell.* 138, 177.
Dieterich *Untersuch.* 11.

[2] Τέσσαρα in the B text only in Jer. Ez. and Minor Prophets (Jer. xv. 3,
Ez. i. 6 BA, 8 BA, Zech. i. 18, vi. 1). The same group writes masc. acc.
τέσσαρας.

[3] See Moulton *Prol.* ed. 2 p. 243 f. for the predominance of this form
in business documents.

lation of acc. to nom. plur., of which there are other instances
(§ 10, 15): but the *frequency* of this assimilation in the numeral
appears to be due to the weakening influence of the liquid.
The nom. conversely appears twice in the B text of 2 Esdras
(ii. 15, 64) as τέσσερας. The rule appears to be that ᾰ
cannot retain its place both before and after ρ: one of the
vowels must be weakened to ε: in τέσσερα τεσσεράκοντα the
first α was altered, in τέσσαρες = acc. assimilation to the nom.
suggested alteration of the second.

> The same influence is seen at work in the papyri in the
> transition from Σαράπις (Ptolemaic age) to Σεράπις (Roman
> age): Mayser 57 quotes two examples only of Σεραπιεῖον before
> the Roman age. Σεράπις and τέσσερα appear to have come into
> general use together, about i/A.D. Cf. περά for παρά (i/B.C.).
> Mayser 56.

3. In the verb καθαρίζω Cod. A in 14 passages[1] has -ερ-
for -αρ-, but, with the exception of N. xii. 15 καθερισθῇ A
(read ἐκαθαρίσθη with BF), only where there is an augment
or reduplication: ἐκαθέρισα, ἐκαθερίσθην κεκαθερισμένος, but
always καθαρίζω[2], καθαρῶ, καθαρίσασθε -ίσαντες etc.

> B only once has -ερ-, 2 Es. vi. 20 ἐκαθερίσθησαν B*A, ℵ never:
> F has it in Lev. viii. 15, Q in Ez. xxiv. 13, V three times in 1 and
> 2 Macc., always preceded by an augment.
> In this instance the prefixing of a syllable with ε appears to
> produce the change: assimilation of first and third syllables
> and the weakening force of ρ upon the vowel are jointly re-
> sponsible. The avoidance of the sequence of the vowels
> ε- a- a where the second a is preceded or followed by ρ
> observable in the two examples quoted (τέσσερα, ἐκαθέρισα)
> is curious[3].

4. Connected with the preceding exx. is a group of words[4],

---

[1] As against seven with ἐκαθαρ. κεκαθαρ.
[2] The sub-heading καθερίζω in Moulton-Geden s. v. is therefore mis-
leading.
[3] Cp. Dieterich *op. cit.* 8. Dr J. H. Moulton suggests that the verb
was popularly regarded as a compound of κατά, and ἐκαθέρισα is an example
of double augment.
[4] Thumb *Hell.* 75 f. regards the ε forms as Ionic and thinks that

in which the ancient grammarians pronounce the forms with
α to be Attic, those with ε Hellenistic : the vowel is in most
cases followed by a liquid. In a few words containing υ
(μυελός, πύελος, πτύελον) the ε form is said to be Attic, the
α form Hellenistic. LXX prefers the ε forms, viz. (for Attic
μιαρός etc.) it has μιερός[1] and compounds, μυσερός[2], σίελ(ος)[3]
and σιελίζειν, ψέλιον[4] (Att. ψάλιον) : also (with Attic according
to the grammarians) μυελός[5], πτύελ(ος)[6] : similarly ψεκάς[7] for
Attic ψακάς. On the other hand LXX retains the Attic α in
κύαθος, ὕαλος[8], φιάλη. The MSS are divided as to ἀττέλεβος
(Bℵ : the Ionic form) and ἀττέλαβος (AQ) in Na. iii. 17.

The words σκι(α)ρός, χλι(α)ρός, ψί(α)θος are absent from LXX.

5.　For ἕνεκα > ἕνεκεν see § 9, 8. Assimilation of vowels
produces πέντες = πάντες 2 Ch. xiv. 8 A (so τετεγμένος Μεκεδόνος
ἐδέφους etc. in Ptolemaic papyri). Analogy of -ω verbs accounts
for forms like ἐδύνετο 4 M. ii. 20 A, analogy of the imperfect for
forms like ἔδωκες Ez. xvi. 21 A (so in the papyri).

6.　E > A.　The reverse change of ε to α is less common ·
two formations in -άζω may be mentioned. Ἀμφιάζω takes
the place of classical ἀμφιέννυμι : the verb occurs four times
only, in two, Job xxix. 14, xxxi. 19, all the uncials have ἠμφιασάμην (-ίασα), in 4 K. xvii. 9, Job xl. 5, B keeps the class.
aor. with ε (A, ℵA having the later form). Πιάζω is used

Hellenistic Greek arrived at a compromise between these and the Attic
forms : in modern Greek the α form has prevailed.
　[1] So Cod. A always (with μιεροφαγεῖν -φαγία -φονία) in 2 and 4 M.
(the only two books which use the word) except in 2 M. vii. 34 : ℵ has -ε-
six times, V once.
　[2] Lev. xviii. 23, BAF.
　[3] 1 K. xxi. 13 τὰ σίελα, Is. xl. 15 ὡς σίελος : προσσιελίζειν Lev. xv. 8
BA (-σιαλ- F).
　[4] So in a papyrus of iii/B.C. : otherwise the Ptolemaic papyri have
Attic forms only, Mayser 16.
　[5] Gen. xlv. 18, Job xxi. 24, xxxiii. 24 : but μυαλοῦν Ψ lxv. 15.
　[6] Job vii. 19 (τὸν πτ.), xxx. 10.
　[7] Job xxiv. 8, Cant. v. 2.
　[8] Job Θ xxviii. 17.

along with the Attic πιέζω "press," but takes on another meaning, "seize" (§ 24 s.v.).

The MSS A and א afford other examples, mainly due to assimilation. A has λακάνη Jd. v. 25, ταλαμῶνι 3 K. xxi. 38, ἀρωδιός 'heron' Ψ ciii. 17 (ἤρωδ. T: ἐρωδιός BאR was the usual form, but there is early authority for ῥωδιός, and the initial vowel may have been an aftergrowth). א has e.g. σαραφείν Is. vi. 6, τάσσαρας Jer. xxv. 16, ἀνυπνιάζεσθαι ib. xxxvi. 8.

Preference for the first aor. forms accounts for words like ἀναλάβατε Jer. xxvi. 3 A, ἔβαλας etc. (§ 17, 2), Confusion of aor. and fut. inf. for ἐκφεύξασθαι 2 M. ix. 22 V (=fut. inf.: similar confusion in the papyri from ii/B.C., Mayser 385).

7.   A and H.   The following exx. of ᾱ where η might be expected are noticeable.   (1) 'Αρεταλογία, Sir. xxxvi. 19, "the story of thy majesty" (Heb. הוד: scribes have misunderstood the word and corrupted it to ἆραι τὰ λόγια: the word ἀρεταλόγος appears first in the κοινή, where it means a prater about virtue, a court-jester or buffoon).   (2) Μαρυκᾶσθαι is so written (not μηρ.) in both passages, Lev. xi. 26 = Dt. xiv. 8, μηρυκισμὸν οὐ μαρυκᾶται: the subst. is always μηρυκισμός. (So (ἀνα)μαρυκᾶσθαι, Ep. Barn. 10, but subst. μηρυκισμός, ἀναμηρύκησις Aristeas 153 f., 161.)   (3) 'Οσφρασία (= class. ὄσφρησις) is a ἅπ. λεγ. in Hos. xiii. 7 BA (ὀσφρησία Q) coined from the late verb ὀσφράομαι for ὀσφραίνομαι.

Thumb (*Hell.* 66 f., cf. 61) mentions ἀρεταλόγος and μαρυκᾶσθαι among the few instances of κοινή forms which appear to be of Doric origin.   Another "Doric" κοινή form quoted by Thumb is δίχαλον: LXX uses only the verb διχηλεῖν.   LXX similarly uses only κυνηγός, ὁδηγεῖν -ός, never ὁδαγ. as in some N.T. MSS. 'Ράσσω is the LXX form of ἀράσσω, which is not used (a before ρ tends to be dropped or weakened to ε): it is not an alternative for ῥήσσω ῥήγνυμι.

8.   The Hellenistic (Ionic) inf. χρᾶσθαι appears in 2 M. vi. 21 A beside Attic χρῆσθαι ib. iv. 19, xi. 31, Est. viii. 11 etc.: the Ptolemaic papyri have both forms (Mayser 347).

The LXX MSS have only the regular forms ἀναλίσκειν, ἀνάλωσις with a in the second syllable; in the Ptolemaic papyri, however, the augment has invaded all parts and derivatives of the verb : ἀνηλίσκειν, ἀνηλωτικός etc. are usual, and ἀνήλωμα is almost universal down to ii/A.D., when ἀνάλωμα begins to reassert itself (Mayser 345 f.). The extensive use of these forms under the Ptolemies excites suspicion as to the trustworthiness of the uncials.

9. A and O. Βιβλιαφόρος Est. iii. 13, viii. 10 (corrected by אᶜ·ᵃ· to βιβλιοφ.) is supported by Polyb. iv. 22. 2 and a papyrus of 111 B.C. βυβλιαφόροις (Mayser 102, 61) and by the similarly-formed βιβλιαγράφος, in which the first half of the compound seems to be the neuter plural : but βιβλιοθήκη, βιβλιοφυλάκιον.

Illiterate scribes confused a and o, much as a and ε were confused : assimilation and the weak pronunciation of a in the neighbourhood of a liquid account for many examples (Mayser 60 f.). So μολλον (=μᾶλλον) Is. liv. 1 א : μετοξύ (for μεταξύ) 3 K. xv. 6 A is a curious example, found in the papyri from i/A.D. (BM² 177. 11 = 40 A.D., OP² 237 col. v. 11 = 186 A.D., AP App. I. Pt. I. iii. (c) = iv/A.D.), apparently due to false etymology (ὀξύς).   Conversely βαρρᾶ (for βορρᾶ) Jer. vi. 1 א : cf. βράματα (for βρώματα) Jl. ii. 23 א.

10. AI and A.   LXX writes κλαίω, not the old Attic κλάω, and καίω : for the few exx. in the MSS of κλάω κάω (rare in Ptol. papyri, Mayser, 105) see § 24 s.v. Αἰεί (Epic and Ionic) appears in 1 Es. i. 30 B, elsewhere the Attic ἀεί, and always ἀετός.

11. AI and E. Some time before 100 A.D. αι ceased to be pronounced as a diphthong and was pronounced as *e*. The interchange of αι and ε, which resulted from the change in pronunciation, begins c. 100 A.D. in the Attic inscriptions[1]. At about the same date the interchange becomes common in the Egyptian papyri, although the beginnings of it may be traced back in the vulgar language to the second century B.C.[2]

---

[1] Meisterhans 34.
[2] Mayser 107 cites half a dozen examples of ε for αι, less than a dozen of αι for ε, from Ptolemaic papyri, mainly illiterate, beginning about 161 B.C.

The change seems to have begun in final -αι -ε in verbal forms.

The appendices to the Cambridge Manual LXX afford innumerable instances of this change, which must, however, be mainly attributed to later scribes. Cod. ‏א‎, in particular, abounds in spellings like τες ημερες=ταῖς ἡμέραις in the prophetical books. B is more free from such spellings especially in the historical books, but even this MS has nearly 300 examples (mainly of final -αι for -ε or final -ε for -αι), which can hardly all go back to the autographs. The statistics for B, collected from the Appendices to the Cambridge LXX, show a curious rise in the frequency of this usage from the Historical Books to the Psalms group and from this to the Prophetical group. The Pentateuch has 24 examples in all, Joshua to 2 Esdras only 11, the Psalms[1] and Wisdom group 63, the Prophets 188. A few of the more frequent examples may be noted. Ἐξέφνης has preponderant support as in N.T. (B 6 out of 8 times, A 8/10, ‏א‎ 4/6): ἐφνίδιος (-ίως) is read by A in 2 and 3 Macc., but αἰφνίδιος is certainly original in W. xvii. 15. The proximity of one of the liquids specially tends to convert αι into ε (the liquid having the same weakening effect as in τέσσαρα > τέσσερα): hence frequent examples in B, often supported by ‏א‎A, of forms like ἔρετε (=αἴρετε) ἐρετίζει (=αἱρετ.) etc., and of ἔλεον = ἔλαιον. It may be noted that among the few Ptolemaic examples of this interchange other than in final -αι -ε occur αὐθεραίτως = αὐθαιρέτως, ἔλεον = ἔλαιον (Mayser 107). The reverse change takes place in παιδίον[2] = πεδίον, which is common in B and A. An idiosyncrasy of B is αἴδεσμα = ἔδεσμα, 8 out of 10 times (once in T, Ψ liv. 15). In the circumstances the context alone can show whether e.g. ετεροc = ἕτερος or ἑταῖρος, εcεcθε = ἔσεσθε or ἔσεσθαι.

12. AY and EY. The Ptolemaic papyri exhibit only the classical forms ἐρευνάω ἔρευνα : ἐραυνάω ἔραυνα make their appearance in papyri of i/A.D.[3], and subsequently made way again for the older forms. In the LXX uncials the forms are about equally divided, and once again the papyri suggest that the MSS are not to be relied on as representing the auto-

---

[1] The examples in the Psalms (31) are limited to the first half, the last being παιδίῳ lxxvii. 12 (see § 5, p. 69).
[2] This form supplies the only examples of αι for ε in the B text of 2—4 Kingdoms (2 K. xvii. 8, 3 K. xi. 29, xvi. 4).
[3] Mayser 113. The earliest example is dated 22 A.D.

graphs[1]. The theories once held that the form ἐραυνάω was a peculiarity of Jewish or of Alexandrian Greek have to be given up : a special association with Egypt is just possible[2].

> Cf. κολοκαύει=κολακεύει 1 Es. iv. 31 B and πέταυρον written by correctors of B and א in Prov. ix. 18 (πέτευρον B*א*A seems to have been the older form of the word). The converse, ευ for αυ, is seen in ἐντεῦθα 1 Es. v. 66 A.

13. AY—A[3]. No examples in the LXX uncials have been noted of the dropping of υ in forms like ἀτός (=αὐτός), ἐματήν, ἑατούς etc., which appear from the papyri to have been in vogue in i/A.D. Assimilation accounts for καταγάζειν (=καταυγ.) in W. xvii. 5 B and for τραματίαι (=τραυμ.) in Jer. xxviii. 4,‍52 א : the influence of εὔθλαστος probably produced εὔθραστα (=εὔθραυστα) in W. xv. 13 אAC.

14. E and H. A prominent instance of ε replacing η is seen in the preference shown by the κοινή for the termination -εμα in a group of neuter nouns which in the classical language ended in -ημα, due apparently to the analogy of cognate words in -εσις (-ετος)[4]. The same preference for the short radical vowel appears in πόμα (like πόσις : class. πῶμα), δόμα, χύμα (class. χεῦμα), and so apparently κρίμα κλίμα. Words in -μα and -σις had come to be used with little, if any, difference of meaning (e.g. δόμα, δόσις), and it was natural that they should be formed on the same pattern. H is retained in the neuter where the cognate feminine nouns have it : where the cognates ended in -ἄσις η is either retained (στάσις, -στῆμα, not -στᾰμα)[5] or shortened to ε, on the model of the majority of these neuter

---

[1] The statistics are as follows : ἐξ- δι- ερευνάω and the substantives ἔρευνα ἐξερεύνησις are included. B has 13 examples of ευ to 13 of αυ : A 17 ευ, 20 αυ : א 11 εὐ, 14 αυ. Passages where the -αυ- forms are strongly attested are Dt. xiii. 14 BA, Jd. v. 14 BA, 1 Ch. xix. 3 Bא‍A, Ψ *passim*, Prov. ii. 4 Bא‍A, Wis. vi. 3 Bא, xiii. 7 Bא, Est. A 13 Bא‍A, Jer. xxvii. 26 Bא‍A.

[2] Thumb *Hell.* 176 f.

[3] Cf. J. H. Moulton *Prol.* 47.

[4] Cf. Mayser 65 f., Schweizer *Perg. Insch.* 47 ff.

[5] Ἀνάσταμα should perhaps be read in Or. Sib. 8. 268.

nouns. New words are formed with the short vowel (LXX
ἄφεμα, κάθεμα, ἀφαίρεμα). The LXX exx. are as follows :—

with ε	with ε and η	with η
εὕρεμα	ἔψεμα -ημα²	βῆμα
θέμα	ἀνάθεμα -ημα³	μνῆμα
ἔκθεμα	σύνθεμα -ημα	ὑπόμνημα⁶
ἐπίθεμα	ἀνάστεμα -ημα	ὑπόδημα
παράθεμα	(διάστεμα)⁴ -ημα	διάδημα
περίθεμα	σύστεμα -ημα	
πρόσθεμα	(ὑπόστεμα)⁵ -ημα	
κατάστεμα¹		

The two forms ἀνάθεμα ἀνάθημα appear in different senses,
the Hellenistic form being used in the translated books for
a thing devoted to destruction, accursed (=חרם), whereas the
more literary books (Jdth, 2 and 3 Macc.) use the classical form
with the classical meaning, a votive offering given for the
adornment of a temple. We cannot, however, point to an
example of the distinction of meanings being made in a single
book, and ἀνάθημα in Deut. (B text) is used to translate חרם,
while ἄνθεμα is used by Theocritus of a temple offering (Ep. v.
[xiii] 2). In N.T. Luke possibly observes the distinction (Lc.
xxi. 5 ἀναθήμασιν WH with Acts xxiii. 14 ἀναθέματι), but there
is good authority in the first passage for ἀναθέμασιν⁷.

15. Connected with the foregoing words is the form
ἀνυπόδετος (five times in LXX), the κοινή form of class.
ἀνυπόδητος (once restored by A in Is. xx. 2), on the analogy of
(σύν)δετος etc.

16. Two exx. of Hellenistic shortening of η in the verb
are referred to elsewhere (§ 18, 1): (1) in the fut. and aor.

¹ 3 M. v. 45.
² The former in Genesis (3 times), 4 K. B (twice), Hg. ii. 12, Dan. Θ
(once): the latter in 4 K. iv. 38 A, 39 A, 40 BA, Dan. O (once).
³ Ἀνάθημα Dt. vii. 26 B *bis*, Jdth. xvi. 19 B, 2 M. ii. 13 V, ix. 16,
3 M. iii. 17: elsewhere ἀνάθεμα.
⁴ Four times in the A text of Ezekiel.
⁵ Twice in A text: 2 K. xxiii. 14 = 1 Ch. xi. 16.
⁶ But ὑπόμνεμα in a papyrus of iii/B.C., PP ʒ9 (5). PPゴ
⁷ See Trench *N.T. Synonyms* 1st series (v) and Lightfoot on Gal. i. 8.
Deissmann has shown that ἀνάθεμα = " curse " is not confined to " Biblical
Greek," ZNTW ii. 342.

of a group of verbs with pure stems, πονέσω ἐπόνεσα, φορέσω ἐφόρεσα etc., (2) in the aorist pass. ἐρρέθην (presumably due to assimilation, as the long vowel is retained where there is no augment, ῥηθείς etc.).

Ἤνυστρον (the form used by Aristophanes) becomes ἔνυστρον in the κοινή: so in LXX Dt. xviii. 3, Mal. ii. 3.

17. The interchange of η and ε continued, though less frequent than that of ω and ο, till about ii/ or iii/A.D., when η began to be pronounced like ι (Meisterhans 19). It will be noted from the foregoing examples that the short vowel is specially frequent in conjunction with λ, μ, ν, ρ. So A has ἐρεμάζων 2 Es. ix. 3 (but in the next v. ἦρ. with B), κωπελάται Ez. xxvii. 9, σελένη Dan. Θ iii. 62. A also has ζετεῖν 1 K. xxiv. 3, B πεντέκοντα N. iv. 3.

The examples of the converse lengthening of ε to η are few. In two adjoining passages in Isaiah another meaning is made possible by the use of the long vowel in B: in xxxii. 4 we must read προσέξει τοῦ ἀκούειν with ℵAQ "attend" (B προσήξει) and in xxxiii. 6 ἐκεῖ with the same MSS (B ἦκει). Πέντη N. vii. 53 'Bᵉᵈⁱᵗ' (Swete's Appendix) occurs also in a papyrus of iii/B.C. (Mayser 63): this and πεντέκοντα above due apparently to assimilation of the two numerals. B has μετοικησίαν Na. iii. 10 (confusion of forms in -ησις and -εσία), A ἔννηα 2 K. ii. 30 (so in an illiterate papyrus of ii/B.C., LP pap. C), V γονυπητίας 2 M. xii. 24. A writes Ἰηρεμίας in 4 K. xxiv. 18, Sir. xlix. 6 and often in Jer., B only once, Jer. xli. 6. For ἀλώπηκος etc. see § 10, 20.

18. E and EI. Attic Greek often dropped the ι in the diphthong ει *before vowels*, just as it dropped it in the diphthong αι (ἐλάα ἀεί etc.)[1]. Hellenistic Greek almost always wrote the diphthong, although Ptolemaic papyri still yield sporadic instances of its omission[2].

In the LXX the writing of ε for ει, in two words where the omission of ι is specially common in Attic, is practically confined to literary books. Πλέον for πλεῖον is certain only in 4 Macc. (i. 8, ii. 6, ix. 30 ℵ): it has good authority in Mal. iii. 14 ΒΑΓ (πλ(ε)ῖον ℵQ) and is a v. l. in L. xxv. 51 A,

---

[1] Meisterhans 40 ff.   [2] Ib. 44: Mayser 67 ff.

W. xvi. 17 אC, Sir. prol. 6 א : πλέονα is read by BQ in Am. vi. 2, by א in Sir. xxxi. 12 : elsewhere the diphthong is universal before long and short vowels alike[1]. (Derivatives, πλεονάκις πλεονεκτεῖν etc., were always so written.) The writer of 3 Macc. has the adverbs τέλεον i. 22, and τελέως vii. 22 A (but τελείως iii. 26 AV): elsewhere LXX has τέλειος, τελειοῦν etc.[2] The literary translator of Job writes φορβέα for φορβεία "a halter" (xl. 20).

Only in the case of two late derivatives from ἀχρεῖος (which itself keeps the diphthong, 2 K. vi. 22, Ep. J. 15) is there strong evidence for a more general omission of ι[3], viz., ἀχρεοῦν (ἠχρεώθησαν Ψ xiii. 3, lii. 4, Jer. xi. 16, ἀχρεῶσαι 1 Es. i. 53 B) and ἀχρεότης Tob. iv. 13 BA *bis*; ἀχρειοῦν stands in 4 K. iii. 19 Dan. O iv. 11, vi. 20 (1 Es. i. 53 A).

Δωρεά is universal, and had begun to replace the older δωρειά in classical times[4].

19. As regards ε and ει *before consonants*, LXX always has ἔσω, but εἰς (Attic has εἴσω ἐς as well). LXX commonly has ἕνεκεν (ἕνεκα § 9, 8), while εἵνεκεν (Ionic and poet.), apart from Lam. iii. 44 εἵνεκεν προσευχῆς, is curiously confined to the phrase οὗ εἵνεκεν "because" (Gen. xviii. 5, xix. 8, xxii. 16, xxxviii. 26, N. x. 31, xiv. 43, 2 K. xviii. 20 B, Is. lxi. 1 = Lc. iv. 18 quot.), which replaces Attic οὕνεκα.

Οὗ εἵνεκεν for οὕνεκα appears to be due in the first place to the avoidance of crasis in the κοινή, while attraction of the diphthong οὗ may account for the use of the Ionic diphthongal εἱν. (Crönert 114 quotes examples of οὗ εἵνεκα.) Εἵνεκεν is unattested in the Ptolemaic papyri, which have only one example each of εἵνεκα οὕνεκα τοὕνεκα, Mayser 241 f.: in Attic Inscriptions

---

[1] The Ptolemaic papyri show a great and increasing preponderance of the forms with the diphthong, Mayser 69. The Attic rule was ει before a long vowel (πλείων etc.): before a short vowel either ει or ε, except in the neut. which was always πλέον, Meisterhans 152.

[2] Τελεωθησόμενον occurs in a private letter of 103 B.C. (Witkowski, *Epist. Privatae Graecae*, no. 48, line 18).

[3] Χρέα=χρεία occurs in a papyrus of iii/B.C. (Mayser 68) and on an Attic inscription of iv/B.C. (Meist. 40).

[4] Meisterhans 40.

it appears first in Roman times, Meist. 217 : N.T. has three examples of it apart from the quotation in Lc.

20. **H and EI.** The two examples quoted by WH (ed. 2 App. 158) of change of η to ει call for note also in the LXX. Both appear to be due to the approximation in the pronunciation of η and ει.

’Ανάπειρος for ἀνάπηρος, " maimed," or more particularly "blind," is the reading of the uncials in the only two LXX passages, Tob. xiv. 2 א, 2 M. viii. 24 AV (Swete ἀναπήρους in the latter passage), and has overwhelming authority in the two N.T. passages (Lc. xiv. 13, 21)[1].

Εἰ μήν in asseverations for ἦ μήν occurs in the papyri from ii/B.C. and is quite common in i/A.D.[2] In the LXX it is abundantly attested[3], the classical ἦ μήν occurring in the uncials only in Genesis (xlii. 16 D), Exodus (xxii. 8, 11), and Job (xiii. 15 BאC, xxvii. 3 אC). Deissmann was the first to point to the papyrus examples of εἰ μήν as exploding the old theory of a " Biblical" blending of the classical ἦ μήν with εἰ μή, the literal rendering of the Heb. form of asseveration אם לא. A further argument against that theory might be drawn from the fact that εἰ μήν renders other Heb. words, viz. כי (in Genesis) and אם, and may be followed by a negative (N. xiv. 23 εἰ μὴν οὐκ ὄψονται). Still εἰ μήν most commonly renders אם לא, and the similarity between it and εἰ μή naturally caused confusion between the two[4]. The Pentateuch written

---

[1] Cf. the note of WH on Heb. xi. 37 ἐπειράσθησαν, which should probably be corrected to ἐπειρώθησαν = ἐπηρ.

[2] Mayser 78, Deissmann *BS* 205 ff., Moulton *CR* xv. 33, 434, xviii. 107, *Prol.* 46. 112 B.C. is the date of the earliest example yet found. On the other hand papyri of iii/B.C., e.g. the Revenue papyrus of 258 B.C., have ἦ μή.

[3] Gen. xxii. 17, xlii. 16 AF : N. xiv. 23, 28 BF, 35 Bᵃᵇ AF : Jd. xv. 7 B : 2 K. xix. 35 B : Job i. 11, ii. 5 Bא, xxvii. 3 BA : Jdth i. 12 : Is. xlv. 23 אᶜ·ᵇ AQ : Bar. ii. 29 : Ez. v. 11 B and five times in " Ez. β," xxxiii. 27, xxxiv. 8, xxxv. 6, xxxvi. 5, xxxviii. 19.

[4] So εἰ μή is read by one or more of the uncials for εἰ μήν in N. xiv. 28 (A), 35 (B) : Job ii. 5 (A) : Is. xlv. 23 (Bא : no equivalent in Heb.) : Ez. v. 11

in iii/B.C. may, like the papyri of the same date, have contained ἢ μήν throughout in the autographs, and the literary translator of Job no doubt wrote the classical form : the other LXX books all adopted the spelling which was in vogue from ii/B.C.

21. The converse change of ει to η appears in Jd. v. 13 B, τότε κατέβη κατάλημμα = κατάλειμμα (Heb. "then came down a remnant") : similarly in 4 K. xix. 4 B λήμματος = Heb. "remnant" (A λίμματος), and in 2 M. v. 20 καταληφθείς appears to be intended for καταλειφθείς (V* καταλήμφθης exhibits the same change in the final syllable). These examples are accounted for by the change of ει to ι, which was then altered to η (see below). BℵA unite in writing σήσματι for σείσματι in Sir. xxvii. 4 : a papyrus of about the date of the Greek Sirach has the word in its usual form[1].

For εἴρηκα εἴρημαι = ἥρηκα ἥρημαι, ἠργασάμην—εἰργασάμην etc. See § 16, 5.

22. E and I. Ἁλεεῖς, as in N.T., always replaces ἁλιεῖς (Is. xix. 8, Jer. xvi. 16, Ez. xlvii. 10), apparently through dissimilation, i.e. from avoidance of the double *i* sound[2] : the change does not take place in ἁλιέων, Job xl. 26, or the verb (Jer. xvi. 16, ἀποστέλλω τοὺς ἁλεεῖς...καὶ ἁλιεύσουσιν).

Assimilation (specially frequent in the case of two vowels flanking λ μ ν or ρ) accounts for the spelling σιμίδαλις (for σεμ.) 4 K. vii. 1 A, Is. i. 13 B, lxvi. 3 ℵ and πιρί (for περί) Is. lii. 15 ℵ (so in papyri of ii/B.C., Mayser 81). The influence of Egypt has been traced in the interchange of ῐ and ĕ Thumb *Hell.* 138 (Coptic had no short ῐ, Steindorff *Kopt. Gramm.* p. 13) : but it

(AQ), xxxiv. 8 (Q). In 3 K. xxi. 23 εἰ μή BA=אֹל אִם is probably a literalism of the original translator.
   [1] Teb. 41. 22 σείσματα = 'extortions,' c. 119 B.C.
   [2] Blass N.T. § 6, 3 : W.-S. § 5, 20 a. The Ptolemaic papyri always have ι in the second syllable, ἁλιεύς, ἁλιέως, ἁλιέων and one example of ἁλιεῖς, Mayser 82, 269 f.: the originality of the ε form in LXX is therefore uncertain. LXX has no examples of the Latin words in which ε for ι is common in the papyri from i/A.D., λεγεών etc.

is to be noted that it is not limited to that country, being found in Asia as well (Thumb ib.).

23. H and I. The change in the pronunciation of η from an open *ē* sound to an *i* sound fell within the period 150—250 A.D., at least within the district of the Attic Inscriptions, in which the mixture of η and ι begins about 150 A.D.[1] The change may have taken place at a rather earlier date in Egypt, but the Ptolemaic papyri show very few indications of it. It speaks well for the three principal uncials that examples of this interchange of η and ι are distinctly rare in B and not much commoner in אA : they occur most frequently in two late MSS of viii/ or ix/A.D. Γ (Isaiah) and V (1—4 Macc.).

'Αναπηδύει, Prov. xviii. 4 BאA = ἀναπιδύει is due to an incorrect etymological association of the word with πηδάω (see LS s.v. πιδύω).

The following examples of confusion of the vowels may be noted as occurring more than once or as occurring in B or as affecting the sense. (1) H > I :—'Απορρίξει Lev. xiii. 56 B · ἱλικία Sir. xxvi. 17 A with ἵλικίας 4 M. viii. 2 A, ἱλικιώτης ib. xi. 14 A: κτίσεως (for κτήσεως) Ψ. civ. 21 אARᵛⁱᵈ: ῥιτίνη Gen. xxxvii. 25 AE, xliii. 11 AF, Jer. viii. 22 A: σμίγμα Est. ii. 9 A (=σμῆγμα Bא). Here may be added two examples where B, by writing ει for η, imports a new meaning : εἰμεροῦτο W. xvi. 18 (which might be intended for 'was charmed': read ἡμεροῦτο), εἴξουσιν Mic. vii. 12 (for ἥξουσιν יבוֹאוּ). (2) I > H. Οὐχ ἡδίαν (for οὐκ ἰδίαν) Jdth. v. 18 B, so Prov. v. 19 א (in the next *v.* A has ἦσθι=ἴσθι), cf. § 8, 3 : ἀνακλήσει (for ἀνακλίσει) Cant. i. 12 C : ἐξεχώρησεν 1 Es. iv. 44 and 57 A (in act. sense "removed," B ἐχώρισεν : a similar confusion ἐπιχωρίσαντος for -ρήσ. in a papyrus of ii/B.C., Mayser 84): ἐπιμηγῆναι 1 Es. viii. 84 B : μηαινομένη Jer. iii. 1 B.

24. I and EI[2]. It is needless to dwell long on the interchange of these two methods of spelling. For more than a century before our era ει had ceased to be a diphthong : ι and ει were pronounced alike and scribes had no guide but

---

[1] Meisterhans 19.
[2] See especially Blass N.T. 6 f., Mayser 87 ff.

classical models to tell them which was the correct method of writing. The alteration in pronunciation thus brought it about that ει and ι could be used indifferently to represent long *i*: the use of ει for ῑ is an indication of greater illiteracy and is more restricted. Some scribes used the old diphthong ει for a new purpose, namely, to indicate long *i* (so generally the scribe of B): others practically dispensed with it or used the two spellings indiscriminately. This use of ει and ι as equivalent does not, however, become common in the Egyptian papyri till ii/B.C.[1]: those of iii/B.C. for the most part observe the classical orthography. The earlier Ptolemaic papyri usually write τιμάω, τιμή, χίλιοι etc. (beside the classical ἔμειξα, τείσω etc.): it is only towards the end of ii/B.C. that τειμή, γείνεσθαι, γεινώσκειν, ἡμεῖν and ὑμεῖν etc. become common. It is thus *a priori* probable that the LXX autographs, at least of the earlier books, preserved the correct classical spelling.

The only rough conclusion that can be drawn with regard to the LXX uncials is that the orthography of B in this matter is more correct and perhaps goes back to an earlier age than that of א and A. In general it may be said that B prefers writing long *i* as ει (e.g. μεικρός, κλείνη, μεισεῖν, ῥείπτειν), and that many of these forms are well attested in papyri of ii/B.C. א, on the other hand, and (to a less degree) A, prefer ι as representing the sound of long *i* (e.g. ἐκῖνος, ἀπέστιλα, ἔμινα, χίρ, τῖχος).

25. It will be noted that in most of the instances cited the *i* sound is preceded or followed by one of the letters λ, μ, ν, ρ: and it might be laid down as a general, though not an exhaustive, rule that B writes λει- μει- νει- ρει- while א writes -ιλ. -ιμ. -ιν. -ιρ. Exceptions to this rule in the case of B are ἀλίφειν, λιτουργεῖν and forms from λείπειν (ἐκλίψει, ὑπελίφθην etc.).
B is fond of writing ι for ει in the dat. sing. of words in -ις, e.g. δόσι κρίσι δυνάμι[2]: on the other hand it almost invariably has ἰσχύει for ἰσχύι.

[1] In Attic Inscriptions the interchange did not make itself widely felt till later, *c.* 100 B.C., Meisterhans 48.
[2] So πόλι βασίλι in HP 110 (270—255 B.C.), παρευρέσι Teb. 5 (118 B.C.)

As regards ει for ῑ B is not impeccable : ὄρειον is frequently attested in this MS¹ ; but forms like ἀληθεινός are more characteristic of A. Πόλεις for nom. πόλις is common in B.

26. As regards abstract nouns in -εια -ία the following examples of forms in -ία are well attested by the uncials : ἀγυία (attested 4/5 : by B*AF in N. vi. 2), ἀκριβία (attested 5/6 : by B*A in Dan. Θ), ἀσφαλία (Lev. xxvi. 5 B*, Dt. xii. 10 B*, all uncials in the one example in Ψ, ciii. 5 : elsewhere in ℵ, A and V), δουλία (well supported throughout : only in three passages δουλεία appears unquestionable, 3 K. xii. 4 BA, 2 Es. vi. 18 BA, Jdth. viii. 23 BℵA), ἑρμηνία (Sir.), εὐσταθία (Est. and Wis.), ἱερατία (always attested, by B in Pent., by A in later Hist. books, by BℵA in Sir., by BQ in Hos.), λατρία (B* Hex., AℵV 1 M.), μαντία (Isaiah), μεταμελία (BA in the only passage), μυία (BℵA in Jer. β), νηστία (Ψ and Min. Proph.), παιδία (certain in Ψ and Is.), πλημμελία (certainly on MS evidence to be preferred to -λεια), πορία (attested throughout, except in Jdth. ii. 19, but mainly by ℵA), πορνία (mainly ℵA, Bℵ in Is. xlvii. 10, BℵA Jer. iii. 2), πτωχία (always attested, certain in Ψ and Job Θ), χηρία, ὠφελία (always attested, certain in Job, Ψ, Jer. β). Inferior support (mainly that of ℵ) is given to forms like ἀπωλία βοηθία δυναστία εὐσεβία etc.

In the Psalter we have evidence that the orthography in this case goes back to an earlier date than that of B : the book was divided either in the autograph or in an early copy of it into two parts after Ψ 77 : the scribe of the earlier portion preferred the forms in -ία, the scribe of the latter part wrote -εια (see § 5, p. 69).

For the omission of the first ι in words in -ιείον -ίεια see § 5, p. 63 ff.

27. O and E. Assimilation, analogy and the weakening of pronunciation in an unaccented syllable produce some interchange of these short vowels²

(1) E > O. The late derivatives from ὄλεθρος, first used apparently in the LXX, where they abound, are there, according to the preponderant evidence of the uncials, correctly written

and frequently in business contracts from i/A.D. onwards in the formula βεβαιώσω πάσῃ βεβαιώσι.

¹ Possibly to avoid the tribrach. The writing of ῑ as ει is specially common in diminutives where it is apparently due to a desire to avoid ‿‿‿. Βιβλείδιον is common in the papyri (I have counted seven examples between i/ and iii/A.D.) : so ἀλυσείδιον, δακτυλείδιον etc.

² Cf. Meisterhans 22 f., Mayser 94 ff.

(ἐξ)ολεθρεύειν -ευμα -ευσις. The spelling ἐξολοθρεύειν, which has survived in mod. Gk. ξολοθρεύω, and is due to assimilation of the vowels flanking the liquid[1], is quite rare in the first hands of the principal uncials and cannot be attributed to the autographs.

Out of upwards of 250 examples in the LXX B* has only 22 instances of -ολοθρ., A 8, ℵ* 9. The only books where the ο form is well supported are 3 Kings (ii. 4 B, xii. 24 m B, xvi. 33 B, xviii. 5 B, xx. 21 B' A, as against seven examples where ο is unattested) and the first half of Ψ (B 5, ℵ 1, A 1): in Jer. xxxi. 8 ἐξολοθρ. has the weighty support of BℵAQ[2], elsewhere this book has ἐξολεθρ., though in the simple verb the ο form is attested in three out of four passages by ℵ or B. The later ο form is introduced into the Vatican MS with indefatigable regularity by one or more of its correctors. The subst. ὄλεθρος remains constant in this form.

The same change appears in another verb in -εύειν, κατερόμ βευσεν, N. xxxii. 13 B (-ρέμβ. AF), where it is due apparently to the influence of ῥόμβος ῥομβέω: for the causative meaning "made to wander," cf. Syntax and contrast Is. xxiii. 16, ῥέμ βευσον πόλεις, "wander through."

The ε in the penultimate syllable of τετράπεδος (λίθος), "a squared (or hewn) stone," is usual in Hellenistic Greek in this phrase and in similar adjectives: but τετράποδος is strongly supported in Jer. lii. 4 (B*AQΓ), and is attested in the two other LXX passages, 2 Ch. xxxiv. 11 A, 1 M. x. 11 ℵV[3].

(2) O > E. The substitution of ε for ο in an unaccented syllable is strongly attested in two verbal forms: ἐπελάθεντο

---

[1] Perhaps we may find a parallel in Attic in the two forms ὀβελός, ὀβολός. The assimilation takes another form in ἐξελεθρεύειν Zech. xiii. 2 ℵ, Ez. xxv. 13 Qᵛⁱᵈ, 16 Q*ᵛⁱᵈ.

[2] Here perhaps may be traced the hand of the redactor who combined Jer α and Jer. β.

[3] The usual Attic adjectives are τετράπους, ἑξάπους etc. The forms in -πεδος (τρίπεδος, ἑξάπεδος, ἑκατόμπεδος etc.) are mainly used of length, as is τετράπεδος in Polyb. 8. 4 (6). 4. But the Heb. מצחב ('hewn') which is rendered by τετρ. in 2 Ch. xxxiv. 11 and the use of τετράγωνος as a synonym in 1 M. x. 11 A (so Jos. *A. J.* xiii. 2. 1) seem to fix the meaning of λίθος τετρ.

= ἐπελάθοντο (Jd. iii. 7 A, Jer. iii. 21 Bℵ, xviii. 15 BℵA, xxiii. 27 Bℵ, xxvii. 6 ℵA, xxxvii. 14 ℵ, Hos. xiii. 6 B, Ψ lxxvii. 11 B)[1] and ὀμώμεκα[2] = ὀμώμοκα, 1 K. xx. 42 B, ὀμώμεχα, Ez. vi. 9 A. With ἐπελάθεντο (? on the analogy of ἐτίθεντο) cf. the termination -εσαν which occasionally replaces the more usual -οσαν (κατεφάγεσαν, Jer. x 25 ℵQ and in papyri ἐλαμβάνεσαν ἀφίλεσαν · see § 17, 5 and 10).

28. O and Ω. The distinction between the long and short vowels, after the formal adoption of ω into the Attic alphabet at the end of v/B.C., is on the whole strictly observed in Attic Inscriptions down to 100 A.D.[3] In Egypt the distinction became obliterated at an earlier date, earlier, it would seem, than in any other province of the κοινή: the papyri of iii/B.C., however, are practically free from the mixture, which only becomes common in ii/B.C., and is then mainly confined to illiterate documents[4]. It is another testimony to the value of the principal uncials that the instances in them of confusion of o and ω are comparatively rare: it is only in late MSS such as E (Genesis), Γ (Prophets), T (Psalms), and V (Macc.) that it is frequent.

29. A few words claim special notice.

The verb ἀθῳοῦν (a late formation, perhaps coined by the translators, from ἄθῳος, θῳή) in all the 21 passages where it occurs in the uncials takes o in the second syllable, ἀθοωθήσομαι, ἠθόωμαι etc., apparently owing to the difficulty felt in pronouncing the long vowel twice consecutively[5]

---

[1] So in Mark viii. 14 B. The regular ἐπελάθοντο in 1 K. xii. 9, Job xix. 14, xxxix. 15 B, Ψ cv. 13, 21, cxviii. 139 and as v. l. in loc. citt.

[2] So ὀμόμεκα ὀμώμεκα in papyri from i/B.C., Mayser 95: add ὀμώμεκα OP³ 478. 44 (132 A.D.).

[3] Meisterhans 24. There are a few examples of mixture as early as iii/B.C., but it does not become common till Hadrian's time.

[4] Mayser 97 ff. He reckons seven examples of mixture in iii/B.C. (a few more must be added from the Hibeh Papyri) to 140 in ii/B.C.

[5] Ἀθῳος remains unaltered, even where there is a double ω (Jer. ii. 34,

Πρόιμος should be written in all the (eight) passages¹, but πρωινός. The former word means "early" in the year (of rain and fruit), is opposed to ὄψιμος, and is apparently derived from πρό: the latter means "morning" (as in morning-sacrifice, morning-watch), is opposed to ἐσπερινός, and derived from πρωί².

Ἀγαθωσύνη, ἁγιωσύνη, μεγαλωσύνη are the forms in use in LXX as in N.T.: T alone (in Psalms) consistently writes -οσύνη: B has μεγαλοσ. in Dan. Θ (iv. 33, v. 19), and B*ℵ* in Zech. xi. 3. Ἱερωσύνη (ἀρχιερωσ.) has also the best authority: in Macc. ἱεροσ. is read sporadically by each of the three uncials. A occasionally writes δικαιωσύνη, treating the αι as a short vowel (3 K. viii. 32, x. 9, Is. i. 26, xxxii. 17).

For the short vowel in πόμα (Att. πῶμα), δόμα cf. 14 above: for ἑώρακα-ἑόρακα³ § 24 s.v. ὁράω.

30. The remaining examples in Cod. B of the interchange of ω and o are (unless others have escaped notice) confined, apart from two in Exodus, to the books contained in vol. II. of the Cambridge LXX. (1) Ω > O : ἰσοθήσεται Job Θ xxviii. 17. (2) O > Ω : καθωμολογήσηται Ex. xxi. 9 (καθωμολογήσεται A : so ἀνωμολογησάτω in a papyrus of ii/B.C., Mayser 99), πεπτωκώς (=-κός) Ex. xxiii. 5 (cf. τὸ ἠσθενηκώς Ez. xxxiv. 4 A and τὸ γεγονώς in a papyrus of *c*. 115 B.C., Teb. 115. 23), θυρεωφόρος 1 Ch. xii. 24 (to avoid five short vowels: usually -οφόρος or ἀφόρος), πώρρω 2 Ch. xxvi. 15, ἀνθωμολόγησις 2 Es. iii. 11 (Σωμωρών B = Σομορών A = Samaria ib. iv. 10), ἀνώνητοι⁴ (for

Est. E 5), but ἀθόῳ is read by B in 2 Ch. xxxvi. 5 d, ἀθόων by ℵ in Jer. xix. 4.

¹ In the two where it is used of early figs (Hos. ix. 10, Jer. xxiv. 2) A has πρώιμος.

² The distinction between the uses and forms of πρόιμος πρωινός is carefully observed in LXX. Πρώιμος appears to be a later form due to a false etymology, as from πρωί (but see Blass N.T. 22 who, accepting the derivation from πρωί, compares πλώιμος πλόιμος). In Is. lviii. 8 τότε ῥαγήσεται πρόιμον τὸ φῶς σου (כשחר 'as the dawn': Ottley renders the Gk. 'early in the morning') πρωινόν would be nearer the original: the translator seems to have meant 'early,' 'soon' (cf. ταχὺ ἀνατελεῖ which follows) and to have dropped the Hebrew simile.

³ Ἑόρα 4 M. iv. 24 A.

⁴ In Wis. this form improves the metrical balance with the previous

ἀνόν.) W. iii. 11 B*ℵ (and so A in 4 M. xvi. 7, 9). In Sirach the writing of ω for ο is more frequent and goes back apparently to the autograph or to an early copy : prol. 22 βιωτεύειν BℵAC, μεσοπωρῶν (for μεσοπορῶν) xxxiv. 21 BAC(ℵ)[1], ἄκμωνος xxxviii. 28 B, εὐωδία (for εὐοδία) xliii. 26 B and so xx. 9 A, xxxviii. 13 ℵC (εὐοδία is confirmed by the Heb. in two of the passages, by the sense in xx. 9 where the Heb. fails), φωτίζων (agreeing with τόξον) l. 7 Bℵ.

31. In view of what has been said as to the correct use in general of ω and ο in the uncials, their evidence as regards e.g. fut. (or pres.) ind. and conj. gains in importance : in the LXX at least we shall not expect ἔχομεν and ἔχωμεν to be confused in Cod. B[2]. It is clear, for instance, from the following passages that the Pentateuch translators were fond of using a fut. ind. in the first clause of a sentence, followed by a deliberative conj. in the later clauses : Gen. xxii. 5 διελευσόμεθα...καὶ...ἀναστρέψωμεν, xliii. 4 καταβησόμεθα καὶ ἀγοράσωμεν, xliv. 16 Τί ἀντεροῦμεν...ἢ τί λαλήσωμεν ἢ τί δικαιωθῶμεν ; Ex. viii. 8 ἐξαποστελῶ...καὶ θύσωσιν.

32. O and Y. The heterogeneous Attic adjective πρᾶος -εῖα -ύ has been rendered uniform, πραΰς replacing πρᾶος : the substantive is consequently πραΰτης, not the older πραότης (§ 12, 11).

33. OY and O. Of this interchange (fairly frequent in Ptolemaic papyri, Mayser 116 f.) the uncials yield but few examples. ℵ has ὀκ (ὀχ) for οὐκ (οὐχ) (no examples quoted by Mayser) in Is. xl. 16, lviii. 10, Jer. xii. 4, xxii. 12, so F in Ex. vii. 23 : ℵ also has Ἰόδα Jer. xxxvi. 22. A has νομηνία Ex. xl. 1, δολεία (=δουλ.) Ez. xxix. 18, and conversely διαβουλῆς for διαβολῆς Sir. li. 2.

34. OY and Ω. Δῶναι for δοῦναι (on the analogy of γνῶναι) Est. ii. 9 B is not attested in the papyri before i/A.D. (FP 109. 4, letter early in i/A.D., ἀναδῶναι AP 77. 24, 130 A.D., μεταδῶναι OP[2] 123. 11, letter of iii/ or iv/A.D.).
The uncials always write οὖς, not ὦς (as often in Ptolemaic papyri on the analogy of the oblique cases, Mayser 5).

---

clause, ending with ταλαίπωρος, but it can hardly be original: the writer's sense of rhythm (cf. Syntax) would be sufficiently satisfied by ταλαίπωρος—ἀνόνητοι.

[1] LS cite the same form from Dioscorides.
[2] Contrast Moulton *Prol.* 35 on the text in Rom. v. 1.

35. OY and Y. The Ptolemaic papyri offer a few examples of their interchange[1]. In LXX κολλούρα, "a roll" or "cake," κολλουρίς, κολλουρίζειν are read by B in 2 K. xiii. 6, 8, beside κολλυρίς, κολλυρίζειν, κολλύριον in the same MS (as always in A) in 2 and 3 Kingdoms. The two forms are attested in the single N.T. passage (Ap. iii. 18), and elsewhere[2].

Two examples of ου for υ appear close together in Jer., λεπτουνοῦσιν xxxi. 12 B*, λουμενόμενος (=λυμαιν.) xxxi. 18 ℵ*vid, which *may* go back to the compiler of the two portions of the Greek book. B has ἡμίσου for ἡμίσυ Is. xliv. 16 (so in a papyrus of ii/A.D., Mayser 118).

An instance of υ for ου is apparently to be found in λυτρῶνας[3] 4 K. x. 27 BA (for λουτρῶνας, a euphemism for the Heb. 'draught-house' : cf. *latrina* = *lavatrina*).

We find also ὑρανοῦ Sir. i. 3 ℵA, δῦλος (=δοῦλος) 1 K. xiv. 21 A, Ψ cxxii. 2 T.

36. OI > I. ℵ has λύχνι=λύχνοι Zech. iv. 2 and apparently ἐμιχῶντο Jer. xxxvi. 23, πιήσατε ib. xlii. 15, A has Φινίκης Is. xxiii. 2. (LXX uses στίχος only, not στοῖχος, for "a row"; and so στιχίζειν (not στοιχ.) "to arrange in a row" Ez. xlii. 3.)

37. OI > EI. Δυεῖν is the form assumed by δυοῖν in two literary LXX books, 4 M. i. 28 ℵV (δυοῖν A), xv. 2, Job xiii. 20 = ix. 33 A, as also in late Attic Inscriptions (329—229 B.C.)[4], in a literary papyrus of ii/B.C.[5] and in some literary κοινή writers (Polybius, Strabo, Plutarch). The form seems to reflect a stage in the change in the pronunciation of οι which was on the way to becoming equivalent to υ (cf. 41 infra). It is almost the only vestige of the dual remaining in the κοινή.

[1] Mayser 118, cf. Thumb *Hell.* 193 f. Thumb holds that υ in the κοινή was pronounced in at least three different ways (as German *ü, i, u*).
[2] Blass N.T. § 6, 4 pronounces the -ου- form to be certainly of Latin origin.
[3] The form is not quoted in LS.
[4] Meisterhans 157.
[5] Mayser 314, where the literature is quoted. Phrynichus sanctions δυεῖν but only as a genitive (Rutherford *NP* § 185).

38. OI and O. The ι in the diphthong οι is sometimes dropped, as it is in αι and ει, before a vowel, both in classical and in κοινή Greek[1]. Ποεῖν for ποιεῖν is the commonest example: the only example noted in LXX is ποῆσε (= ποιῆσαι) Jer. xxxix. 35 א. The loss of the ι before a consonant is unknown in class. and rare in κοινή Greek[2]: B* has ὀκίας (= οἰκ.) Jer. lii. 13, ἀποκία (= ἀποικία) 2 Es. i. 11, ii. 1, x. 8, and τόχοις (= τοίχοις) ib. v. 8.

39. On the other-hand, in the κοινή an ι was sometimes inserted between ο and another vowel (α or η), e.g. βοιηθεῖν, ὀγδοιήκοντα, or an original ι in this position, which was dropped in Attic, was retained. Attic Greek wrote πόα, ῥόα, χλόη, ψόα (or ψύα), a muscle of the loins: but ποία (-η), ῥοιά (-ή), χλοίη appear in the dialects, in late Attic and occasionally in the papyri[3]. LXX always has the Attic ῥόα and χλόη. Πόαν should be read in Prov. xxvii. 25 (BאC, ποίαν A), but ποία in Mal. iii. 2 (BAΓ), and probably in Jer. ii. 22 (B*Q*). Ψόα Lev. iii. 9 and three times in the B text of 2 K. (A ψοία): in Ψ xxxvii. 8 αἱ ψύαι of AT must be the original text (corrupted to αἱ ψυχαί and thence to ἡ ψυχή of Bא*).

LXX has no examples of forms like βοιηθεῖν, ὀγδοιήκοντα (found in Attic Inscriptions and Ptolemaic papyri).

40. OI and Ω. א* has ἀνέγνοι (= ἀνέγνω) Is. xxxvii. 14, ἔγνοις ib. xlviii. 8, ἔγνοι 1 M. i. 5. For δοῖς, δοῖ = conj. δῷς, δῷ see § 23, 10.

41. OI and Y. Οι in the Attic Inscriptions is the last of the diphthongs to lose its diphthongal character: interchange of οι and υ is first found in them *c.* 240 A.D.[4] In Egypt

---

[1] Meisterhans 57, Mayser 108 f. Ποεῖν etc. appears in Attic Inscriptions in v/B.C. and is common in iv/B.C.: in the papyri its flourishing period is ii/B.C., though the examples of ποι- are even then twice as many as those of πο-: in i/ and ii/A.D. ποιεῖν is replaced by πυεῖν (οι = υ).

[2] Λοπός for λοιπός several times in Tebtunis papyri (end of ii/B.C.), Mayser 109.

[3] Meisterhans 58, Mayser 15, 110.   [4] Meisterhans 58 f.

the equalisation of οι and υ begins considerably earlier, in illiterate papyri of ii/B.C., but does not become frequent till i/A.D.[1] It is noteworthy that the earliest instances in the papyri are also the only examples which, on the authority of the uncials, are deserving of consideration in the LXX.

(i) B* has forms from ἀνύγειν (= ἀνοίγειν) in 2 Es. xvii. 3, Ψ xxxviii. 10, Na. ii. 7 (with ‭א‬) and Jer. xxvii. 25, and these forms are fairly common in ‭א‬ (and A) in the Prophetical and Wisdom groups: ἀνύγειν is the earliest example of υ for οι in the papyri (160 B.C. : so ὔξει = οἴξει, 99 B.C.).

Συνδοιάσω (for -δυάσω) read by B*A* in Ψ cxl. 4 may be original. B* also has σύ=σοί 1 Ch. xxix. 11 (=‭לך‬=σοί A : cf. Dan. Θ Sus. 50 A : the earliest papyrus example noted by Mayser is dated 90 A.D.) and ἀλυφῆς Mic. vii. 11. A and ‭א‬ afford other examples : στυβῆς Jd. xv. 5 A, τύχοις 3 K. vi. 10 A (so in a bank receipt of 112 B.C., Mayser op. cit.), σχῦνος A, σχυνίον and σχύνισμα ‭א‬, φῦνιξ Sir. xxiv. 14 A, φυνικοῦν Is. i. 18 ‭א‬ etc.

(ii) Of the converse use of οι for υ the only example claiming consideration is λοιμαίνεσθαι for λυμαίνεσθαι, which has strong support in Proverbs (xviii. 23 B*, xxiii. 8 B*C, xxv. 26 B*, xxvii. 13 B*‭א‬AC : but xviii. 9 λυμ. B‭א‬A) and in Sirach (xxviii. 23 B*‭א‬)[2], and is moreover attested in a papyrus dated as early as "about 147 or 136 B.C." (G. 17. 15). A real or supposed etymological connection between λοιμός and λύμη probably accounts for the adoption of this form.

Σοί for σύ is read by BAC in Job xv. 4, by A ib. xxxiv. 17, ‭א‬ ib. xxxv. 2, also by A in Jer. xlv. 24, and by ‭א‬ in 1 Ch. xvii. 27, Is. xxvii. 8, Zech. ii. 2. B has κλοιδωνισθήσονται Is. lvii. 20. Οἰποίσω (for ὑποίσω) occurs in Job Θ xxxi. 23 ‭א‬A and Prov. xviii. 14 ‭א‬, and these two MSS yield some other examples of οι=υ. F has ἐνδεδοίκει (= ἐνδεδύκει) in Lev. xvi. 23, which appears to be the only example in the uncials in the Pentateuch.

---

[1] Mayser 110 ff. Dr J. H. Moulton points out to me that in the matter of *pronunciation* the κοινή by no means followed the lead of Attic.
[2] The first hand of ‭א‬ probably wrote this form in Jer. xxxi. 18: " λουμενόμενος ‭א‬*vid " in the Cambridge edition (App.).

42. Υ and Ι. The change in the⸴ pronunciation of *v* to that of *i*[1] did not become general in the κοινή till about 100 A.D. In two words, however (in addition to some proper names), other causes had before this produced interchange between the two vowels, even in Attic Inscriptions[2]. These words are ἥμισυς and βιβλίον (βίβλος). Assimilation of the unaccented ι to the following υ produced ἥμυσυς (-συν -συ : but ἡμίσεος etc. where there is no υ in the 3rd syllable) as early as iv/B.C. : in the Ptolemaic papyri this form predominates in iii/B.C., in ii–i/B.C. ἥμυσυς and ἥμισυς are represented by nearly equal numbers. LXX has ἥμυσυ only in Dan. ℮ vii. 25 B, elsewhere ἥμισυ: the preference for ἥμυσυς in the early Ptolemaic age casts some doubt on the trustworthiness of the uncials.

On the other hand LXX has some examples of assimilation of the 3rd syllable to the 2nd. Ἡμίσει for ἥμισυ has good authority at the end of Joshua (xxii. 1 B*, 10 A, 11 B*A, 13 A, 21 A) and is attested by F in N. xv. 9, 10, Jos. ix. 6. Conversely, ἥμισυ stands for dat. ἡμίσει in N. xxxii. 33 BAF, xxxiv. 13 F, Dt. xxix. 8 A, Dan. ℮ ix. 27 BA. B* writes ἥμισον for ἥμισυ in 3 K. iii. 25, Is. xliv. 16. Cf. § 12, 10.

43. The same doubt attaches to the constant use of the Attic spelling βιβλίον, βίβλος in LXX (βύβλος in 2 Ch. xvii 9 B, Dan. ℮ ix. 2 B) in view of the predominance in Ptolemaic papyri of βυβλίον, βύβλος. Attic Greek had at an early time assimilated the original υ in the first syllable of βυβλίον to the accented ι in the second and βίβλος followed suit : there was also perhaps a desire to discriminate between the material βύβλος and the papyrus-roll formed from it. In the vernacular in Egypt, from which the word came, this distinction (to judge from the papyri) does not seem to have been generally made. In Is. xviii. 2 ἐπιστολὰς βυβλίνας B, "letters

---

[1] Thumb *Hell.* 139 ff. conjectures that it originated in Phrygia.
[2] Meisterhans 28 ff., Mayser 100 ff.

written on papyrus," is no doubt the true text (βιβλ. אAQΓ), as is Βυβλίων, Ez. xxvii. 9 B*Q*, the Greek name of Gebal being Βύβλος (Strabo xvi. 755).

LXX, with the Ptolemaic papyri, always writes μαρσίππιον, not μαρσύπιον (Lat. *marsupium*), which was an alternative way of writing the foreign (? Semitic) word.

44. Μόλιβος is written by the uncials (with variants μόλιβδος μόλυβος, § 7, 34), the Epic and κοινή form[1] of Attic μόλυβδος. Σμιρίτης (-τος A) λίθος is the reading of the uncials in Job xli. 6, not σμυρίτης, as cited by LS: assimilation of the unaccented vowel accounts for it, if the word is etymologically connected with μύρον.

LXX has the Attic ἁλυκός, the uncials again conflicting with the papyri, which write ἁλικός (on the analogy of other adjectives in -ικός)[2].

Other examples, mainly in Aא, are due to later scribes. (i) I > Υ. A has γύνεται (=γίνεται) 2 K. xiv. 27, καθυδρύσαντες 3 M. vii. 20, ὑδρυμένη 4 M. xvii. 3: Γ has σύντρυμμα Is. xxii. 4.

(ii) Υ > I. א has in Is. σινωρίδος xxi. 9, δάκριον xxv. 8, ἀργιρίου xlviii. 10, σινήχθησαν xlix. 18, ἐρίθρημα lxiii. 1, in Zeph. διuατή i. 14, ἐπελίφθησαν iii. 3, in Cant. v. 2 βόστριχοι. A* appears to have written ἀρχίφιλοι for ἀρχίφυλοι 1 Es. ii. 7: C has ῥείπου for ῥύπου Job xiv. 4.

45. Υ (ΕΥ) and Η (Ε). Πανουργεύω (not class. πανουργέω) is the verb in use (1 K. xxiii. 22) and has the corresponding noun πανούργευμα (used in good sense): Jdth. xi. 8 B*א (-ημα ABᵃᵇ), Sir. i. 6 B (-ημα אAC), xlii. 18 BC (-ημα א*A).

46. The following examples in one or other of the uncials of interchange of υ (ευ) and η (ε) are due to assimilation of vowels and to the later pronunciation (υ=ι=η):
(i) Η > Υ: θῦλυ Gen. i. 27 D, Lev. xii. 7 A, ῥύγνυται 3 K. xiii. 3 A, θυσαυρούς Prov. viii. 21 B, πυλός (=πηλός) Job xli. 21 א, πολλυ (=πολλῇ) Sir. xviii. 32 A.

---

[1] In the papyri μόλιβος first occurs in i/B.C.: μολύβδινος twice in ii/B.C. and μολυβδ[in iii/B.C.: Mayser 101.
[2] Mayser 102: ἁλικός *passim* in iii/B.C., the only example quoted of ἁλυκός is iii/A.D.

(ii) Υ > Η (always with assimilation): ὑποδήτην Ex. xxviii.
27 A, ῥησθήσῃ (=ῥυσθ.) 4 K. xix. 11 A, φηλῆς (=φυλ-) Hg. ii. 2 א,
ψηχή. (=ψυχή) Is. xxi. 4 א, ὑποχητῆρας Jer. lii. 19 B.
(iii) Ε > Υ, Υ > Ε: πέλυκυς Jer. xxiii. 29 A: ἐνέπνιον Jer. xxiii.
28 א, τετρεπημένον (=τετρυπ.) Hg. i. 6 א.
(iv) ΕΥ > Ε (assimilation of vowels flanking λ, μ, ρ, ψ):
δευτερέων Est. iv. 8 א, διελέσεται Jer. xiii. 1 B, ἐψέσατο 1 M. xi.
53 V, πεπιστεμένα 2 M. iii. 22 V: early Attic inscriptions yield
a few examples of loss of υ in final -ευς (Meisterhans 62) as in
βασιλές (= -εύς) Jer. xliv. 17 א.

47. ΕΥ and Υ. Πρεσβύτης, owing to its constant use
_ senex_, is, by a natural error, written for πρεσβευτής = *legatus* in
several passages[1]: 2 Ch. xxxii. 31 B, 1 M. xiv. 22 אV, xv. 17 אV,
2 M. xi. 34 AV.

Omission of ε also appears in (?) ἱερατύσουσιν Ex. xl. 13 B*
(second ε small, possibly first hand), ἀποσκυήν N. xxxi. 9 F,
καταφύξονται Jer. xxvii. 5 A, γῦμα ib. xxxi. 11 א*ᵛⁱᵈ, σκύη ib.
xxxv. 3 and 6 א: insertion of ε in ἰσχεύς Lam. i. 14 א. For ΑΥ
and ΕΥ, ΑΥ and Α see 12, 13 above.

48. Prothetic Vowel.

The Attic ἐκεῖνος is used to the exclusion of (Ionic and
poetical) κεῖνος[2], and Attic ἐχθές has supplanted (Ionic) χθές[3]
On the other hand ἐθέλω disappears, θέλω alone being used.
Σταφίς, στάχυς are written without euphonious α[4]. Ὀμείρεσθαι
"to long for" is read by the uncials in Job iii. 21 (corrected
by B^b to ἱμείρ.) as in 1 Thess. ii. 8, but is unattested elsewhere[5]
Ὀδύρεσθαι is used, not the Tragic δύρεσθαι.

---

[1] Cf. Philemon 9 πρεσβύτης with Lightfoot's note. He keeps the MS
reading but renders it "ambassador." "There is reason for thinking that
in the common dialect πρεσβύτης may have been written indifferently for
πρεσβευτής in St Paul's time."
[2] א* has κείνων, a corruption of κρίνων, in W. xii. 10.
[3] As to the Attic and Ionic forms see Rutherford *NP* 370 ff. Χθές is
confined in the uncials to Gen. xxxi. 42 A (after σε), Ex. ii. 14 A (τὸν
Αἰγύπτιον χθές) and 1 M. ix. 44 V (ὡς χθές): it is also written in nearly all
cases by one or both of the correctors of B (usually B^b).
[4] Attic Greeks apparently wrote ἀσταφίς but στάχυς: the Ionic ἄσταχυς
(Hom. *Il.*, Hdt.) reappears in Josephus, *A. J.* 17. 13. 3=*B. J.* 2. 7. 3.
[5] Dr J. H. Moulton tells me that the ὀ in this word as in ὀδύρεσθαι
ὀκέλλειν etc., comes from a derelict preposition ὠ (seen in ὠκεανός participle

א affords an example of *anaptyxis* (the reverse of syncope) in σάραξ = σάρξ Zech. ii. 13 (cf. Mayser 155). The same MS writes ὁμοροοῦντες (= -ροῦντες) 1 Ch. xii. 40, ἀναγάοντες (= ἀνάγοντες) ib. xv. 28. The LXX does not contain examples of prothetic ι before σ (ἰστήλη εἰστρατιώτης etc.), which appears to be a peculiarity of Asia (Thumb *Hell.* 144 ff., Schweizer 103).

49. Contraction and Syncope.

The κοινή generally prefers contracted forms, and introduces some contractions unknown to the older language. The Attic word for a young bird was νεοττός[1], and this is used by the Atticizing writer of 4 M. (xiv. 15), while two other literary books, Job and Proverbs[2], have the almost equally orthodox νεοσσός. The remaining books have the κοινή vernacular form νοσσός[3]. The derivatives all take the κοινή form : νοσσιά (16 times : νεοσσιά only in N. xxiv. 22 B*), νοσσίον, νοσσεύειν, νοσσοποιεῖν.

The LXX, in common with the Ptolemaic papyri, retains the Attic contracted form νουμηνία in most books (B 26 times, A 29, א 4): νεομηνία (Ionic) does not make its appearance in papyri or inscriptions[4] till the Roman epoch, and its originality where it occurs in the LXX is therefore extremely doubtful[5].

The coalescence of the two ι sounds in the forms ταμεῖον, ὑγεία, πεῖν has been discussed elsewhere (§ 5 p. 63 ff.), and it was shown from the papyri that the shortened forms found in the LXX uncials can hardly be attributed to the autographs.

of ὤ-κειμαι 'circumambient') which is shortened in the unaugmented tenses from the notion that ὤ contained the temporal augment. The root is *smer* seen in *memor*. There is therefore no connexion between ὀμ. and ἱμείρεσθαι.

[1] Rutherford *NP* 287.

[2] Job v. 7, xxxviii. 41, xxxix. 30, Prov. xxiv. 22ᵉ, 52.

[3] So all the uncials in Dt. (three times), and B in all the dozen other passages, while A, *more suo*, introduces the Attic form (νεοσσός). א twice sides with B, once with A.

[4] Mayser 153 (example of 191 A.D.), Nachmanson 69 (earliest example 213 A.D.). Lobeck (ap. Rutherford *NP* 225) "Νεομηνία...perrarum est etiam in vulgari Graecitate."

[5] N. xxviii. 11 B, 1 K. xx. 5 BA, 18 A, 4 K. iv. 23 BA, 1 Ch. xxiii. 31 BA, 2 Ch. ii. 4 A, Ψ lxxx. 4 (all uncials), Ez. xxiii. 34 B.

The hypothetical particle retains its usual classical form ἐάν in LXX as in the papyri[1]. The form ἄν, used by some literary writers (Plato, Thuc.), is practically confined in LXX to two phrases where there is crasis or elision (κἄν, οὐδ' ἄν) and to a small group of books (Wisdom, Sirach, 4 Macc., Isaiah)[2] The only instance of its use apart from καί or οὐδέ is Tob. xiii. 16 א μακάριος ἔσομαι ἂν γένηται. Ἐάν also frequently supplants the indefinite particle ἄν after a relative pronoun etc. (ὃς ἐάν etc., see § 5, p. 65 ff.).

The LXX retains the uncontracted forms, usual in Attic prose, in ἔαρ, στέαρ, ἐλεεινός.

For κανοῦν and ὀστοῦν ὀστᾶ (but ὀστέου -έων -έοις) see § 10, 8 : πηχῶν § 10, 21 : ἀργυροῦς etc. § 12, 2 : ἡμίσους § 12, 10 : contracted comparative adjectives in -ων § 12, 21 : ἀργός (ἀεργός Prov.) § 12, 2.

50.   LXX uses only the *syncopated forms* καμμύειν[3] = καταμύειν (Is. vi. 10, xxix. 10, xxxiii. 15, Lam. iii. 45 : B καμβ. in the first and last of these passages) and σκόρδον[4] = σκόροδον (N. xi. 5). (Δίφορον read by BF^corr in Dt. xxii. 9, where AF* have διάφορον, which is also read by BAF in the parallel passage, Lev. xix. 19, may be taken, not as an example of contraction but as an alternative rendering, = "bearing fruit twice a year," of כלאים.)

Other syncopated forms in the uncials are ὑπερδεῖν (=ὑπεριδεῖν) 1 Es. ii. 18 B*, so ὕπερδες (=ὑπερεῖδες) Zech. i. 12 א*: ἀκούσμεθα (=ἀκουσόμ.) 2 Es. xxiii. 27 א*, ἐπιχθήσονται (=ἐπιχυθήσ.) Job xxxvi. 27 א*, ἔλαλσεν (=ἐλάλησεν) Is. xxxvii. 22 B*,

---

[1] Meisterhans 255 (only 6 examples of ἄν in Attic Inscriptions from v/ to iii/B.C.): Mayser 152 f.: Moulton *Prol.* 43 note 2.
[2] κἄν Lev. vii. 6 B, W. iv. 4, ix. 6 (xiv. 4, xv. 12 = καί), Sir. iii. 13 B, ix. 13, xiii. 23, xiv. 7, xvi. 11, xxiii. 11, xxx. 38 [but καὶ ἐάν ib. xxxvii. 12, xxxix. 11, xli. 9 *bis*], 4 M. ii. 8, 9, x. 18, xviii. 14 [quoting Is. xliii. 2 which has καὶ ἐάν], Is. viii. 14 B. Οὐδ' ἄν 4 M. v. 30, x. 4, xvi. 11, Is. i. 12.
[3] Condemned by Phrynichus (Rutherford *NP* 426).
[4] So Ptolemaic papyri, Mayser 146 : in Attic Inscriptions from ii/A.D., Meisterhans 69.

πατοῦσν (=πατοῦσιν) ib. xlii. 5 א *, παρδόθη (=παρεδόθη) Jer. xxvii. 2 B*.

The MSS occasionally write a single *a* in transliterating proper names for the more usual double vowel: 'Αρών (= אהרן) Cod. A in Ex. vi. 26, vii. 8 (so vii. 1 F), N. xii. 10, Sir. xlv. 6, Tob. i. 7: 'Ισάκ Gen. xxvii. 1 A, Ex. ii. 24 B, Sir. xliv. 22 Bא, Jdth. viii. 26 B, and א in 1 Ch. xvi. 16, Ψ civ. 9, 4 M. xiii. 12, 17, xvi. 20, 25, xviii. 11. (The distinction between 'Αβράμ=אברם and 'Αβραάμ=אברהם is strictly observed in Genesis.) The prophet is always 'Ιερεμίας but a syncopated form 'Ιερμ(ε)ιά 'Ιερμίος is used of others of the name (יִרְמְיָהוּ יִרְמְיָה) in 1 Ch. and 2 Es.: cf. 'Ιρουσαλήμ Jer. ii. 28 א.

§ 7. The Consonants.

Interchange of consonants.

1. The consonants in the κοινή are subject to fewer widespread changes than the vowels. The general adoption of σσ for Attic ττ and such individual phenomena as the temporary substitution of οὐθείς for οὐδείς, the omission of the second γ in γίγνεσθαι and γιγνώσκειν, and the insertion of μ in the tenses of λαμβάνω (λήμψομαι etc.) are features which distinguish the κοινή as a whole from the classical language.

2. Phonetic changes, however, produced some new spellings which have a more limited range in the vernacular: consonants belonging to the same class are interchanged, gutturals with gutturals, dentals with dentals, etc. An interest attaches to some of these, because they appear to be confined to certain localities, and they have been attributed to idiosyncrasies in the pronunciation of the native languages of the countries in which they are found. In particular, the interchange of τ and δ and of κ and γ is specially characteristic of Egypt[1]. The examples of such changes in the LXX uncials

---

[1] Thumb *Hell.* 133 ff., with two papers in *Indogermanischen Forschungen*, vi. 123 ff. (J. J. Hess) and viii. 188 ff. (Thumb). It appears probable that Egyptians, in the early centuries of our era, could not pronounce Greek γ and δ. The evidence is as follows. (1) Hess shows that in demotic papyri of ii/A.D. containing Greek transliterations κ is used as the

have, therefore, a certain value in connexion with the question of their *incunabula*, although it is unlikely that many of them go back to the autographs.

3. **The gutturals.** K > Γ. The only example of weakening of κ to γ in the LXX uncials which can confidently be ascribed to the autographs is the form γναφεύς (4 K. xviii. 17, Is. vii. 3, xxxvi. 2), which replaces the older (and apparently original) form κναφεύς in the κοινή[1].

4. In other particulars the evidence of the uncials as regards interchange of these consonants is not supported by the Ptolemaic papyri.

On the one hand the conversion of ἐκ to ἐγ before certain consonants (ἐγ δέ, ἐγβάλλειν etc.) which is common in Attic Inscriptions and almost universal in the Egyptian papyri down to about ii/—iii/A.D.[2], is practically unrepresented in the uncials : ἐγλεκτός in the B text of Ψ civ. 43, cv. 23, and ἐγ γῆς Is. xxxix. 3 ℵ, xlix. 12 A, have been noted. Ἔκγονος is commonly written : ἔγγονος occasionally in Codd. A and ℵ[3]. For the similar absence of assimilation of ἐν cf. § 9, 4. Anomalous forms with γκ for κ are ἐγκλεκτοῖς Jer. x. 17 ℵ*, ἀγκμή 2 M. iv. 13 A.

5. On the other hand A has examples of γ for κ, some of which may indicate the Egyptian origin of that MS, but they are not likely to be older than i/A.D. The commonest example is -δειγνύω etc. which occurs nine times in this MS (Dt. i. 33 with F, Tob. xii. 6, W. xviii. 21, Ep. J. 25, 58, Dan. Θ iii. 44, 2 M. ix. 8, xv. 10, 3 M. v. 26). A also has γνήμην Jd. xv. 8 A (cf. ἀντιγνημίω CPR 78, 221—6 A.D.), οἶγον 1 K. v. 5, γαρπῶν Prov. xii. 14, δάγνοντες Hb. ii. 7. ℵ appears to read ἀπογρύψω in W. vi. 22 (see Swete): D has γυνηγός Gen. x. 9. The inter-

equivalent of both demotic *g* and demotic *k*. Demotic has no sign for *d*: τ and δ correspond to demotic *t*. (2) In Sahidic the consonants ꞅ and ⲝ, along with a few others, are rarely used except in Greek words (Steindorff, *Koptische Gramm.* p. 7). (3) In Greek papyri instances occur of interchange of κ and γ (not due, as in Attic γναφεῖον, to the influence of a neighbouring consonant) and of τ and δ.

[1] Mayser 169 f. The initial γ is found already in an Attic Inscription of iv/B.C. (γναφεῖον) Meisterhans 74.

[2] Mayser 226 f. In ii/A.D. the standing formula in the papyri καθάπερ ἐγ δίκης begins to be written καθάπερ ἐκ δίκης.

[3] Is. (xiv. 29 AΓ and five times in ℵ: xxx. 6, xlviii. 19, xlix. 15, lxi. 9, lxv. 23), Prov. xxiii. 18 A, Dt. vii. 13 F^vid. The papyri have both forms.

change of κ and γ, in which Thumb traces the influence of Egyptian pronunciation (*Hell.* 134), only comes to the front in illiterate papyri of i/A.D. (Mayser 170)[1].

6. Γ > K. The reverse change is represented in A by κῆν (=γῆν) 1 K. v. 4, ἠκούμενος 3 K. ix. 5 (=ἠγούμενος B : Heb. "upon the throne"), Κοργίας 1 M. iv. 5. ℵ has λέκι (=λέγει) Zech. i. 3, ἀκαλλιώμεθα Is. xxv. 9. B has χυτρόκαυλος 3 K. vii. 24 *ter*, 29 (A -γαυλος correctly from γαυλός "a milk-pail"). Familiarity with the native country of the founder of Alexandria might account for the appearance of Megiddo as Μακεδών 4 K. xxiii. 30 B, Μακεδδώ ib. ix. 27 A. One instance which appears with some frequency, πακίς for παγίς "a trap" or "snare," is partly due to the fact that it is often used to render the Heb. פח which has the same meaning, though the form occurs where other Hebrew words are rendered : B has πακίς twice (=פח in both places) Jos. xxiii. 13, Hos. v. 1, ℵ has it 13 times viz. Tob. xiv. 10 *bis* and 11 times in Ψ[2]: as against these 15 passages there are 47 where παγίς is read by all the uncials.

7. X > K (KX). Confusion between aspirate and tenuis is common in LXX and in the papyri when θ follows : in the uncials alteration of aspirate to tenuis is also met with before λ, μ, ν.

Ἐκθρός (found in a papyrus of 118 B.C., Teb. 5, 259) occurs sporadically in each of the three main uncials, B (Mic. iv. 10, vii. 10), ℵ (Na. iii. 11, 13) and A (Job xxxiv. 26, 2 M. x. 26): similarly A has ἐκθρεῦσαι 2 M. x. 26, ℵ ἔκθιστος 4 M. v. 27. In ℵ and A we more frequently meet with the spellings, paralleled in post-Ptolemaic papyri, ἐκχθρός -ία -αίνειν : so once in B*, Bar. iv. 25 (this portion of the book was written in i/A.D.). Ἐκθές for ἐχθές stands in the A text in 1 K. xiv. 21, xix. 7, 2 K. iii. 17, Job Θ xxx. 3.

Μοκλός is confined to the B text which has 16 examples of it to 19 of μοχλός : ℵ has ἀναμοκλεύοντες 4 M. x. 5. Κλίδων occurs in Sir. xxi. 21 A and Is. iii. 20 ℵ. Ἐκμαλωσία (for αἰχμ.) and

---

[1] The earliest examples I have noted are as follows :
κ>γ i/A.D. γυρίου BU 975 (45 A.D.), πατριγῆς and εὐδογὶ (=-κεῖ) BM ii. 154 (68 A.D.).
   ii/A.D. γρεάγρα BM ii. 191, πρόγιται (=-κειται) BU 153.
γ>κ i/A.D. ὁμολοκῶ BU 189 (? 7—8 A.D.), καστροκνημιο ib. 975 (45 A.D.).
   ii/A.D. ἐπιστρατήκων ib. 587, ἀρκυρίου ih. 416, διαιέκραψε (=διέγρ.) ib. 662, ὑτρακωγός (=ὑδραγ.) ib. 71, ἠκοράκαμεν ib. 153, Ἀκρικούλας BM ii. 189.
[2] Between Ψ x. 6 (where ℵ is joined by R) and xc. 3: at the beginning and end of the book (Ψ ix. 16, 30, cxviii. 110 etc.) ℵ unites with the other uncials in reading παγίς.

cognate forms occur nine times in א. B has λυκνίας Sir. xxvi. 17, A καλκοῦ N. xxxi. 22 (Swete ed. 2 App.). Κιτών[1] occurs in B* in Ex. xxviii. 35, xxxvi. 35, in א* in Is. iii. 16, 24, xxxvi. 22.

8. *Transposition of the aspirate* or repetition in the second syllable is seen in κύθρα (Ionic)=χύτρα 1 K. ii. 14 B, Sir. xiii. 2 א (so κυθρόποδες Lev. xi. 35 BF) and χύθρα N. xi. 8 F, Na. ii. 11 א : κύθ. and χύτ. in Ptolemaic papyri, Mayser 184. (Κιθών, χιθών of the papyri are absent from LXX.)

9. K—X. ʼΕκ is occasionally written ἐχ before θ χ φ in Attic inscriptions and Ptolemaic papyri[2]. So in the uncials (1) ἐχθέσει W. xi. 14 אAC (RV^{mg} 'cast forth *in hatred*' unwarrantably assumes a word ἔχθεσις=ἔχθρα : the papyri show ἔχθεσις ἔχθεμα etc., Mayser 228), ἔχθεσμος 4 M. v. 14 א, ἔχθες (=ἔκθες) Dan. Θ vi. 8 B*A : (2) ἐχ Χαρράν Gen. xxix. 4 A, ἐχ χειμάρρου Lev. xxiii. 40 A. Other examples of irregular χ are εἴχοσι 3 K. ix. 11 A, λιχμωμένους W. xi. 18 A (not from λιχμᾶν 'to lick,' cf. λικμηθέντες v. 20 : but the exact meaning of the passage is doubtful), ψεχάδων Cant. v. 2 א, χαλλίπαις 4 M. xvi. 10 A*^{vid}.

10. X > Γ. This change is unrepresented in the Ptolemaic papyri : in the LXX it appears, mainly in late MSS, in two pairs of words : (1) δραγμή in V (2 M. iv. 19, x. 20, xii. 43 3 M. iii. 28 : in the last passage A has δραγχμάς) and δίδραγμον in F (N. iii. 47 : Jos. vii. 21) and once in A (2 Es. xx. 32) : (2) in א αἰγμάλωτος Na. iii. 10, αἰγμαλωσία Jer. xxv. 19 : this MS usually has ἐκμάλωτος etc. (see above).

11. **The dentals.** The interchange of τ, δ, θ is characteristic of Egyptian Greek, probably on account of the difficulty which natives of the country found in distinguishing between the sounds represented by these letters[3]. In the circumstances the examples in the LXX uncials are fewer than might be expected.

12. T and Δ. The only examples noted of interchange (common in papyri, mainly illiterate, from ii/B.C.) are (1) πάνδες 4 K. xxiv. 16 B*, αὐδῷ=αὐτῷ 1 Es. iii. 5 B*, κασσιδέριον Zech. iv. 10 א* (so κασιδέρινα BU 1036, 15, 108 A.D.): (2) δεκατάρχους[4]

---

[1] So in an Attic Inscription of iv/B.C. and in papyri, mostly post-Ptolemaic: the Ptolemaic documents usually have χιτών (or the Ionic κιθών), Mayser 41, 184.
[2] Meisterhans 106, Mayser 228.
[3] Thumb *Hell.* 134.
[4] Due, perhaps, to the analogy of δεκατός.

1 M. iii. 55 א* (so in papyri of iii/B.C., PP ii. 13 (1) and 4 (1) and (2), not quoted by Mayser: δεκάδαρχος is read by BAF in the three Pentateuch passages).

13. T and Θ. Uncertainty as to whether the aspirated letter should be used or not is specially evident in words containing two aspirated letters or one aspirated and one tenuis. Ἀναφάλαντος -φαλάντωμα is read by the uncials in L. xiii. 41 ff.: the papyri of iii/B.C. fluctuate between this and ἀναφάλανθος, which is probably the older form (Mayser 177 f.). Κολόκυνθα has the best authority in Jon. iv. 6, 7, 9, 10: κολό-κυντα is read by A (Q): κολοκύντη is the Attic form according to Phrynichus (Rutherford *NP* 498): similar fluctuation in the papyri.

(i) Further examples of insertion of aspirate. Κάλλυνθρον is certain in L. xxiii. 40 (BAF), and probably φόβηθρον should be read in Is. xix. 17 with B* (φόβητρον cett.) as in Luke xxi. 11 (WH with BD). The following are due to attraction of a second aspirated letter: καθόπισθεν Zech. vi. 6 B*א*, βαθράχους Ex. viii. 9 F. Μασθός for μαστός is read by A in Is. xxxii. 12, Lam. ii. 20, by Q in Ez. xvi. 4 (the reverse, στ for σθ, is frequent in Ptolemaic papyri, Mayser 179). (ii) Examples of omission. The 2nd pers. of the 2 aor. imperat. pass. has its termination in -τι (for -θι), like the 1 aor. imperat. pass.: ἐντράπητι Sir. iv. 25 B*AC (-ηθι אBᵇ), χάρητι Tob. xiii. 13 B*A. Assimilation to preceding τ may account for κατορτώθη 2 Ch. xxix. 35 B*, ἐνταῦτα 4 K. ii. 2 A, 2 M. xiii. 6 V. Νεχωτά Is. xxxix. 2 א* (transliteration of נבתה: νεχωθά cett.).

14. Δ and Θ. Under this head come the forms οὐθείς, μηθείς, which have already been considered in the Introduction (§ 5, p. 58 ff.). They are not peculiar to Egypt: for some centuries they enjoyed a wide currency in the κοινή and then disappeared again in the first two centuries of our era. That they are not due to mixture of οὔτε and οὐδέ is shown by the fact that the fem. οὐδεμία remains unaltered. Their explanation lies in a coalescence of δ with the aspirate of εἷς to form θ (= δ + h)[1].

15. There is a curious distinction between the late derivatives from οὐθείς, οὐδείς. Each form had a progeny of its own. These derivatives are apparently unattested outside Biblical

---

[1] See Meisterhans 104, Mayser 180 ff., Schweizer 112 ff.

and ecclesiastical Greek¹ and are unrepresented in certain portions of the LXX, e.g. the Pentateuch, Isaiah and Job (excluding Θ)². Οὐθείς produced (1) ἐξουθενέω (-ημα), while οὐδείς produced (2) ἐξουδενόω (-ωμα -ωσις). Two rarer and doubtful forms, due to mixture, are (3) ἐξουδενεῖν, (4) ἐξου-θενοῦν. (1) must have been coined while οὐθείς was still in vogue, probably in the earlier part of ii/B.C. : it is preferred by literary writers, including the translator of Proverbs (though he wrote οὐδείς) : it is the form used by Luke and Paul in N.T. (2) apparently came later, when οὐδείς had begun to reassert itself : it is the form used in the later LXX books. 1 Kingdoms uses both (1) and (2), in juxtaposition in viii. 7 B οὐ σὲ ἐξουθενήκασιν, ἀλλ' ἢ ἐμὲ ἐξουδενώκασιν. In Sirach (the Greek of which was written during the period of transition from οὐθείς to οὐδείς) all four forms are attested.

The evidence for the verbs is as follows :
(1) 'Εξουθενεῖν 1 K. ii. 30, viii. 7 (7 A), x. 19 B : Prov. i. 7 : Wis. iii. 11, iv. 18 : Sir. xix. 1, xxxiv. 31 B : Am. vi. 1 : Jer. vi. 14 : Dan. O iv. 28 : 2 M. i. 27, and occasionally as a v.l. elsewhere.
(2) 'Εξουδενοῦν Jd. ix. 38 B : 1 K. viii. 7 B, x. 19 A, xv. 9, 23 *bis*, 26 *bis*, xvi. 1, 7 : 2 K. vi. 16, xii. 10 : 4 K. xix. 21 A : 1 Ch. xv. 29 : 2 Ch. xxxvi. 16 B : Jdth xiii. 17 : Ψ 18 times : Job Θ xxx. 1 BC : Eccl. ix. 16 : Cant. viii. 1 Bℵ, 7 B : Sir. xxxiv. 22 ℵAC, 31 ℵ, xlvii. 7 : Zech. iv. 10 : Mal. four times : Dan. Θ xi. 21 : 1 M. iii. 14 ℵA.
(3) 'Εξουδενεῖν 4 K. xix. 21 B : Ez. xxi. 10, xxii. 8 BQ : Sir. xxxiv. 22 B : Cant. viii. 1 A, 7 A.
(4) 'Εξουθενοῦν is read by B in Ψ xliii. 6, l. 19, by A in Sir. xxxiv. 31, by ℵ in Jdth xiii. 17.

16. **The labials.** Π > Β. 'Αμβλάκημα, ἀμβλακία (cf. Doric ἀμβλακεῖν)³ are the forms attested by the uncials in the only passages where the words occur, Dan. Θ vi. 4, 3 M. ii. 19.

---

¹ Plutarch has ἐξουδενίζω, and ἐξουθενίζω is cited by LS from a Scholiast on Aristophanes.
² These books use other verbs to render מאס, בזה e.g. ἀπειθεῖν, ἀφιστάναι, ὑπεριδεῖν, φαυλίζειν, ἀπαναίνεσθαι, ἀπειπεῖν, ἀποποιεῖσθαι, ἀπαρ-νεῖσθαι etc.
³ And cf. the fluctuation between 'Αμπρακία 'Αμβρακία in Attic inscriptions of iv/B.C., Meisterhans 77.

B > Π. ℵ has πορρᾶ (=βορρᾶ) Jer. i. 14, A προπλήταις
(=προβλῆτες) 4 M. xiii. 6.

17. Φ > Π. ℵ has σπόνδυλος ἐκσπονδυλίζειν in 4 M. x. 8,
xi. 18 (Ionic and in some κοινή writers, e.g. Strabo: Crönert 85):
A keeps the Attic form with σφ, and so all the uncials in
Lev. v. 8. (Σπόγγος, σπυρίς, which show similar fluctuation,
are absent from LXX.) Ἰωσήφ in Hellenized form appears in
the uncials as Ἰώσηφος and Ἰώσηπος: the latter form has
Ptolemaic support and was invariably used by the historian
Josephus of himself and of the patriarch.

18. Π—Φ. Σκνίψ has cases σκνίφα σκνίφες in Ex. viii. 16 ff.
in BA(F) (with variants σκνίκες and κνίφες F, σνίφαν A), and
the same forms appear as variants in Ψ civ. 31, W. xix. 10,
where the B text has the more regular σκν(ε)ῖπες, σκν(ε)ῖπα.
The two forms go back to iii/B.C. (ὑπόσκνιπος, ὑπόσκνιφος,
Mayser 174).

In the case of φάτνη[1], φατνοῦν, φάτνωμα (which have preponderant authority) individual MSS exhibit a variety of
spellings with transposition or loss of aspirate, transposition
of the first two consonants, and substitution of μ for ν:
(1) πάθνη Jl. i. 17 ℵ. (2) πάθμη Job vi. 5 ℵ, xxxix. 9 ℵ. (3) ἐτά-
φνωσεν 3 K. vii. 40 A. (4) πεφατμωμένα Ez. xli. 15 B, φατ-
μώματα Am. viii. 3 B, Zeph. ii. 14 B. (5) πατμώματα Cant. i. 17 ℵ.

19. B and M. The labial and nasal are occasionally
interchanged, mainly when flanked by vowels and in the
neighbourhood of a liquid or another nasal. (1) Alteration of
β to μ is seen in the reading of A ἐφ᾽ ἡμῶν in 2 M. iv. 12, a
corruption of ἐφήβων which V reads (cf. *v.* 9 ἐφηβίαν): also in
Σαναμάσσαρος 1 Es. ii. 11 BA* (=Sheshbazzar), εὐσέμιαν
(=εὐσέβειαν) 4 M. xv. 3 ℵ. Assimilation causes μόλιμος (=μόλι-
βος, μόλυβδος) in Jer. vi. 29 B, βόλιβον in Sir. xxii. 14 A[2].
(2) The converse change is more frequent[3]. Τέρμινθος, apparently
the oldest form for the turpentine tree (in LXX thus only in
Gen. xiv. 6 E, xliii. 11 F), develops into τερέμινθος (B 5 out of
7 times, A 2/7), and thence to τερέβινθος read by all the uncials

---

[1] Thumb (*Hell.* 71) conjectures that πάθνη is an Ionism taken over by
the κοινή. This is the form which has survived in modern Greek παχνί
(=παθνίον) with Asiatic varieties παθενίν παυθίν παθιμίν (ib. 81). LS suggest
derivation from √ΠΑΤ (πατέομαι).

[2] LS quote περιβολιβῶσαι from a Rhodian Inscription.

[3] Attic Inscriptions show βαρνάμενοι (=μαρν.) and fluctuation in Σερ-
μυλία (Σερβ.), Ἀδραμυτηνός (Ἀδραβ.), Meist. 77. Ῥύβην=ῥύμην is the
only Ptolemaic example cited by Mayser 199. Γερβανικόν is attested in
Rhodes and Asia Minor, Nachmanson 82. The proximity of ρ in all these
examples is noticeable.

in Isaiah (i. 30, vi. 13), and four times elsewhere (by E, A, אA). In the case of στίμι, a pigment for the eyelids, and στιμ(μ)ίζειν, the forms with β receive slightly better support (cf. Lat. *stibium*): στίβι Jer. iv. 30 Bא (στίμη A, στεῖμι Q), ἐστιβίζου Ez. xxiii. 40 BAQ, but ἐστιμίσατο 4 K. ix. 30 B* (β in AB^ab). Ἀνὰ βέσον 1 K. vii. 12 A, οἰκουβένην Is. xiv. 26 א, βέλη (=μέλη) 4 M. x. 20 א. Π is converted to μ in μοιμαινες (=ποιμένες) Jer. x. 21 A.

20. **The liquids.** In the vulgar language from the Hellenistic period down to modern Greek (which has e.g. ἀδερφός ἦρθα ἐρπίδα) ρ replaces λ, especially before consonants : instances occur, also, of the reverse change in the κοινή where no consonant follows[1]. Two examples of the interchange appear to have become stereotyped: σικνήλατον "a cucumber-bed" (from ἐλαύνω = "plant") becomes σικνήρατον (so in the only LXX passages, Is. i. 8, Ep. Jer. 69 with variants with υ in the first syllable): conversely κρίβανος (the Attic form according to Phrynichus), a small covered cooking-vessel, always appears as κλίβανος in LXX (as previously in Ionic, Hdt. II. 92). The papyri support the LXX in these two instances (Mayser 188). In the following passages the interchange affects the meaning. In 1 Macc. the word φάλαγξ which should certainly be read in all five passages, in four of them has a v. l. φάραγξ in one or other of the uncials (vi. 35 A, where Swete retains φάρ., 38 V, 45 A, x. 82 א* (V)). In the same book (1 M. ix. 42) the reading of א εἰς τὸ ἕλος τοῦ Ἰορδάνου (cf. v. 45) must be preferred to εἰς τὸ ὄρος of AV : the vulgar pronunciation and the influence of ὄρος in vv. 38 and 40 have produced ορος out of ελος. In Sir. xxii. 18 the converse change has occurred : it is the χάρακες (Bא) or "pales set on a high place" that cannot stand against the wind, not the χάλικες (AC), "pebbles" or "rubble."

The MSS yield the following further examples : (1) Λ > Ρ · οἰνοφρυγεῖ Dt. xxi. 20 B, βερτίων Is. xvii. 3 א*, ἀργηρά Jer. x. 19 א*, ἔθρασεν Job xx. 19 A (= ἔθλασεν cett.), χαρβάνη Sir. xxiv. 15 A

---

[1] Mr W. E. Crum tells me that in several Sahidic sub-dialects the two consonants are confused.

and χαβράνη Ex. xxx. 34 A (for χαλβάνη = חלבנה), Ἀμερσάρ Dan. Θ i. 11 and 16 A (= המלצר): (2) P > Λ: φαλέτρας Jer. xxviii. 11 B*, ἐσπέλας Is. xxi. 13 א*, κλιμάτων Ψ cxviii. 102 א*, Καλχαμύς 1 Es. i. 23 A (=כרכמיש), φλουράν 1 M. xi. 66 A.

21. **The spirants σ ζ.** Z₁ which in classical times was probably pronounced like *zd*, in the Hellenistic period had the weaker sound of voiced *s* (as in 'those'), as is shown by the substitution of ζ (or σζ) for σ, especially before β and μ[1]. א has ζμύρνα five times (Cant. iii. 6, iv. 6, 14, v. 13, Sir. xxiv. 15) and once ζσμαράγδου Sir. xxxv. 6: elsewhere all the uncials have σμύρνα, σμάραγδος. The same change appears in the form ζιβύνη, "a spear," attested by all the uncials in Is. ii. 4, Jer. vi. 23 (also Mic. iv. 3 AQ*, where it is a gloss from the Isaiah passage): Judith alone keeps σιβύνη, i. 15 B*א* (altered to ζιβ. in A and correctors of B and א): this foreign word of doubtful extraction appears outside the LXX in a variety of forms, συβίνη, σιγύνη etc., but it is clear that the older form had initial σ[2]

Attic ξύν for σύν survived after 400 B.C. only as a literary affectation and is unrepresented in LXX[3]. א writes ὡσμίλας for ὡς σμίλαξ Na. i. 10.

22. **Insertion of Consonants.** A remarkable feature of the κοινή (or rather, excepting one instance, of local varieties of the κοινή) is the tendency to insert the nasal μ before a labial (β or π), especially when the labial is followed by another consonant, usually σ: in other words μψ replaces ψ.

23. One instance is distinguished from the rest by its greater frequency: it also appears to owe its origin, in part at least, to another cause. The use of λήμψομαι (for λήψομαι) together with cognate forms ἐλήμφθην, (ἀνά)λημψις, (ἀνα)-λημπτέος etc. became for a considerable period universal. The papyri and the later uncials enable us to distinguish three periods. (1) In the Ptolemaic age, from iii/ to i/B.C., both the classical λήψομαι and the newly-introduced λήμψομαι were

---

[1] Meisterhans 88 (Attic examples from 329 B.C.), Mayser 204, 209: the latter's suggestion that σζ in ἀνασζητήσας etc. is intended to mark off the syllables more clearly will not suit initial σζ in the above instance.

[2] Sturz *de dialecto Macedonica* 46 f.

[3] ξυνωρίδος, written by a seventh century corrector of א in Is. xxi. 9, is the only trace.

employed, the former slightly preponderating[1]. (2) Under the Empire, from i/A.D. until after iv/A.D., λήμψομαι and its kin are uncontested, having driven the classical forms off the field[2]. (3) The reappearance of the latter in the uncials of the Byzantine epoch and in the correctors' revisions of the older uncials suggests that the μ forms again went out of use between vi/ and viii/A.D.[3]

Now the orthography attested in the three oldest LXX uncials is that of the second period, that is to say, the classical forms are practically absent. If, as is suggested by the Ptolemaic papyri, the autographs contained both λήμψομαι and λήψομαι, scribes of the Roman period have produced uniformity by writing the former throughout.

There are some 450 examples (including the compounds) where the μ forms occur in all three of the main uncials or in one or two of them. On the other hand, examples of forms like λήψομαι in the original script of B, א and A do not amount to a dozen in all : B has 3, one doubtful (Mic. vi. 16, Is. ii. 4ʳⁱᵈ, Jer. xxxi. 7), א has 3, one doubtful (Zech. xi. 7, Is. x. 29ᶠᵒˡᵗ, Jer. xli. 3), A 5 (Jd. vii. 5 λήψη [read λάψη and contrast λήμψη ib.], 1 K. xxv. 11, Jer. xli. 3, Ez. xlv. 18, Sir. iii. 24 : in 2 M. v. 20 καταληφθείς is probably a case of itacism = -λιφθείς)[4]. The classical forms become more frequent in later MSS and corrections of MSS[5], occurring sporadically in C (v/A.D.), T (vii/A.D.) and Γ (viii/ix/A.D.), constantly in Q* (vi/A.D.) in Min. Proph. and Isaiah (in Jer., except xxxi. 1, 41, and in Ez. they are due to correctors), always in Cod. 87 of Daniel (ix/A.D.), and nearly always in V (viii/ix/) and Bᵇ (probably xiv/A.D.).

---

[1] Mayser 194 f.

[2] Crönert 66 asserts "nullum reperiri in Berolinensium corpore exemplum nasali carens." The huge Berlin collection consists mainly of papyri from i/ to iv/A.D.: I have noted one example wanting the nasal, BU 1060. 30 προσδιαλη|φθέντος (14 B.C.): J. H. Moulton (*CR* xv. 34) adds one instance of ii/A.D. where the μ has been afterwards written above the line. The only other examples dated A.D. which I have noted are BM ii. 276. 4 προσειλ]ῆφθαι (15 A.D.), OP iv. 724. 8f. λήψομαι, λήψη (155 A.D.). Συνλήβδην FP 21. 7 (134 A.D.) is differentiated by the δ following the labial.

[3] So Crönert 67, who fixes the date of their disappearance from the living language at about the end of viii/A.D.

[4] F (iv/v/A.D.) has none (always λήμψομαι etc.).

[5] Cf. Gregory *Prol.* 72 for a similar distinction in the MSS of the N.T.

24. Apart from these forms from λαμβάνειν the LXX contains only four instances of words showing insertion of μ before ψ, all in Cod. A, viz. λάμψασιν (for λάψασιν) Jd. vii. 7, καμψάκης "a flask," 3 K xvii. 12, xix. 6 (from κάπτω, cf. Lat. *capsa*: elsewhere A unites with B (‭א‬) in writing καψ.), ἀντάμιμψιν (= ἀντάμειψιν) Ψ cxviii. 112, ἀνακύμψαι Job x. 15.

25. The origin of this inserted nasal has not yet been finally decided: Thumb (*Hell.* 136) thinks it unnecessary to assume a uniform explanation for all the instances. Λήμψομαι may be a mixture or compromise between Attic λήψομαι and Ionic λάμψομαι[1] (which retained both the α and μ of the present stem) or it may be an independent formation due to the same phonetic law which produced the other nasalised κοινή forms. These other forms (συμψέλιον etc.) are specially characteristic of parts of Asia Minor (Καμπαδοκία, Παμφλαγόνες are attested) and Dieterich (*Untersuch.* 92 ff.) traces their origin to that region. Egypt, however, yields examples other than λήμψομαι, and Thumb (*op. cit.*) suspects the influence of Egyptian pronunciation: the four examples in the preceding section which are peculiar to A may be taken as supporting the Egyptian origin of that MS.

It should be added that the older Attic, like the LXX, shows fluctuation in the use of the nasal in πί(μ)πλημι, πί(μ)πρημι, and in some proper names (Τλη(μ)πόλεμος etc., Meist. 84).

26. The combination μψ recurs in another instance, where the *p*, not the *m*, is the intruder, viz. in the name Σαμψών (= ‭שמשון‬), which is always so written in Judges (B and A texts)[2].

---

[1] The Ionic form occurs once in a papyrus of c. 250 B.C. παραλάμψεσθαι (Mayser 195), in the LXX in Job Θ xxvii. 21 C ἀναλάμψεται δὲ αὐτὸν καύσων. It is noticeable that the Hellenistic -λιμπάνω for -λείπω (§ 19, 3) appears to be of Ionic origin (Hippocrates).

[2] Schmiedel (W.-S. 64) compares Lat. *sumo sumpsi*.

27. As euphony requires the insertion of π between μ and σ, so between μ and ρ there is a tendency to insert another labial, β (cf. μεσημβρία = μεσημερία). Μαμβρή (ממרא) is written by the uncials in Genesis, Ζαμβρ(ε)ί renders both זמרי and עמרי · in other names there is fluctuation, as between 'Αμβράμ (-άν) and 'Αμράμ (עמרם)[1]

Ezra (עזרא) in LXX becomes Ἔσρας ('Εσρά) in B, Ἔζρας ('Εζρά) in A, Ἔσδρας ('Εσδρά) in א[2]. Probably the δ in the last form, familiarised by its adoption in our Apocrypha, is euphonic, like the β in Μαμβρή: but it is conceivable that σδ is used to represent Heb. ז[3] with a reminiscence of the old pronunciation of ζ (*zd*), see 21 above.

א inserts a nasal before δ in Jl. i. 6 ὄνδοντες=ὄδ., Ψ cxxxix. 2 ἀνδίκου=ἄδ.

28. **Omission of Consonants.** Under this head we have to deal with the omission of consonants, γ in particular, (1) between vowels, (2) in other positions, and we are brought into contact with some peculiarities of Greek as pronounced by Egyptians.

29. The curious phenomenon of the omission of *inter-vocalic* γ suggests that the guttural, in this position at least, was pronounced as a spirant, with the sound of *y* or (*g*)*h*[4].

---

[1] The nasal and liquid are sometimes separated by a: N. xxvi. 20 B Σαμαράμ Σαμαρανεί, 1 Ch. xxvii. 18 A 'Αμαρί.

[2] Ἔσδρας in B in the subscriptions to 1 and 2 Esdras, which are therefore later than the books themselves: also once in the body of the work, 1 Es. viii. 19.

[3] Cf. 'Εσδρ(ε)ί BA, 'Εσδρεικάν 1 Ch. ix. 44 B, 'Εσδριήλ BℵQ, 'Εσδρ(α)η-λών BℵA (=יזרעאל Jezreel), in all of which σδ corresponds to ז. On the other hand in 4 K. xix. 37 it answers to ס: 'Εσδράχ B='Εσθράχ A=MT נסרך.

[4] As in modern Greek: Thumb *Handbuch* 1. Conversely in the papyri (Mayser 167 f.) it is occasionally *inserted* between vowels, seemingly to avoid hiatus: ὑγι(γ)αίνω, κλά(γ)ω=κλαίω, ἀρχι(γ)ερεύς etc. In papyri of iii/ and ii/B.C. an ι is interpolated for the same purpose between the vowels ο and η: βο(ι)ηθεῖν, ὀγδο(ι)ήκοντα (Mayser 110).

In the case of one word, ὀλί(γ)ος, the omission of γ in writing began c. 300 B.C. and spread over a wide area in the Greek-speaking world[1]. Apart from this and one or two other words the usage was apparently restricted to Egypt[2].

The uncials B, ℵ and A always write ὀλίγος, but in two derivatives—ὀλιγοῦν (a Hellenistic creation, perhaps coined by the translators)[3] and ὀλιγοστός—the γ is omitted, four times in all, by the original scribe of B: Jd. x. 16 ὠλιώθη, 4 K. iv. 3 ὀλιώσῃς, 2 Es. xix. 32 ὀλιωθήτω ("B*vid"), Is. xli. 14 ὀλιοστός[4].

Ἀγ(ε)ίοχα[5] (so constantly in the uncials, see § 16, 7 · ἀγήοχα usually in Hellenistic writers), the perfect of ἄγω (condemned by Phrynichus, who prescribes ἦχα), is probably another instance of omission of "spirantic" γ[6]; ἀγήγοχα appears in Inscriptions.

30. The omission of intervocalic γ in other instances, usually between ευ, αυ and a long vowel, appears to be a peculiarity of Egypt during the Roman period: it is unknown to the Ptolemaic papyri. In the LXX it is almost confined to one section of ℵ (Prophets: once in Proverbs), and the

---

[1] Meisterhans 75 (Attic Inscr. show ὀλίος ὀλιαρχία ὀλιωρέω: also Φιαλεύς = Φιγ.): Mayser 163 f.: Schweizer 108 (who mentions as places, other than Egypt, where ὀλίος is found Boeotia, Arcadia, Tarentum, the Tauric Chersonese, Imbros, Pamphylia and the extreme East of the Empire).

[2] Thumb, *Hell.* 134 f., distinguishes two groups: (1) the older forms attested outside Egypt viz. ὀλίος Φιάλευς (to which should be added Boeot. ἰών = ἐγώ and perhaps ἀγήοχα pf. of ἄγω), (2) the 'Egyptian' forms φεύω — φεύγω etc. In the latter he traces the native's difficulty in pronouncing γ, which in other instances produced in Egyptian Greek the alteration of γ to κ (see § 7, 2 ff. above). In the earlier group it is curious to note that (adopting the LXX form ἀγίοχα) the lost γ was in each case preceded by ι.

[3] The verb is confined in LXX to a late group of books.

[4] As against these four passages there are eight and 18 respectively where ὀλιγοῦν ὀλιγοστός are written by all the uncials. Aquila is cited as writing ὠλιώθησαν in Jer. xiv. 2.

[5] The papyri have (as Dr J. H. Moulton informs me) ἀγήγοχα HP 34 (iii/B.C), ἀγείοχα Teb. 19 (ii/B.C.), ἀγέοχα Teb. 124 (ii/B.C.) and ἀγέωχα (ii/—i/B.C.).

[6] The omission has been otherwise explained as due to dissimilation.

Prophetical portion of that MS or of a parent MS was therefore, presumably, written by an Egyptian scribe.

The examples are as follows :—

Φεύειν in ℵ occurs in Is. x. 18, xiii. 14, xvi. 3, xxii. 3, xxxi. 9,
xliii. 14, Jer. xxvii. 28, xxxi. 44, xlv. 19, Jon. i. 3 (φοῦν=φυ[γε]ῖν),
Na. ii. 9 (φθυο̄|τες *sic*), Prov. xii. 13 (ἐκφεύει).　In all cases, except
Jer. xlv. 19 πεφευότων, the lost γ is followed by a long vowel.
The γ is written where a short vowel follows (φεύγετε -ετω
Jer. iv. 6, xxvi. 6, xxviii. 6, xxx. 8, xxxi. 6), less frequently before
a long vowel.　B and A have no examples of loss of γ in this
word.

Κρανή for κραυγή is consistently written by the first hand of ℵ
in the Prophetical books, 17 times including Jer. xxxii. 22 καυῆς:
the only exceptions (all in ' Jer. a ') are Jer. iv. 19 where the MS
has κραγήν and viii. 19, xviii. 22, xx. 16 where it has the usual
form.　On the other hand κραυγή is always written by this MS
in the historical and literary books (14 examples between 2 Es.
and Judith).　B writes κρανή in Is. xxx. 19 (with ℵ) and Ez. xxi. 22.

Ζεύη for ζεύγη Is. v. 10 ℵ*.

'Εξερευόμενα for -ερευγ. is written by A in Ψ cxliii. 13, and the
same MS in W. xix. 10 has the aorist ἐξηρεύσατο formed as from
ἐξερεύεσθαι.　(ℵ keeps γ in this word, which however is not
found in the Prophetical portion.)

('Ανεείγνωσκον Job xxxi. 36 A, cf. 32 below.)

'Ανοίει for ἀνοίγει Is. l. 5 ℵ*.

Λεῖ for λέγει Zech. ii. 8 ℵ* (cf. mod. Greek λέει).

The weak pronunciation of intervocalic γ occasionally produces its *insertion* in the wrong place[1].　ℵ writes λέγοντες for
λέοντες Jer. ii. 15 : hence too the mistaken reading attested by
ℵℵA in Est. vii. 3 ὁ λόγος μου for ὁ λαός μου (עמי).

31.　While γ is the consonant most frequently omitted
between vowels, there are certain others which are liable to
omission in a similar position.　These are κ (χ), τ, δ, λ, σ (ρ, ν).
Most of the instances occur again in the Prophetical portion
of Cod. ℵ and doubtless reproduce the Egyptian pronunciation.
As a contribution to the study of Graeco-Egyptian phonetics
and as bearing on the history of the uncials, it may be useful
to collect them here.

---

[1] Cf. papyri examples in note 4 on p. 111.

Examples of omission of intervocalic consonants other than γ.

κ. ℵ has πρωτότοα (= -τοκα) Ψ cxxxiv. 8. Cf. (? from haplology) διαθης = διαθήκης Zech. ix. 11, διος (=δίκαιος) 2 Es. xix. 33.

χ. B has ἀπέεσθε (= ἀπέχ.) Mal. iii. 7. Cf. the variants ψυχαί ψύαι ψόαι in Ψ xxxvii. 8, and ἐξεαν=ἐξέχεαν Dt. xxi. 7 F.

τ. ℵ has ἀποσταε (= ἀποστάται) Is. xxx. 1, σιος (= σῖτος) Hg. i. 11, καάλοιποι (=κατ.) Zech. xiv. 2, συνεελέσθησαν (= -ετελ.) Job i. 5. B has a parallel to the last in ἀποελεσθῆναι 1 Es. v. 70: cf. Is. ii. 13 μεώρων B=μετεώρων. A has τοὖο (=τοῦτο) Ex. ix. 5.

δ. ℵ has παῖ|α (= παῖδα) Is. xxvi. 16, ὕωρ xlviii. 21, Ἰουμέᾳ (=Ἰδουμαίᾳ) Jer. xxix. 8. A likewise has Ἰουμαίας Lam. iv. 21. (Conversely, as γ is inserted in ὑγιγαίνω etc. of the papyri, so is δ in πραδέων=πραέων Is. xxvi. 6 ℵ.)

λ. ℵ has μέεσιν=μέλεσιν Job ix. 28, θά|ασσαν Jer. xxviii. 36, βασιέως xxxiv. 9, cf. βασια=βασιλέα Jon. iii. 6. Similarly A has βασι|ως=-σιλέως 2 K. xv. 3 and καταβάω=-βάλω Ez. xxix. 5: V has ἀντιπάους = -πάλους 3 M. i. 5: B πουπειρία (=πολυπ.) Sir. xxv. 6.

σ. ℵ has ἐποίηε=-ησε Is. xii. 5 (cf. ποιηες=ποιῆσαι Jer. vi. 25 BℵA), κιθάριον=-ισον xxiii. 16, κρίιν=κρίσιν xlii. 3, πλησίον (=πλησ.) Jer. xxii. 13, ὀλιγώεις (=-ώσεις) Hb. iii. 12. B has ἐπιλεύεσθαι=ἐπελεύσεσθαι 1 Es. iv. 49 (in the same section which has the omission of τ noted above) and κριν=κρίσιν Is. i. 17. A has θραύ=θρασύ N. xiii. 29, σύνεις=σύνεσις Is. xlvii. 10 (cf. συνε|εις Ψ xxxi. 9 U).

ρ. A has μιεός for μιερός 2 M. iv. 19.

μ and ν. ℵ has μεγαρηονήσῃς (=-μεγαλορημ.) Ob. 12, ἐσφραγισμέου Is. xxix. 11.

32. Of omission of a consonant *in another position than between vowels* there are two examples which were universally adopted. The second γ in γίγνομαι, γιγνώσκω ceased to be written after c. 300 B.C.[1]: vulgar Attic, as attested by vase inscriptions, had led the way[2]. Γ(ε)ίνομαι γ(ε)ινώσκω are all but universal in the LXX uncials as in the papyri. The classical spelling was revived by some of the Atticists.

Γίγνομαι in the leading uncials is confined to the A text of 1 and 2 Esdras, Job xl. 27 A, and to a unique example in B (1 Es. vi. 33). A has it five times in 1 Esdras (from v. 43

---

[1] Meisterhans 75, Mayser 164 f. The latter compares (g)natus, (g)nosco, and assumes an intermediate stage when -γν- was written -νν-.

[2] Thumb *Hell.* 207.

παραγίγν. to viii. 90 ἡγνέσθω *sic*, clearly a corruption of ΓΙ to Η: in i. 30, iv. 16, vi. 33. vii. 3 γιν.) and nine times in 2 Esdras (ἐγιν. only in xv. 18 with γιγν. ib.). It appears that among the ancestors of A was a small volume comprising 1 and 2 Esdras, written by an Atticizing scribe probably after ii/A.D.

Γιγνώσκω appears sporadically as a v.l. of B, ℵ, A in a wider circle of books: 1 Ch. xxviii. 9 B: 1 Es. ix. 41 A: Est. iv. 11 A, c 5 A, vi. 1 A: Job? xxxi. 36 A (ANEEIΓ. for ANEΓIΓ. cf. 30 above), xxxvi. 5 Bℵ: Tob. v. 14 A, vii. 4 A *bis*: Jer. xliii. 13 A: Dan. Θ i. 4 B: 1 M. v. 14 ℵ.

33. Other examples of omission by the original scribes of the uncials of consonants in positions other than intervocalic have their interest in the history of phonetics. They are not to be treated as mere blunders. Here, as in the cases of omission of intervocalic consonants, ℵ again affords the majority of the instances, but there are not a few in the other MSS, and we cannot be so confident in all cases as to their "Egyptian" origin. The omitted consonants are partly the same as in the former case, partly different: omission of ρ, which does not occur between vowels, is specially common here.

Omission of gutturals.

γ. The γ in the nom. of nouns ending in -γξ gen. -γγος is sometimes dropped, on the analogy, it would seem, of e.g. μάστιξ -ιγος. Φάραξ is written by ℵ in (Zech. xiv. 5 πάραξ), Is. lvii. 5, Jer. vii. 32, by Q in Is. lxv. 10, λάρυξ by C in Job Θ xxxiv. 3. (Conversely μάστιγξ appears in 3 K. xii. 24 r B: 2 Ch. x. 11 B, 14 B: Sir. xxiii. 11 ℵ.) Similar omission before ξ (κ) is seen in ἐλέξει Is. xi. 3 ℵ, ἀνεξέλεκτος Prov. x. 17 B.

Elsewhere omission takes place in the proximity of ρ or a nasal. In ℵ: ὀρ[γ]ῆς[1] Jer. xxvii. 13, κρεά[γ]ρας lii. 18, κατα-νένυ[γ]μαι Is. vi. 5, δή[γ]ματα W. xvi. 9, ἔ[γ]νω Zeph. iii. 5. In A: τελεσιουρ[γ]εῖ Prov. xix. 4.

κ. In ℵ: ἔ[κ]στασις Zech. xiv. 13, ἐ[κ]φεύξεσθαι Est. Ε 4. In B: διε[κ]βολῇ Ἐz. xlvii. 11, ἐκλε[κ]τοί 1 Ch. vii. 40: cf. πρω-τοτο[κο]ν[2] Ex. xi. 5, ἀ[κα]θαρτος Lev. xv. 11. In A: σ[κ]νίφαν Ex. viii. 18, cf κατα[κα]λύπτον Lev. iv. 8. In F cf. συμβολο-[κο]πῶν Dt. xxi. 20.

---

[1] The omitted consonant is inserted in square brackets throughout this section.

[2] This and some of the following examples may be merely cases of haplology.

χ. In א: ἐτέ[χ]θησαν 1 Ch. xiv. 3. In C cf. ψυ[χη]σου Sir. xxx. 39.

34. *Omission of dentals.*

Two words uniformly appear without the dental throughout the LXX. Ἄρκος replaces ἄρκτος and the older (Epic) μόλιβος (or μόλυβος Ez. xxvii. 12 BAQ, Zech. v. 7 א) is used to the exclusion of μόλυβδος[1].

τ is omitted in Αἴγυπ[τ]ος in the א text of Jer. xxvi. 17, xlix. 14, li. 30 and in ἔσ[τ]ιν Is. xliii. 11, 13 א (elsewhere the σ is lost, see below). B has τέταρ[τ]ον Ez. v. 12. A has δακ[τ]ύλῳ Lev. xvi. 14, σκῆπ[τ]ρον Ep. Jer. 13 (cf. δευ[τε]ρα R. i. 4).

δ disappears after β (as in μόλυβ[δ]ος) in ῥάβ[δ]ον Zech. viii. 4 א. Cf. in F δω[δε]κα Gen. xliv. 32, ἐ[δε]ται Ex. xii. 45, [δα]-μάλεως N. xix. 9: and in D [δι]δωμι Gen. xlviii. 22.

θ is dropped after the other aspirated letters χ (κ) φ. א has ἐκ[θ]λίψω Is. xxix. 2, ἀπεκαλύφ[θ]η liii. 1, αὐτόχ[θ]ων Jer. xiv. 8. A writes κατεφ[θ]είρετο 2 Ch. xxvii. 2. The omission in the case of ἐχ[θ]ρός seems to go back to an early copy of the Greek Lamentations: Lam. i. 9 א, ii. 3 B, i. 7 A: A has this spelling (ἔχραν) also in Mic. ii. 8, F in N. xxxv. 20, Q in Ez. xxxv. 5.

35. *Omission of liquids.*

λ. א omits (in proximity of κ and β): ἐσκ[λ]ήρυνας Is. lxiii. 17, cf. σκ[λ]ηροκαρδίαν Jer. iv. 4, ἐπεκ[λ]ήθη xli. 15, εἴ[λ]κον 4 M. xi. 9: βιβ[λ]ίῳ Jer. xxviii. 60, ἐκβ[λ]ύζωσιν Prov. iii. 10. A has ἐξῆ[λ]θες Ex. xxiii. 15, πολυοχ[λ]ίας Job xxxix. 7, F has ἀδε[λ]φῷ Lev. xxi. 2.

ρ. Omission is frequent especially after the dentals τ (στ) δ θ (ρθ). א has γαστ[ρ]ί Is. xl. 11, (ἐπι)στ[ρ]έψει etc. Jer. ii. 24, xviii. 20, xx. 16, ἄστ[ρ]ων ib. xxviii. 9, ἀροτ[ρ]ιαθήσεται xxxiii. 18, ἐπαρυστ[ρ]ίδ(ες) Zech. iv. 2 (with A), 12: κέδ[ρ]ου Is. xxxvii. 24, σφόδ[ρ]α Jer. ii. 10, Zech. ix. 9, τετράδ[ρ]αχμον Job xlii. 11: ἄνθ[ρ]ωπος Is. vi. 5, ἐχθ[ρ]ός Jer. xx. 5. Loss of the second ρ in ὄρθ[ρ]ος ὀρθ[ρ]ίζειν is shared by א with the other uncials: so א in Jer. vii. 25, xxv. 4, xxxiii. 5, xxxix. 33, xlii. 14, li. 4, Prov. vii. 18, xxiii. 35: B in Ex. ix. 13, Hos. xi. 1: A in Gen. xix. 2, Ex. xxxiv. 4: C in Sir. iv. 12. א has further μικ[ρ]ός Is. xxii. 5, Jer. xlix. 8, σά[ρ]ξ Is. xlix. 26, κατά[ρ]ξει etc. Jl. ii. 17, Zech. vi. 13, ix. 10, β[ρ]οῦχος Jl. i. 4, Na. iii. 15, φ[ρ]ύαγμα Jer. xii. 5, σκο[ρ]πίου 4 M. xi. 10. B has also πάτ[ρ]αρχον Is. xxxvii. 38, μέτ[ρ]ου Ez. xlii. 17, τ[ρ]αχεῖα Sir. vi. 20, ἄνδ[ρ]ες 1 K. xxix. 2, σφόδ[ρ]α 2 Es. xxiii. 8. A (besides ἐπαρυστίδες, above) has ἐρυθ[ρ]ᾷ ἠρυθ[ρ]ο-δανωμένα Ex. xv. 4, xxxix. 21, Ψ cv. 7, ἔξαρθ[ρ]ος 4 M. ix. 13, κ[ρ]εάγρας Ex. xxxviii. 23, N. iv. 14, Jer. lii. 18. F has μίτ[ρ]αν Lev. viii. 9, Q στ[ρ]ουθία Jer. viii. 7 and C κατασφ[ρ]αγίζει Job xxxvii. 7.

---

[1] Cod. A writes μόλιβδος in Ezekiel.

36. *Omission of* σ occurs most often before τ and π.
א has γα[σ]τρί Is. xxvi. 18, ἔ[σ]τιν Is. xxvii. 9, xxxi. 3, Zech. i. 9,
ἀγρω[σ]τις Is. xxxvii. 27, ἀκου‖[σ]τήν Is. xxx. 30, ἴα[σ]πιν Is. liv.
12, διε[σ]παρμένους lvi. 8, μό[σ]χον lxvi. 3, ἔκα[σ]τος Jer. xvi. 12,
xxviii. 6, νεανί[σ]κοι ib. xxx. 15, ἐπί[σ]τάτην xxxvi. 26, χρη[σ]τός
xl. 11. The omission of σ in the verb ἐκ[σ]πᾶν is shared by א
with A: ἐκ[σ]πασθῆναι Hb. ii. 9 אA, ἐκ[σ]πάσατε Zech. xiii. 7 א, so
(in A) Am. ix. 15, Ψ xxi. 10 (ARU), xxiv. 15 and (in R) Ψ cxxviii. 6.
A has also παιδίι[σ]και Gen. xii. 16, ἐξόπι[σ]θεν (Epic) 2 K. xvii.
21, ἀπε[σ]χίσθη 2 Ch. xxvi. 21, ἐ[σ]φραγίσθη Est. viii. 10: [σ]τέγος
Ep. Jer. 10 AQ has classical authority. B has προσοχθί[σ]ματι
4 K. xxiii. 13, ἀπε[σ]χίσθη 2 Ch. xxvi. 21 (with A). E has
ἐνυπνιά[σ]θη Gen. xli. 5: F ἰ[σ]χνόφωνος Ex. iv. 10, ἐπί[σ]παστρον
Ex. xxvi. 36, ἐνδο[σ]θίων Lev. viii. 16. V has [σ]κῦλα 1 M. v. 51.
    Less frequent is *omission of labials* (א has παρεμ[β]ολῆς Is.
xxi. 8, ὑπερ[β]ήσετε Jer. v. 22, ἄμ[π]ελον Is. xvi. 9) and of
nasals: ν is dropped by א in ἀναγ[ν]ώσῃ Jer. xxviii. 61, στρωμ[ν]ή
Job xli. 21, by B in ἐ[ν]στάντος 1 Es. v. 46 (with A), ἄκα[ν]θαι
Is. v. 6 (with Q), βρο[ν]τῆς Is. xxix. 6, ποίμ[ν]ιον Jer. xiii. 17, by
Q in Ez. xlii. 20 πε[ν]τακοσίων.

37. **Single and double consonants.** Doubled consonants in Attic Greek owe their origin to a fulness of pronunciation given to some of them, particularly to liquids and
nasals[1]. From the Hellenistic period onwards (in Egypt
from about 200 B.C.) the tendency has been in the direction
of simplification, and in modern Greek, with the exception
of certain districts of Asia and the islands, the single consonant
has prevailed[2]. This phenomenon, together with the less
frequent doubling of simple vowels, appears to have arisen
from a shifting of the dividing-line between the syllables.
Ἄλ|λος became ἄ|λλος and so ἄλος : reversely the closing of the
open syllable in e.g. νῆ|σος produced νῆσ|σος. In the LXX
uncials the Attic forms are usual, with some exceptions in
Cod. א and in the case of ρρ (ρ), where there was fluctuation
even in the Attic period.

    [1] In Homer an initial λ lengthened a preceding vowel (πολλὰ λισσομένη
Il. ε. 358).
    [2] Thumb *Hell.* 20 ff. From the diversity of practice in the modern
dialects he infers the existence of "geminierende und nichtgeminierende
Κοινή-Mundarten."

38. The two following examples do not come under the head of simplification.

Καταράκτης is always written with single ρ in the uncials in accordance with the κοινή derivation[1] of the word from κατ-αράσσειν (not καταρραγῆναι).

Γένημα (unrecorded in LS ed. 8) is a new κοινή formation from γίνομαι = "produce of the earth," "fruit," and is carefully distinguished from γέννημα, "offspring" (from γεννάω)[2].

Γένημα (with πρωτογένημα) is common in LXX, always being used of the fruits of the ground except in 1 Macc. (i. 38, iii. 45) where it is applied to Jerusalem's offspring. Γέννημα appears in Jd. i. 10 BA (="descendant"), Sir. x. 18 (γεννήμασιν γυναικῶν): both books use γένημα="produce" elsewhere. In three passages there are variants, but the difference in the spelling imports a different meaning. (*a*) Gen. xlix. 21 Νεφθαλεί, στέλεχος ἀνειμένον, ἐπιδιδοὺς ἐν τῷ γενήματι (BDF) κάλλος. The comparison to a tree fixes the spelling: γεννήματι of A drops the metaphor. (*b*) Job Θ xxxix. 4 (of the wild goats) ἀπορρήξουσιν τὰ τέκνα αὐτῶν, πληθυνθήσονται ἐν γενήματι (BΝ), i.e. "they will multiply among the fruits of the field," RV "in the open field" (בָּבָר): γεννήματι of A gives בַּר its more familiar Aramaic meaning "son" i.e. "they will abound in offspring." (*c*) W. xvi. 19. The flame that plagued the Egyptians burnt more fiercely ἵνα ἀδίκου γῆς γενήματα (BC) διαφθείρῃ. The contrast with the "angel's food" in the next verse shows that the reference is to the destruction of the "herb of the field" and the "tree of the field" (Ex. ix. 25): γεννήματα of ΝA refers to the Egyptians, who themselves were struck by the hail (ibid.).

39. PP and P. The Attic rule was (to quote Blass) that "ρ, if it passes from the beginning to the middle of a word (through inflexion or composition), preserves the stronger pronunciation of the initial letter by becoming doubled." But exceptions are found in Attic Inscriptions from v/B.C.[3]

In the LXX ρρ is usual in the simple verbs: ρ is fairly frequent in the compounds. The same distinction is found in the Ptolemaic papyri.

---

[1] Strabo 667 (xiv. 4).
[2] Cf. Deissmann *BS* 109 f., 184, Mayser 214.
[3] Meisterhans 95. Cf. Mayser 212 f.

A distinction is also observable between groups of books. In general it may be said that, while in certain verbs ρρ is attested throughout, in others it is characteristic of the Pentateuch and some literary books, while ρ appears in the later historical books, in Psalms, in Jeremiah and Minor Prophets (in Bℵ) and in Theodotion.

Ἄρρωστος -εῖν -ία -ημα but εὔρωστος, as in Attic, are constant in LXX. So is ἐρρέθην (five times: Jon. iii. 7 ἐρέθη ℵ). Ῥέω has ρρ in the augmented tenses, but ἐξερύημεν Is. lxiv. 6 BℵAQ, ἐξερύησαν I M. ix. 6 AℵV (ἐρύησαν Ψ lxxvii. 20 T). Ἔρρηξα ἐρράγην etc. (including compounds) are usual: ρ in the simple verb appears once only in the B text (2 Es. xix. 11), in composition it is strongly supported in Prov. xxvii. 9 καταρήγνυνται BℵC and is read by Bℵ in Jl. ii. 13, Na. i. 13, by B in 4 K. viii. 12, by ℵ in Is. and Jer., by A in 1 K. xxviii. 17, 2 M. iv. 38. Ἐρρίζωκα -σα in Sirach: elsewhere (ἐξ)ερίζωσα etc. Ἔρριψα ἔρριμμαι etc. are usual, but ἔρ(ε)ιψα and other forms with ρ are uncontested in Dan. Θ (viii. 7, 12) and (in composition) in Job Θ xxvii. 22 and are strongly supported (usually by Bℵ) in Jer. and Minor Prophets: in the compounds ρ is more common than ρρ. The perf. pass. loses the second medial ρ in Jer. xiv. 16 B, Bar. ii. 25 BAQ, while it sometimes takes on an initial ρ (ῥέριμμαι): Jd. iv. 22 B, xv. 15 B, Tob. i. 17 B (ἔριμμ. A), Jdth. vi. 13 A (ἐριμμ. B), Jer. xliii. 30 A (ἐριμμ. BℵQ). Ῥύεσθαι has ρρ in the augmented tenses in the Pentateuch (Exodus five times: v. 23 ἐρύσω AF), but ἐρύσασθε Jos. xxii. 31 BA: in the subsequent books the MSS fluctuate between the two forms.

Ἀρραβών seems to have been the older Hellenized form of ערבון and is so written by all MSS in the three passages of Genesis where it occurs (Gen. xxxviii. 17 f., 20)[1].

40. Weakening of ρρ to ρ in words other than verbs and of λλ to λ is mainly confined to ℵ: C and V have examples of σ for σσ.

ℵ in the Prophets has πόρω and πόρωθεν (Is. x. 3, xxii. 3, xxix. 13, xlvi. 11: Jer. v. 15, xxxviii. 3), βοράν for βορρ. Is. xlix. 12 (so in a papyrus of i/B.C., the only Ptolemaic example quoted by Mayser of this form of simplification), πυρός for πυρρός Zech. i. 8, vi. 2 (with A). Weakening of λλ to λ (in papyri from ii/B.C., especially in ἄλ[λ]ος and derivatives) occurs in παραλάσσον Est. B 5 B*,

[1] So in a papyrus of iii/B.C. Papyri of later centuries write ἀραβών almost as often as ἀρρ-: Mayser 40, J. H. Moulton *CR* xv. 33 b and *Prol.* 45, Deissmann *BS* 183 f.

διαλάσσ. W. xix. 18 א, μεταλάσσ. 2 M. vii. 14 V, εὐκατάλακτον 3 M. v. 13 AV, cf. μεταλ|ευομένη W. xvi. 25 A. א has also ἀγαλίαμα Is. xvi. 10, li. 3, lxv. 18, ἀγαλιᾶσθαι xxix. 19, στραγαλία lviii. 6, μέλων (=μέλλ.) lix. 5, ἀλά 4 M. iii. 1, βαλάντιον Tob. viii. 2 (elsewhere in LXX. correctly βαλλάντιον).

The single μ in ἀπέρριμαι Ψ xxx. 23 B*א*U (so ἔρρειμαι in a papyrus of iii/B.C., Mayser 214) seems due to the presence of another double consonant (elsewhere ἔριμμαι, above). א* has ἄμον Jer. v. 22.

Cod. V writes δυσεβής (δυσεβεῖν) in 2 and 3 Macc., on the analogy of εὐσεβής: so A once in 3 M. iii. 1. V further has ταράσοντας 1 M. iii. 5, C κασίτερον Sir. xlvii. 18.

Mutes are dropped in σαβάτων Ez. xxii. 26 B*, συγνούς 2 M. xiv. 31 A, νεοτῶν 4 M. xiv. 15 A*V*.

41. There is one instance of *doubling of single consonant* which the LXX contributes to the study of Greek orthography : it is unrecorded in the grammars. In all the 21 instances where the word occurs the classical οἴμοι is written with double μ either as οἴμμοι or ὄμμοι (the two forms in conjunction in Jer. li. 33, ὄμμοι οἴμμοι B*): the class. form is limited (in the three leading uncials) to 3 K. xvii. 20 A.

42. New verbs are coined, on the model of κεράννυμι etc., in -ννω (§ 19, 2): βέννω (for βαίνω) in the A text, ἀποκτέννω (for -κτείνω), ἀποτιννύω, φθάννω, χύννω[1].

'Αέναος and ἔνατος retain the classical spelling (ἀέννaos in 2 M. vii. 36 V: ἔννατος [in the corrector of the same MS] does not deserve the recognition as a " LXX " form which Redpath and Mayser accord to it).

B writes 'Ελλυμαίδα Tob. ii. 10 (elsewhere 'Ελυμ.). Later MSS afford: πολλύν (on the analogy of πολλήν) Job xxix. 18 A, θρύλλημα θρυλληθείην Job xvii. 6 C, xxxi. 30 C, ἀσύλλου 2 M. iv. 34 V, ἔλλαττον xii. 4 V.

B* has νῆσσος in Ez. xxvi. 18, xxvii. 6: א βύρσσης Job xvi. 16, γεῖσσος Jer. lii. 22, εὑρίσσκοντες Lam. i. 6, ἠσσθένησεν ii. 8: A ἐρρύσσω 3 M. vi. 6: C πάσσης Sir. xxxvii. 21, κλῖσσον (=κλεῖσον) xlii. 6: Q μίσσγουσιν Hos. iv. 2.

Doubling of κ, as in ἐκξελεύσεται Is. ii. 3 א, ἐκξοίσω Zech. v. 4 א, in the papyri appears to be not earlier than i/A.D. (ἐκξουσίαν OP ii. 259. 18 of 23 A.D.). Μογγιλάλος, a late reading (QΓBᵃᵇ)

---

[1] Cf. πίννω in the corrector of Q: Is. xxiv. 9, xxix. 8.

in Is. xxxv. 6, is said (Thayer) to be derived not from μόγις but
from the adj. μογγός, which occurs, as Dr J. H. Moulton tells
me, in BM iii. p. 241. 16 (iv/A.D.).

43. **Doubling of the aspirate.** The incorrect doubling
of the aspirate where tenuis + aspirate should be written (χχ,
θθ, φφ for κχ, τθ, πφ) appears occasionally in the uncials : it
has good authority in some late books or portions of books.

(1) φφ. Σαφφώθ 2 K. xvii. 29 BA, Jer. lii. 19, Σαφφάν
(Σεφφάν) 4 K. xxii. 3 ff. BA, Σαφφάθ 4 K. xxii. 14 B (=Σαφάν A):
so κεφφωθείς Prov. vii. 22 A (κεπφ. Bℵ). On the other hand
Σαπφείν, ʽΑπφείν, Σαπφαάδ are read by B in 1 Ch. vii. 12, 15,
Σαπφούς 1 M. ii. 5 ℵV (Σαφφούς A). (2) θθ. Μαθθάν (Μεθθανίαν)
4 K. xxiv. 17 BA, Μαθθαθά, Μαθθανιά and similar forms frequently
in 2 Esdras A (and ℵ : B writes Μαθανία etc.): B has ὑποτίθθια
in Hos. xiv. 1. On the other hand in 1 and 2 Chron. and 1 Es.
A writes correctly Ματθανίας etc. (B Μανθανίας etc.). (3) χχ.
Βάκχουρος is correctly written by BA in 1 Es. ix. 24 and in
1 Μαcc. Βακχίδης is usual: Βαχχίδης[1] only in vii. 8 ℵ, ix. 49 ℵV,
Βακχχ. ix. 1 ℵ (so Βαχχί N. xxxiv. 22 F).

Σάπφειρος is written correctly (not σαφφ.), but assimilation
is sometimes produced by dropping the aspirate altogether :
B has σάππ(ε)ιρος in Is. liv. 11, Ez. i. 26, Tob. xiii. 16, so F in Ex.
(xxiv. 10 σα . π: third letter illegible) xxviii. 18.

44. **ΣΣ and ΤΤ.** The Hellenistic language as a whole
adopted the σσ of non-Attic dialects and abandoned the
peculiarly Attic ττ. The latter was still employed by literary
writers, even before the age of the Atticists. But the general
statement that the κοινή used σσ requires some modification,
and there is ground for believing that, in certain words at
least, ττ still survived in the living language[2].

[1] Βαχχιάδος is found already in a papyrus of iii/B.C. (Mayser 182).
[2] See Thumb *Hell.* 78 ff. In MSS of the Apostolic Fathers ττ is frequent even in documents ordinarily addicted to vulgarisms, Reinhold 43 f.
The underlying principle has now been explained by Wackernagel, *Hellenistica*, 1907, pp. 12—25. Hellenistic writers retained ττ in certain words
which were taken over directly from Attic and were not current in another
form in κοινή-speaking countries. Among these words was ἡττᾶσθαι, shown
by its termination to be an Attic formation (Ionic ἑσσοῦσθαι) : the ττ of the
verb influenced the form of the adj., ἥττων, and of its synonym ἐλάττων,
and to a less degree that of the antithetical κρείττων.

In the LXX the use of ττ is practically confined (1) to the three words ἐλάττων, ἥττων, κρείττων, and derivatives of the first two, (2) to the three literary writings 2, 3 and 4 Maccabees, which introduce the forms with ττ in words other than those mentioned.

45. Ἐλάττων is used in Ex. Lev. Num. Jdth. Dan. O ii. 39 and 2 Macc. (also Job xvi. 7 BAC and Sir. xx. 11 A)—16 times in all, against six examples in all of ἐλάσσων, in Genesis (i. 16, xxv. 23, xxvii. 6), Proverbs (xiii. 11, xxii. 16) and Wis. ix. 5. The distinction here is not one between vulgar and literary Greek: σσ is found in distinctly literary writings. Ἐλαττοῦν is the normal form of the classical verb in LXX, though the pass. part. appears as ἐλασσούμενος in 2 K. iii. 29 and in the latter part of Sirach (xxxiv. 27, xxxviii. 24, xli. 2, xlvii. 23 BAC: also ἠλασσώθη xlii. 21 ℵA)[1]. The post-classical verbs ἐλαττονεῖν, ἐλαττονοῦν (which appear to be unexampled outside the LXX[2]: cf. ἐξουθενέω, ἐξουδενόω, 15 above) always have ττ (excepting ἐλασσονοῦσι Prov. xiv. 34 BℵA): so also do the substantives ἐλάττωμα, ἐλάττωσις.

Ἥττων occurs 11 times (of which six are in 2 Macc.), ἥσσων only twice (Job v. 4: Is. xxiii. 8). Ἡττᾶσθαι (ἡττᾶν)[3] is always so written (common in Isaiah, four times elsewhere) and ἥττημα in the one passage where the word occurs (Is. xxxi. 8).

The proportion is reversed in the case of κρείσσων, which occurs without variant in the uncials in 47 instances (mainly in Proverbs and Sirach) as against four examples only of ττ without variant (Prov. iii. 14 κρεῖττον, Sir. xxiii. 27 do., Est. i. 19 κρείττονι, Ez. xxxii. 21 κρείττων) and seven with variant σσ (Jd. viii. 2 A: Prov. xxv. 24 Bℵ: W. xv. 17 B: Sir. xix. 24 BℵA, xx. 31 ℵA: Is. lvi. 5 BΓ: Ep. Jer. 67 B).

46. The three literary writings which stand at the end of the Septuagint, among other Atticisms, make a freer use of Attic ττ, but not to the entire exclusion of σσ.

2 Macc. has

γλωττοτομεῖν vii. 4 V (σσ A)　　but γλῶσσα (3 times).
θᾶττον iv. 31, v. 21, xiv. 11.
πράττειν (ἀντι-) (3 times).
κατασφάττειν v. 12 V (-σφάζειν A).
ταράττειν xv. 19 V (σσ A)　　but ἐπιταράσσειν ix. 24 AV.

---

[1] Contrast ἐλαττούμενος Sir. xvi. 23, xix. 23, xxv. 2. The distinction suggests an early division of the book into two parts (cf. § 5).

[2] The former in an O.T. quotation in 2 Cor. viii. 15.

[3] See note 2, p. 121.

τάττειν x. 28 AV   but {ἐπιτάσσειν ix. 8 V.
                                {προστάσσειν xv. 5 AV.
φρυάττεσθαι (φρύττ.) vii. 34 AV.
διαφυλάττειν vi. 6, x. 30 V but -φυλάσσειν iii. 22 A, x. 30 A.
2 Macc. further keeps σσ in μεταλλάσσειν, βδελύσσεσθαι,
δράσσεσθαι, περισσῶς, (ἐκ)πλήσσειν, ἐντινάσσειν.
3 Macc. has:
προστάττειν v. 37   but -τάσσειν v. 3, 40.
                                φυλάσσειν etc.
4 Macc. has:
βδελύττεσθαι v. 7.
γλῶττα x. 17, 21   but γλῶσσα x. 19, xviii. 21.
γλωττοτομεῖν x. 19 ℵ (σσ A), xii. 13.
νεοτ(τ)ός xiv. 15   but {νοσσία xiv. 19.
                                {νοσσοποιεῖν xiv. 16.
πράττειν iii. 20.
φρίττειν xiv. 9, xvii. 7.
It further keeps σσ in μέλισσα, φυλάσσειν.

Apart from this triplet of books and the triplet of words
above-mentioned σσ is universal in the LXX, except that
φυλάττειν occurs twice in the last chapter of Jeremiah (probably
a later appendix to the Greek version) lii. 24 B, 31 A, and twice
as a variant reading elsewhere: Job xxix. 2 A, W. xvii. 4 AC.
Σήμερον, σευτλίον (Is. li. 20) have initial σ, not τ.

47. **PΣ and PP.** The use of the later Attic ρρ is in
the following words practically restricted to a few literary
portions of the LXX.

Ἄρσην, ἀρσενικός, θαρσεῖν, θαρσύνειν (Est. C 23, 4 M. xiii.
8 παρεθ.) are the ordinary forms in use. Ἄρρην is confined to
Sir. xxxvi. 26, 4 M. xv. 30, cf. ἀρρενωδῶς 2 M. x. 35 (a ἅπ. λεγ.),
θαρρεῖν to Prov. i. 21 BℵAC, xxix. 29 ℵ (θαρσεῖ BA), Bar. iv. 21
B (ρσ AQ), 27 B (do.) (but ρσ iv. 5, 30), Dan. O vi. 16, 4 M.
xiii. 11, xvii. 4, θαρραλέος (-έως) to 3 M. i. 4, 23, 4 M. iii. 14,
xiii. 13.

In addition to these examples, the adjective πυρρός, with
derivatives πυρράκης πυρρίζειν, keeps ρρ throughout the LXX,
as in the papyri (Mayser 221): πυρσός was an alternative Attic
form, used in poetry. The later Attic forms πόρρω πόρρωθεν
are used to the exclusion of the older πρόσω (πόρσω).

The contracted form βορρᾶς (ρρ resulting from ρj, Kühner-
Blass i. 1. 386) which appears in Attic inscriptions from
c. 400 B.C., is practically universal in the LXX, as it is in the
papyri (Mayser 252). The older βορέας appears only in Proverbs

(xxv. 23, xxvii. 16), Sirach (xliii. 17, 20: in 20 B has the Ionic βορέης) and Job Θ xxvi. 7.

On the other hand μυρσίνη, μυρσινῶν, χέρσος are written.

§ 8. THE ASPIRATE.

1. The practice of dropping the aspirate, which began in early times in the Ionic and Aeolic dialects in Asia Minor, gradually spread, until, as in modern Greek, it ceased to be pronounced altogether[1]. In the Alexandrian age it appears to have been still pronounced[2], but the tendency towards deaspiration has set in.

2. **Irregular insertion of the aspirate.** On the other hand, there is considerable evidence for a counter-tendency in the κοινή, namely to insert an aspirate in a certain group of words which in Attic had none. The principal words are ἐλπίς, ἔτος, ἰδεῖν and cognate words, ἴδιος, ἴσος. These forms are attested too widely to be regarded as due to ignorance —to a reaction against the prevailing tendency, causing the insertion of the *h* in the wrong place: they represent a genuine alternative pronunciation. Grammarians are divided on the question whether these forms are "analogy formations within the κοινή,"[3] καθ' ἔτος, e.g., being formed on the analogy of καθ' ἡμέραν, or whether they go back to the age of the dialects[4], and the aspirate is a substitute for the lost digamma, which once was present in all the five words mentioned. The older explanation of the aspirate by the lost digamma has the support of Blass and Hort and it does not appear why it should be given up[5]. Another explanation must be sought for

---

[1] Thumb, *Untersuch. über den Spiritus asper* 87, puts its final dis-appearance at about iv/–v/ A.D.

[2] Ib. 79.

[3] Thumb *Hell.* 64.

[4] Schwyzer *Perg. Inschriften* 118 ff.

[5] Dr J. H. Moulton (*Prol.* 44 note) regards it as untenable, but without giving reasons. Thumb in his earlier work admits the possibility of this explanation in some cases (*Spir. Asp.* 71 ὑφιδόμενος, 11 ἔτος).

a recurrent instance like ὀλίγος, which never had a digamma, and in some cases analogy is doubtless responsible.

3. The LXX examples of these words are as follows:

(1) ἐλπίς[1] in ἐφ᾽ ἐλπίδι twice in B, Jd. xviii. 27, Hos. ii. 18 (as against eight examples of ἐπ᾽ (μετ᾽) ἐλπ., including Jd. xviii. 7 B, 10 B). Ἀφελπίζειν has good authority in Sirach (xxii. 21 Bℵ, xxvii. 21 B*AC): ℵ has it in Est. C 30, Jdth. ix. 11, while (A)T have ἐφελπίζειν in Ψ (li. 9 T, and six times in Ψ 118 AT): in all there are 11 examples of ἀφ- ἐφελπίζειν against three of ἀπ- ἐπ- without variant (4 K. xviii. 30: Is. xxix. 19: 2 M. ix. 18).

(2) ἔτος in ἐφέτιον Dt. xv. 18 BAF (=ἐπέτειον) (so the papyri have καθ᾽ ἔτος, ἐφ᾽ ἔτη since 225 B.C.[2] beside κατ᾽ (ἐπ᾽) ἔτ. which are more common: LXX has κατὰ (κατ᾽ V) ἔτος in 2 M. xi. 3, the only example of the phrase). The analogy of καθ᾽ ἔτος seems to have produced καθ᾽ ἐνιαυτόν[3] Dt. xiv. 21 B* (elsewhere in LXX κατ᾽ ἐπ᾽ μετ᾽ ἐνιαυτόν regularly, 27 examples).

(3) ἰδού, ἀφιδεῖν[4] etc. are exceedingly common in LXX. In the B text οὐχ ἰδού is practically universal, occurring no less than 27 times, as against six examples only of οὐκ ἰδού (Dt. xi. 30 BAF, xxxii. 34 BF: Jos. xxii. 20 BA: 3 K. viii. 53 B, xvi. 28 c B: Is. lxvi. 9, where ℵ has οὐχ). A unites with B in reading οὐχ ἰδού in 1 K. xxiii. 19, usually in 3 and 4 K., Sir. xviii. 17 (B*ℵA) and Zech. iii. 2 (B*ℵAΓ). Οὐχ ἴδ(ου) occurs in 4 K. ii. 12 A: Dan. Θ x. 7 B*: κάθιδε in Dt. xxvi. 15 B, while A and the other uncials furnish nine examples of similar forms, ἐφίδοι Gen. xxxi. 49 A, ἔφιδ(εν) Ψ liii. 9 R*T, xci. 12 AT, cxi. 8 ℵT, ἐφιδεῖν 1 M. iii. 59 AℵV, 2 M. viii. 2 AV, ἔφ(ε)ιδε 2 M. i. 27 A, ἀφιδών 3 M. vi. 8 A, 4 M. xvii. 23 Aℵ. Even οὐχ ὄψομαι (which Blass calls a "clerical error") has an established position: there are nine examples (as against 24 of undisputed οὐκ ὄψ.); N xiv. 23 B*: Ψ xlviii. 10 B*, 20 B*T, lxxxviii. 49 T, cxiii. 13 T, cxxxiv. 16 T: Jdth. vii. 27 A: Jer. v. 12 B*A, xii. 4 B*. With these instances may be classed οὐχ οἶδας Zech. iv. 13 ℵ.

For οὐχ ἰδού, οὐκ ἰδού in 3 K. see p. 70.

The almost universal employment of ΟΥΧΙΔΟΥ in B may be partly due to the influence of the form οὐχί. Οὐχὶ ἰδού occurs in Acts ii. 7 B, but not apparently in LXX. The origin of this rendering of הלא, *nonne*, is not clear, as there is no equivalent in the Heb. for ἰδού. Only in 2 Ch. xxv. 26 do we find the combination הלא הנם כתובים "Behold are they not (written)?,"

---

[1] So in an Attic Inscription as early as 432 B.C. (Meisterhans 86).
[2] Mayser 199 f. Cf. Moulton *CR* xv. 33, xviii. 106 f.
[3] So μεθ᾽ ἐν. (158 B.C.), ἐφ᾽ ἐν. in the papyri, Mayser 200, *CR* xviii. 107.
Ἐφιδεῖν in a papyrus of iii/B.C. and frequently under the Empire, Mayser 201.

contrast xxxvi. 8 הנם. The present writer would suggest that
οὐχ ἰδού originated in a doublet. The interrogative הלא is only
an alternative mode of expressing the positive הנה, and in
Chron. הנה sometimes replaces הלא in the parallel passages
in Kings. הלא is principally rendered by (1) οὐχ ἰδού, (2) οὐκ or
οὐχ, (3) ἰδού nine times e.g. Dt. iii. 11. It is suggested that at
least in the earlier books the oldest rendering was in all cases
ἰδού, the translators preferring the positive statement to the
rhetorical question. Οὐχ(ί) was an alternative rendering, and
out of the two arose the conflate ογχιΔογ. This in time
became the recognised equivalent for the classical ἆρ' οὐ; The
textual evidence given in the larger Cambridge LXX in the
first passage where οὐχ ἰδού appears (Gen. xiii. 9) favours this
explanation.

(4) ἴδιος appears in καθ' ἰδίαν[1] 2 M. ix. 26 V* (κατ' A), as
against three examples of κατ' ἰδ. all in this book: also in the
three chief uncials in Jdth. v. 18 (οὐχ ἰδίαν אA, οὐχ ἠδ. B).

The itacism in B in the last passage recurs in Prov. v. 19 א
and causes occasional confusion between ἡδύς and ἴδιος. In
Sir. xxii. 11 e.g. ἥδιον κλαῦσον of Bא "weep more tenderly" (for
the dead than for the fool) is doubtless the meaning, though
ἴδιον κλαῦσον of AC would yield a tolerable sense "keep a
special mourning for the dead" (the Heb. is not extant here).

(5) ἴσος[2] is aspirated in ἔφισος Sir. ix. 10 BאC (εφ'ιcoc B*),
xxxiv. 27 Bא (the only occurrences in LXX : unaspirated in the
editions of Polyb. 3. 115. 1) and in οὐχ ἰσωθήσεται Job Θ xxviii.
17 B*אA, 19 B*א (the only other example of the verb is
indeterminate as regards aspirate).

Another form well-attested elsewhere is ἐφιορκεῖν -ια: so
1 Es. i. 46 B: W. xiv. 28 A, 25 C (but ἐπίορκος Zech. v. 3 all
uncials): due to throwing back the aspirate of ὅρκος[3].

4. Ὀλίγος seems to belong to a later period[4] than the preceding cases of aspiration and is not so uniformly attested in
LXX as in N.T.: with οὐχ Is. x. 7 אA, Job x. 20 B*, 2 M. viii.
6 V (οὐκ ὀλ. 2 M. x. 24, xiv. 30), with μεθ' only in Jdth. xiii. 9 B*
(as against five examples of μετ' ἐπ' κατ' ὀλ.).

There being no digamma here to explain the aspirate, its
explanation may perhaps be found in the gamma. The word
often appears in the papyri as ὀλίος (§ 7. 29): the weak spirant

---

[1] So in Attic Inscriptions from 250 B.C. (Meisterhans 87) and elsewhere
in the κοινή.

[2] As early as iv/B.C. in the phrase ἐφ' ἴσῃ (καὶ ὁμοίᾳ): Thumb *Asp.* 71,
Schwyzer 119 f.

[3] Or to mixture of ἐφορκέω ἐπιορκέω (Thumb *ib.* 72).

[4] In papyri of ii/iii/A.D., *CR* xv. 33 (add οὐχ ὀλ. BM ii. 198 c. 170 A.D.,
ib. 411 c. 346 A.D.) but not in those of the Ptolemaic age.

sound of the γ may have been thrown back on to the first
syllable. For initial γ replacing the usual aspirate cf. τὴν δὲ
γίσην (?=ἴσην) Teb. 61. 233 (118 B.C.): but see p. 111, n. 4.
Καθ᾽ ἐμαυτόν 2 M. ix. 22 AV is due to analogy (καθ᾽ ἑαυτόν).
Ἰσχυ(ρος) in οὐχ ἰσχυραί 1 Es. iv. 32 B*, 34 AB*vid, οὐχ ἰσχύω
Is. l. 2 A and Q, has old authority[1]

In transliterated proper names such as Ἰούδας (e.g. οὐχ
Ἰούδα Dan. Θ, Sus. 56 BAQ) the aspirate in the second radical in
the Heb. (יהודה) is sometimes thrown back to the first syllable.

5. Sporadic examples of irregular aspiration follow, mainly
clerical errors. Οὐχ ἀγαπᾷ Prov. xxii. 14 a A, οὐχ ἀνοίγει Is. liii.
7 B* *bis*: καθ᾽ εἰκόνα Sir. xvii. 3 B*ℵ* (? due to lost digamma or
to preceding καθ᾽ ἑαυτούς), οὐχ εἰσακούσομαι Jer. vii. 16 B*A, οὐχ
εἰσήνεγκαν Dan. Θ vi. 18 B*: ἀφήλιψα Is. xliv. 22 ℵ* with οὐχ
ἠλειψάμην Dan. Θ x. 3 B, οὐχ ἤκουσαν Is. lxvi. 4 B* (due to οὐχ
ὑπήκ. *ib.*): clerical errors in ℵ are ἐφ᾽ ὄνων Is. xxx. 6, ἐφ᾽ οὐδενός
4 M. xv. 11: ἐφ᾽ ὤμοις Ep. Jer. 25 B* is a solitary example in
LXX of aspiration of this word (cf. Lat. *humerus*), ἐπ᾽ being
used before it 13 times, once in this Epistle: οὐχ ὠδίνες Jer. xiii.
21 ℵA may be a corruption of οὐχὶ ὠδ.

(LXX has only ἀπ- ἐξαπ- ἐπ- ἐσταλκα, not ἀφέσταλκα etc.
[reduplication as in ἕστηκα, Thumb *op. cit.* 70] as often in the
κοινή.)

6. **Loss of aspirate (psilosis).** As the tendency
towards deaspiration continually increased between the dates
of the LXX autographs and of the uncials, the evidence of the
latter is of doubtful value. The most noticeable feature in it
is the marked preference in Cod. B for unaspirated ὐ (and
for εὐ in εὑρίσκω).

7. One example stands apart from the rest and is well
attested in the κοινή, namely the dropping of the aspirate in
the perfect of ἵστημι. This, however, does not in the LXX
take place as a rule in the old perf. ἕστηκα, "I stand," but in
the new transitive perf. -έστακα, "I have set up," with its corresponding passive -έσταμαι, the psilosis being perhaps due to
the analogy of the trans. aorist ἔστησα[2].

[1] Meisterhans 87 (Ἰσχύλος).
[2] Or to that of ἔσταλκα, Thumb *op. cit.* 70. Mayser 203 quotes two
examples of ἀπέστηκα from Ptolemaic papyri, in one of which the verb is
transitive: the intrans. perf. is elsewhere ἀφέστηκα.

Κατέστακα has strong support in Jer. i. 10 BℵA, vi. 17 BℵA, 1 M. x. 20 ℵV (but ἀφέστακα trans. Jer. xvi. 5 BQ, ἀφέστηκα ℵA: 1 M. xi. 34 ἐστάκαμεν is indeterminate). Κατεσταμένος is written by B seven times[1], once being supported by A, which also has this form in Jer. xx. 1 and ἐπεσταμένη *ib.* v. 27. Psilosis in other forms of the perfect and in the present occur sporadically: (*a*) ἐπεστῶτα Jdth. x. 6 B, ἐπεστηκώς Zech. i. 10 ℵ, κατεστήκεισαν 3 M. iii. 5 V: (*b*) ἐπιστημει *sic* Jer. li. 11 A, ὑπίσταται Prov. xiii. 8 ℵ, ἐπίσταται W. vi. 8 B (so in N.T., 1 Thess. v. 3 BℵL).

8. The following examples occur of unaspirated tenuis ·

(i) Before *a*(η). Οὐκ ἡγιάσατε N. xxvii. 14 B, οὐκ ἡγνίσθησαν 2 Ch. xxx. 3 A (cf. ἅγος ἄγος). Οὐκ ἅψεσθε (-εται) has good support in the Pentateuch: Ex. xix. 13 B, Lev. xi. 8 BA, xii. 4 BF, N. iv. 15 B (cf. ἐπάπτοιτο in a Phocian Inscription, Thumb *Asp.* 36 f.). Οὐκ ἀρπ(ᾷ) L. xix. 13 BAF. Οὐκ ἁμαρτήισ(ομαι) Sir. xxiv. 22 B, Eccl. vii. 21 C, perhaps due in both cases to the οὐκ in the balancing clauses: cf. οὐκ ἡμάρτηκεν 1 K. xix. 4 B. Confusion of αὐτή and αὕτη is natural: οὐκ precedes the pronoun where αὕτη is clearly meant in e.g. 4 K. vi. 19 A *bis*, Is. xxiii. 7 ℵ, Dan. Θ iv. 27 A.

(ii) Before ε. Οὐκ ἑκών Ex. xxi. 13 BA (on the analogy of ἄκων: conversely ἀκούσιος on an Attic Inscription): οὐκ ἕνεκεν Jos. xxii. 26 BA, 28 BA, Is. xlviii. 10 ℵAQ: οὐκ ἑτοιμασθήσεται 1 K. xx. 31 B: οὐκ ἑψήσεις Ex. xxiii. 19 B=Dt. xiv. 20 B: οὐκ ἑωράκα(σιν) Dt. xxi. 7 B, xxxiii. 9 B: κατ᾽ ἑκάστην Ψ xli. 11 ℵ (so in iii/B.C., Mayser 202, and earlier, Thumb *op. cit.* 61). Ἕλκω loses its aspirate in οὐκ εἵλκυσεν Dt. xxi. 3 B, Sir. xxviii. 19 ℵ and in Ep. J. 43 ἀπ- ἐπ- ελκυσθ(εῖσα) AQ (against four examples of ἐφελκ- without v.l.).

(iii) Before η. Οὐκ has strong support before forms from ἡσυχάζειν viz. Jer. xxix. 6 BAQ, Prov. vii. 11 BℵA (but μεθ᾽ ἡσυχίας Sir. xxviii. 16) and ἥκειν, Jer. v. 12 ℵQ, xxiii. 17 Bℵ, xxv. 16 ℵ, Hg. i. 2 AQ, cf. Prov. x. 30 B[2]. The loss of the aspirate in ἡμεῖς (2 M. vi. 17 ταῦτ᾽ ἡμῖν εἰρήσθω) is common elsewhere: Mayser 202 gives an example of iii/B.C. Ἀπηλιώτης "east" appears to have been an Ionic coinage which was adopted in Attic Greek and is the invariable form in LXX and papyri (Mayser 203).

(iv) Before ι. The MSS afford a few examples: οὐκ (ὸκ) ἱκανός Is. xl. 16 ℵ *bis*, οὐκ ἱλάσθης Lam. iii. 42 AQ, μετ᾽ ἵππου

---

[1] N. iii. 32, xxxi. 48: 2 K. iii. 39: 3 K. ii. 35 h (with A), iv. 7, v. 16: 2 Ch. xxxiv. 10. On the other hand there are eight examples of καθεστ. without v.l.

[2] The only examples of undisputed οὐχ before ἥκειν are 1 K. xxix. 9: Jer. ii. 31.

1 Es. ii. 25 A (cf. the old form ἴκκος, Lat. *equus*), κατιπτάμενα Sir. xliii. 17 B.

(v) Before ο, ω. Ὅμοιος loses its aspirate in Prov. xxvii. 19 C οὐκ ὅμοια : cf. οὐκ ὁμοεθνῶν 2 M. v. 6 AV. The definite art. twice loses its aspirate in the same phrase οὐκ ὁ φόβος Job iv. 6 BℵC, xxxiii. 7 Bℵ, apparently owing to the aspirated consonant which follows it : so in Job xxxii. 7 B, Bar. ii. 17 A (Mayser 203 gives an example of ii/B.C.). Οὐκ is used before ὡδήγησεν Ex. xiii. 17 B, ὡραῖος Sir. xv. 9 ℵ, ὡς Is. viii. 14 ℵ.

(vi) Before ευ, υ[1]. Loss of aspirate in εὑρίσκω (partly perhaps through analogy with compounds of εὖ) is frequent in the B text, which has 12 examples of οὐκ εὑρεθήσεται etc. (nine in the historical books between Ex. xii. 19 and 2 K. xvii. 20) to 57 of οὐχ : in A the proportion is 4 to 69. Other uncials supply half a dozen examples between them. The later papyri from ii/A.D. afford parallels (Grönert 146), but there is no certain instance in the Ptolemaic age of εὑρίσκω or of ὑ, so that B in the above examples and in those which follow is unreliable.

B has some 20 examples of initial ὑ, ℵ 5, A 3, Q 2, C and V one each. The commonest examples are οὐκ ὑπάρχ(ει) Job Θ xxxviii. 26 BℵA, B in Sir. xx. 16, Tob. iii. 15, vi. 15 (with ℵ), Q in Am. v. 5, Ob. 16 and οὐκ ὑπελεί(φθη) which B writes seven times. Οὐχ, however, largely preponderates with both verbs. It is needless to enumerate other examples of οὐκ before compounds of ὑπό, ὑπέρ : κατυφανεῖς Ex. xxviii. 17 B, κατύπερθε 3 M. iv. 10 AV (as in Ionic, Hdt. ii. 5) may be mentioned.

For οὐθείς, μηθείς and other peculiarities of aspiration in the middle of words see § 7.

§ 9.   EUPHONY IN COMBINATION OF WORDS AND SYLLABLES[2].

1. **Division of words.** The practice of dividing the individual words in writing did not become general till long after the time of the composition of the LXX. This accounts for an occasional coalescence of two words, particularly where the first ends and the second begins with one of the weak

---

[1] The Boeotian dialect was the one exception to the old rule that every initial υ was aspirated (Thumb *Asp.* 42).

[2] A comprehensive term embracing Assimilation of consonants, Variable final consonant, Elision, Crasis and Hiatus seems wanting, analogous to the German Satzphonetik.

final letters ς or ν (cf. οὕτω(ς), μέχρι(ς), ἐστί(ν) etc.). Instances like εἰστήλην τὰσπόνδας appear already in Attic Inscriptions of iv/B.C.[1] and become common in papyri from ii/B.C. onwards[2]. The LXX remains practically free from this blending of words, the only well-supported example being πρὸστόμα, 2 Es. xii. 13 BאA.

> Of individual MSS, Cod. א has several examples in the Minor Prophets : εἰσκότος Jl. ii. 31, ὡσμῖλας (ὡσμῖλαξ A) Na. i. 10, ἵππουσου Hb. iii. 8, ὡσφραγῖδα Hg. ii. 23 (cf. ἐνάγεβ Ob. 19) : so εἰσκάνδαλον 1 K. xviii. 21 A, Ψ cv. 36 A, ἀνοίξῃστόμα Sir. xxii. 22 A, ἕωσπινθῆρος xlii. 22 C, ὡσφραγίς xlix. 11 B*, τῆσβεστικῆς W. xix. 20 A, εἰσφαγήν Job xxvii. 14 C.

2. A rather different kind of blending of words takes place where a final κ and an initial σ are amalgamated into the compound letter ξ. B has ἐξαβά for ἐκ Σαβά in Is. lx. 6, and ἐξοῦ (Swete ἐξ οὗ) for ἐκ σοῦ (ממך) in Mic. v. 2 : א has the same orthography in Na. i. 11. א further has ἐξ for ἐκ in Mal. ii. 12 ἐξ σκηνωμάτων[3]

3. **Assimilation of consonants.** In contrast with the occasional coalescence of words referred to in the last section is the general tendency of the Hellenistic language towards greater perspicuity by isolating not merely individual words but also the constituent elements of words. Dissimilation, rather than assimilation, is the rule. This tendency is observable not only in the absence of assimilation in many words compounded with ἐν and σύν, but also in the rarity of elision and crasis, and in the formation of compound words in which an unelided vowel is retained[4].

---

[1] Meisterhans 90 f. (with one exception, only where the second word begins with σκ στ σπ or σφ): cf. 111 ἐστήλη = ἐν στ. etc. from v/B.C.

[2] Mayser 216, 191 f., 205 ff.

[3] Cf. ἐξαλαμῖνος and ἐξ Σαλαμῖνος (iv/B.C.) Meisterhans 105 f., and for examples in the papyri Mayser 225.

[4] E.g. in LXX γραμματοεισαγωγεύς, ἀρχιεταῖρος, ἀρχιευνοῦχός (ἀρχευν. Dan. Θ i. 9, 11, 18 B), ἀρχιἱερωσύνην 1 M. xiv. 38 A, μακροημερεύειν, ἀλλοεθνής, ὁμοεθνής, μισούβρις 3 M. vi. 9 A (cf. κατᾳοικοῦσα Jer. xxvi. 19 א).

4. This tendency, however, did not at once become universal in the Hellenistic period. There is a well-marked division in this respect between the earlier papyri (c. 300—150 B.C.) and the later (after 150 B.C.). In the earlier period not only is *assimilation* in compounds usual[1], but it is extended to *two contiguous words*. There are numerous examples in papyri of iii/B.C. of the assimilation of final ν (mainly in monosyllabic words) to μ before labials, to γ before gutturals (τὸμ παῖδα, ἐμ μηνί, ἐγ κροκοδίλων πόλει etc.), though the practice is going out and the non-assimilated forms predominate[2]. After 150 B.C. these forms practically disappear, though the assimilation of κ to γ in ἐγ δίκης etc. lingers on as late as iii/A.D.

Of this class of assimilation the LXX only exhibits two recurrent examples, one of which is limited to Cod. A, while the other is most widely attested in that MS. Ἐγ γαστρί[3] is confined to A which has 19 examples of it (once ἐκ γαστρί, Job xv. 35) to 14 of ἐν γαστρί. Ἐμ μέσῳ or ἐμμέσῳ ("apparently Alexandrian" WH) occurs some 200 times in A, while B has 17 examples (mainly in Ψ and Sir.), and א 3: there are also instances of it in the uncials E, F, T (in Ψ), C (Sir.), Γ (Prophets): the only passages where it is supported by all the principal uncials are Lev. xxv. 33 BAF, Is. vi. 5 Bא ΑΓ.

Apart from these two phrases, the only similar forms noted in the uncials are ἐμητρός (=ἐκ μ.) Gen. xx. 12 A*, ἐχειρός (=ἐκ χ.) Ex. xviii. 8 A*, Ψ xxi. 21 U, xxx. 16 U, ἀπαρχὴμ τῶν Ψ lxxvii. 51 R, ἐμμεσημβρινῇ Is. xvi. 3 א. Assimilation never takes place, as in the papyri, in ἐν μηνί, ἐκ δεξιῶν, ἐκ μέρους etc. The papyri would lead us to expect more examples of such assimilation, at least in the Pentateuch, and it is probable that a larger number of them stood in the autographs. Cf. § 7, 4 and 9.

---

[1] Mayser 233 ff.
[2] Ib. 229 ff.: cf. Meisterhans 110 ff. Contrast the usual opening formula of a will of iii/B.C. εἴη μέμ μοι ὑγιαίνοντι κ.τ.λ. with εὐορ]κοῦντι μέν μοι εὖ εἴη BM ii. 181 (64 A.D.), εἴη μέν μοι ὑγιαίνειν Lp. 29 (295 A.D.).
[3] Found in a papyrus of iii/B.C., Mayser 231.

5. A few instances occur of *irregular assimilation within the word*: βοββήσει (for βομβ.) 1 Ch. xvi. 32 B*, cf. ἐβόββησεν Jer. xxxviii. 36 ℵ, σάππιγγος (=σάλπ.) Jer. vi. 17 ℵ, ἄσσει (=ἄλσει) 4 K. xxi. 7 A, παρράσιν (=πατρ.) Ez. xlvii. 14 A, ἐκλιμμήσει (=-λικμ.) W. v. 23 A, συνμίσσει (=-μίσγ.) 2 M. xiv. 16 A.

6. As regards *assimilation of final ν in composition* (compounds of ἐν, σύν etc.), the papyri show that assimilation was still the rule in iii/B.C. and the first half of ii/B.C., while after *c.* 150 B.C. the growing tendency to isolate the separate syllables produces a great increase in the number of unassimilated forms. Before labials assimilation remains longer in force than before gutturals. Mayser's table[1] exhibits the contrast between these two centuries.

According to the oldest MSS of the LXX the general rule is that ἐν and σύν remain unassimilated before the gutturals, but are assimilated before the labials. Newly-formed words generally retain the constituent parts unassimilated, whereas assimilation is usual ın old and common words, in which the preposition has begun to lose its force. As regards individual books, Ψ, Prov. and Dan. Θ nearly always have the later un-assimilated forms. The following list shows the normal practice of the uncials with regard to individual words: words in which the evidence is indecisive are omitted[2]

Unassimilated	Assimilated
Compounds of ἐν.	
Before gutturals:	
γ- ἐνγαστρίμυθος, ἔνγραπτος. ἐνγράφειν.	

[1] 234. Final ν in composition

	before labials		before gutturals	
	is assimilated	not assim.	assim.	not assim.
in iii/B.C.	58 times	8	58	14
in ii/B.C.	44	35	45	52

[2] Cf. WH[2] App. 156 f.

κ- ἐνκάθετος ἐνκαθίζειν   ἐγκαλεῖν
ἐνκαλύπτειν ἔνκαρπος   ἐγκαταλείπειν (except in Ψ)
ἐνκατάλειμμα -λιμπάνειν   ἐγκλείειν
ἐνκαταπαίζειν ἐνκαυχᾶσθαι   ἐγκρατής -κράτεια
ἐνκρατεῖν ἐνκρούειν   ἐγκώμιον -κωμιάζειν.
ἐνκυλίειν.

χ- ἐνχρίειν ἐνχρονίζειν.   ἐγχεῖν.

Before labials, on the other hand, there is undisputed authority for ·

β-   ἐμβάλλειν ἐμβατεύειν
           ἐμβιβάζειν ἐμβίωσις
           ἐμβλέπειν etc.

π- ἐνπαραγίνεσθαι (Prov.)   ἐμπαίζειν (and derivatives)
ἐνπεριπατεῖν (Prov. BℵA,   ἐμπειρεῖν -ος -ία
and elsewhere in one of   ἐμπιπλάναι ἐμπιπράναι
the uncials) ἐνπηγνύναι   ἐμπίπτειν ἐμπλατύνειν
(1 K. Ψ).   ἐμπλέκειν ἐμποδίζειν
           ἐμπορεύεσθαι ἐμπορία
           -πόριον ἔμπροσθεν.

φ-   ἐμφαίνειν ἐμφανής
           ἐμφανίζειν ἔμφοβος
           ἐμφράσσειν ἐμφυσᾶν.

μ-   ἐμμανής ἐμμελέτημα
           ἐμμένειν ἔμμονος (except
           Sir) ἐμμολύνειν.

Compounds of σύν.

Before gutturals :

γ- συνγραφή συνγράφειν.   συγγενής -γένεια (-νία).

κ- συνκαίειν συνκαλεῖν
συνκαταβαίνειν συνκαταφαγεῖν
συνκλᾶν -κλασμός συνκλείειν
συνκλύζειν συνκρίνειν.

χ-   συγχεῖν.

Before labials etc. :

β-   συμβίωσις -τής (except
           Dan. Θ)
           σύμβουλος -εύειν.

π- συνπαραγίνεσθαι (Ψ) συν-   σύμπας[1] συμποδίζειν

---

[1] In Eccles. σὺν πάντα etc. should be read as two words, σύν being Aquila's rendering of אֵת : alteration to σύμπαντα was natural and B so reads in every passage except the first (i. 14). Of σύνπας for σύμπας the only examples are Na. i. 5 ℵA, Ψ ciii. 28 R, cxviii. 91 AR.

-παραμένειν (Ψ) συνπαρεῖναι   συμπορεύεσθαι (except Dt)
συνπαριστάναι (Ψ) συνπερι-   συμπόσιον -σία.
-φέρεσθαι συνπίνειν συνποιεῖν
συνπονεῖν συνπροπέμπειν.

φ-   συμφέρειν συμφορά
                       συμφράσσειν σύμφυτος.

μ-   σύμμαχεῖν -ία -ος
συνμίσγειν (1 and 2 M.)   σύμμετρος συμμιγνύναι
συνμιγής (Dan. Θ)   σύμμικτος σύμμιξις.

λ-   συλλαμβάνειν συλλέγειν.

σ-   συνσεισμός (late word)   συσκοτάζειν σύσσημον
                       σύστασις σύστεμα (-ημα)
                       συστρέφειν -στρεμμα
                       -στροφή.

LXX compounds of σύν followed by ρ are few: συνράπτειν, συνράσσειν, συνρέμβεσθαι are attested.

In compounds with παν- (mainly in 2, 3 and 4 M.) the MSS are divided, but want of assimilation (e.g. πανκρατής, πανβασιλεύς, πανμελής, πανπόνηρος) is the prevailing rule, many of these words being new. On the other hand παρρησία, παρρησιάζεσθαι are always so written.

7. **Variable final consonants.** It has been well established that the insertion of the so-called "νῦ ἐφελκυστικόν" was not, either in Attic times or in the earlier Hellenistic period, mainly due to a desire to avoid hiatus. In Attic Inscriptions from 500—30 B.C. it is inserted more frequently before consonants than before vowels[1]. Traces of a growing tendency to use the variable final consonant to avoid hiatus may perhaps be found in the papyri[2], "but as far as we know the [modern] rule was only formulated in the Byzantine era[3]." The difference between Attic and Hellenistic Greek consists in the greatly increased use in the latter of the final ν, which in some forms has practically become an invariable appendage.

In the MSS of the LXX, as in the Ptolemaic papyri[4], the insertion of ν in ἐστί(ν) and in verbal forms in -ε(ν) is almost universal before both consonants and vowels. In other verbal

---

[1] Meisterhans 114.
[2] Mayser 245.
[3] Blass N.T. 19.
[4] Mayser 237.

and in nominal forms in -ι(ν), however, such as ποιοῦσι(ν), Μακεδόσι(ν), omission is also allowed: well-attested instances in the LXX of its omission are πᾶσι τούτοις 2 Es. xix. 38 BℵA, Jdth. xiv. 3 ἐγεροῦσι τοὺς...BℵA. Εἴκοσι never takes the ν ἐφελκ- in LXX or in Ptolemaic papyri. ΄As regards the Hellenistic dative of δύο—δυσί(ν)—here the LXX MSS do on the whole insert or omit the ν according as the letter following is a vowel or a consonant: δυσίν is always (14 times) used before a vowel, δυσί is attested without v. l. before a consonant 12 times: on the other hand, δυσίν precedes a consonant without v. l. five times (Dt. xvii. 6, Jos. vi. 22 B, 3 K. xxii. 31 B, Is. vi. 2 *bis*), while in four passages δυσί and δυσίν appear as vll. before a consonant.

The vernacular language inserted an irrational final ν very freely (Mayser 197 ff.): so in LXX ℵ has διέλθατεν Jer. ii. 10, cf. ἐμέν (=ἐμέ) Is. xxxvii. 35 ℵ. The latter form, like χεῖραν ὑγιῆν etc., may be partly due to assimilation to nouns of the 1st declension (see § 10, 12).

8.   The Attic form ἕνεκα has been largely superseded by the Ionic and poet. ἕνεκεν (εἵνεκεν, limited in the best MSS to οὗ εἵνεκεν, except in Lam. iii. 44).

῞Ενεκα is not found before 2 K. xii. 21 B: it occurs in all only 37 times (15 in Ψ), including variants, out of 141 examples of the preposition.   It is probably the original form in 3 K. (2), Prov. (1), 2 M. (4): 1 Es., Ψ, Sir., Min. Proph., Ez. and Dan. O have both forms, the remaining books ἕνεκεν only.

The use of one form or the other is not governed by the fact that the following word begins with a vowel or a consonant (ἕνεκα ὀνόματος in 3 K. viii. 41 A): but in the first half of Ψ (to lxviii. 19) the distinction seems to be made that ἕνεκεν τοῦ is written, but ἕνεκα τῶν (to avoid the triple ν)[1].

Εἶτεν, ἔπειτεν are not found.

---

[1] ῞Ενεκα τῶν Ψ v. 9, viii. 3, xxvi. 11, xlvii. 12 B, lxviii. 19: ἕνεκεν τοῦ vi. 5, xxii. 3, xxx. 4, xliii. 27.

9. The **final** s of οὕτω(s) is likewise inserted on preponderant authority of the LXX MSS, as in the papyri, before both consonants and vowels. Οὕτω is strongly attested only in Lev. vi. 37 (BAF before καί), x. 13 (BAF before γάρ), Dt. xxxii. 6 (BA before λαός), 1 K. xxviii. 2 (BA before νῦν), Job xxvii. 2 BℵC (before με), Is. xxx. 15 (Bℵ before λέγει). Elsewhere οὕτω receives occasional support from single MSS, especially ℵ, which uses this form fairly consistently in Est. (six out of seven times), 4 M. and the latter part of Isaiah (from xlix. 25).

Μέχρι and ἄχρι are usually so written, as in Attic, without final s, even before a vowel. Μέχρις οὗ, however, is well attested in Est. D 8 (BℵA), Jdth. v. 10 (Bℵ), Tob. xi. 1 (BA), 1 Es. vi. 6 (B), Dan. ⊛ xi. 36 (AQ: μέχρις τοῦ B*); μέχρι οὗ on the other hand, is read by B*AF in Jos. iv. 23, cf. 1 Es. i. 54 B*, Jdth. xii. 9 B*A, Tob. v. 7 ℵ (μέχρι ὅτου), and ἄχρι οὗ in Job xxxii. 11 by BℵC (ἄχρις οὗ A). Apart from this phrase the (Epic and late) forms ἄχρις μέχρις are confined to Jd. xi. 33 B ἄχρις Ἀρνών, Job ii. 9 A μέχρις τίνος. Ἄντικρυς...αὐτοῦ 3 M. v. 16 = "opposite" is a late usage : Attic uses (κατ)αντικρύ in this sense.

The poetical ἑπτάκι is written before a consonant in Prov. xxiv. 16 Bℵ and in the B text of 3 K. xviii. 43 f. *ter*, 4 K. v. 14 (contrast 10 ἑπτάκις ἐν): elsewhere always ἑπτάκις ἑξάκις πεντάκις ποσάκις.

10. **Elision.** Elision, owing to the prevailing tendency to isolate and give a distinct individuality to each word is the exception, and is in most books of the LXX confined to prepositions (and particles), though even with these the *scriptio plena* is more common. The few rules that are observable in the MSS of the N.T. apply also to those of the LXX.

(1) *Proper names* in particular are kept distinct and apart : before them the prep. is nearly always written in full, e.g. 1 M. x. 4 μετὰ Ἀλεξάνδρου (but μετ' αὐτῶν, καθ' ἡμῶν in the

same verse): exceptions are ἐπ᾽ Αἴγυπτον Is. xxxvi. 6, κατ᾽
Αἴγυπτον 4 M. iv. 22, καθ᾽ Ἡλιόδωρον 2 M. iii. 40 A (κατά V).

(2) Elision of the final vowel of *prepositions* often takes
place in combinations of frequent occurrence and before pronouns, e.g. ἀπ᾽ ἀρχῆς, ἀπ᾽ ἐχθές, κατ᾽ ἀνατολάς, ἀπ᾽ ἐμοῦ, μετ᾽
αὐτῶν, ἀντ᾽ αὐτ(οῦ)[1], ἀνθ᾽ ὧν. Elsewhere, the *scriptio plena* of
the prep. is the rule even where an aspirate follows, e.g.
N. xv. 20 ἀπὸ ἅλω (ἅλωνος), W. ix. 17 ἀπὸ ὑψίστων : we find
even (with pronoun following) ἐπὶ ὧν N. iv. 49.

(3) Of *particles* ἀλλά and οὐδέ occasionally suffer elision,
but are more commonly written in full. Ἵνα undergoes elision
in Ex. ix. 14 B ἵν᾽ εἰδῆς (ἵνα A), Jos. iii. 4 B ἵν᾽ ἐπιστησθε
(ἵνα AF): contrast Jos. xi. 20 ἵνα ἐξολεθρ. BAF.

(4) 4 Maccabees shows a more frequent and bolder use
of elision. Not only does this book contain such examples
as δι᾽ ἀνάγκην, δι᾽ ἔργων, δι᾽ εὐσέβειαν, καθ᾽ ἡλικίαν, κατ᾽ οὐδένα,
κατ᾽ ἐνιαυτόν, κατ᾽ οὐρανόν, καθ᾽ ὑπερβολήν, ἀλλ᾽ οὐδέ, ἀλλ᾽ ὥσπερ,
but it also has συμβουλεύσαιμ᾽ ἄν, μακαρίσαιμ᾽ ἄν and similar
phrases (i. 1, 10, ii. 6, v. 6), τοῦθ᾽ ὅτι ii. 9 A (τοῦτο ὅτι אV),
δ᾽ ἔστιν *ib.* A, δ᾽ ἄν vii. 17. Another literary book, 2 Macc., has
τοῦτ᾽ ἐπιτελέσαι xiv. 29 V (no doubt the right reading : τοῦ ἐπιτ.
A) and ποῦ ποτ᾽ ἐστίν xiv. 32. But even the literary and poetical
books prefer the *scriptio plena* in combinations not involving a
prep., e.g. πτῶμα ἄτιμον W. iv. 19, ἄνδρα ἀκάρδιον, Prov. x. 13
BA (ΑΝΔΡΑΚΑΡΔΙΟΝ א)—one of the iambic endings that are
so frequent in this book.

11. **Crasis**, again, is quite rare in LXX, and practically
confined to some stereotyped combinations with καί. The only
frequent example is κἀγώ which is attested in nearly every
instance : καὶ ἐγώ has good authority only in 2 Ch. xviii. 7 (BA),
Job xxxiii. 5 f. (BA, Bא A), Ez. (xxxiv. 31 BAQ, xxxvi. 28 AQ),
and in the Minor Prophets. Κἀμέ is the reading of the uncials

---

[1] Jd. xv. 2 A (ἀντὶ αὐτ. B), 4 K. x. 35, 1 Ch. i. 44 etc., 1 M. ix. 30.

in Gen. xxvii. 34, 38, Ex. xii. 32 and 4 M. xi. 3 (so κάμοῦ
ib. v. 10) : κάμοί is read by A in Jd. xiv. 16, by B in Job xii. 3.
Κἄν for καὶ ἐάν is doubtless original in 4 M. x. 18, and is
attested by B elsewhere (Lev. vii. 6, Sir. iii. 13, Is. viii. 14).
Καὶ ἐκεῖ is usually and καὶ ἐκεῖθεν always written *plene*: κἀκεῖ
is no doubt original in 3 M. vii. 19, is read by BA in R. i. 17,
and also attested in 3 K. xix. 12 A, Is. xxvii. 10 Q, lvii. 7 אQ.
Κἀκεῖν(ος) is certain in W. xviii. 1, Is. lvii. 6, 2 M. i. 15, and
is read by AQ in Dan. Θ Sus. 57 (*ib.* Dan. O καὶ ἐκ. and so
3 K. iii. 21). The literary books 2 and 3 Macc. alone[1]
contain examples of crasis with the definite article : τἀνδρός
2 M. xiv. 28, 31 V, τοὐναντίον 3 M. iii. 22, τἀληθές *ib.* vii. 12 ·
4 Macc. always writes καλοκἀγαθία (but καλὸς καὶ ἀγαθός as
in 2 M.) and it affords apparently the only example of crasis
in compounds of προ-, προυφάνησαν iv. 10 Aא (προεφ. V).

    א* has ἐσταγαθόν for ἔσται ἀγ. in Prov. xiii. 13 a: C writes
ἡμαρτία in Job xxiv. 20 for ἡ ἁμαρτία.

12. **Hiatus** and the harsh juxtaposition of consonants at
the close of one word and the beginning of the next were
avoided by followers of the rules of Isocrates by the use of
some alternative forms. Πᾶς and ἅπας, ὅτι and διότι are the
chief examples. In the LXX, as in the Ptolemaic papyri[2],
the employment of ἅπας appears to be due in most books to
regard for euphony, whereas διότι is used indiscriminately after
vowels and consonants.

    The LXX always writes (εἰς) τὸν ἅπαντα (not πάντα) χρόνον:
Dt. xxii. 19, 29: 1 Es. viii. 82: Est. E 24, ix. 28: 1 M. x. 30,
xi. 36, xv. 8. Only in the following passages do the uncials
unite in attesting ἅπας after a vowel: 2 K. iii. 25 γνῶναι ἅπαντα,
1 Ch. xvii. 10 ἐταπείνωσα ἅπαντας Bאα (cf. xvi. 43 Bא), 1 Es. viii.

---

[1] Apart from τοὐνιαυτοῦ Ex. xxxiv. 23 A*. The papyri show a fair
number of examples of crasis with the article, τἄλλα τἀντίγραφον etc., but
scriptio plena is the rule, Mayser 158.
[2] Mayser 161 f.

63 (after a pause), 2 M. iv. 16 καθ' ὃ ἅπαν AV, 3 M. v. 2 ἀκράτῳ ἅπαντας: elsewhere there is always a v. l. πᾶς.

Διότι occurs altogether in 358 instances, of which 201 are after a vowel, 157 after a consonant. With the meaning "because" (300 examples) the number of examples following a vowel and a consonant are about equal: with the meaning "that" the word is used with greater regard to euphony, there being only 10 examples following a consonant.

Out of the 358 examples of διότι 250 are found in the Minor Prophets (145), Ezekiel *a* (75) and Jeremiah *a* (30), a fact which illustrates the close connexion existing between these portions of the LXX. Jer. β has only three examples, two of which are incorrect readings (xxx. 1 ℵ, xxxi. 44 A, xxxvii. 6): Ez. β has four (in three of which other readings are preferable). Ez. *a* writes ἐπιγνώσονται διότι ἐγὼ Κύριος where Ez. β has γνώσονται ὅτι ἐγώ εἰμι Κύριος.

ACCIDENCE.

1. Assimilation is here seen at work. There is a tendency to obliterate distinctions within each declension and between the several declensions. In particular we note some signs of the movement in the direction of the absorption of the consonantal (third) declension in the α and ο (first and second) declensions.

2. **First declension.** *Nouns in a pure.* The Attic rule that nouns ending in α pure (-ρα -ια -εα) keep α in the gen. and dat. sing. undergoes modification in the κοινή in two classes of words, which it will be well to keep distinct: (1) nouns and perfect participles in -υια (-υῖα), (2) nouns in -ρᾰ. These now tend to have gen. and dat. sing. in -ης -η like the majority of fem. words in Declension I. Nouns in -ειᾰ etc. and in -ρᾱ are unaffected: ἀληθείας -είᾳ, ἡμέρας -ρᾳ are written as before.

The LXX exx. of (1) are κυνομυίης Ex. viii. 21 B, 24 B, τετελευτηκυίη L. xxi. 11 B, N. vi. 6 B, ἐπιβεβηκυίης 1 K. xxv. 20 B (A -κύεις = -κύης = -κυίης), ἑαλωκυίης Is. xxx. 13 ℵ, ἑστηκυιηστήλη (= ἑστηκυίης στήλη, § 9, 1) ἁλός W. x. 7 ℵ*. Only in the passage in 1 K. is the η form attested by more than one of the uncials: elsewhere the MSS have the usual forms, e.g. ἐξεληλυθυίας L. xxvii. 21.

(2) The exx. of the η forms with nouns in -ρᾰ are also quite in a minority, so far, at least, as the only word which occurs

repeatedly is concerned. Out of 79 exx. of the use of μάχαιρα in gen. or dat. sing. in LXX there are only 2 where the η forms are universally supported and certainly original. These are μαχαίρῃ Gen. xxvii. 40 A*D*E (no witness to -ρᾳ in the larger Cambridge LXX), Ex. xv. 9 B*AF: both passages, it is important to note, are poetical—the blessing pronounced upon Esau and the song after the crossing of the Red Sea. The η forms with μάχαιρα occur also in Gen. xlviii. 22 A*D* (-ρᾳ BF) and in a single uncial in the following: in E Gen. xxxiv. 26, in B* N. xxi. 24, 2 K. xv. 14, in A Dt. xiii. 15, Jos. xix. 47, Bel Θ 26 and 11 times in the A text of Jeremiah (in both parts)[1].—Σφῦρα has dat. σφύρῃ Is. xli. 7, gen. σφύρης, Sir. xxxviii. 28 (cf. ὁλοσφύρητος Sir. l. 9 with Rutherford *NP* p. 286). 2 Macc. yields 3 exx.: σπείρης viii. 23, xii. 22, παλαίστρῃ iv. 14.

As to the origin of these forms, they cannot be entirely due to mere assimilation to δόξης -η : for why should participles in -κυῖᾰ have the η forms, while ἀλήθειᾰ retains the α forms?

The forms -υίης -υίῃ owe their existence, no doubt, as Blass says[2], to the non-pronunciation of the ι in the diphthong υι, which produced such spellings as παρειληφῦα, ὑός in Attic Inscriptions of iv/B.C. and earlier[3]. Though the older spelling again revived in the Hellenistic period, the declension -υίης -υίῃ maintained its place and is very common in papyri of the early Empire.

As to the forms -ρης -ρη there is a division of opinion. They are explained by the majority of critics[4] as due to analogy with other nouns in α, e.g. δόξα δόξης, while others[5] are convinced that they are the result of Ionic influence upon the κοινή. The probability is that both influences have been at work, and that the η forms were *originally* Ionic survivals, specially frequent with words having Ionic associations: afterwards analogy came into play (the η forms only became common in the *later* κοινή) and extended their use to all words in -ρᾰ[6].

[1] As against 11 exx. of the α forms in the A text of Jer.: the other uncials have the α forms throughout the book.
[2] N.T. p. 25. Cf. ἐπιβεβηκυεις = -κυης in 1 K. loc. cit. A.
[3] Meisterhans 59 f.
[4] So Blass, J. H. Moulton, Mayser.
[5] So Thumb *Hell.* 68 ff., Schwyzer *Perg.* 40 ff., W.-S. 80 f.
[6] Cf. modern Greek ἐλεύτερος fem. ἐλεύτερη.

(i) This is suggested by the piece of LXX evidence given above. It is most remarkable that the two passages in LXX where μαχαίρῃ is certainly original are poetical sections. The Pentateuch translators, according to their usual practice[1], adapted their language to their subject-matter and, writing at a time when the papyri show that the α forms were still the rule in prose, appear to have consciously selected the η form as an Ionism and therefore appropriate in these poetical passages.

(ii) It is further to be observed that the two words which most commonly take the η forms in the papyri of the early Empire have Ionic associations. The use of ἄρουρα for γῆ was an old Ionism taken over by the Tragedians (Rutherford *NP* 14) : one of the uses of σπεῖρα was of the mouldings on an Ionic column (LS).

(iii) The contrast between the LXX and the N.T. is instructive and indicates the value of the uncial evidence. Whereas we have seen that in the LXX μαχαίρας -ρᾳ are normal and there are only 2 undisputed exx. of the η forms out of 79, in the N.T. μαχαίρης -ρῃ are read by WH in all the 8 passages where the cases occur : an almost exclusive use of the η forms is found in the other N.T. words in -ρᾰ (WH ed. 2 App. 163).

(iv) This distinction between O.T. and N.T. is borne out by the papyri, which show that it is one of time, not of country (Egypt and Palestine). The η forms are absent from papyri of iii/B.C. : exx. with words in -ρᾰ begin at the close of ii/B.C. with ὀλύρης (118 B.C.), μαχαίρης -ρῃι (114 and 112 B.C.)[2]. On the other hand under the early Empire these forms are practically universal[3].

3. Κόρη[4] (originally κόρϝη) was one of two words (with δέρη) where Attic prose retained η in the nom. after ρ. It is not surprising to find the word brought into line with others in -ρᾱ: there is evidence for the form κόραν in all 3 passages in LXX where the acc. appears, Dt. xxxii. 10 B*F, Ψ xvi. 8 B*א*, Sir.

---

[1] Thiersch 61.

[2] Mayser 12 f.

[3] I have noted upwards of 30 exx. of ἀρούρης between 67 A.D. (BU 379) and vii/A.D. (BU 319), about a dozen of σπείρης in ii/A.D. alone. Σπίρας gen. occurs in BM ii. 256 (early i/A.D.). Apart from the last ex. the cases of these two words do not seem to occur in the earlier papyri : we should expect to find the η forms, if, as appears, the words are Ionic in their origin : a recrudescence of a dialectical peculiarity at a late stage in the language would be unnatural.—The forms -υίης etc. begin with καθηκυίης (= καθηκούσης) in 161 B.C. (BM i. 41. 5) : εἰδυίης is common under the Empire.

[4] See J. H. Moulton *Prol.* ed. 2, 244.

xvii. 22 א (-ρην BAC) : the Attic gen. κόρης stands, however, in Zech. ii. 8.

4. In proper names, as previously in Attic Greek, α impure replaces η in gen. and dat.: ῎Αννᾳ 1 K. i. 2, ῎Αννας Tob. i. 20, Φεννάνᾳ 1 K. i. 2, 4, Σουσάννας Dan. O Sus. 30, Dan. Θ Sus. 27 AQ (-άννης B), 28 B^{ab}AQ (-άννης B*), 63 AQΓ.

5. Τόλμην as from τόλμη (not τόλμᾰ) stands in Jdth xvi. 10 A (-μαν Bא) : cf. the fluctuation between πρύμνα πρύμνη etc. in Attic poetry. Conversely κολόκυνθα (-κυντα AQ) acc. -θαν replaces Attic κολοκύντη (Rutherford *NP* p. 498) in the κοινή : Jon. iv. 7.

6. The (Doric) gen. plur. ψυχᾶν occurs as a v. l. of א* in W. ii. 22.

The rare plural forms of γῆ[1] occur in the B text of 4 K. · τὰς γᾶς xviii. 35, ταῖς γαῖς xix. 11. Elsewhere the Heb. ארצות is rendered by χῶραι or by the poetical γαῖαι (4 K locc. citt. A text, 2 Es. 4 times, Ez. xxxvi. 24, Ψ xlviii. 12) or the plur. is replaced by the sg. (e.g. Gen. xli. 54 ἐν πάσῃ τῇ γῇ, Jer. xxxv. 8 ἐπὶ γῆς πολλῆς, Dan. Θ xi. 42).

7. The contracted form βορρᾶς, which already in Attic Greek was an alternative for βορέας[2], was used almost exclusively in the κοινή. It is the normal form in papyri[3] and LXX: βορέας -έου -έαν is confined to the literary version of Proverbs (xxv. 23, xxvii. 16 : corrected in later hands of B to βορρέας), Sirach (xliii. 17, 20 : in 20 B has βορέης) and Job Θ xxvi. 7. Elsewhere gen. βορρᾶ, dat. βορρᾷ, acc. βορρᾶν, voc. βορρᾶ (Cant. iv. 16).

א sometimes appends an irrational ν to the gen. ἀπὸ (γῆς) βορρᾶν, ἐκ τοῦ βορρᾶν etc., Is. xlix. 12 (ἀπὸ βορᾶν : Mayser 213), Jer. iii. 18, xiii. 20, xvi. 15, xxiii. 8, xxv. 9, xxvii. 9, 41, xxix. 2,

---

[1] LS cite Aristotle for γαῖ, Strabo for γᾶς : γᾶς and γῶν occur in papyri of ii/B.C. (Teb. 6. 31, BU 993. 3, TP 1. 2.)

[2] Meisterhans 100. The change seems to have begun with βορρᾶθεν, which first appears c. 400 B.C.

[3] Always in the Ptolemaic papyri, Mayser 252, 221. Βορέας seems to have been partially reinstated later: an ex. from i/A.D. is cited by Thumb *Hell.* 65.

Zech. vi. 6, cf. Ez. xlvii. 17 Q : while the ν is dropped in the acc. in Dan. Θ viii. 4 B (κατὰ θάλασσαν καὶ βορρᾶ καὶ νότον) and elsewhere in Q.

For gen. -α or -ου in proper names in -ας see § 11, 4 f.

8. **Second declension.** The κοινή, or some portions of it[1], used the *uncontracted* as well as the Attic *contracted forms*. In the LXX there is a curious distinction in one word. The rule as regards ὀστέον ὀστοῦν in LXX is that the contracted forms are used in the nom. and acc., the uncontracted in the gen. and dat.: ὀστοῦν ὀστᾶ but ὀστέου ὀστέων ὀστέοις. See e.g. Gen. ii. 23 Τοῦτο νῦν ὀστοῦν ἐκ τῶν ὀστέων μου, Ez. xxxvii. 1 ὀστέων (-των Q), 3 f. ὀστᾶ (*ter*), 5 ὀστέοις (-τοις Q), 7 and 11 (*bis*) ὀστᾶ.

'Οστῶν Ez. xxxii. 27 breaks the rule : there are also variant readings ὀστέα in Ψ l. 10 Tℵca, Lam. iii. 4 BQ, iv. 8 B, ὀστῶν Job Θ xxxiii. 19 Bℵ, ὀστοῖς Jer. xx. 9 B.

On the other hand the contracted forms only of κάνεον are used : κανοῦν κανοῦ κανῷ plur. κανᾶ (Pent. and Jd. vi. 19 A).

Χειμάρρους -ουν is still so written : the later χείμαρρος is confined in LXX to Ψ cxxiii. 4 and to vll. in N. xxxiv. 5 (A), Jer. xxix. 2 (ℵ*).
('Αρχι)οινοχόος, χρυσοχόος are uncontracted as also in Attic Greek : the papyri have the contracted forms as well[2]
For νοῦς νοός, χοῦς χοός etc. see § 10, 31 : for contracted adjectives § 12, 2.

9. The so-called **Attic second declension** for the most part disappears from the κοινή, words in -ως being transformed or replaced by new words. Excepting one word (ἅλως) the forms in -ως in LXX are confined to the literary books. The old ἅλως and the new ἅλων -ωνος (already attested in Aristot.) appear side by side in the LXX, the new form prevailing[3]. ῞Αλως appears only in the form ᾰλω which does

---

[1] Thumb *Hell.* 63 says they are specially characteristic of the Eastern κοινή and regards them as of Ionic origin.
[2] Mayser 258.
[3] The uncials (Camb. Manual LXX) have forms from ἅλως without v. l.

duty not only for gen. dat. and acc. sing. (not ἄλων), but also
for acc. plur., τοὺς ἄλω 1 K. xxiii. 1 BA: this form of the acc.
plur., due to the weak sound of final ς, is attested in papyri of
ii/B.C. and in MSS of Josephus (*A.J.* vi. 272)[1]. The preponderance of the forms from ἄλων in the LXX is remarkable, as
the Ptolemaic papyri only yield one example (ἀλώνωι = ἀλώνων
118 B.C.) as against numerous examples of the other forms[2].
The gender as well as the form is variable, B on the whole
preferring the masc. and A the fem.

Ἕως appears only in 3 M. v. 46. Κάλως "rope" is replaced
by κάλος N. iii. 37, iv. 32 (A κλάδους *bis*), λεώς by λαός
throughout, and νεώς by ναός except in 2 M., which, beside
ναός, has nom. νεώς x. 5, gen. νεώ iv. 14, acc. νεώ A (νεών V)
vi. 2, ix. 16, x. 3, xiii. 23, xiv. 33. Λαγώς is replaced by
δασύπους (Aristot.).

For adjectives in -ως see § 12, 3.

10. The vocative of θεός is the unclassical θεέ, even in
the literary books (Jd. xvi. 28 B, xxi. 3 B: 2 K. vii. 25 B:
Sir. xxiii. 4: 3 M. vi. 2, 4 M. vi. 27) as in N.T. (Mt. xxvii. 46).
The class. voc. θεός occurs in N. xvi. 22 BA (θεὲ θεέ F). More
often, however, the voc. is expressed by ὁ θεός (see Syntax).

11. *Gender in Declension II.*

The tendency towards uniformity shows itself in the occasional transference of some feminine words in Decl. II. into
the larger class of masculines. Ὁ ἄμπελος Hb. iii. 17 ℵ,
ὁ βάσανος 1 M. ix. 56 ℵ, ὁ ῥάβδος Gen. xxx. 37 A, are vagaries
of a single MS: the classical fem. is kept elsewhere. Ὁ βάτος
of LXX (Ex. iii. 2 ff.: Dt. xxxiii. 16) appears to be vulgar and
Hellenistic (Aristoph., Theophr.). Ὁ ληνός has the support

in 13 passages, from ἄλων without v. l. in 24: in 6 passages the two
forms are attested by different MSS. The -ως forms occur in Numbers,
Ruth, 1—3 K., 1—2 Ch., Hg. ii. 19.
[1] Mayser 259, 207.
[2] Ib. 287, 258 f.

of a group of cursives in Gen. xxx. 38, 41 : the uncials here and elsewhere keep the fem. Ὁ λίθος, as in N.T., is used in all senses, including that of precious stones, where Attic writers often used ἡ. Ὁ στάμνος Ex. xvi. 33 is 'Doric[1].' Ὁ λιμός, the older Attic gender, is usual in LXX : the 'Doric' ἡ (Rutherford *NP* p. 274) is read by all uncials in Is. viii. 21, by B in 3 K. xviii. 2, and by A in Jer. xvii. 18, xxiv. 10, 1 M. ix. 24, xiii. 49. Ἡ (usual in Attic) and ὁ τρίβος (already in Euripides) are both found, sometimes in the same book, the former slightly preponderating[2]. The gender of the probably Semitic ὕσσωπος also fluctuates : it is masc. in Lev. xiv. 6, 51 f. in B*A, fem. ibid. in F (B^ab) and in 3 K. iv. 29 BA.

Ἀνεβιβάσθη ἡ βάτραχος Ex. viii. 6 A (ὁ β. B) is no doubt due to the collective use of the noun as in (classical) ἡ ἵππος = "cavalry," Gen. xiv. 11 etc.

12. Third declension.

Accusative sing. in -αν for -α. The assimilation of accusatives of the 3rd decl. ending in a vowel to those of the 1st decl. by the addition of final ν had begun as early as iv/B.C. in the case of a few proper names and appellatives in -ης (Σωκράτην, τριήρην etc.)[3]. The addition of ν to accusatives in -α did not come till later : it begins in the Egyptian papyri in ii/B.C.[4] and does not become common before ii/A.D. It is always a vulgarism, and is connected with a wider tendency, specially common in Egypt, to append an irrational ν to other cases of the noun and to other parts of speech[5]. The LXX examples are

[1] The N.T. in the single passage in Hebrews keeps Attic ἡ.
[2] Ὁ is attested in 1 K. vi. 12, 1 Ch. xxvi. 18, Ψ xliii. 19, cxviii. 35 ℵ (elsewhere ἡ in this book), Prov. iii. 17 (do.), Jer. xviii. 15 (do.), Jl. ii. 7 A and in one or more of the uncials in Is. iii. 12, xxx. 11, xlii. 16, xlix. 9, 11, lviii. 12.
[3] Jannaris p. 542. His list of LXX exx. of accusatives in -αν needs checking.
[4] Χῖραν in a letter of 160 B.C. and τρίποδαν in i/B.C. are the only examples in the Ptolemaic age quoted by Mayser 199.
[5] Ib. 197 ff.

practically confined in the uncials to the two MSS A and א, where they probably represent the Egyptian spelling of a later age than the autographs.

The examples noted in A are Ex. x. 4 ἀκρίδαν, xiii. 21 νύκταν, N. xv. 27 αἶγαν : R. iv. 11 γυναῖκαν : in 1 K. νύκταν θώρακαν χεῖραν γυναῖκαν μερίδαν : in 2 K. ii. 29, iv. 7 νύκταν, v. 18 κοιλάδαν, xiii. 10 κοιτῶναν : 3 K. i. 45 βασιλέαν : 4 K. xxii. 3 and 2 Ch. xxxiv. 15 γραμματαίαν, 2 Ch. xxxiv. 9 ἱερέαν : 1 Es. iv. 19 πρᾶγμαν, viii. 8 ἱερέαν : Ψ xxviii. 7 φλόγαν : Is. vii. 19 ῥαγάδαν : Jdth xiii. 10 φάραγγαν : Sir. xiii. 6 ἐλπίδαν : 1 M. x. 1 Πτολεμαΐδαν. In א these forms are exceedingly common in the Prophetical books (αἰῶναν and χεῖραν furnish the majority of instances): cf. the pronominal forms in א τίναν Na. iii. 19, ἐμέν Is. xxxvii. 35. In B, on the other hand, the only exx. noted are Is. xxxvi. 2 βασιλέαν, xxxvii. 29 ῥ(ε)ῖναν (with א)[1], Zeph. i. 4 χεῖραν.

Cf. § 12, 5 for adjectives.

13. *Accusative plural.* The old termination of the acc. plur. of stems in υ (ου)—viz. ς unpreceded by α (e.g. τὰς βοῦς)— is replaced in Hellenistic Greek by -ας, possibly to prevent confusion with the nom. sing. So in LXX βόας always, 29 times[2]: ἰχθύας 8 times with ἰχθῦς twice as a v.l., Ez. xxix. 4 B (contrast 5), Hb. 1. 14 א (ἠχθῦς): μύας 1 K. vi. 1, 4 A, but μῦς vi. 5, 11 (similar variety in the nom.: μύες v. 6 but μῦς vi. 18): ὀσφύας 10 times (including L. xiv. 9 B) with v.l. ὀσφῦς in Is. xxxii. 11 B*: ὀφρύας L. xiv. 9 A (ὀφρῦς B^{ab}F): στάχυας[3] Gen. xli. 7, 24, Jd. xv. 5 A, but στάχυς Ex. xxii. 6, Dt. xxiii. 24.

14. The assimilation of the acc. to the nom. plur. in words in -ευς (on the model of αἱ and τὰς πόλεις) begins in Attic Inscriptions as early as c. 300 B.C.[4] The LXX accord-

---

[1] Cod. B in the central chapters of Isaiah has other instances of Egyptian or vulgar spellings not found elsewhere in the MS : κραυῆς xxx. 19 (= κραυγῆς, § 7, 30), προσήξει (for -έξει) xxxii. 4, ἥκει (for ἐκεῖ) xxxiii. 6.

[2] The only ex. of the acc. pl. in Ptolemaic papyri is in the Attic form τὰς βοῦς (iii/B.C.), Mayser 268. Papyri of the Imperial age have βόας: OP iv. 729 (137 A.D.), GP 48 (346 A.D.).

[3] Ptolemaic papyri have one ex. of στάχυς, none of -υας, Mayser 267.

[4] Meisterhans 141.

ingly has τοὺς βασιλεῖς, γονεῖς, ἱερεῖς, ἱππεῖς etc. The older form βασιλέας occurs in 4 K. vii. 6 *bis* BA [contrast iii. 10, 13] and as a v.l. in 2 Es. xix. 22 B, Jer. xxxii. 12 ℵ, Hos. vii. 3 Q. Γονέας 4 M. ii. 10 V may have been written by the Atticizing author of that book.

15. *Assimilation of acc. to nom. plur.* occurs also in the substitution of -es *for* -as. This seems to have begun with the numeral τέσσαρες and then to have been extended to other words. Dr J. H. Moulton has acutely suggested a reason for the special tendency to equate the nom. and acc. of τέσσαρες, viz. that this is (excepting εἷς) "the only early cardinal which ever had a separate acc. form[1]."

In the papyri[2] τέσσαρες (acc.) furnishes most of the examples. I have counted 49 exx., of which 8 are B.C. and 41 between i/ and ii/A.D.: from i/A.D. it is more frequent than τέσσαρας which is still in use. Next comes πάντες (9 exx.), then participles in -ντες: exx. like γυναῖκες occur sporadically. Two exx. are as early as iii/B.C., the first being τέσσαρες HP 90, 15: in the other the -es has been corrected to -as, πάντ]ε̃ς τούς ap. Mayser 59.

In the LXX, as in the papyri, the commonest instance is τέσσαρες which is normal in B* (Ex. xxv. 11, 25 *bis* [A *semel*], 34 etc.) and frequent in A[3]. The -es form appears also, but far less frequently, in another numeral. As against upwards of 100 examples of χιλιάδας (without v.l.) the acc. is written as -δες in 1 Es. i. 7 A, Jdth ii. 5 ℵ, Is. xxxvii. 36 ℵ = ‖ 1 M. vii. 41 A[4]. (Μυριάδας is constant.)

---

[1] *Prol.* (ed. 2) 243. A possible contributory cause has been suggested elsewhere (§ 6, 2).

[2] Mayser 59, Moulton *CR* xv. 34, xviii. 108.

[3] The statistics for the uncials are as follows. B has 27 exx. of τέσσαρες to 13 of τέσσαρας: A 22 -ρες, 26 -ρας: ℵ 3 -ρες, 2 -ρας. The evidence of B cannot be quoted in N. xxix. 13 ff. where it writes ιδ′, but -ρες ih. 29 shows how the symbol should be read. The statistics include Jos. xxi. 18 ff., where πόλεις τέσσαρες of BA should perhaps be taken as a new sentence (cf. 39) and not in apposition with the preceding accusatives.

[4] Also perhaps in 3 K. viii. 63 B = ‖ 2 Ch. vii. 5 B, 3 K. xii. 21 BA = 2 Ch. xi. 1 B, 1 Ch. xviii. 12 A, Ez. xlv. 5 *bis* (AQ, BAQ). But these passages

Apart from these two numerals the LXX instances of acc.
in -ες are quite rare: it is noteworthy that two of them occur
in connexion with τέσσαρες. 1 Ch. xxv. 5 A καὶ ἔδωκεν θεὸς τῷ
'Α. υἱοὺς δέκα τέσσαρες καὶ θυγάτερες τρ(ε)ῖς: 2 Ch. xxiii. 2 B
συνήγαγεν τοὺς Λευείτας...καὶ ἄρχοντες: Zech. i. 20 א ἔδειξέν μοι
Κύριος τέσσαρες τέκτονες[1]. The B text of 2 Es. xxiii. 15 εἶδον
ἐν Ἰούδᾳ πατοῦντας...καὶ φέροντες...καὶ ἐπιγεμίζοντες...καὶ φέροντες *may* be merely an instance of "drifting into the nominative[2]," but the papyri show that this form of acc. was common
in participles.

The converse use of -ας for -ες in the nom. plur. occurs in
4 K. xiii. 7 A χιλιάδας, 1 Ch. xii. 36 A χιλιάδας, 2 Es. xvi. 9 א χεῖρας.

16. *Relation of the nominative to the cases* (inflection with
or without consonant). The inflection κέρας κέρως dat. κέρᾳ
has disappeared, the cases being formed with τ: dat. κέρατι
(Is. v. 1: Dan. O Θ vii. 8), plur. κέρατα κεράτων. Κρέας, on the
other hand, which is used mainly in the plural, keeps the
shorter forms κρέα κρεῶν[3]. Γῆρας in Attic is declined like
κέρας, γήρως γήρᾳ: in LXX the anomalous dat. is replaced by
γήρει (Gen. xv. 15 etc., 1 Ch. xxix. 28, Ψ xci. 15, Dan. O vi. 1),
except in Sirach which has γήρᾳ (iii. 12, viii. 6 אΑ, xxv. 3): the
gen. keeps the classical form γήρως in the literary books
(W. iv. 9, 2—4 Macc.) and Gen. xliv. 20, elsewhere γήρους has
undisputed (Gen. xxxvii. 3, Sir. xlvi. 9) or good authority
(Gen. xlviii. 10 B: 3 K. xi. 3 B [xiv. 4 A = Aquila], xv. 23 A:

may be merely instances of "drifting into the nominative" and of the
tendency to place a numerical statement in a parenthesis. This is clearly
the case in 3 K. v. 14 B καὶ ἀπέστειλεν αὐτοὺς εἰς τὸν Λίβανον—δέκα χιλιάδες
ἐν τῷ μηνί, ἀλλασσόμενοι. In Jd. vii. 3 B εἴκοσι καὶ δύο χιλιάδες is subject,
not object.
  [1] In Dt. ii. 25 B* ταραχθήσονται καὶ ὠδῖνες (-νας BᵇAF) ἕξουσιν, ὠδῖνες is
apparently the subject: cf. Job xxi. 17, Is. xiii. 8.
  [2] Cf. BM ii. 154. 14 (68 A.D.) μηδὲ τοὺς παρ' αὐτοῦ κυριεύοντα[ς αὐτῶν]
καὶ εἰσοδεύοντας καὶ ἐξοδεύοντας καὶ κατασπῶντες.
  [3] Ex. xxix. 14 "κρεατα F" Swete: the MS, I learn from Mr Brooke,
has κερατα. Κρέατος once in an Attic inscription of iv/B.C., Meist. 143.

Ψ lxx. 9 BR, 18 B*אR : Is. xlvi. 4 א*A). Πέρας, τέρας keep τ in the cases, as in Attic.

17. Κλείς has acc. sing. κλεῖδα Jd. iii. 25 BA (and in a Hexaplaric insertion in Is. xxii. 22 κλῖδα(ν) Aא) and acc. plur. κλεῖδας Dan. Ο Bel 11 : the usual Attic forms κλεῖν, κλεῖς do not occur[1]. Χάρις keeps the classical χάριν throughout except twice in Zech. (iv. 7, vi. 14) where χάριτα is used : the latter (which has some classical authority : it appears to be Ionic and poetical) is absent from the papyri before the Roman period[2]. Γέλωτα is the only acc. known to LXX (Attic also used γέλων in poetry).

> According to Moeris κλεῖν χάριν γέλων are Attic, κλεῖδα χάριτα γέλωτα Hellenic.

Θερμαστρίς -ίδος has acc. θερμάστρ(ε)ις 3 K. vii. 31 BA : ib. vii. 35 B has τὰς ἐπαρύστρις, A τὰς ἐπαρυστρίδας.

18. Egyptian (Ionic) words in -ις are declined like πόλις : βᾶρις (§ 4, p. 34) dat. βάρει[3], plur. βάρεις βάρεων βάρεσιν: θῖβις (ib.) θῖβιν θίβει Ex. ii. 3, 5, 6 (θείβην is probably merely an itacism and not from θίβη LS): (ε)ῖβις -βιν, nom. plur. (ε)ῖβ(ε)ις Is. xxxiv. 11.

> The plural of ἔρις is not used : in Ψ cxxxviii. 20 read ἐρεῖς.
> ΑΝΟΡΑϹ 1 K. viii. 22 A may be a mere slip for ΑΝΔΡΑϹ or a relic of the Epic ΑΝΕΡΑϹ.

19. Διῶρυξ has gen. -υχος etc. in Attic writers, -υγος etc. in Hellenistic writers from Polybius onward and throughout the Ptolemaic papyri[4] and so in LXX (Ex. vii. 19, viii. 5, Jer.

---

[1] But they are found in N.T. (Ap.) and the papyri.

[2] Mayser 271 f., Crönert 170 n. 6 : but χάριτας once at end of ii/B.C. (Mayser).

[3] So in a papyrus of ii/B.C. (Mayser 266). Literary writers (Euripides, Plutarch) have the consonantal inflection βάριδι βάριδας (*Iph. in A.* 297). Hdt. has βᾶρις, βᾶριν, βάρισι (ii. 179). He also writes gen. ἴβιος, plur. ἴβιες, τὰς ἴβις (ii. 75 f.): LS cite ἴβιδος ἴβεως from Aelian.

[4] Mayser 18 : the classical forms reappear in the papyri at the end of ii/A.D.: the B text in Isaiah is therefore open to suspicion.

xxxviii. 9): the classical forms appear in the B text of Isaiah (xix. 6, xxvii. 12, xxxiii. 21).

20.   *Assimilation of the nominative to the cases* appears in ἡ ὠδίν Is. xxxvii. 3 (so N.T.).   (The cases only of the class. nominatives ἀκτίς, ῥίς are used in LXX: in the papyri forms like ὀξύρριν abound.)   Conversely, the consonant or the vowel of the nom. is retained in the dative plural: ἐλέφανσιν 1 M. i. 17 A (-ασιν א*, with metaplasmus ἐλεφάντοις V), vi. 34 A (-ασιν אV): χειρσίν 1 Ch. v. 10 B[1].   It may be a merely orthographical matter that the long vowel of the nom. ἀλώπηξ is retained in the cases in Jd. i. 35 B (-πηκες), xv. 4 B (-πηκας), 3 K. xxi. 10 B^ab (-πηξιν), Ez. xiii. 4 A (-πηκες).   Cf. θυγατῆρος Sir. xxxvi. 26 א[2].   Assimilation to σάλπιγξ etc. produces μάστιγξ 3 K. xii. 24 Γ B, Sir. xxiii. 11 א, μάστιγξιν 2 Ch. x. 11 B (§ 7, 33).

21.   *Open and contracted forms.*   As in the case of neuter words in -ov in the 2nd declension (8 *supra*), the κοινή preferred the (Ionic) uncontracted form of the gen. plur. in certain 3rd declension neuters in -os[3].   So LXX always has ὀρέων and χειλέων, and usually τειχέων (τειχῶν 4 K. xxv. 4 A, Is. xxii. 11 B, lxii. 6 B, Dan. O iv. 26, 1 M. xvi. 23 אV).   But ἐτῶν, σκευῶν are written, and in the other cases the contracted forms are retained: ὄρους ὄρη, τείχους τείχη, χείλους χείλη, πάχη etc.

Conversely, the gen. plur. of πῆχυς, in classical Greek πήχεων, in the κοινή, through assimilation to neuters in -os, takes on a contracted form πηχῶν.   So in the LXX in Judith, Esther and Ezekiel α (with occasional v.l. -εων in the last-named book): on the other hand in Genesis, Exodus and Chronicles[4] the classical πήχεων is retained: elsewhere the MS evidence is uncertain.

The gen. sing. in LXX is πήχεος (Ex. xxv. 9 etc.) corrected occasionally in A(F) to the classical πήχεως.

---

[1] So in "late inscriptions" (LS): cf. Epic χείρεσσι.
[2] LXX keeps θυγατρός etc. (not poet. θυγατέρος).
[3] Cf. Mayser 17, 277, Moulton *CR* xv. 435.
    Also (without variant) 1 K. xvii. 4, Zech. v. 2, Jer. lii. 21 f. (ib. 21 -χῶν BאQ), Dan. Θ iii. 1 *bis* (= O -χῶν).

22. *Miscellaneous peculiar forms.*

Of τὸ ἅλας gen. ἅλατος (for ὁ ἅλς) the only fairly certain instance in LXX is Sir. xxxix. 26 ἅλας A (ἅλα cett.: as nominatives precede and follow A appears to preserve the true text): in other passages (L. ii. 13, Jd. ix. 45, 2 Es. vi. 9, Ez. xliii. 24 A) ἅλας may equally well be acc. plur. and is almost certainly so in the first of them (ἁλί, ἅλα in same verse). In the Ptolemaic papyri τὸ ἅλας appears as early as iii/B.C., but forms from ἅλς preponderate[1]: in the N.T. the new form has gained the ascendancy.

The oblique cases of ἀμνός—rare in classical Greek which uses ἄρνα ἀρνός etc. instead—in LXX are frequent, though the classical forms are still fairly well represented[2]. (In N.T. the only forms found are ἀμνός [nom.] and ἀρνίον.) The new fem. form ἀμνάς (Theocr. v. 3 with v.l. ἀμνίδες) usually renders the Heb. fem. כבשה (כשבה) "ewe-lamb."

Γόνα for γόνατα (3 K. viii. 54 A) may, if not a slip, be compared with Epic γοῦνα.

Ναῦς is on the way to becoming a literary word, πλοῖον supplanting it in most books of the LXX. Νῆας (= Att. ναῦς) occurs in 3 K. xxii. 49 A (a section apparently interpolated from Aquila) and the Epic. gen. νηός in Prov. xxiv. 54 νηὸς ποντοπορούσης BℵA—naturally as the translator is imitating Homer (νεώς C, νηώς ℵ^{c.a}): elsewhere the Attic forms ναῦν, νηί, νῆες 3 K. xxii. 49 A, ναυσί.

Ὄρνις, like ναῦς, makes way for a second declension form—

---

[1] Mayser 286, *Expositor*, Feb. 1908, v. 177.

[2] In the Pentateuch (or a portion of it) there is a curious differentiation in the use of the Hellenistic and the classical forms, based on a slight variation in spelling of the Hebrew. כֶּבֶשׂ, the ordinary word for "lamb," is constantly rendered by the forms from ἀμνός : in some dozen passages the radicals are transposed to כֶּשֶׂב, and in five of these (Gen. xxx. 32, 33, 35, L. i. 10, iii. 7) the forms of ἄρνα are used, ἀμνός only once (Gen. xxx. 40), elsewhere (L. iv. 35 etc.) πρόβατον. In Ex. xii. 5 כבשים read ἀμνῶν A (not ἀρνῶν B).

ὄρνεον (ὀρνίθιον)—being found only in 3 K. ii. 46ᵉ = iv. 23 (ὀρνίθων ἐκλεκτῶν one of Solomon's delicacies).

Πέλεκυς is shortened to πέλυξ in Jer. xxiii. 29 BאQ (πέλυκυς A), Ez. ix. 2 (so once in Aquila).

Πληθύς (Epic) replaces πλῆθος in 3 M. iv. 17.

The contracted form στῆρ (for στέαρ) is limited to Theodotion (Bel 27): the LXX proper has στέαρ, φρέαρ in common with the papyri (Mayser 273)[1].

Συγγενής has dat. plur. συγγενεῦσι in 1 M. x. 89 A (-νέσι[ν] א*V) as from συγγενεύς[2].

23. Metaplasmus.

We may group under this general head further instances of the mixture of forms and declensions which grammarians subdivide into (a) *abundantia*, viz. double forms for *nominative* and other cases, e.g. λεώς, λαός: (b) *heteroclita*, viz. a single nom. form with diverging forms in the oblique cases, e.g. ὁ and τὸ σκότος: (c) *metaplasta*, viz. formation of a new nom. out of the oblique cases, e.g. ἡ ὠδίν. Mixture of this kind was common in the κοινή and has already been illustrated in the preceding sections: several of the instances which follow have classical precedent.

24. *Fluctuation between masculine and neuter in Decl. II.*

Τὸ ἀλάβαστρον (Theocr. N.T.) for class. ὁ ἀλάβαστος is read by A in 4 K. xxi. 13 (B ὁ ἀλάβαστρος).

The same MS has masc. ἄχυρος[3] (τὸν ἄχυρον) in 3 K. iv. 21: elsewhere in LXX τὸ ἄχυρον (class.).

Γαῖσος (ὁ) "javelin" (an imported word, said to be Iberian)

---

[1] Theodotion's spelling is supported by φρητός as from φρῆρ in a contemporary papyrus of ii/A.D.: Moulton *CR* xv. 435ᵃ.

[2] Cf. Mayser 296 (τὸν συγγενέα ii/B.C.) and WH (ed. 2) App. 165: Dr Moulton calls my attention to συγγενέας in Dittenberger *Sylloge* 258. 20 (end of iii/B.C., Magnesia). The identity of forms in some of the cases of nouns in -ής and -εύς (e.g. acc. plur. in -εῖς) produced mixture throughout: cf. εὐθύς—εὐθής, § 12, 7.

[3] There is some doubtful authority for it in Comedy (see LS).

in Jos. viii. 18 BA has the support of Polybius (xviii. 1-8. 4, Teubner): F reads τὸ γαῖσον.

Δεσμός in Attic Greek has plural δεσμοί and δεσμά: the neuter,[1] in the κοινή has passed over to the literary forms, being restricted in LXX to 3 M. vi. 27, 4 M. xii. 3 (2 Es. vii. 26 A), in N.T. to Luke: commonly in LXX δεσμοί (even in the proverbial κύων ἐπὶ δεσμούς Prov. vii. 22, found elsewhere with δεσμά). (Δέσμη Ex. xii. 22 has a distinct meaning "bundle": a vulgar word found in Comedy and the papyri.)

Τὸ ζυγόν, apparently the older gender (Lat. *jugum*), is replaced almost everywhere in LXX (as in N.T. in the only determining passages) by ὁ ζυγός: with the meaning "balances" the neuter remains in L. xix. 36 ζυγὰ δίκαια, a passage which has influenced the text in Ez. xlv. 10 ζυγὸν δίκαιον AQ (ζυγὸς δίκαιος B: the other books use the masc. with this meaning also, Hos. xii. 7, Prov. xi. 1, xx. 17).

As regards θεμέλιος (sc. λίθος) and θεμέλιον we cannot speak with certainty as to the earlier usage. In the plural οἱ θεμέλιοι has good authority in Attic prose, while τὰ θεμέλια is poetical: on the other hand ὁ θεμέλιος appears to be vulgar and late: the dictum of Moeris that θεμέλιον and θεμέλια are the only true Attic forms is questionable[2]. In LXX τὰ θεμέλια is frequent (Dt. xxxii. 22, 2 K. xxii. 8, 16 [= Ψ xvii. 8, 16], Ψ lxxxi. 5, Prov. viii. 29, Sir. iii. 9 etc, Prophets *passim*). The masc. form is limited to the following: τὸν θεμέλιον 3 K. vi. 2 B (= v. 17 A), 4 K. xvi. 18: θεμέλιοι, θεμελίους, 2 Ch. xxxi. 7, 1 Es. vi. 19, 2 Es. iv. 12, v. 16, Job Θ xxii. 16: Ψ beside the neuter plurals locc. citt. has οἱ θεμέλιοι lxxxvi. 1, ὁ θεμέλιος cxxxvi. 7 (v.l. τῶν -ων). (In N.T. Lc. alone has τὰ -λια Acts xvi. 26: Paul, Hebrews and Apoc. have the masculine forms.)

---

[1] Absent from Ptolemaic papyri (Mayser 28₅). Dr Moulton reminds me of the original *collective* character of these old neuters : so *loca* of a region, *loci* of several isolated places.

[2] Kühner-Blass I. i. 499, Mayser 289 (Ptolemaic papyri -ον -α).

It looks as if the earlier and later κοινή differed in their method of producing uniformity, the former using the neuter throughout, the latter the masc.

Τὸ κλοιόν is read by A in 3 K. xii. 4 (LS cite Byzantine grammarians for plur. κλοιά): elsewhere ὁ κλοιός (class.).

Ὁ λύχνος has plur. οἱ λύχνοι only (Att. also τὰ λύχνα).

Ὁ νῶτος, οἱ νῶτοι are the usual forms in LXX[1], the Attic neuter form being confined to Gen. ix. 23 (τὰ δύο νῶτα), Jer. ii. 27 (νῶτα).

Οἱ ὄνειροι W. xviii. 19 replaces Attic neuter plur. ὀνείρατα or ὄνειρα (Attic sing. ὁ ὄνειρος, τὸ ὄνειρον or τὸ ὄναρ). The word itself has joined the 'literary' vocabulary, ἐνύπνιον being used in the translations.

(Ὁ) σίελος (with Ionic ε) replaces Attic τὸ σίαλον in Is. xl. 15 (neut. σίελον A): the neuter plur. occurs in 1 K. xxi. 13 (τὰ σίελα).

Ὁ σῖτος, τὰ σῖτα of Attic Greek are retained, but the latter is restricted to two literary books (Job and Proverbs), the plur. in any form being absent elsewhere.

Τὸ στάδιον (Dan. O Sus. 37) has plur. σταδίους in the literary 2 M. (xi. 5 V, xii. 10 etc.) as in Attic Greek, which also uses στάδια. The latter appears to have been usual in the κοινή vernacular[2].

Ὁ σταθμός has plur. οἱ σταθμοί in all senses[3]. Attic wrote σταθμός "a halting-place," plur. σταθμοί and -μά, but σταθμόν -μά of "a weight[4]"

Τὸ χειμάρρουν 4 K. xxiii. 6 A is no doubt a slip for τὸ χ. On the whole a tendency is traceable to replace all anomalous neuter plurals by masculine forms.

---

[1] 1 K. iv. 18, 3 K. vii. 19, 4 K. xvii. 14, 2 Es. xix. 29 (ἀπειθοῦντα), Ψ [lxv. 11 Rא·ᵃ], lxviii. 24, lxxx. 7 [cxxviii. 3 R], Zech. vii. 11, Is. l. 6, Ez. i. 18, x. 12. Elsewhere the gender is indeterminate.
[2] Mayser 289, Crönert 175.
[3] N. xxxiii. 1 f., Prov. viii. 34, Is. xxviii. 17. So the papyri, Mayser 263.
[4] K.-Bl. I. i. 500. A has τὸ σταθμόν 4 K. xxi. 13 (B στάθμιον).

25. *Fluctuation between Declensions I. and II.* Nouns compounded from ἄρχω have their termination in -αρχος in Attic Greek : in the κοινή the form -άρχης (which originated in Ionic districts) is usual and gradually ousts the other form. The Attic termination maintains its hold longest in compounds of numerals and in old official titles : new compounds nearly all end in -άρχης[1]. The Attic forms retained in LXX are δεκάδαρχος, ἑκατόνταρχος[2], ἔπαρχος, μόναρχος, πεντηκόνταρχος, ὕπαρχος (1 Es. vi. 26 B), χιλίαρχος. On the other hand LXX writes the following more newly-coined words with -άρχης : γενεσιάρχης, ἐθνάρχης, ἐλεφαντάρχης, Κυπριάρχης (governor of Cyprus 2 M. xii. 2), κωμάρχης, μεριδάρχης, πατριάρχης[3], τοπάρχης. In the following old words both forms occur : ἱππάρχαι[4] 2 K. i. 6 B, ἵππαρχοι A : φύλαρχος Dt. xxxi. 28, 1 Es. viii. 58, 92, but φυλάρχης 2 M. viii. 32.

The N.T. shows an advance upon the LXX in one word : ἑκατόνταρχος of LXX appears in N.T. with few exceptions as ἑκατοντάρχης : χιλίαρχος is however still universal. Ἑκατοντάρχης is also the predominant form in Josephus and δεκαδάρχης is universal in his *Jewish War* : χιλίαρχος is still the usual form, but there is some slight MS evidence even for χιλίαρχης[5].

26. The following words show the converse change— transition from the first to the second declension. Ἀμφίταπος 2 K. xvii. 28, Prov. vii. 16 replaces ἀμφιτάπης (Comedians of iv/B.C. ap. LS). Ἔνεδρον has supplanted the classical ἐνέδρα, which occurs only in Jos. viii. 7, 9 (beside ἔνεδρον 6 times in the same chap.) and Ψ ix. 29, in all three passages with the meaning "place of ambush," whereas ἔνεδρον in Joshua (and

---

[1] Mayser 256 f., where the literature is quoted. Cf. Moulton *CR* xv. 34. 434, xviii. 108 for the post-Ptolemaic papyri. It is noticeable that all specially Egyptian titles end in -άρχης : Θηβάρχης, Λιβυάρχης, νομάρχης (so Hdt.).

[2] Excepting 4 K. xi. 10 B, 15 B -άρχαις (ib. 9 Bᵇ -άρχαι).

[3] Πατρίαρχον Is. xxxvii. 38 Q is an incorrect reading for the adj. πάτραρχον "ancestral" (sc. θεόν).

[4] So in the papyri from iii/B.C.: the B text is therefore right.

[5] W. Schmidt *De Jos. eloc.* 485 ff.

usually in LXX) means the ambuscading party. Ἦχος (ὁ or τὸ, 29 *inf.*) has entirely replaced Attic ἠχή.

Μανδράγορος[1] for μανδραγόρας has good authority in Gen. xxx. 15 (-όρους AD cursives: -όρας E): the older form is kept in Cant. vii. 13 -γόραι Bא (for A see 27 below). Ἕσπερος for ἑσπέρα, a v.l. of A in Jos. v. 10 (ἀφ᾽ ἑσπέρου: ἀπὸ [ἀφ᾽] ἑσπέρας BF), is poetical. Ἁμάξοις Is. xxv. 10 א*vid and πύλοις 1 M. xiii. 33 V may be clerical errors (the latter receives doubtful support from Hom. *Il.* v. 397). Τὸ βασίλειον in addition to its old meaning "palace" (Hdt.) takes on that of "crown" (2 K. i. 10, 2 Ch. xxiii. 11, W. v. 16) and "royal dominion" and so in some late portions of LXX becomes identical with ἡ βασιλεία "kingdom" (which is frequent elsewhere in LXX): Hexaplaric additions (from Aquila apparently) in 3 K. iv. 19 A, xiv. 8 A, 4 K. xv. 19 A: 1 Es. iv. 40, 43: Dan. O iv. 30 c etc. (in vii. 22 = τὴν βασιλείαν Θ): 2 M. ii. 17 (and perhaps in W. i. 14 οὔτε ᾅδου βασ. ἐπὶ γῆς, R.V. "royal dominion," mg. "a royal house": in 1 Ch. xxviii. 4 γένος should be supplied). Both forms πλευρά and πλευρόν are classical, and both are used in LXX, the former slightly more often than the latter: there is diversity of reading in 2 K. xiii. 34, πλευρᾶς B (-ρου A), Dan. Θ vii. 5 τρεῖς πλευραὶ B = τρία πλευρά A (Dan. O ib. πλευροῦ), 4 M. vi. 6 τὰ πλευρά Aא* (τὰ πλευράς *sic* אc.a): in Ez. xli. 5 f. the two forms are found in conjunction. There is also diversity of reading in 2 M. vii. 1 νευραῖς A (-ροις V) "cords": both forms are classical.

27. *Fluctuation between Declensions I and III.*

Τὸ νῖκος[2] supplants ἡ νίκη universally in the later versions (α'σ'θ') and largely in the LXX: the latter is now restricted to 'literary' writings (1 Es., Prov., 1—4 M. with 1 Ch. xxix. 11), but νῖκος has even invaded books of that type (2 M. x. 38, 4 M. xvii. 12). Ἡ δίψα and τὸ δίψος (both classical) are used interchangeably even in the same context[3]. Βλάβη W. xi. 19 (βλάβος, also classical, is not found).

Ἀκάν (4 K. xiv. 9 τὸν ἄκανα B, τὴν ἄκανα[ν] A) supplants in

---

[1] So in Test. XII. Patr. Is. i. 3, ii. 2, 4.
[2] In a papyrus of 56 B.C.: νίκη in ii/ and i/B.C. (Mayser 93).
[3] W. xi. 4 δίψης, 8 δίψους: Am. viii. 11 δίψαν, 13 δίψει.

this LXX passage and elsewhere in a'σ'θ' the classical ἡ ἄκανθα (still common in LXX)[1].

The following variants are of interest. Δόξεως Is. lxvi. 11 א gen. as from δόξις (= δόξα) is attested elsewhere[2]. Μανδράγορες Cant. vii. 13 A (-αι cett.) and φιάλες ib. v. 13 A (-αι cett.) anticipate modern Greek, which uses these plurals in all words of the old 1st declension (καρδιές, θάλασσες etc.). The same MS has the datives πύλει, πύλεσιν in K. γδ (3 K. xxii. 10, 4 K. vii. 18), as if from a nom. τὸ πύλος (cf. πύλοις 26 *supra*).

28. *Fluctuation between Declensions II and III.* Interchange of nouns in -ος masc. (Decl. II) and in -ος neut. (Decl. III) began in classical times. The general tendency in κοινή Greek is in the direction of the neuter third declension forms, as will be seen from the following table:

Classical Greek.	LXX.		N.T.[3]
	masc.	neut.	
ὁ ἔλεος	ὁ ἔλ. sporadically (literary)[4]	τὸ ἔλεος usually	τὸ ἔλεος always
ὁ ζῆλος	ὁ ζῆλ. usually	τὸ ζῆλ. rarely[5]	τὸ and ὁ ζ.
ὁ and τὸ θάμβος	θάμβοι Eccl. xii. 5	gen. θάμβους Cant. iii. 8 (W. x. 19 א)	τὸ θ. (Acts iii. 10 gen. -βους)

---

[1] Ὁ ἄκανος occurs in Theophrastus and Symmachus.

[2] LS cite " Democrit. ap. Sext. Emp." The form, we may conjecture, comes from the later writer.

[3] WH (ed. 2) App. 165.

[4] The literary translator of Prov. uses the masc. only (iii. 16ᵃ, xiv. 22 *bis*), as does the writer of 4 M. in his single use of the word (ix. 4). The following sporadic exx. occur: Ψ v. 8 τοῦ ἐλέου σου BA, which might be a case of dropping one σ out of two (§ 9, 1), but it is noticeable that Ψ, which has upwards of 100 exx. of the neut., has only one other of the masc., viz. lxxxiii. 12 ἔλεον, i.e. the masc. is written *on the first appearance of the word in either part of the Greek book* (p. 68 f.): Job x. 12 A, Tob. viii. 17 א (ib. ἔλεος neut.), W. vi. 6 A, Sir. li. 3 B* : Hos. xii. 6, Mic. vi. 8 B, vii. 20 B : Is. lx. 10 BאQ, lxiii. 7 (ib. τὸ ἐλ.), lxiv. 4 : Jer. xlv. 26 B ῥίπτειν τὸν ἐλ., a phrase imitated in Dan. Θ ix. 20, Bar. ii. 19, in which the noun = "a pitiful supplication": Dan. Θ i. 9, 1 M. iii. 44 A, 2 M. vi. 16, viii. 5, 3 M. iv. 4 τὸν κοινὸν ἔλ. "the general misery."

[5] Τὸ ζ. W. v. 17 א : gen. ζήλους Zeph. i. 18 BאA, iii. 8 B*Q, 1 M. ii. 58 א, and in interpolations from Θ in Ez. viii. 3 Q, 5 A.

Classical Greek.	LXX.		N.T.
	masc.	neut.	
ὁ (and τό: Aristotle πάγεσι) πάγος "frost"	πάγοι Dan. O iii. 69	τὸ π. Na. iii. 17 gen. πάγους BℵQ (-ου A): Job Θ xxxvii. 10 acc. πάγος	unused (τὸν Ἄρειον πάγον)
ὁ πλοῦτος	ὁ πλοῦτος usually	τὸ πλ. Is. xxix. 2 ℵΑΓ (ὁ BQ)	ὁ and (8 times in Paul) τὸ πλ.
ὁ (and rarely ' τό) σκότος	—	τὸ σκότος always	τὸ σκ. always

The following isolated exx. occur.

Τὸ γνόφος gen. -ους Est. A 7 A (γνόφου Bℵ and masc. elsewhere in LXX as in N.T., Heb. xii. 18): ὁ δνόφος was the class. (poetical) form, ὁ γνόφος begins with Aristotle.

Τὸ ῥύπος Is. iv. 4 Γ (masc. in the other MSS and elsewhere in LXX and N.T.: the plur. ῥύπα is Homeric).

χιρογc stands for χειρός in Jer. xli. 3 ℵ.

29. In the following a classical first declension word in -ή has passed over first to the second declension and then to the third:

Classical Greek.	LXX.		N.T.
	M. and F.	N.	
⎧ ἡ ἠχή ⎨ ὁ ἦχος (from ⎩ Aristot.)	ὁ ἦχ. usually	τὸ ἦχ.[1] occasionally	ὁ Heb. xii. 19 (ἤχῳ) τὸ Lc. xxi. 25 (ἤχους : WH ἠχοῦς)
⎧ ἡ ταραχή ⎨ ὁ τάραχος ⎩ (Xen.)	ἡ τ. frequent ὁ τ. Jd. xi. 35 B, 1 K. v. 9, Est. A 7	τὸ τ. Job Θ xxiv. 17 BℵC, Is. xxii. 5 ℵ (gen. -χους)	ἡ. τ. 'Jo.' v. 4 ὁ τ. twice (Acts)

30. Examples of the reverse change (gen. -ου for -ους) are confined to readings of single MSS: βάθου Sir. li. 5 B*, ἔθνου

[1] In Jer. xxviii. 16 ἦχος appears to be accusative. It is probable therefore that the gen. ηχους should be accented ἤχους, not as the classical ἠχοῦς from ἠχώ, in Ψ ix. 7, xli. 5 ART (ηχου Bℵ), lxxvi. 18, Sir. xlvii. 9.

Prov. xxviii. 15 A, τεμένου 2 M. i. 15 A (before initial σ), ὕψου Ψ ci. 20 א: so τῖχον Jer. i. 18 A (as acc. of τεῖχος).

31. Transition from Declension II to Declension III in the κοινή occurs also in some contracted words in -οῦς which are now declined like βοῦς. So even in the Atticizing writer of 4 Macc. νοῦς has gen. νοός[1]. Χοῦς " earth " (probably originally second declension)[2] similarly has gen. χοός Eccl. iii. 20, dat. χοΐ 2 K. xvi. 13 B (χοει A) and is therefore indistinguishable from χοῦς (or χοεύς) the liquid measure (third declension in Attic).

An accus. τὸν ἴκτερα occurs in L. xxvi. 16 B (ἴκτερον AF: class. ὁ ἴκτερος). The dat. δένδρ(ε)ι Dt. xxii. 6 B*A has Attic authority (elsewhere in LXX -ου -ῳ).

Transition from Declension III to II in dat. plur. is illustrated by the variants ἐλεφάντοις 1 M. i. 17 V, τεσσάροις Ez. i. 10 A (but τέσσαρσι in same verse)[3].

§ 11. Proper Names.

1. In the translated books we find a medley of transliterated (indeclinable) *personal names* and names which are, partly at least, Hellenized and declined. The general distinction made is that names which in the Hebrew end in a consonant remain unaltered (Ἀδάμ, Ἀβραάμ, Δαυείδ, Ἰσραήλ, Ἰωσήφ etc.), while those which end in a vowel, especially in ה‎ׇ, are in most cases declined like nouns of the first declension, the feminines requiring no addition in the nominative, the masculines taking on the termination -ίας and being declined like Νικίας. Names ending in other vowels are either Hellenized by the addition of s and form a new class of first declension names in -ᾶς, -ῆς, -οῦς etc. (Ἰωνᾶς, Μωυσῆς, Ἰησοῦς etc.) or remain indeclinable (Ἡλειού).

---

[1] i. 35. So N.T. νοός νοΐ, πλοός. Elsewhere LXX has no exx. of gen. or dat. of νοῦς and there are none of πλοῦς: 3 M. iv. 10 has the Attic κατάπλῳ.   [2] K.-Bl. I. i. 498.

[3] Ῥινόν Job xl. 20 C is not another form of ῥῖνα BאA (from ῥίς) but a different word, "hide."

2. Names declined according to Declension II (in -ος)[1] or Declension III (-ης, -ους : -ών, -ῶνος etc.) are almost unrepresented in the translations. Literary writers like Josephus and the paraphrastic writer of 1 Esdras[2], on the other hand, employ these freely, carrying out the Hellenization in all cases (Ἄβραμος, Δαβίδης etc.). In N.T. times a few of these Hellenized forms have permeated into the popular language (Σολομών -μῶνος).

3. Feminines declined like Declension I are e.g. Ἄννα, Βάλλα[3], Γοθολία[4], Δείνα[5], Ἐλιβέμα ('Ολ.)[6], Ζέλφα, Ζωσάρα or Σωσ. (Haman's wife Zeresh), Κασ(σ)ία Job xlii. 14, Λεία, Ὀλδα, Ὀολα (Ὄλλα), Ὀόλιβα (Ὄλ.), Ῥεβέκκα, Σαρου(ε)ία[7], Σάρ(ρ)α, Σουσάννα, Χεττούρα. The genitive and dative, wherever attested, are in -ας, -ᾳ, whether the α of the nom. be pure or impure, the only exception being Σουσάννης Dan. ☉ Sus. 27 f. B (the other uncials -ας and so Dan. O Sus. 30 : cf. § 10, 4).

4. A large number of Hebrew masculine proper names end with the Divine name Yahweh in a more or less abbreviated form, usually יָה (also יָהוּ, יְ, יָ). These are in the majority of cases Hellenized by the adoption of the old termination -ίας (as in Νικίας), and forms in -(ε)ίας, -αίας declined according to the first declension abound. The genitive termination of these names is commonly -ου, as in Attic and in the Ptolemaic papyri[8],

---

[1] Ἀγγαῖος: Νεεμιος 2 Es. ii. 2 B seems to be a slip for -ίας.

[2] He shows much ingenuity in dealing with the long lists of names, which in the other version (2 Esdras) are baldly reproduced, and even some sense of humour, when he renders "Rehum the Chancellor" by Ῥάθυμος ὁ (γράφων) τὰ προσπίπτοντα (ii. 16, 21), "Slack the Secretary."

[3] 1 Ch. vii. 13 A (υἱοὶ) Βαλλα may be indecl. (Βαλλά) or gen. as from Βάλλας.

[4] But τὴν Γοθολιά 2 Ch. xxiii. 21 B (-αν A).

[5] Τὴν Δεινά Gen. xxxiv. 26 A (-αν D^vid E): ih. xxx. 21 read Δείνα not Δεινά (Swete), the nom. being usual after verbs of naming.

[6] Indecl. in Gen. xxxvi. 2 AD (-βαιμαν E with O.L.), 18 E. Ib. xxxvi. 41, 1 Ch. i. 52 Ἐλ(ε)ιβαμας may be nom. masc. (-ᾶς Swete) or gen. fem.

[7] In 1 K. xxvi. 6 B, 2—3 K. and 1 Ch. xviii. 12 BA. But indecl. Σαρουιά (=gen.) 1 K. xxvi. 6 A, 2 K. ii. 13 A, 18 B, and in 1 Ch. *passim* (B text).

[8] Mayser 250 f.

not the 'Doric' -*a* : so always (or with a rare v.l.) e.g. 'Aναviov, 'Eζεκίου, Zαχαρίου, 'Hσαίου, 'Iερεμίου, 'Iεχονίου, Mαασ(σ)αίου, Σελεμίου, Σοφονίου, Xελκίου. The use of the gen. in -*a* appears to be vulgar and late. The following examples are certain : Mειχαίας gen. -*a* Jd. B text (xvii. 8 ff.), 2 Ch. xxxiv. 20 (-*ου* 4 K. xxii. 12), Nεεμίας -*a* 2 Es. (but -*ου* in 1 Es. Sir. 2 M.), Tωβ(ε)ίας -*a* Tob. i. 20 א, vii. 7 א, xi. 17 א, 19 BA (-*ου* i. 20 A, ix. 5 א). There is also strong attestation for the gen. 'Iωσεία (throughout Jeremiah, i. 2 etc., 4 K. xxiii. 23 B, 2 Ch. xxxv. 16, 19, 26). Jeremiah also occasionally has Σεδεκία (i. 3 BאA, xlvi. 1 B, 2 Bא, lii. 11 א) in place of the usual -*κίου*: add further Jdth xiv. 6 'Oζεία BA.

> 5. Much difficulty, however, presents itself, especially in the long lists and genealogies in Chron. and 2 Es., in determining whether a form in -*ια* represents a Doric gen. (therefore -*ία*) or a mere transliteration (therefore -*ιά*). These lists exhibit a strange mixture of declined names in -*ιας* and indeclinables, nom. -*ιά*. The practice of the books with regard to nom. and acc. (e.g. Nεεμίας -*αν*) can alone determine the accent in the case of the gen. (Nεεμία). Possibly the lists in the original version were omitted or were much shorter, and they have subsequently been supplemented from another source in which the names were undeclined: we often find two or three declined names at the beginning followed by a string of indeclinables. Take for instance 2 Es. xviii. 4 (the brackets indicate the possibly later additions): καὶ ἔστη "Eσρας...καὶ ἔστησεν ἐχόμενα αὐτοῦ Mατταθίας καὶ Σαμαίας [καὶ 'Aνανιὰ καὶ Oὐρειὰ καὶ 'Eλκειὰ καὶ Mαασσαιὰ] ἐκ δεξιῶν αὐτοῦ, καὶ ἐξ ἀριστερῶν Φαδαίας καὶ Mεισαὴλ καὶ Mελχείας καὶ Zαχαρίας or vii. 1 "Eσρας υἱὸς Σαραίου υἱοῦ Zαρείου [υἱοῦ 'Eλκειὰ κ.τ.λ.].
>
> The longer Heb. forms in יהו are in some names kept in the Greek as indeclinables in -(ε)ιού. Elijah in the historical books is 'Hλ(ε)ιού: the N.T. form 'Hλ(ε)ίας only in Mal. iv. 4 and in apocryphal books (Sir., 1 M.). Obadiah appears as 'Aβδειού or 'Oβδειού·

6. The declension of Hebrew masc. proper names ending in a vowel sound other than יה follows what Blass (N.T. § 10, 3) calls the '*mixed declension*.' In this the pure stem stands unaltered in three cases (G. D. V.), while in the nom. it has s

appended to it, in the acc. *v.* The nominatives end in -αs (-âς), -ῆς, -(ε)ίς, -οῦς.

This declension has nothing exactly answering to it in the papyri, where the proper names are usually of the third declension (-âς -âτος: -ῆς -ῆτος: -οῦς -οῦτος etc.: Mayser 273 ff.). A desire to adhere as closely as possible to the Hebrew names and also perhaps to avoid the familiar forms of common life in rendering Scripture may account for this new departure.

(1) In -αs (âς). Ἰούδας -δαν -δα -δᾳ is the constant declension for patriarch, tribe and country. Occasionally the name remains indeclinable, Ἰουδά being used for nom. and acc.[1] The gen. Ἰούδου is confined to 1 and 2 Maccabees, and there to Judas Maccabeus[2], while Ἰούδα is used of the tribe and country (ἄρχοντες, γῇ Ἰούδα etc.). Ἔσδρας and Ἰωνᾶς similarly have acc. -αν (-âν), other cases -α. Σατανᾶς (שָׂטָן) is found in the acc. Σατανᾶν Job ii. 3 A, Sir. xxi. 27 (elsewhere Σατάν or διάβολος). Other words are found only in the nom., e.g. Εἰρᾶς (Εἴρας), Ἐλιωνᾶς, Ὠνᾶς.

(2) In -ῆς. Μωυσῆς[3] in LXX is with few exceptions declined according to the 'mixed' declension: -ῆν, -ῆ, -ῆ, voc. ῆ. In the first century A.D., on the other hand, both literary writers

---

[1] So in its first appearance, where the original Hebrew form seemed more appropriate: Gen. xxix. 35 ἐκάλεσεν τὸ ὄνομα αὐτοῦ Ἰουδά (=nom., cf. iii. 20 ἐκάλεσεν...τὸ ὄν....Ζωή). Otherwise rare, except in 2 Ch., 2 Es., Jer. (mainly β), which have πᾶς Ἰουδά, πάντα τὸν Ἰουδά etc. fairly frequently of the tribe. Once only in a 'Greek' book does Ἰουδά (? Ἰούδα) stand for acc., 2 M. xiv. 13 (N. and A. -ας -αν in the same chapter).

[2] 1 M. iv. 13 (ΙΟΥΛΟΥ A), 19 (do.), v. 61 A, ix. 12 A, 22 AV etc., 2 M. xii. 21 AV etc. The unusual gen. naturally puzzled the scribes and -δα is a constant variant.

[3] This is clearly the older orthography: Μωσῆς, which is nearer to the Heb. מֹשֶׁה, has quite inferior support. Though the Egyptian etymology given by Philo (*Vit. Mos.* 1. 4) and Josephus (*Ant.* 11. 9, 6, *c. Ap.* 1. 31), viz. μῶυ=ὕδωρ, ἐσῆς=σωθείς, is now abandoned by Coptic scholars, at least it attests the antiquity of the form with υ. Whatever the origin of the name, there can be little doubt that the diphthong ωυ is an attempt to reproduce the Egyptian pronunciation, being found in the Greek rendering of Egyptian proper names and months such as Θωῦθ, Σαμῶυς (Mayser 138). The υ disappeared later: Θωῦθ (Θωῦτ) was written in the earlier Ptolemaic age, Θώθ (Θώτ) under the Roman Empire (ib. 185).

(Philo and Josephus) and the vernacular writers of the N.T. used the third declension forms for gen. and dat., Μωυσέως, Μωυσεῖ, keeping -ῆν in the acc.[1] In LXX the gen. Μω(υ)σέως is confined to a few passages, several occurring in a group of books which we have reason to believe are of late date[2]. The dat. Μωυσεῖ is more frequent, but this is really a mere matter of orthography : the gen. Μωυσέως appears to have grown (on the analogy of βασιλέως -λεῖ) out of Μωυσεῖ, which originally was only another way of spelling Μωυσῇ (§ 6, 21).

Like Μωυσῆς are declined Πετρεφῆς (Πετεφρῆς), Potiphar, gen. -η, dat. -η, and Μανασσῆς gen. -η when used of King Manasseh, Judith's husband and other individuals (Tob. xiv. 10, 1 Es. ix. 33 A) : on the other hand Μανασσή indecl. is used of the tribe[3] and its progenitor.

(3) In -(ε)ις. Λεύ(ε)ις = לוי Gen. xxxiv. 25 E, xxxv. 23 AE, 1 Es. ix. 14, acc. -ειν 4 M. ii. 19 AℵV : elsewhere indecl. Λευ(ε)ί. Τώβεις -ειν in Cod. ℵ, 2 Es. xiv. 3 (= Τωβίας cett.) and in Tob. x. 8, xi. 10 (= -βείτ BA), 18, xii. 4 : once in B as an indeclinable[4], 1 Es. v. 28. Χάβρεις -ειν and Χάρμεις[5] -ειν Jdth vi. 15, viii. 10, x. 6. Χανάν(ε)ις -ειν N. xxi. 1 BF, 3 BF, xxxiii. 40 BAF = כנעני an inhabitant of Canaan (usually Χαναναῖος, also Χαναρείτης 3 K. iv. 32 B and Χαναν(ε)ί N. xxi. 3 A, 2 Es. ix. 1)[6].

(4) In -ους. Ἰησοῦς (Joshua) has, like Ἰησοῦς (Χριστός)

---

[1] Lc. once even has acc. Μωυσέα (xvi. 29) : elsewhere in N.T. always Μωυσῆν -έως -εῖ (-ῆ Acts vii. 44).

[2] In Pent. only Ex. iv. 6 A (BF αὐτοῦ with Heb.) : Jd. i. 16 B (but -σῆ iii. 4 BA, iv. 11 BA), 3 K. ii. 3 BA, 4 K. xxiii. 25 A, 2 Es. iii. 2 A, Dan. Θ ix. 11 B (but -σῆ 13) : in the literary 1 Esdras v. 48 BA, vii. 6 BA, 9 BA, viii. 3 BA, ix. 39 B : in other apocryphal books Sir. xlvi. 7 BℵAC (but -σῆ 1), Tob. vi. 13 ℵ, vii. 11 ℵ, 12 BAℵ, 13 ℵ : and two or three times as a v.l. in late MSS (T, V, Γ).

[3] Μανασσῆς Jd. i. 27 A, Ψ cvii. 9 ART.

[4] The same section of 1 Es. has indecl. Ἀννείς, v. 16 B.

[5] Also indecl. Jer. xxvi. 2 ἐν Χαρμείς (= Carchemish). In Hexateuch and 1 Chr. indecl. Χαρμεί.

[6] In τὸν Ῥαβσαρείς 4 K. xviii. 17 A, Ναβουσαρείς Jer. xlvi. 3 the final ς comes from the Heb. and the words are indeclinable.

in N.T., acc. -οῦν gen. -οῦ, but differs from the N.T. name in the dative, which throughout Dt. and Jos. is consistently written Ἰησοῖ[1], the N.T. form Ἰησοῦ appearing as an occasional variant. In the other books the dat. only occurs in three passages and there in the N.T. form Ἰησοῦ : Ex. xvii. 9 B*AF (but Bᵇ -σοῖ), 1 Ch. xxiv. 11 BA, 1 Es. v. 65 BA. Ἰησοῖ even stands in three passages for the genitive ; Ex. xvii. 14 B, 2 Es. ii. 36 B, xxii. 7 BA.

In the papyri, on the other hand, as Dr Moulton informs me, we find a gen. Ἰησοῦτος BM iii. p. 25 (105 A.D.) : cf. OP 816. Ἐλιοῦς -οῦν in Job. Other names are only represented in the nom., e.g. Σαμμοῦς, Ἐλεισοῦς, Θηησοῦς, 2 K. v. 14 ff. Φαλλού N. xxvi. 5 AF (= dat.) 8 (= gen.) is probably correctly accented as an indeclinable : the nom. Φαλλοῦς, however, occurs elsewhere.

7. Names in -ών, the termination being taken over from the Hebrew[2], are as a rule indeclinable in LXX : Ἀαρών, Σαμψών etc.

To one of these—the name Solomon—a special interest attaches. The process of Hellenization gradually affected both the first two vowels and the declension. As in the case of Moses, the LXX and the N.T. represent earlier and later stages respectively. The steps in the evolution, speaking generally, appear to have been in the following chronological order : as regards orthography Σαλωμών—Σαλομών—Σολομών[3] :

---

[1] On the analogy of datives of feminine names in -ώ, which in the papyri were declined (e.g.) Δημώ -οῦν -οῦς -οῖ (Mayser 268). A more frequent type, applicable also to masculine names, was (e.g.) Πατοῦς -οῦν -οῦτος -οῦτι (ib. 274 f.). The acc. -οῦν, which is common to both types and to the Biblical name, facilitated mixture of types in the other cases. Ἰησοῦς (= gen.) 1 Es. v. 8 A (cf. 2 Ch. xxxi. 15 B) may be another instance of transition to the -ώ type.

[2] The ν is sometimes appended to a final ο in the Hebrew.

[3] Σαλωμών represents most nearly the Heb. שְׁלֹמֹה of the M.T., except for the final ν, which is the first step towards Hellenization. The long vowel in the middle unaccented syllable could not long maintain its place, hence the transitional form Σαλομών arose: lastly, the short vowels flanking the liquid were assimilated, as they often are in this position (or with intervening μ) where a long syllable follows: cf. ἐξολοθρεύειν (p. 88), Σομόηλος (= Σαμουήλ) Aristeas § 47.

as regards declension (1) indeclinable: (2) -ῶντα, -ῶντος;
(3) -ῶνα, -ῶνος.

(1) Σαλωμών indeclinable is the normal form throughout
the LXX (including the literary 1 Esdras)[1]

(2) Σαλωμῶν -ῶντα -ῶντος (like Ξενοφῶν and the Greek
equivalents of Egyptian names in the papyri, e.g. Πετεχῶν)[2]
appears in Proverbs (probably translated not earlier than i/B.C.)[3]
i. 1 Bℵ, xxv. 1 B : also in 3 K. i. 10 A, 4 M. xviii. 16 ℵ.

The same form of declension with o in the second syllable
is found in ℵ (Prov. xxv. 1 and subscription, Wis. title and
subscr.) and in 4 M. loc. cit. A.

Σολομῶντος occurs in 2 K. viii. 7 BA (in what is clearly a
Greek gloss : the passage is absent from the M.T.)[4] and as a
v.l. of A (C) in the passages from Prov. and Wis. cited.

(3) The declension Σολομών -ῶνα -ῶνος is that found in
N.T.[5], Josephus and later writers[6]. In LXX the nom. Σολομών
is read by A in 3 K. ii. 12, 2 Ch. vii. 1, 5 ; by ℵ(A) in Sir.
xlvii. 13, 23: the cases have even slenderer support, Wis[subscr] A,
4 M. xviii. 16 V, with Σαλωμῶνος Wis[subscr] B, Σαλομῶνα Ψ
lxxi.[tit] R.

8. Names of *places* and *peoples*, like those of individuals,
appear either as indeclinable transliterations or as Hellenized
and declinable. Here, however, the Hellenized forms largely
predominate. The translators, for the most part, had a fair
knowledge of the geography, not only of Egypt, but also of
other countries, and adopted the current Hellenized forms[7].

---

[1] And so in the headings to each of the Psalms of Solomon (the Greek
dates from the end of i/B.C.) Ψαλμὸς τῷ Σαλωμών (Σαλομών). The declined
form Σολομῶντος (-μῶνος) appears in the inscription and subscription to the
whole work.

[2] Mayser 275 f.

[3] See p. 61.

[4] The gloss comes from 2 Ch. xii. 9 (where the usual Σαλωμών is written).
There are two similar glosses from 2 Ch. in the next verse in 2 K. LXX.

[5] Always (WH) except Acts iii. 11, v. 12 Σολομῶντος.

[6] For Cyprian see C. H. Turner in *J. T. S.* ix. 86 f.

[7] E.g. Αἰθιοπία (Cush), Ἀντιλίβανος (Dt. i. 7, iii. 25, xi. 24, Jos. i. 4,

Sometimes we meet with a name in both forms, e.g. Ἐδώμ—Ἰδουμαία, Συχέμ—Σίκιμα: cf. Φυλιστιείμ—ἀλλόφυλοι (Φιλιστιαῖοι).

Rarely, apart from the later historical books, do we find places of importance like Damascus or Tyre transliterated. Τὴν Δαμάσεκ 3 K. xi. 14 B (passage not in M.T. or A). Σόρ (for Τύρος) in Jer. a (xxi. 13) and Ez. a (xxvi. 2 etc.): but Τύρος in Ez. β (xxviii. 2 etc.). Σηδαμείν, Σωρείν 2 Es. iii. 7 B: cf. ib. ix. 1 ὁ Μοσερεί = ὁ Αἰγύπτιος. Σομορών, Σεμερών etc. (for the more usual Σαμαρ(ε)ία) 3 K. xvi. 24, 2 Es. iv. 10, xiv. 2, Is. vii. 9 *bis*. Χερμέλ (τὸ and ὁ) Is. xxix. 17 *bis*, xxxii. 15 *bis*, xxxiii. 9 B (but Κάρμηλος ib. xxxii. 16, xxxiii. 9 אAQ, xxxv. 2 as elsewhere in LXX). Cf. τὸ Κεχάρ 2 K. xviii. 23 (= the Jordan valley, elsewhere ἡ περίχωρος τοῦ Ἰορδάνου as in N.T.).

9. Many place-names end in -α and are declined like *feminines* of Declension I: e.g. Γάζα -αν, -ης, -η: Σαμαρεία -αν, -ας, -ᾳ: Παθούρης (Φαθωρῆς) gen., Παθ(ο)ύρῃ dat. (§ 10, 2) = Pathros or Upper Egypt (nom. wanting, but cf. Φαθούρα = Pethor, N. xxii. 5): Χαρρά = Haran Ez. xxvii. 23 BQ, Χαρρᾶς gen. Gen. xxix. 4 E (usually indecl. Χαρράν).

10. Names of *towns* as a rule end in -α and are declined like *neuters* of Declension II, with occasional transition (metaplasmus) to Declension I, especially where the nom. ends in -(ρ)ρα. The article stands in the fem. (sc. πόλις). Thus:

τὴν Ἄδιδα -δοις[1]	τὴν Βεθσούρα (or -ούραν), G. -σού-
(Ἀρβηλα) -οις[2]	ρων[3], D. -οις (or -ᾳ)
τὴν Βαίθαρρα N. xxxii. 36 A	Βόσορρα[4], G. -ας
(-ά(ρ)ραν BF)	

ix. 1: elsewhere Λίβανος), Ἰόππη, Καππαδοκία (Caphthor), Καρχηδών -δόνιοι (Χαρκ., = Taishish Is. xxiii. 1 etc., Ez. xxvii. 12, xxxviii. 13: elsewhere Θαρσ(ε)ίς, Μεσοποταμία and Συρία (Aram etc.), Ῥόδιοι (Dodanim). The translators are of course thoroughly familiar with Egyptian geography. The identification of "the brook of Egypt" as Rhinocorura (Is. xxvii. 12) may be mentioned, and the introduction of tribes living by the Red Sea, Troglodytes and Minaeans, into Chronicles LXX, which, with other indications of Egyptian colouring, somewhat discredits the theory that the version of that book is the work of Theodotion.

[1] 1 M. xii. 38 (not Ἀδιδά, Swete), xiii. 13 (Ἀδείνοις א, Ἀδίμοις V).
[2] 1 M. ix. 2.
[3] 2 M. xi. 5 συνεγγίσας Βεθσούρων (not -ρῶν, Swete): for the gen. after ἐγγίζειν cf. 1 M. xi. 4, xiii. 23 and for the form 1 M. vi. 49, xiv. 7.
[4] 1 M. v. 26 V (εἰς Βοσσορά Swete as indecl.). Probably it is neut. plur.

Γάζαρα Acc. -αρα (or -άραν) -ων -οις[1]
Γάλγαλα -α -ων -οις[2]
Γέραρα -α -ων -οις
Γόμορρα -α -ας[3]
Γόρτυνα Acc.[4]
Ἐκβάτανα -α -ων -οις
Ζόγορα (Zoar) Acc.[5]
Ἱεροσόλυμα -α -ων -οις (below)
Μέρρα[6] Acc. (or -αν), G. -ας
(Ῥάγα)[7] -ων -οις, also (as from

Ῥάγη -αι) Acc. plur. -ας Tob. ix. 2 א, 5 א, Dat. -η ib. vi. 10 BA
(Ῥινοκορούρα) -ων Is. xxvii. 12
Σάρεπτα -ων Ob. 20
Σίκιμα -α -ων -οις[8]
Σόδομα -α -ων[9] -οις
(Σοῦσα) -οις Est. i. 2 etc.: in the same book Acc. Σοῦσαν (which might also be indecl. as in 2 Es. xi. 1 ἐν Σουσάν)

11.   The following names in -α are *indeclinable*: Βαιτ(ο)υλουά (Jdth : Βαιτούλια א ii. 21, iv. 6), Λουζά (Swete Λοῦζα), Λομνά Λοβνά Λοβενά etc. = Libnah (but Λόβναν, Λόμναν Is. xxxvii. 8 Bא), Ῥαμά (another transliteration Ἀρμαθάιμ in 1 K.), Σαββά (βασίλισσα Σ. etc.)[10], and the mountains Σ(ε)ινά, Φασγά.

Names in -ή are usually indeclinable, the termination of acc. or gen. being sometimes appended: Μαμβρή (but G. xiii. 18 τὴν δρῦν τὴν Μαμβρήν AE), Νινευή (but acc. -ήν Jon. iii. 2 א, Zeph. ii. 13 א, gen. -ῆς Jon. iii. 6 א), Ῥαμεσσή (but gen. -σῶν N. xxxiii. 3 ABᵃ, -σῆς 5 Bᵃᵇ).

Ἱερουσαλήμ is consistently written in the translations and in several of the apocryphal books (1 Esdras, Sirach, Esther, Judith, Baruch, and as a rule 1 Macc.).   The Hellenized form Ἱεροσόλυμα (as from ἱερός, Σόλυμοι) is limited to 2—4 Macc. and (beside Ἱερ) Tobit and 1 Macc.

---

like Γόμορρα. The gen. in Gen. xxxvi. 33, 1 Ch. i. 44.   The indeclinable form used elsewhere is Βοσόρ.
[1] Also indecl. Γαζηρά 2 K. v. 25 or Γάζερ.
[2] Also indecl. τῆς Γαλγαλά 1 K. x. 8 A or Γαλγάλ.
[3] So always in conjunction with Σοδόμων: Γομόρρων only Gen. xviii. 20 D, λαὸς Γομόρα (-ρά) Jer. xxiii. 14 א.
[4] 1 M. xv. 23 אV (Γόρτυναν A).
[5] Probably neut. plur.: also indecl. Ζόγορ and Σήγωρ.
[6] Probably neut. plur. (not Μερρά, Swete): Ex. xv. 23 εἰς Μέρρα B (εἰς Μέρραν AF).   Indecl. τῆς Μερράν Bar. iii. 23.
[7] Nom. not found: this is more probable than Ῥάγοι (Redpath).
[8] Also indecl. Συχέμ, frequent in Jd. (B text).
[9] I find no instance of gen. Σοδόμης cited by Redpath.
[10] But acc. τὸν Σάβαν Gen. xxv. 3 AD (personal name).

12. Place-names in -ων are declined or indeclinable mainly according to their rank and situation on or away from the main routes. This accounts for the declension of Ἀσκάλων -ωνα etc. (on the coast and on or close to a main trade-route), while Ekron which lay off the route appears as indeclinable Ἀκκαρών[1]. Two other names are declined: ἡ Βαβυλών -ῶνα -ῶνος -ῶνι[2] and similarly Σ(ε)ιδών (voc. -ών Is. xxiii. 4, Ez. xxviii. 22)[3]. The gentilic Μακεδών is regularly declined -όνα etc.: Μακεδών Μαγεδαών etc. (elsewhere Μαγεδ(δ)ώ) representing Megiddo are indeclinable. To the indeclinables belong further Ἀερμών (Ἑρμών: Mount H.), Ἀμμών, Ἀρνών, Γαβαών (Gibeon)[4], Κεδρών[5] (the brook Kidron), Κ(ε)ισών (ὁ of the brook, ἡ of the city), ὁ Σαρών, Σ(ε)ιών, Χεβρών.

13. The following towns end in -ις (-ιδα -ιδος): Πτολεμαΐς (1—3 M.: acc. -αΐδαν 1 M. x. 1 A, § 10, 12), Φασηλίς -ιδα 1 M. xv. 23 אV (Βασιλεῖδαν A). The river Τίγρις (Τίγρης Dan. O x. 4) has acc. Τίγριν, gen. Τιγρίδος (Tob. vi. 2 א). Compounds of πόλις are declined like the noun: Διοσπόλει (Ez. β), Πενταπόλεως (W. x. 6), Περσέπολ(ε)ιν (2 M. ix. 2 A: Περσιπ. V), Τρίπολιν (2 M. xiv. 1). Similarly Egyptian place-names in -ις: Μέμφις -ιν -εως -(ε)ι, Σάις -ιν (Ez. β), Τάνις -ιν -εως -(ε)ι.

14. Names of *countries* or *districts*, when not simply trans-literated, are expressed by *adjectival forms* (sc. χώρα). These in the case of countries outside Palestine end in (1) -ίς -ίδος:— ἡ Ἐλυμαΐς, Dan. O viii. 2, Tob. ii. 10 (Ἐλλ. B), 1 M. vi. 1[6]: ἡ

---

[1] In Jos. xv. 11 A εἰς Ἀκκαρωνά the final vowel represents the Heb. הָ of direction: the name is indeclinable in the same verse (B and A texts).

[2] Βαβυλόνα -όνος Jer. xlvii. 7 א, [lii. 12 אd], Ez. xxiii. 17 B. Acc. Βαβυλῶναν Jer. xxviii. 9 א (§ 10, 12). Gen. Βαβυλως (corruption of -ῶνος) 2 Es. v. 17 B*.

[3] Σ(ε)ιδόνα Jer. xxix. 4 B, Ez. xxvii. 8 A.

[4] 1 Ch. xxi. 29 ἐν Γαβαῶνι A.

[5] It was natural that it should come to be regarded as gen. plur. of κέδρος, hence ἐν τῷ χειμάρρῳ τῶν κέδρων, 2 K. xv. 23 BA (the words are absent from M.T. and are doubtless a gloss): ib. τὸν χειμάρρουν Κεδρών B (A again writes τῶν κ.). The same Hellenization appears in N.T., John xviii. 1 (see Lightfoot *Biblical Essays* 173 f.).

[6] Read (cf. Josephus *A. J.* XII. 9. 1) ἤκουσεν ὅτι ἐστὶν Ἐλυμαῒς ἐν τῇ

Καρίς -ίδα, 1 M. xv. 23 A (τὴν Καρίαν אV): ἡ Περσίς (so already in Hdt.); (2) -(ε)ία:—(ἡ) Βαβυλωνία (1 Es. and Dan. O, Is. xi. 11, xiv. 23, xxxix. 1, Jer. xxviii. 24 A, 2 M. viii. 20, 3 M. vi. 6 A), Μηδ(ε)ία(apocr. books), Σειδωνία 3 K. xvii. 8; (3) -ική:—ἡ Ἰνδική. The transliterated names of the districts of or on the borders of Palestine (Ἐδώμ, Μωάβ etc.) begin to be replaced by adjectives either in (4) -αία or (5) -(ε)ῖτις, forms which appear to have come into use c. 200 B.C.[1]; (4) Ἡ Γαλ(ε)ιλαία, Ἰδουμαία (beside Ἐδώμ), Ἰουδαία (beside γῆ Ἰούδα); (5) (beside Ἀμμών, Γαλαάδ etc.) ἡ Ἀμμανῖτις (2 M. iv. 26, v. 7), Αὐραν(ε)ῖτις (Ez. a: with v.ll. Ὠραν. Λωραν.), Αὐσ(ε)ῖτις (= Uz, Job), Βασαν(ε)ῖτις (Jos., Ez. a and Minor Proph.), Γαλααδ(ε)ῖτις (in the same group: also Jd. x. 8 A, 1 K. xxxi. 11, 2 K. ii. 4, 5, 9, 1 Ch. xxvi. 31, 2 Ch. xviii. 2 f, 1 M.), Θαιμαν(ε)ῖτις (= Teman: Job), Μωαβ(ε)ῖτις (Is., Jer. xxxi. 33, xxxii. 7), Σαμαρ(ε)ῖτις (1 M.)[2], Χανα(α)ν(ε)ῖτις (Zech. xi. 7), to which must be added the curious Μαβδαρ(ε)ῖτις (Μαδβ.) = מדבר "the desert" (Jos. v. 5, xviii. 12)[3]. The cases are -ίτιδος -ίτιδι -ῖτιν (only once acc. -ίτιδα, Jos. xiii. 11 B Γαλααδείτιδα).

15. *Mountains* also are expressed adjectivally in two cases: τὸ Ἰταβύριον[4] (= Tabor) Hos. v. 1, Jer. xxvi. 18 (elsewhere

Πέρσιδι πόλις (A ἐν Ἐλύμαις, אV ἐν Λύμαις): the description of Elymais as a city is of course incorrect and accounts for the reading of A. Elsewhere in LXX Αἰλάμ (Ἐλάμ) or (in 2 Es. and 1 Es. v. 12 A) Ἠλάμ.

[1] They are absent from the Pentateuch, but perhaps from a feeling of the anachronism of using them of the patriarchal age. Isaiah has Ἰουδαία, Ἰδουμαία. The translators of Joshua, Ez. a and Minor Prophets are partial to them. The literal School (Jd, K βδ) avoids them.

[2] Elsewhere Σαμαρ(ε)ία as in N.T. of district as well as city.

[3] Βαλλαργεις Jos. xv. 6⊦ is also probably a corruption of Μαλ-Βαρειτις. The historian Eupolemus (c. 150 B.C.) ap. Eus. *P. E.* ix. 449 is an early extra-Biblical authority for these forms in -ῖτις: the extent of Solomon's kingdom is described in a letter of the monarch as τὴν Γαλιλαίαν καὶ Σαμαρεῖτιν καὶ Μωαβῖτιν καὶ Ἀμμανῖτιν καὶ Γαλαδῖτιν. Aristeas § 107 refers to τὴν Σαμαρεῖτιν λεγομένην. In Polyb. v. 71 τὴν Γαλᾶτιν appears from the context to stand for τὴν Γαλααδῖτιν. Josephus supplies us further with Γαυλανῖτις (or Γαυλων.: Golan), Ἐσεβωνῖτις (Σεβ., Heshbon), Τραχωνῖτις (also in N.T.).

[4] So in Josephus τὸ Ἰταβύριον ὄρος: Ἀταβύριον in Polyb. v. 70. 6. The

Θαβώρ): (τὸ) ὄρος τὸ Καρμήλιον, 3 K. xviii. 19 f. (contrast 42 τὸν Κάρμηλον as elsewhere in LXX), 4 K. ii. 25, iv. 25.

16. *Gentilic names*—of tribes and inhabitants of towns or districts—in Hebrew end in -ī and in LXX are either transliterated (rarely and mainly in the later historical books)[1] or (more often) Hellenized, usually with the termination -αῖος or -(ε)ίτης. Thus a Canaanite appears as (1) Χαναν(ε)ί 2 Es. ix. 1, N. xxi. 3 A; (2) Χανανείς[2] N. xxi. 1, 3, xxxiii. 40; (3) Χαναneίτης 3 K. iv. 32 B; (4) elsewhere always Χαναναῖος.

It is difficult to determine what principle governed the choice of -αῖος or -ίτης. Generally speaking, the former denotes a member of a tribe or clan ('Εβραῖος, 'Αμορραῖος etc.), the latter the inhabitant of a town (Βηθλεεμίτης etc.). But the distinction is by no means universal. Γαζαῖος and Γεθθαῖος denote inhabitants of cities (like 'Αθηναῖος, Θηβαῖος): 'Αμμανίτης, Γαλααδίτης, 'Ισμαηλίτης, 'Ισραηλίτης, Μωαβίτης are tribal names. The tendency in the later books seems to be to form all new gentilic names in -ίτης, fem. -ῖτις (-ιν -ιδος -ιδι), because these terminations corresponded most nearly to those of the Hebrew (-ī -īth). In English this termination has been given a still wider range : it is not from the LXX that we get e.g. the names Hittite (Χετταῖος) and Amorite. Sometimes we find alternative forms in -αῖος and -(ε)ίτης such as Μαδιηναῖος, Μαδιαν(ε)ίτης : one of Job's comforters is called Βάλδαδ ὁ Σαυχίτης in the body of the work (viii. 1 etc.) but B. ὁ Σαυχαίων τύραννος in the proem and conclusion (ii. 11, xlii. 17 e). In 2 K. xxiii. 25 ff. the interposition of a series of names in -(ε)ίτης between others in -αῖος (contrast 25 'Αρωδαῖος A with 33 'Αρωδείτης) points to an interpolated text.

Other terminations are (1) -ιος : 'Αζώτιος, 'Αράδιος, 'Ασσύριος, Σύριος, Σιδώνιος ; (2) -ηνός : Γαζαρηνός 1 M. xv. 28 A, 35 A (cf. Τασβαρηνός 2 Es. i. 8 B); (3) -εύς plur. -εῖς, in the Greek books 'Αλεξανδρεύς and Ταρσεῖς, in the translations Κιτιεῖς (Is. xxiii. 12, 1 M. viii. 5 : elsewhere Κίτιοι Κιτιαῖοι or transliterated) and 'Αμαζονεῖς, 'Αλειμαζονεῖς, 2 Ch. xiv. 15, xxii. 1.

latter was also the name of heights in Rhodes and at Agrigentum, where there were temples to Ζεὺς 'Αταβύριος (art. Tabor, *Enc. Bibl.*), the name having been carried westward by Semitic colonists. The origin of the Hebrew name and of the prothetic vowel in its Greek dress is uncertain : we may perhaps compare Τουραίων B 'Ιτουραίων A 1 Ch. v. 19.

[1] Contrast the names of the aboriginal inhabitants of Palestine in 2 Es. ix. 1 (τῷ Χανανεί, ὁ 'Εθεί, ὁ Φερεσθεί κ.τ.λ.) with the forms in -αῖος used elsewhere.

[2] Cf. ὁ "Αμορις Gen. xiv. 13.

§ 12. ADJECTIVES.

1. **Declension.** *Adjectives in* -ος, -η (-α), -ον *and* -ος, -ον. On the whole the LXX follows classical precedent in the use of two or three terminations for adjectives in -ος. The movement towards the uniformity of modern Greek, in which every adjective has a special feminine form (ἄδικη, ἥσυχη etc.), has hardly begun.

Two exx. of compound words with fem. termination occur in Numbers: ἀθῴα N. v. 19 BAF, 28 BAF (-ῷος ℵ*): ἀτειχίσταις xiii. 20 B* (-οις Bᵃᵇ AF, so Prov. xxv. 28).

The direction in which the language is moving may be indicated by the fact that several adjectives which in Attic fluctuate between 2 and 3 terminations in LXX are only found with 3: such are e.g. ἄγριος, βέβαιος, δίκαιος, ἐλεύθερος, ἐνιαύσιος (except N. vii. 88 F ἀμνάδες ἐνιαύσιοι), μάταιος, ὅμοιος (except Ez. xxxi. 8 A *semel* ἐλάται ὅμοιοι), ὅσιος. Similarly ἕτοιμος always has fem. ἑτοίμη except in Jdth ix. 6 BℵA.

Other words in -ιος fluctuate as in Attic. Such are αἰώνιος[1], ἀνόσιος (-α 3 M. v. 8, but -ος W. xii. 4), παραθαλάσσιος, παράλιος, ὑποχείριος (-ίαν Jos. vi. 2 B: else fem. -ος, as usually in Attic).

Attic fluctuates also in the declension of words in -λος -μος -ρος. Under this head we may note the following (the only passages in which the fem. is used): θυγατέρα λοιμήν, 1 K. i. 16 (the adjectival use "pestilent" is new), φρονίμη Sir. xxii. 4, χρησίμης Tob. iv. 18.

On the other hand ἡ ἔρημος is used to the exclusion of ἡ ἐρήμη: similarly οὐράνιος -ος. Noticeable also is 4 K. iii. 18 B κοῦφος καὶ αὕτη (κούφη A) and σῶοι (with σφραγῖδες) Bel Θ 17 *bis* (A once corrects to Attic σῷαι).

2. The *contracted* adjectives in -οῦς are usual in LXX as in Attic: ἀργυροῦς, χρυσοῦς, σιδηροῦς, χαλκοῦς, ἐρεᾶ Ez. xliv. 17, φοινικοῦν Is. 1. 18: ἁπλοῦς, διπλοῦς etc. The following *uncon-*

---

[1] Usually 2 term. as also in Attic and N.T.: fem. -ία L. xxv. 34, N. xxv. 13, Hb. iii. 6 BℵQ, Jer. xxxviii. 3 A, xxxix. 40 B, Ez. xxxv. 5 [9 Bᵃ], xxxvii. 26 [contrast xvi. 60], 1 M. ii. 54 ℵV, 57 A.

tracted forms occur: in Sir. χρύσεος vi. 30 BℵAC, χρύσεοι xxvi. 18 Bℵ (ib. ἀργυρᾶς): so χρύσαιοι (= -εοι) 2 Es. viii. 27 A, and as a proper name Καταχρύσεα Dt. i. 1 (κατάχρυσος is the usual form of this late word): ℵ* has σιδηρέας 4 M. ix. 26, σιδηραίαις ib. 28.

Ἀθρόος (3 M. v. 14 -όους) is the usual Attic form.

The Epic form χάλκε(ι)ος occurs in Job (vi. 12 BℵC, xl. 13 BℵC, xli. 6 B, 19 Bℵ) and elsewhere: Jd. xvi. 21 B, 1 Es. i. 38 BA, Sir. xxviii. 20 B (χάλκεοι ℵA, χαλκοῖ C). Cf. σιδηρίῳ Job xix. 24 ℵ (= -είῳ).

Want of contraction in word-formation is seen in the poetical ἀεργός used in Prov. xiii. 4, xv. 19, xix. 12 (elsewhere Att. ἀργός).

3. The *Attic declension* in -ως is, as was stated (§ 10, 9), disappearing. Of the few adjectives of this class found in LXX two are on the way to becoming indeclinables. Ἵλεως alone is used with any frequency, and, except for one book, only in the nom., in the phrases ἵλεώς μοι "God forbid," ἵλεως γενέσθαι etc.: in 2 Macc. ἵλεως is used also for the acc.—vii. 37 A (ἵλεων V), x. 26 AV* (-ων Swete)—and for the gen., ii. 22 A ἵλεως γενομένου (ἵλεω V)[1]. Similarly ἐσχατογήρως stands for the gen. in Sir. xlii. 8 B ἐσχατογήρως κρινομένου (-γήρους ℵ, -γήρῳ -μένῳ AC), where the text of B is supported by a contemporary papyrus, ἐσχατογήρως ὄντος TP i. 7. 29 (117 B.C.)[2]: the dat., however, is regular, ἐσχατογήρῳ Sir. xli. 2. Ὑποχρέως appears in 1 K. xxii. 2 B (nom.) with dat. ὑπόχρεῳ Is. l. 1: the nom. of καταχρέῳ W. i. 4 is unattested.

Κάθιδρος is read by the uncials in Jer. viii. 6 (LS cite καθίδρως -ωτος from Basil).

4. Πᾶς. There are a number of instances in the LXX where πᾶν appears to be used for πάντα (acc. sing.). A solitary

---

[1] So ἀνίλεως = nom. plur. neut. in Test. XII. Patr. Gad v. 11 ἔκειτο τὰ ἥπατά μου ἀνίλεως κατὰ τοῦ Ἰωσήφ.
[2] Mayser 294. Perhaps influenced by γῆρας gen. γήρως.

example of this use of πᾶν in the papyri[1] rescues it from the suspicion of being a 'Biblical' usage. Assimilation of the masc. to the neuter form of the accusative is not surprising in the κοινή: the analogy of μέγαν and the preference for accusatives in ν (such as νύκταν, εὐγενῆν) might be responsible for the vulgarism.

On the other hand, the context of the first passage in the LXX and other considerations throw some doubt on the equation πᾶν = πάντα and suggest that in some of the passages at least we have to do with a *syntactical* colloquialism rather than a vulgarism of *accidence.*

The idiomatic use of the neuter of persons in the common LXX phrases πᾶν ἀρσενικόν, πᾶν πρωτότοκον etc. allows us, though with hesitation, to explain πᾶν as a true neuter in the following phrases containing an adjective or participle: ἐπάταξαν ..ὡσεὶ δέκα χιλιάδας ἀνδρῶν, πᾶν λιπαρὸν καὶ πάντα ἄνδρα δυνάμεως Jd. iii. 29 B: πᾶν δυνατὸν ἰσχύι 4 K. xv. 20 BA: πᾶν δυνατὸν καὶ πολεμιστήν κ.τ.λ., 2 Ch. xxxii. 21: perhaps also πᾶν προσπορευόμενον, τοῦτον...ἔνταξον 2 Es. vii. 17 BA: πᾶν ἔνδοξον Is. xxiii. 9 BℵAΓ (of persons): πᾶν περικειρόμενον τὰ κατὰ πρόσωπον αὐτοῦ Jer. ix. 26 ℵAQ with πᾶν περικεκαρμένον κ.τ.λ. ib. xxxii. 9 BA.

It is less easy to explain on this principle πᾶν followed by the accusative of a masc. *substantive.* Yet, in the earliest occurrence of this, the participle and the relative clause following show that πᾶν is regarded as a true neuter: Ἰδοὺ δέδωκα ὑμῖν πᾶν χόρτον σπόριμον σπεῖρον σπέρμα ὅ ἐστιν ἐπάνω πάσης τῆς γῆς Gen. i. 29. (In the next verse the uncials have πάντα χόρτον: in ii. 5 E again has πᾶν χόρτον, perhaps influenced by πᾶν χλωρόν ib.)

---

[1] Πᾶν τὸν τόπον in a Paris papyrus of 163 B.C. (37. 11: Mayser 199) differs from the LXX exx. in the presence of the article. The Paris collection was edited half a century ago (1858) and one cannot be quite so sure of the accuracy of the editors as in more recent editions.

It seems possible therefore in the remaining passages to explain πᾶν as a neuter in apposition with the masc. substantive, a sort of extension of πᾶν ἀρσενικόν etc. (πᾶν οἰκέτην e.g. = πᾶν οἰκετικόν), though it is simpler on the whole to regard it in all these passages as = πάντα. It is to be observed that the article is never present and that the meaning is usually "every": the recurrence of certain phrases is also noticeable.

Πᾶν οἰκέτην, Ex. xii. 44 B*.
Πᾶν ὃν ἐὰν εἴπω...αὐτὸς οὐ πορεύσεται Jd. vii. 4 B.
Πᾶν λόγον R. iv. 7 B (τὸν λ. A): so 1 Ch. xxvii. 1 BA, 1 B, 2 Ch. xix. 11 *bis* BA.
Πᾶν ἄνδρα 1 K. xi. 8 B.
Πᾶν πόνον[1] 3 K. viii. 37 B, and so in the parallel 2 Ch. vi. 28 BA and Sir. xxxviii. 7 A(C)[2].
Πᾶν βουνόν 3 K. xv. 22 BA[3], Jer. ii. 20 BאQ, Ez.[4] xx. 28 BªAQ, xxxiv. 6 BQ.
Πᾶν υἱὸν δυνάμεως 3 K. xxi. 15 B.
Πᾶν τέκτονα 4 K. xxiv. 14 BA.
Πᾶν οἶκον "every house," ib. xxv. 9 B. Πᾶν οἶκον Ἰσραήλ Ez. xxxvi. 10 BAQ, Jdth iv. 15 BA: πᾶν οἶκον Ἰούδα Jer. xiii. 11 Bא.
Πᾶν δὲ ὑβριστήν Job xl. 6 Bא.
"Ez. β" further supplies πᾶν λίθον xxviii. 13 BQ, πᾶν φόβον xxxviii. 21 BA.
Dan. Θ has πᾶν ὁρισμὸν καὶ στάσιν vi. 15 BA and πᾶν θεόν xi. 37 B (πάντα AQ and so BAQ in 36).
Cf. πᾶν ἄνδρα ὅσιον, πᾶν σοφὸν ἐν βουλῇ Ps. Sol. iii. 10 r, viii. 23 r.
The converse use of πάντα for πᾶν appears once in א, πάντα τεῖχος Is. ii. 15 (under the influence of the 2 exx. of πάντα preceding).
In Bel Θ 2 πας B* must be a mere slip for πάντας. For πάντες = πάντας see § 10. 15.

5. *Adjectives in -ης and -υς.* Examples of the *accusative in*

---

[1] Πᾶν συνάντημα, πᾶν πόνον, πᾶσαν προσευχήν shows the vernacular accusative πᾶν—πᾶσαν—πᾶν.
[2] Here τὸν πόνον Bא appears from the Heb., which has no לֹ, to be right.
[3] But πάντα βουνόν ib. xiv. 23.
[4] This use of πᾶν appears clearly to go back to the translator or an early scribe of "Ezekiel β" (πάντα acc. sing. only in xxxvii. 21, xxxix. 20 in all uncials): Ez. α, on the other hand, writes πάντα ἄνεμον etc. v. 12, vi. 13, xiii. 18, xvi. 15, xvii. 21 and we should therefore read πάντα βουνόν in xx. 28 with B*.

-ῆν *for* -ῇ in adjectives in -ής are, like those of νύκταν etc. (§ 10, 12), with two exceptions, absent from the B text. We have ὑγιῆν Lev. xiii. 15 B*Aᵃ: ἀσεβῆν Ψ ix. 23 A, x. 5 A, Prov. xxiv. 15 ℵ, Job xxxii. 3 A, Sir. xxi. 27 A, Is. v. 23 ℵ [xi. 4 ℵᶜ·ᵃ]: εὐσεβῆν Sir. xiii. 17 Bℵ: μονογενῆν Ψ xxi. 21 AR, xxxiv. 17 ℵᶜ·ᵃ AR, Bar. iv. 16 A : πολυτελῆν Prov. i. 13 ℵ: ἐπιφανῆν Jl. ii. 31 ℵ: ψυδῆν Zech. viii. 17 ℵ [ἀναιδῆν Jer. viii. 5 ℵᶜ·ᵇ].

The acc. of ὑγιής is ὑγιῆ(ν) L. xiii. 15, Tob. xii. 3, not the Attic ὑγιᾶ.

6. **Πλήρης.** A mass of evidence has recently been collected demonstrating beyond a doubt that this adjective was at one time treated as an indeclinable[1]. The LXX contributes its share, but the evidence is not as a rule so strong as to warrant our attributing the form to the autographs : in most cases it is certainly due to later scribes. Indeclinable πλήρης is common in the papyri from i/A.D. onwards, but only one instance B.C. has yet been found[2].

We have seen in the case of the Attic declension in -ως (3 *supra*) that forms on the way to extinction become indeclinable before finally disappearing. The old adjectives in -ής have disappeared from the modern language[3], and this might account for *all* adjectives in -ης becoming indeclinable, but such is not the case. Why is this adjective alone affected?

Nestle has quoted an apt parallel in the indeclinable use of German *voller* in the phrase "eine Arbeit voller Fehler": but it is precarious to explain the Greek use by an idiom, however similar, in a modern language. The explanation is perhaps partly to be found in the tendency to assimilate the vowels flanking ρ or the nasals. At a time when η, ει and ε had come to be pronounced alike, there would be a tendency

[1] C. H. Turner in *J.T.S.* i. 120 ff., 561 f.: Blass N.T. 81: Moulton *CR* xv. 35, 435, xviii. 109: Crönert 179 : Reinhold 53.
[2] Μαρσείπειον πλήρης (= πλῆρες) Leiden Pap. C. p. 118 col. 2, 14 (160 B.C.).
[3] Thumb *Handbuch* 49.

to write πλήρης for πλῆρες and for πλήρεις as well as for the nominative. Subsequently this form would also replace πλήρη and πλήρους.

The LXX instances (only once without v.ll.) are as follows.
Πλήρης =(a) acc. sing. (πλήρη): L. ii. 2 B, N. vii. 20 Bℵ*, 62 BA, xxiv. 13 A.

(b) nom. and acc. neut. sing. (πλῆρες): Ex. xvi. 33 B, 4 K. vi. 17 A, Is. xxx. 27 ℵ, Ψ lxxiv. 9 Rℵ^{c.a}, Sir. xlii. 16 Bℵ.

(c) gen. sing. (πλήρους) Gen. xxvii. 27 ὡς ὀσμὴ ἀγροῦ πλήρης DE cursives (-ρους AM cursives)[1].

(d) nom. acc. plur. (πλήρεις) Gen. xli. 24 D, N. vii. 86 BF, Is. i. 15 Γ, li. 20 B, Jer. v. 27 ℵQ, Job xxxix. 2 B, W. v. 22 ℵ, xi. 18 ℵ, 3 M. vi. 31 V*.

(e) neut. plur. (πλήρη) N. vii. 13 F, 19 ℵ, 79 B, Ψ cxliii. 13 R^{vid}, Job xxi. 24 τὰ δὲ ἔγκατα αὐτοῦ πλήρης στέατος BℵAC with the parallel in Sir. xix. 26 τὰ δὲ ἐντὸς αὐτοῦ πλήρης δόλου B*Cℵ^{c.a} (A -ρεις : -ρη ℵ*B^b).

It will be seen that in the last two passages alone is there really strong authority for the indeclinable form and in Job πλήρης might partly be accounted for by the initial σ of the next word (cf. Mark iv. 28 πλήρης σῖτον with WH. App.). Several examples occur in Numbers, but it should be noted that in chap. vii which has 6 exx. of indeclinable πλ., there are 19 exx. without v.l. in the uncials of the declined forms.

Conversely, πλήρη = πλήρης Ez. xliii. 5 B*. The following are merely itacisms, which illustrate the tendency referred to above : πλήρεις = πλήρης (nom. sing.) 1 Ch. xxix. 28 A, Job vii. 4 B, Ψ xlvii. 11 B: πλῆρες = πλήρης Job xlii. 17 A : πλήρη — πλήρει 4 K. xx. 3 B.

7. **Εὐθής—εὐθύς.** In this word we find in the LXX a strange mixture of forms : the fem. of the old εὐθύς εὐθεῖα εὐθύ is retained, while the masc. and neuter in the singular are supplied by the new forms **εὐθής** -ές (like ἀληθής) and in the plural we meet with forms as from a nominative **εὐθεῖος** (like ἀνδρεῖος). The whole declension, so far as represented, runs as follows : the new forms are in thick type.

---

[1] And possibly in Is. lxiii. 3 (ὡς ἀπὸ πατητοῦ ληνοῦ) πλήρης καταπεπατημένης BAQ*: πλήρους is read by ℵQ^{mg}, and the Latin Fathers took πλ. as agreeing with ληνοῦ (see Ottley *in loc.*). It seems however preferable to take πλήρης as nom. beginning a fresh sentence, with ellipse of εἰμί.

Singular	M.	F.	N.
N.	εὐθής[1]	{εὐθής[2] / εὐθεῖα[3]	{εὐθές (-ής)[4] / εὐθύ[5]
A.	εὐθῆ (-ῆν)[6]	εὐθεῖαν	εὐθές
G.	εὐθοῦς[7]	εὐθείας	—
D.	—	εὐθείᾳ	—
Plural			
N.	εὐθεῖς	εὐθεῖαι	εὐθεῖα[8]
A.	εὐθεῖς	εὐθείας	{εὐθεῖα[8] / (εὐθέα)
G.	εὐθ(ε)ίων[9]		—
D.	εὐθέσι(ν)	εὐθείαις	—

We cannot speak of two distinct words and say that the old εὐθύς forms, so far as preserved, are used in the literal sense and the new forms in the metaphorical sense of "straight," "upright," because the fem. forms -εῖα etc. are used in both senses. The fact is that the masc. and neut. sing. εὐθύς and εὐθύ together with εὐθέως (now indistinguishable from gen. εὐθέος) had become stereotyped as adverbs and it was felt that a new nom. for the adjective was required, and the analogy of ἀληθής plur. ἀληθεῖς suggested εὐθής as the proper singular for the old plural εὐθεῖς.

The new forms -ής -ῆ(ν) -οῦς have not yet been found in the papyri, and it is tempting, but would be hazardous, to conjecture that they were an invention of the later translators[10] to render the Hebrew יָשָׁר.

[1] 1 K. xxix. 6 etc. Εὐθύς only as a v.l. of A in Ψ xxiv. 8 (met. sense). In Ez. xxiii. 40 it is an adverb, incorrectly classified as an adj. in Hatch-Redpath.

[2] Ψ cxviii. 137 (ἡ κρίσις), Prov. xxvii. 21 a (καρδία).

[3] Jd. xiv. 3 B (ἐν ὀφθαλμοῖς μου of a woman "well-pleasing"), 4 K. x. 15 and Ψ lxxvii. 37 (καρδία), Prov. xx. 14 etc. (ἡ ὁδός).

[4] Εὐθής 2 K. xix. 6 A, else εὐθές passim.

[5] Only in the phrase κατ᾽ εὐθύ 3 K. xxi. 23, 25, Ez. xlvi. 9.

[6] 4 K. x. 3 (-ῆν A), Jdth x. 16 A, Eccl. vii. 30.

[7] 2 K. i. 18 βιβλίου τοῦ εὐθοῦς (the Book of the Upright or, neuter, of Uprightness).

[8] Ψ xviii. 9 (-έα B^b), lvii. 1, 2 Es. xix. 13 ℵA (-έα B), Dan. Θ xi. 17.

[9] Ψ cx. 1 εὐθίων ℵAT, cxi. 2 -ίων ℵT -είων A, Prov. xi. 3 A and 11 A -είων (probably Hexaplaric).

[10] They are absent from the Hexateuch (where יָשָׁר is rendered by ἀρεστός, δίκαιος and καλός) and not found in N.T.

In the plural, analogy again exercised its influence in
another direction, probably first in the gen. plur., where the
old distinction between εὐθέων—εὐθειῶν—εὐθέων could not long
survive, and the fem. forms suggested masc. and neut. forms
as from εὐθεῖος.

8.   The intrusion of -ος forms into the neuter plural occurs
in other adjectives in -ύς in LXX: βαρ(ε)ῖα 3 M. vi. 5 V
(βαρέα A, and so Sir. xxix. 28): γλυκ(ε)ῖα Ψ cxviii. 103 ARTℵ^{c.a}
(γλυκέα ℵ*), Prov. xxvii. 7 ℵAC (γλυκέα B): ὀξ(ε)ῖα Is. v. 28 all
uncials. (Βαθέα, on the other hand, is undisputed in Dan. OΘ
ii. 22.)   In N.T. cf. τὰ ἡμισ(ε)ῖα Lc. xix. 8.

In modern Greek the -ος forms have encroached still further
and monopolized all cases of the plural and the gen. sing.[1]
Codex A has one instance of gen. sing. in -ου viz. βαθέου Sir.
xxii. 7 (βαθέος cett.), a variant which, although doubtless not the
original reading, is interesting in this connexion.

9.   The genitive singular of these adjectives in -ύς, though
it has not yet gone over to the -ος class, has, however, in the
vernacular begun to undergo a slight change, by taking over
the long ω of the adverb: βαρέως 3 K. xii. 4 BA (but βαρέος
2 Ch. x. 4 BA): δασέως Dt. xii. 2 AF (-έος B), 2 Es. xviii.
15 ℵA^a (-έος BA*), Sir. xiv. 18 ℵA (-έος BC), Hb. iii. 3 ℵAQ*
(-έος B).

In the literary 4 M. γλυκέος is undisputed (viii. 23) and
βαθέος is no doubt the true reading in Sir. xxii. 7.

10.   Ἥμισυς has lost the fem. forms in -εῖα altogether and
adopted the κοινή contracted gen. sing. ἡμίσους (Att. ἡμίσεος)[2].
A word containing three vowels which came to be pronounced
alike was specially liable to confusion and many of the peculiar
LXX forms are due to mere 'itacism' (the equivalence of *i* and
u sounds): but there are clear indications that ἥμισυ is be-

[1] See M. Gr. declension of βαθύς, Thumb *Handbuch* 47.
[2] Mayser 294 f., Moulton *CR* xv. 35^a. The papyri show one form not
found in LXX, neut. pl. ἡμίση.

coming an indeclinable which may stand for all cases: ἥμισυς
indecl. = gen. sing. seems also to deserve recognition. The
LXX declension is as follows·

Singular	M. F.		N.
N. A.	—		ἥμισυ[1]
G.	(τοῦ and τῆς[2])	ἡμίσους	
		ἥμισυς[3]	
		ἡμίσεις[4]	
		ἥμισυ[5]	
		ἡμίσει[6]	
D.	(τῷ and τῇ[7])	ἡμίσει	
		ἥμισυ[8]	

Plural			
N.	(οἱ) ἡμίσεις		(τὰ) ἥμισυ[10]
	(οἱ) (ἡ)μίσει[9]		
A.	(τοὺς and τὰς[11]) ἡμίσεις		
D.	(τοῖς) ἡμίσεσιν[12]		
	(τοῖς) ἡμίσει[13]		

11. The heterogeneous Attic πρᾶος πραεῖα πρᾶον has been
reduced to uniformity by the employment throughout of the
forms from -ύς (as in poetry): πραύς, πραύν[14], dat. sg. πραείᾳ

[1] Also written ἥμισον 3 K. iii. 25 B*, Is. xliv. 16 B*, and -σει Jos.
xxii. 1 B*, 10 A, 11 B*A, 13 A, 21 A.
[2] 3 K. xvi. 9 τῆς ἡμίσους τῆς ἵππου.
[3] Ex. xxvii. 5 B*A ἕως (τοῦ) ἥμισυς, xxx. 15 A ἀπὸ τοῦ ἥμισυς, xxxviii.
1 A *bis*, N. xxxi. 30 B*, 1 Ch. vi. 71 A.
[4] Jos. xxi. 5 A, 1 Ch. xxvi. 32 BA (ἡμίσους Swete).
[5] Ex. xxx. 15 B ἀπὸ τοῦ ἥμισυ, Dan. Θ vii. 25 ἕως καιροῦ καὶ καιρῶν καὶ
γε ἥμισυ καιροῦ.
[6] Jos. xxi. 6 A.
[7] 1 Ch. xxvii. 21 B τῇ ἡμίσει φυλῆς.
[8] N. xxxii. 33 BAF τῷ ἥμισυ φυλῆς, xxxiv. 13 F, Dt. iii. 13 B, xxix.
8 A, Jos. xii. 6 F, Dan. Θ ix. 27 BA, ib. A.
[9] Jos. ix. 6 F* οἱ μισει apparently = οἱ ἥμισυ (cf. M. Gr. 'μισυ μισός).
The more idiomatic οἱ ἦσαν ἥμισυ of B is no doubt right.
[10] Tob. x. 10 BA? (τὸ ἥμ. A*vid).
[11] Ez. xvi. 51, 1 M. iii. 34, 37.
[12] Jos. xiii. 31.
[13] Jos. xxii. 7 A (= τοῖς ἥμισυ). In the same verse A has τοῖς ἡμίσιν
(sic) which may represent τ. ἡμίσεσιν or τ. ἡμίσι (= ἥμισυ) with ν
ἐφελκυστικόν. B has τῷ ἡμίσει in both places.
[14] Πρᾶον 2 M. xv. 12 A (πραύν V).

(Dan. O iv. 16) and plur. πραεῖς, πραεῖς, πραέων[1] occur. At the same time πραΰτης has superseded πραότης (cf. § 6, 32).

12. Πολύς, otherwise regular, has neuter πολύν in Cod. A in a few passages: 4 K. xxi. 16 (αἷμα πολύν), 1 M. iii. 31, 41, iv. 23 (with ἀργύριον, χρυσίον)—the converse of the exchange by which πᾶν replaces πάντα.

We may note the transition from the -ης to the -ος class in ὁμόεθνος 2 M. xv. 31 A (Polyb., Jos.): elsewhere (2 and 3 M.) ὁμοεθνής ἀλλοεθνής. The form περίσσιος for περισσός (classified as 'Neo-hellenic' i.e. after 600 A.D. by Jannaris § 1073) is read by א in 1 M. ix. 22.

13. Comparison.

The use of the degrees of comparison of the adjective in the LXX is affected by two influences, which will be further considered under the head of Syntax. (i) The fact that the Hebrew adjective undergoes no change of form in comparison partly accounts for some restriction in the use of both degrees in the translations. The positive may be used either for the comparative (e.g. ἀγαθὸς ὑπὲρ αὐτόν 1 K. ix. 2) or for the superlative (e.g. ἔτι ὁ μικρός, ib. xvi. 11 "there remains the youngest [of several brothers]")[2]. (ii) The use of the superlative is still further restricted by the tendency of the later language to make one of the two degrees, usually the comparative, do duty for both (e.g. ὁ νεώτερος Gen. xlii. 13 ff. = the youngest of twelve brothers)[3]. The superlative from about the beginning of our era tends to be used solely with *elative* or intensive sense = "very[4]," while "more" and "most" are both expressed by the comparative.

In the papyri of the early Empire true superlatives are quite rare, but superlatives used in elative sense as complimentary

---

[1] Πραέσι Sir. iii. 18 אc.a.
[2] But this use of ὁ μικρός is idiomatic, as Dr Moulton points out, occurring frequently in papyrus letters: it has an affectionate tone.
[3] Blass N.T. § 11, 3.
[4] As in modern Greek, Thumb *Handbuch* 50.

epithets for governors etc., like Ital. *-issimo*, abound : the most frequent are μέγιστος, κράτιστος, λαμπρότατος, ἱερώτατος.

14. In LXX superlatives in **-τατος** are not so rare as in N.T., where Blass finds only two instances, but they occur for the most part in the literary books (Wis., 2—4 Macc., Prov., Est.) and often in elative sense.

The following exx. have been noted in the less literary books. Genesis has several true superlatives: φρονιμώτατος (πάντων) iii. 1, ἐνδοξότατος (πάντων) xxxiv. 19, νεώτατος xlix. 22 (for the more usual νεώτερος). In Jd. xi. 35 A ἐμπεποδεστάτη (!) καὶ σεμνοτάτη the text is a curious perversion of ἐμπεποδεστάτηκας ἐμέ (see Field's Hex.). Ὑψηλοτάτη (καὶ μεγάλη) 3 K. iii. 4 (elative). Ὁ μικρότατος 2 Ch. xxi. 17 (true superlative: usually ὁ μικρός in this sense, as ib. xxii. 1).

In the literary books forms in -έστατος are common: Wis. alone has ἀδρανέστατος xiii. 19, ἀληθέστατος vi. 17, ἀπηνέστατος xvii. 19, ἀτελέστατος iv. 5 A, ἀφρονέστατος xv. 14 BA: Prov. has e.g. ἀφρονέστατος ix. 16, x. 18, xxiv. 25, ἐπιφανέστατα xxv. 14. 4 M. (and to some extent 2 M.) is fond of using comp. and superl. of compound words, e.g. περιεκτικώτατος, πολυτροπώτερος (-τατος), φιλοτεκνώτερος, ἀνοητότερον. Job (vi. 15. xix. 14) has οἱ ἐγγύτατοί μου, for which the other books write (οἱ) ἔγγιστά μου, e.g. Ψ xxxvii. 12 : both are classical.

15. The termination -αίτερος does not occur, unless it is to be found in πλησιέτερον (=-αίτ.) 4 M. xii. 3 ℵ : πλησιότερον of V* shows the tendency to revert to the normal form : πλησιέστερον of A has other late attestation and may be right.

16. The Attic rule as to long or short o before **-τερος** **-τατος** is usually observed. The vowel preceding mute + nasal (liquid) is regarded as short, contrary to Attic practice, in φιλοτέκνώτεραι 4 M. xv. 5 AℵV*: cf. ἐλαφρώτερος Job vii. 6 B*ℵ*, ix. 25 B*. Phonetic changes (αι = ε, interchange of ῐ, ῑ and o, ω) account for other irregularities. The latest LXX book again affords an example : ἀνδρειωτέρα 4 M. xv. 30 AV* (ℵ ἀνδριωτ.): similarly παλαιωτέρων Est. E 7 A (-οτ. Bℵ) and παλαιώτατος 3 times in the colophon at the end of Esther written by correctors of ℵ (strict Attic παλαίτερος -αίτατος). The converse is seen in συνετότερος Gen. xli. 39 E, κυριότατος 4 M. i. 19 A: cf. ἀθλειοτάτης 3 M. v. 49 A.

17. *Adjectival comparative and superlative of Adverbs.* Forms in -τερος -τατος are now augmented by some new adjectives—ἐξώτερος -τατος, ἐσώτερος -τατος[1]—which replace to some extent the classical adverbial forms in -τέρω -τάτω. Of these latter the only exx. are τὴν Βαιθωρὰμ τὴν ἀνωτέρω 3 K. x. 23 B and κατωτάτω read by א in Tob. iv. 19, xiii. 2, by B in Ψ cxxxviii. 15, by A in Job xxxvii. 12. For the comparison of the adverb the κοινή preferred neut. sing. and plur. forms in -τερον -τατα : the former occur in LXX, where they are hardly distinguishable from the simple adv. or prep.—ἀνώτερον (= ἄνω) L. xi. 21 ἔχει σκέλη ἀνώτερον τῶν ποδῶν, 2 Es. xiii. 28 : κατώτερον (= κάτω) Gen. xxxv. 8 AE ἀπέθανεν δὲ Δ. κατ. Βαιθήλ : ἐσώτερον (= ἔσω) Ex. xxvi. 33, L. xvi. 2, 12, 15, 1 K. xxiv. 4, Is. xxii. 11.

The use of the comp. here may be accounted for by the presence of מִן in the Heb.: ἀνώτερον = מִמַּעַל, κατ. = מִתַּחַת, ἐσ. = מִבֵּית.

Whereas the comparative usually encroaches upon the sphere of the superlative, the reverse takes place with πρῶτος, which, besides being used in superlative or elative sense, begins to supplant πρότερος. So e.g. Gen. xli. 20 κατέφαγον αἱ ἑπτὰ βόες αἱ αἰσχραί...τὰς πρώτας τὰς καλάς, Ex. iv. 8 τοῦ σημείου τοῦ πρώτου...τοῦ σημ. τοῦ ἐσχάτου (*former* and *latter*), xxxiv. 1 δύο πλάκας λιθίνας καθὼς καὶ αἱ πρῶται (cf. 4), Dt. x. 1 ff., Jd. xx. 32 B ὡς τὸ πρῶτον (= A καθὼς ἔμπροσθεν), Tob. xiv. 5 א οἰκοδομήσουσιν τὸν οἶκον καὶ οὐχ ὡς τὸν πρῶτον (= BA οὐχ οἷος ὁ πρότερος). Πρότερος, though not half so frequent as πρῶτος, is still well represented, mainly by the adverb (τὸ) πρότερον and by the classical use of the adjective in place of the adverb, as in Ex. x. 14 προτέρα αὐτῆς οὐ γέγονεν τοιαύτη ἀκρὶς καὶ μετὰ ταῦτα κ.τ.λ. This use of πρότερος = πρό may have assisted in

---

[1] Apparently first found in LXX : ἀνώτερος -τατος, κατώτερος -τατος have some classical authority. Cod. A has a similar comparative adj. from ἐντός : Est. iv. 11 τὴν αὐλὴν τὴν ἐντοτέραν (ἐσωτέραν Eא).

producing πρῶτος = πρότερος. Ἔσχατος is similarly used both for superl. and comp.: Dt. xxiv. 3 γένηται ἀνδρὶ ἑτέρῳ καὶ μισήσῃ αὐτὴν ὁ ἀνὴρ ὁ ἔσχατος, Jos. x. 14 οὐκ ἐγένετο ἡμέρα τοιαύτη οὐδὲ τὸ πρότερον οὐδὲ τὸ ἔσχατον¹: ἔσχατον is used as a preposition "after" in Dt. xxxi. 27, 29, ἔσχατον τοῦ θανάτου (τῆς τελευτῆς) μου, ἔσχ. τῶν ἡμερῶν.

Ὕστερος (apart from the adverbial ὕστερον, ἐφ᾽ ὑστέρῳ, ἐξ ὑστέρου) occurs once only (1 Ch. xxix. 29), where it is a true comparative: ὕστατος (= superl.) is also represented by a solitary instance (3 M. v. 49).

18.   In modern Greek the old forms in -ίων -ιστος have been ousted by others in -τερος -τατος (e.g. καλύτερος, χερότερος for καλλίων, χείρων)². In the LXX we see but the beginnings of this transition. Αἰσχρότερος (for αἰσχίων) Gen. xli. 19 may be illustrated from a papyrus of iii/B.C.³ The vulgar ἀγαθώτερος⁴ is confined to the late B text of Judges (xi. 25, xv. 2 · A κρείσσων *bis*).

19.   Ταχύ has the comparative of the earlier period of the κοινή, τάχιον, in W. xiii. 9, 1 M. ii. 40: 2 Macc. alone has class. θᾶττον (iv. 31, v. 21, xiv. 11: used with positive or elative sense).

Ταχύτερον, found in papyri of ii/iii/A.D., has not yet made its appearance: nor does the LXX afford examples of double forms like μειζότερος.

20.   Many of the classical forms in -ιων -ιστος are retained, but few are frequent, and the superlatives are mainly confined to the literary books and used in elative sense.

---

¹ Cf. more doubtful cases in R. iii. 10, 2 K. xiii. 15 B (μείζων ἡ κακία ἡ ἐσχ. ἢ ἡ πρώτη, a gloss, possibly of Christian origin), Hg. ii. 9, Dan. Θ xi. 29. A sentence like (2 M. vii. 41) ἐσχάτη δὲ τῶν υἱῶν ἡ μήτηρ ἐτελεύτησεν has of course classical warrant.

² Thumb *Handbuch* 51.

³ Mayser 298. The superl. αἴσχιστος occurs as a variant for ἔχθιστος in Est. E. 24 A, 3 M. iii. 27 V.

⁴ Ἀγαθώτατος in an undated letter (A.D.), Par. xviii. 3.

Πλείων is frequent, often without comp. force as in the common phrases ἡμέρας πλείους L. xv. 25 etc. (=ἡμ. πολλάς elsewhere) and ἐπὶ πλεῖον (=ἐπὶ πολύ) Ψ l. 4 etc.

Μείζων occurs sporadically.

Ἄμ(ε)ινον only as a v.l. of א in Est. E. 2 (= BA μεῖζον). Βελτίων is fairly frequent (several times in Jer. β).

Κρείσσων is the most frequent comp. form of ἀγαθός.

Ἐλάσσων is used in Pent. (Gen. i. 16 etc., Ex. xvi. 17 f., L. xxv. 16, N. xxvi. 54 etc.) and the literary books.

Ἥσσων Is. xxiii. 8 and in literary books (usually in the phrases οὐδὲν [οὐχ] ἧττον). Χείρων 1 K. xvii. 43 B and literary.

Μᾶλλον is fairly common.

Πλεῖστος occurs sporadically as a true superl., or in elative sense (e.g. Sir. xlv. 9 χρυσοῖς κώδωσιν πλείστοις, l. 18 ἐν πλείστῳ οἴκῳ R.V. "in the whole house" [ἤχῳ should perhaps be read], Is. vii. 22 πλεῖστον γάλα).

Μέγιστος is literary and usually elative as an attribute of θεός (e.g. 2 M. iii. 36, 3 M. i. 9 V).

Ἄριστος literary and elative (4 M. vii. 1).

Βέλτιστος in Pent. and literary books (Gen. xlvii. 6, 11, Ex. xxii. 5 *bis*: 2 M. xiv. 30, 3 M. iii. 26).

Κράτιστος occurs as a true superl. in literary books (2, 3 M.) and elsewhere: 1 K. xv. 15, Ψ xv. 6, xxii. 5, Am. vi. 2.

Ἐλάχιστος also is not confined to the literary books: as a true superl. in Jos. vi. 26 *bis* (opposed to πρωτότοκος), 1 K. ix. 21, 4 K. xviii. 24, Jer. xxix. 21: as elative e.g. ἐλαχίστῳ ξύλῳ, "a diminutive piece of wood," W. xiv. 5.

[Ἥκιστος is not used.]

Χείριστος literary, used as true superl. (Est. B. 5, 2 and 3 M.). Ἔχθιστος literary. Μάλιστα is literary (2—4 M.).

Ὀλιγοστός, apparently a κοινή offshoot from πολλοστός[1] (like πόστος, εἰκοστός), is fairly common in LXX, with the proper etymological meaning of "one of few," "attended by a small retinue," e.g. Gen. xxxiv. 30 ὀλ. εἰμι ἐν ἀριθμῷ, 1 M. iii. 16 ἐξῆλθεν Ἰούδας...ὀλιγοστός, but sometimes hardly distinguishable from ὀλίγος, "few," "inferior.". The converse πολλοστός is classical in the sense of "one of many," "(a) very small (fraction)" or "one of οἱ πολλοί," "plebeian": in LXX it occurs twice only and then with the opposite meaning of "great," "powerful" (=πολύς): 2 K. xxiii. 20 ἀνὴρ αὐτὸς πολλοστὸς ἔργοις, Prov. v. 19 (by conjugal fidelity) πολλοστὸς ἔσῃ.

---

[1] In Soph. *Ant.* 625 Jebb reads ὀλίγιστον χρόνον.

21. As regards the *declension* of comparatives in -ων, the shorter Attic forms in -ω -ους of acc. sing. and nom. and acc. plur., which show signs of waning ın ıı/i/B.C.[1], are still well represented in LXX.

Βελτίων, ἐλάσσων, κρείσσων have the shorter forms only in the cases concerned. Βελτίους Prov. xxiv. 40, Job xlii. 15, Jer. xxxiii. 13, βελτίω ib. xlii. 15 א (the variants show the tendency to introduce the longer form: βελτίων B*, -ιον A, -ιονα Q). Τὸν ἐλάσσω Gen. i. 16, xxvii. 6, οὐκ ἐλάττους 2 M. v. 5, viii. 9, xii. 10. Τόπον...κρείττω Is. lvi. 5 (with v.ll. κρείττων Γ, κρ(ε)ίσσων אA, κρισσον Q), neut. plur. κρείσσω Prov. viii. 19 B (κρίσσων א, κρισσον A) and κρείττω Ep. J. 67 B (κρίσσων A, κρείσσονα Q), κρείσσους Prov. xxvii. 5.—On the other hand ἥττων has the longer forms only: ἥττονα Ep. J. 35, ἥττονες Job xx. 10.—In other words both forms occur. Πλείων has πλείονα in sing. and plur. (once only the shorter form: 1 Es. iv. 42 πλείω τῶν γεγραμμένων): but πλείους is usual (constant in the phrase ἡμέρας πλείους), though πλείονες -ας occur: 2 Ch. xxxii. 7, Jer. xliii. 32, Ez. xxix. 15, 2 M. xi. 12 (Dt. xx. 19 A, 1 Ch. iv. 40 A, Ep. J. 18 A). Μείζονες -ονας -ονα (neut. plur.) only are attested: the acc. sing. is μείζονα in Dan. O xi. 13, μ(ε)ίζω in 3 K. xi. 19 A (τῆς μείζω[2] B) and probably this stood in 4 M. xv. 9 (μείζων AV, μιζον א*, μίζω א^{c.a}). Χείρων has acc. sing. χείρονα 3 M. v. 20 (in 1 K. xvii. 43 Οὐχί, ἀλλ' ἢ χείρω[2] κυνός, the nom. must be meant): the neut. plur. is ˙χείρονα in W. xv. 18, but χείρω ib. xvii. 6.

§ 13. THE NUMERALS.

1. Δύο in LXX, as in the papyri[3], N.T., and the κοινή generally, has gen. δύο and dative δυσί(ν), on the ˙analogy of τρισί(ν). The indeclinable use of δύο ῖor both gen. and dat. (as well as acc.) has classical authority: δυσί(ν) was, however, the normal dative from Aristotle onwards. Δύο for dat. occurs in LXX in the A text of Jos. vi. 22 (AF), xiii. 8, Jd. xv. 13, 3 K. xxii. 31, and so apparently ib. xvi. 24 BA (ἐν δύο ταλάντων ἀργυρίου): cf. Sir. xliv. 23 ἐν φυλαῖς...δέκα δύο. The old dual

---

[1] Mayser 298 f.: the Atticists gave them a new lease of life.
[2] The -ω forms are often used (like πλήρης, ἥμισυ) indeclinably: Moulton *Prol.* 50.
[3] Mayser 3ᵗ3 f. (from end of ii/B.C.).

is preserved in two literary books in the debased form, found
in Polybius and the Atticists, δυεῖν (§ 6, 37): 4 M. i. 28 אV
(δυοῖν A), xv. 2, Job ix. 33 A = xiii. 20 A δυεῖν δέ μοι χρ(ε)ία (or
χρήσῃ Bא in the latter passage, meaning apparently "treat" or
"indulge me in two ways").

2. For the usual declension of nom. and acc. of τέσσαρες
in the LXX uncials viz.:

> N. τέσσαρες τέσσερα,
>
> A. τέσσαρες τέσσερα,

see §§ 5, p. 62, 6. 2, 10. 15. The gen. and, as a rule, the dat.
take the Attic forms (τεσσάρων, τέσσαρσι(ν)). Assimilation of
syllables, apparently, produces the spelling of the dat. as τέρσαρσιν in the opening chapters of Amos in Cod. A (i. 9, 11, ii. 1): the
same MS has the metaplastic τεσσάροις once in Ez. i. 10 (but
τέσσαρσι twice in same v.): the alternative dat. τέτρασιν (poetical
and late prose)[1] occurs once in Jd. ix. 34 B τέτρασιν ἀρχαῖς.

3. To express numbers between ten and twenty the
classical language usually placed the smaller number first. So
always ἕνδεκα, δώδεκα, the composite forms attesting their
antiquity: the component parts of the higher numbers were
linked by καί (τρεισκαίδεκα etc.). But, in certain circumstances,
viz. where the substantive stood before the numeral, the order
was reversed, the larger number preceding: the insertion or
omission of the copula was optional. In the κοινή the second
method (without copula) prevailed and in modern Greek, for
numbers above twelve, has become universal. It was natural
that the order of the symbols (ιγ´ etc.) should ultimately
determine the order of the words when written in full. But
ἕνδεκα (mod. Gr. ἔντ.) δώδεκα had taken too deep root to be
dislodged and have survived to the present day.

Δεκάδυο was a short-lived attempt to displace the latter,
which appears to have been much in vogue in the Ptolemaic

---

[1] Exx. in Crönert 199 note 2.

age[1]. In LXX, as against numerous examples of δώδεκα, δεκάδυο has good authority throughout two books only, viz. 1 Chron. (vi. 63 BA, ix. 22 BA, xv. 10 BA, xxv. 9 ff. B: so 2 Ch. xxxiii. 1 BA, but elsewhere δώδ.) and Judith (ii. 5, 15, vii. 2): elsewhere it receives good support in 2 Es. ii. 6 BA, 18 BA, Sir. xliv. 23 BA and occurs sporadically in B (Ex. xxviii. 21, xxxvi. 21: Jos. xviii. 24, xxi. 40: 4 K. i. 18 a: 1 Es. viii. 35, 54, 63) and, less often, in A.

For 'the teens' the LXX uncials attest the two classical modes of expression (τρ(ε)ισκαίδεκα, δεκατρ(ε)ῖς etc.) in about equal proportions, the latter slightly preponderating.

Occasionally in Genesis, contrary to classical precedent, the copula is inserted with the latter order of words: Gen. xiv. 14 δέκα καὶ ὀκτώ AD, xxxi. 41 δ. καὶ τέσσ., xxxvii. 2 δ. καὶ ἑπτά E, xlvi. 22 δ. καὶ ἐννέα D : so 3 K. vii. 40 A, 1 Ch. xxvi. 9, 2 Ch. xxvi. 1. A, where it does not use δεκαέξ, always writes ἓξ καὶ δέκα, as distinct words: B, except in N. xxxi. 46, 52, writes ἑκκαίδεκα.

4. For numbers above 'the teens' there is no fixed order in LXX, but the tendency is to write the larger number first. The literary 2 Macc. employs πρός with dative for large numbers e.g. v. 21 ὀκτακόσια πρὸς τοῖς χιλίοις, v. 24 V δισμυρίοις πρὸς τοῖς χιλ., x. 31 δισμύριοι πρὸς τοῖς πεντακοσίοις etc. (poetical, cf. Aesch. *P.V.* 774 τρίτος...πρὸς δέκ' ἄλλαισιν γοναῖς, Soph. *Trach.* 45).

5. The *ordinals* retain their place[2]. The strict Attic forms to express 13th—19th—separate declinable words, τρίτος καὶ δέκατος etc.—have been entirely supplanted by the composite words τρισκαιδέκατος etc. (rare in classical Greek, possibly of Ionic origin). The former only survive as variants in 2 M. xi. 33 V πέμπτῃ καὶ δεκάτῃ, Est. ix. 21 ℵ^{c.a} πέμπτην καὶ δεκάτην[3].

[1] Mayser (316) notes only one example of δώδεκα (157 B.C.). On the other hand in the ostraca δώδεκα predominates (Moulton *Prol.*[2] 246). Cod. Bezae writes only δέκα δύο or ιβ (ib. 96).

[2] All above τέταρτος have disappeared from the modern language.

[3] The -τε of πέντε, recalling -τος, perhaps accounts for the tendency in this case: cf. 1 Ch. xxiv. 14 πεμπτεκαιδέκατος *sic* B*.

The form τρισκαιδέκατος, always so written in LXX, for the more correct τρεισκ., has, by analogy, produced the still more impossible form τεσσαρισκαιδέκατος (2 Ch. xxx. 15 B*ᵇA and constantly elsewhere in one or more correctors of B) for τεσσαρεσκαιδέκατος. The ordinals between 20 and 30, 30 and 40 etc. are expressed in Attic by two ordinals connected by καί (δεύτερος καὶ εἰκοστός etc.), except for εἷς καὶ (εἰκοστός): the cardinal is similarly used in this instance in LXX (1 Ch. xxiv. 17 ὁ εἷς καὶ εἰκοστός, 1 M. vii. 1 ἔτους ἑνὸς καὶ πεντηκοστοῦ: and so, with irregular order, Jer. lii. 1 εἰκοστοῦ καὶ ἑνὸς ἔτους, 2 Ch. xvi. 13 A), but we also meet with 3 K. xvi. 23 τριακοστῷ καὶ πρώτῳ, 1 Ch. xxv. 28 εἰκοστὸς πρῶτος, 2 M. xiv. 4 πρώτῳ καὶ ἑκατοστῷ καὶ πεντηκοστῷ (where the order is peculiar). In these compound ordinals the smaller number usually precedes as in Attic, but in the later portions of the LXX, there is a marked tendency to reverse this order, and thus to bring cardinals (whether expressed by words or symbols) and ordinals into line[1].

6. To express certain *days of the month* (the 4th, 20th and 30th) classical Greek employed, in place of the ordinals, the substantives τετράς, εἰκάς, τριακάς. These are retained in the LXX proper[2], but appear to have been unfamiliar to Theodotion and his school: Dan. Θ x. 4 = 2 Es. xix. 1 ἐν ἡμέρᾳ εἰκοστῇ καὶ τετάρτῃ τοῦ μηνός (contrast e.g. 2 M. xi. 21 Διὸς Κορινθίου τετράδι καὶ εἰκάδι).

Τετάρτη appears also (beside εἰκάς) in Dan. O x. 4, 3 M. vi. 38, εἰκοστῇ is read by B in 2 Ch. vii. 10 (εἰκάδι A).

7. The *numeral adverbs* continue in use: for ἑπτάκι (-κις)

---

[1] E.g. 4 K. xiii. 10 ἐν ἔτει τριακοστῷ καὶ ἑβδόμῳ. So regularly in 4 K., 2 Es., Dan. Θ (x. 4) and Jer. lii. (verses 1 and 31): also Jos. xiv. 10, 1 M. i. 10, 20 (the dates in the later chapters follow the Attic order), 2 M. i. 10 and (without copula) xi. 21, 33, 38.
[2] Τριακάς 2 M. xi. 30, the other two frequently. Τετράς in Ψ xciii. tit. is used of the fourth day of the *week*, τετράδι σαββάτων (-του), as in modern Greek.

see § 9, 9. Aquila and his school employ in place of them the plural of κάθοδος to render the Heb. םימעפ (lit. strokes, beats): from this source in "LXX" come 3 K. ix. 25 A τρεῖς καθόδους, Eccl. vii. 23 b καθόδους πολλάς (= πλειστάκις in the doublet 23 a): cf. in mod. Greek μιὰ φορά, τρεῖς φορές.

§ 14. PRONOUNS.

1. **Personal.** The 3rd pers. is represented by αὐτοῦ etc., including (at least in some books) the nom. αὐτός, αὐτοί.

'Απέριψάς μες εἰς βάθη Jon. ii. 4 א, if not a mere slip, may be compared with οὕτω(ς) etc. I have not noted in LXX any exx. of the longer modern Greek forms ἐσύ etc.: μετ' ἐσοῦ occurs in papyri of ii/A.D. (OP iii. 528, 531, Par. 18).

2. **Reflexives.** 'Εμαυτ(οῦ), σεαυτ(οῦ), ἑαυτ(οῦ) remain in use, the last two usually in the longer forms preferred by the κοινή: the alternative Attic forms σαυτοῦ, αὑτοῦ, which are absent from the N.T. (Blass 35), continue to be written in the papyri down to about the end of ii/B.C.[1], and are sporadically represented in the LXX.

Σαυτ(οῦ) in Pentateuch only in Dt. xxi. 11 B (cf. xix. 9 προσθΗσεισαγτω B*vid., -σεις σαυτῷ Swete): frequently in the Kingdom books, 1 K. xix. 11 B, 2 K. ii. 21 B *semel*, 3 K. iii. 5 B, 11 BA *bis*, viii. 53 *bis* (BA, B), xvii. 13 BA, xx. 7 BA, xxi. 34 BA, 4 K. iv. 3 B, vi. 7 B, xviii. 21 BA, 23 A, 24 B: Ez. iv. 9 B *semel* (c'αγτω *sic*), xvi. 52 Q, xxxiii. 9 B, xxxvii. 17 BQ, xxxviii. 7 Q: elsewhere Ψ liv. 11 B, Tob. vi. 5 א, Sir. xiv. 11 A, Is. viii. 1 א. For αὑτοῦ etc. we find e.g. 2 Ch. xxi. 8 B ἐφ' αὑτούς, 1 M. iii. 13 A, μεθ' αὑτοῦ (μετ' αὐτ. אV): of course in many cases it is uncertain whether αὑτ. or αὐτ. is intended.

'Εαυτ(οῦ) for 1st or 2nd pers. sing. is an illiteracy found occasionally as a v.l.: ἑαυτοῦ = ἐμαυτοῦ Job xxxii. 6 C, ἑαυτῷ = σεαυτῷ Job x. 13 A*fortאc.a, Is. xxi. 6 א (see Moulton *Prol.* 87).

The corresponding use of the *plural* ἑαυτῶν, on the other hand, is normal in the κοινή. It had already since c. 400 B.C. supplanted σφῶν αὐτῶν[2], and from ii/B.C. in the papyri further

---

[1] Mayser 305 ff.   [2] Meisterhans 153.

supplants ἡμῶν and ὑμῶν αὐτῶν[1]. So in LXX the 1st pers. plur. is always and the 2nd pers. usually ἑαυτ(ῶν). The Hexateuch, however, a production of iii/B.C., retains the old ὑμ(ῶν) αὐτ(ῶν) together with what appears to be a transitional form ὑμῖν ἑαυτοῖς: the latter might be merely due to mixture of readings, but its frequent attestation and the limitation of this form of reflexive to the dat. of the 2nd plur. are against this.

Ἑαυτ(ῶν): (a)=ἡμ. αὐτ.: Gen. xliii. 22, Jos. xxii. 23 (αὐτοῖς B), 1 K. xiv. 9 etc.: (b)=ὑμ. αὐτ. Ex. xix. 12 BA, Dt. i. 13 BA, Jos. iv. 3 F, ix. 17 BA and frequently in later books.

Ὑμῶν αὐτῶν Ex. xxxv. 5 and frequently in Dt. in the phrase ἐξαρεῖς (ἀφανιεῖς) ἐξ ὑμῶν αὐτῶν (τὸν πονηρόν): Dt. xiii. 5, xvii. 7, xix. 19 (-αρεῖτε AF), xxi. 9, 21, xxii. 21, 24, xxiv. 7, cf. Jos. vii. 12 (ἐξάρητε): the Heb. מִקִּרְבְּךָ "from thy midst" if literally rendered ἐκ σεαυτοῦ would have conveyed another meaning, that of exorcism.

Ὑμῖν αὐτοῖς with variants ὑμῖν ἑαυτοῖς and ἑαυτοῖς. Ex. xix. 12 F ὑμ. ἑαυτ., xx. 23ª ὑμ. αὐτ. B (ἑαυτ. AF), 23ᵇ ὑμ. αὐτ. A (ὑμ. ἑ. BF), xxx. 32 οὐ ποιηθήσεται (A ποιήσεται) ὑμῖν ἑαυτοῖς BAF, xxx. 37 ὑμ. αὐτ. BF (ὑμ. ἑ. A): Dt. iv. 16 and 23 ὑμ. ἑ. B (ὑμ. αὐτ. AF): Jos. iv. 3 ἅμα ὑμῖν αὐτ. AF (ἅμα ὑμῖν καὶ αὐτοῖς B), ix. 17 F ὑμ. αὐτ. (ἑαυτοῖς BA), xxii. 16 ὑμ. ἑ. B (ἑαυτοῖς A), xxiv. 15 ὑμ. ἑ. B (ὑμ. αὐτ. A). [The following are not reflexive: Jos. vi. 18 ὑμεῖς αὐτοί B (ὑμεῖς AF) "even you": 2 Ch. xx. 15 τάδε λέγει Κύριος ὑμῖν αὐτοῖς "to *you*," Heb. לכם אתם, אתם forming part of the Lord's words.]

3. **Demonstratives.** Under Accidence there is little to note. Οὗτος and ἐκεῖνος àre used regularly: ὅδε is much commoner than in N.T., most often in the phrase τάδε λέγει Κύριος and the like, but also elsewhere, in the Pentateuch with correct deictic force idiomatically rendering Heb. הנה = *voici*, e.g. Gen. l. 18 οἴδε ἡμεῖς σοι οἰκέται: but it is going over to the literary class and in some books is used incorrectly for οὗτος. The intensive -ί with οὗτος is unrepresented, but νυνί occurs in literary books (Job, 2 and 4 M., Ψ xvi. 11, xliii. 10).

[1] Mayser 303: the beginnings of this use of ἑαυτῶν go back to Attic Greek. Polybius never has the old forms but only αὐτῶν αὐτούς (for 1st and 2nd pers.) and ἑαυτοῖς (2nd pers.): Kälker 277. Mayser cites no exx. of reflex. 1st and 2nd plur. in any form for iii/B.C.

4. **Relatives.** Ὅς ἥ ὅ is frequent: ὅστις ἥτις ὅ,τι (fem. ἥτιс Jer. vi. 8 א) is less so, and the distinction between the pronouns is not always rigidly observed. The latter, apart from ἧστινος 2 M. v. 10, and the phrases ἕως (μέχρι) ὅτου, is confined to the nom. sing. and plur. and the neut. acc. sing. ὅ,τι. The shorter forms are found only in the phrases quoted: the shorter forms of the interrogative and indefinite pronouns (τοῦ, τῷ, του, τῳ) do not occur. Ὅσπερ in neut. sing. and plur. is literary (5 times in all: in Lev. xxv. 27 read ὃ ὑπερέχει with B^{ab}, in Jos. xxiii. 4 ἐπέρ(ρ)ιφα with A, in 2 K. vi. 8 ὑπὲρ οὗ).

5. **Correlatives.** The following occur. Ποῖος—τοιοῦτος (τοῖος 2 Es. v. 3: τοιόσδε 2 M. xi. 27, xv. 12)—οἷος—ὁποῖος (lit.) 2 M. xi. 37 and in the 'stage-direction' in Cant. v. 10 א. Πόσος—τοσοῦτος (τόσῳ μᾶλλον Sir. xi. 11, xiii. 9)—ὅσος. Πηλίκος Zech. ii. 2 *bis*, 4 M. xv. 22—τηλικοῦτος (lit.: 2—4 M.). Ποταπός only in Dan. O Sus. 54, where it keeps something of its original local meaning, ποτ. τοῦ παραδείσου τόπῳ. (Ὁπόσος, ἡλίκος are unrepresented.)

Τοιοῦτος has neuter in -ο (-ον 2 K. xiv. 13 A, 1 Es. i. 19 B) as also τηλικοῦτος: τοσοῦτος has neut. in -ο in vernacular style (N. xv. 5, 1 M. iii. 17), in -ον in the literary books (Est. E. 7, 11, W. xiii. 9, 2 and 3 M.): both forms are old.

6. Words indicating *duality* as distinct from plurality are disappearing: ἀμφότεροι (not ἄμφω) and ἕτερος alone are frequent (μηθέτερος Prov. xxiv. 21). Ἑκάτερος is correctly used for "one of two" in Gen. xl. 5, Tob. א v. 3 (read ἑκάτερος ἕν), xi. 13 and in the literary books (so ἑκατέρωθεν 4 M.), in Ez. it appears to take the place of ἕκαστος: elsewhere ἕκαστος supplants it, ἕκαστος itself being replaced in the literal books by ἄνθρωπος or ἀνήρ (p. 45). Πότερος is supplanted by τίς, appearing only in Job as an interrogative particle (πότερον).

§ 15. THE VERB. GENERAL CHANGES IN CONJUGATION.

1. The verbal system to a large extent remains unaltered, but in more than one direction shows signs of the shrinkage or retrenchment and the reduction of what appeared to be superfluous varieties to a uniform pattern which characterize the later language as a whole.

Thus, the old three *classes of verbs*—barytones in -ω, contracts, verbs in -μι—have already gone far on the way to being merged into two, since the -μι verbs have in the active in large measure passed over to the -ω class, while the beginnings of a similar amalgamation of three forms into two may be traced in the occasional confusion in the uncials of contract verbs in -άω and -έω (§ 22, 1).

The three *voices* remain as before, but a tendency to eliminate, as in modern Greek, from the middle the only tenses which discriminated it from the passive (1st aorist and future) may be inferred from the more extended use of the aorist passive of deponent verbs (ἀπεκρίθην, ἐγενήθην etc., § 21, 6), and perhaps also from the partial substitution of the future active for the future middle which Attic writers preferred in certain quasi-deponent verbs denoting a physical action or an emotion (ἀκούσω, βλέψω, θαυμάσω etc., § 20, 3).

2. As regards the *moods*, the optative, which is defunct in the modern language, is still commonly used to express a wish: other uses viz. with ἄν in principal sentences (questions etc.) to express possibility and in subordinate clauses (conditional, final etc.) are rare except in the literary essay known as 4 Maccabees, which uses it freely[1]. The conjunctive is still

---

[1] Further instances occur not only in literary versions or writings such as Job, Proverbs, 2 Maccabees and the Epistle of Jeremiah, but also in the Pentateuch (especially in comparisons with ὡς εἰ or simply ὡς), Psalms and elsewhere. The mood thus appears still to show some signs of life in the vernacular of the Ptolemaic age, whereas in N. T. writings it is always an index of a cultivated writer. In its primary use it is occasionally, especially in late texts, replaced by the conj., e.g. Ex. xxxiii. 13 γνωστῶς ἴδω σε, Jd. ix. 15 B ἐξέλθῃ πῦρ...καὶ καταφάγῃ, Job xxxi. 40 A ἐξέλθῃ etc.

frequent, but shows signs of shrinkage in the use of the indicative (imperfect and fut.) after particles such as ἐάν, ὅταν, ἵνα : in other connexions the mixture of conj. and fut. ind. is common, largely owing to changes in pronunciation such as the equalization of ω and ο. The imperative remains but, through the influence of the Hebrew, is often replaced in the second person by the future indicative. The infinitive (defunct in the modern language) is in vigorous life and shows no signs of decay, the anarthrous and the now popular articular form of it being both widely represented : the modern substitution of a clause with ἵνα (νά) can hardly be paralleled from the LXX. The inf. and participle of the future are not often met with outside literary books. The verbal adjective in forms which have become stereotyped as adjectives (αἰνετός "praiseworthy," δεκτός, θελητός etc.) is not uncommon[1]: forms in -έον used as the main verb in the sentence seem to be limited to the Epistle of Jeremiah, which has νομιστέον 39, 56, κλητέον 39, γνωστέον 51, ἐκδεκτέον 56: cf. ἀναλημπτέα 2 M. iii. 13.

3. Turning to the *tense* system, we find new forms of the present evolved out of the perfect (γρηγορέω etc.) and aorist (κρύβω): the partiality of the language for terminations of the present such as -νω (ἱστάνω, λιμπάνω etc.) and its lavish creation of new verbs in -άζω and -ίζω belong to the department of word-formation. The future drops certain forms now regarded as superfluities, and to some extent the limitation which Blass[2] finds in the N.T., viz. that one future now suffices for each voice, is found also in the LXX: i.e. ἕξω is used to the exclusion of σχήσω, μνησθήσομαι (not μεμνήσομαι), στήσω and στήσομαι (not ἑστήξω): but φανοῦμαι (Pent., Prov., Wis.) remains beside φανήσομαι, and the fut. perf. is represented in at least one instance (κεκράξομαι[3]). The most salient

---

[1] Πάντα τὰ ἀρτὰ ὑπ' αὐτῶν N. iv. 27 (=31 τῶν αἰρομένων ὑπ' αὐτῶν) is noticeable. Wisdom has a large number of these adjectives, many of them new.
[2] N.T. § 14, 1.   [3] Cf. κεκλήσομαι, § 24.

alteration, however, in the tense system lies in the terminations and in particular in the encroachment of those of the 1st aorist into the sphere of the 2nd aorist. The new termination affected in the first place the 3rd pers. plur. where it took one of two forms: -oν became either -oσαν or -αν. The LXX is perhaps the principal witness to the -oσαν forms which are found in abundance throughout the whole collection of books with the exception of a single late group: their rarity in the N.T. suggests that they were an earlier transitional form which made way later for -αν. The -oσαν forms invaded the imperfect as well as the aorist. The termination -αν was eventually extended to all the past tenses: its use for -ασι in the perfect no doubt goes back in some instances to the LXX autographs, its employment in the imperfect, though attested, is probably attributable to later copyists. In a few instances an entirely new 1st aor. replaced the old 2nd aor. (ἦξα for ἤγαγον etc.). In the passive correctly formed but unclassical 1st aorists and kindred futures arose, though in one group of words the contrary phenomenon appears, the substitution of new 2nd aorists passive for 1st aorists, probably out of regard for euphony (§ 21, ·4). The periphrastic conjugation widens its range, partly but not entirely owing to the influence of the Hebrew original, the auxiliary verb being now employed with the present participle to represent the imperf., future and more rarely the present tense : periphrasis in the perfect goes back to the earlier language.

The dual has disappeared from the verb as from all parts of speech.

§ 16. AUGMENT AND REDUPLICATION.

1. Three main features under this head distinguish the modern from the classical language, viz. (1) the almost complete disappearance in the former of the temporal augment, (2) the consistently external position of the syllabic augment,

and (3) the disappearance of reduplication. The LXX illustrates the movement towards the first of these changes: the
second and third had hardly begun in the LXX period, but a
few premonitory signs of them appear in some of the uncials.

2. **Loss of syllabic augment.** The syllabic augment
ἐ on the whole retained its place in the κοινή as it has
also, to a considerable extent, in the modern language. The
main exception to this in the κοινή was the pluperfect, the
only tense which contained both augment and reduplication.
The κοινή, as Thumb remarks[1], strove to obliterate the distinction between these two, and ultimately reduplication
disappeared from the language: in the pluperf. the presence
of both aug. and redupl. was felt to be superfluous, and the
augment, as the more easily detachable element, was the one
to disappear. The active forms lost the augment sooner than
the passive[2]. The internal and therefore less conspicuous
augment in compounds was also, it seems, more often dropped
than the initial augment in simple verbs. In the LXX MSS
omission is frequent in the active, insertion is the rule in the
passive[3].

Pluperf. act. The aug. is consistently *retained* in one word,
ἐπεποίθειν: Dt. xxxii. 37, Prov. xxi. 22, Job vi. 13, Zeph. iii. 2 Bℵ,
Is. xxx. 15, 32 (πεποίθει B), Jer. xxvii. 38, xxxi. 7, xlvi. 18 (πε-
ποίθεις ℵ), Bar. iii. 17, Ez. xvi. 15 (κατεπ.), Sus. O 35, Dan. Θ
iii. 95. Πέποιθα had come to be regarded as a present, and

[1] *Hell.* 170 " Die Κοινή strebte ganz allgemein darnach, die Grenzen
zwischen Reduplikation und Augment zu verwischen, d. h. dieses fur jene
einzusetzen." Wackernagel suggests that the loss of the aug. in the pluperf.
may have been due to the influence of the considerable number of verbs in
which the *anlaut* of perf. and pluperf. were identical, e.g. εἴληφα εἰλήφειν.
[2] Owing, perhaps, to their rarer and more literary use. Cf. the longer
survival of the old forms in the passive of verbs in -μι (§ 23, 1).
[3] In the Ptolemaic papyri the passives always have the augment, the
actives more often than not, Mayser 333 f. (320 ff.): in papyri of the Imperial
age the examples of omission increase. Polybius drops the augment in
compounds, mainly in the active (only one ex. of omission in the *simplex* in
Books I—v, Wackernagel *Indog. Forsch.* v. Anz. 1): Josephus likewise
usually omits the aug. in the pluperf. act. and inserts it in the passive,
W. Schmidt 438.

produced a new aorist ἐπεποίθησα: ἐπεποίθει would be regarded as an imperf. like ἐτίθει. Otherwise the augmented forms are practically confined to literary books: ἐγεγόνειν always, Job iv. 12, x. 19 A, 1 M. iv. 27 אV, 2 M. xii. 39, xiii. 17: ἐδεδοίκειν Job iii. 25, xxix. 14 א*A (see below), xxxi. 35 (ἠδ. A): ἐπεπόν-θεισαν W. xviii. 1.

The aug. is *omitted* in βεβήκει W. xviii. 16, ἐπι-βεβ. N. xxii. 22 BF: παρεμ-βεβλήκεισαν Jd. vii. 12 A: ἐν-δεδύκειν L. xvi. 23 (ἐνεδύκει A), Job xxix. 14 BC (ἐδεδοίκ(ε)ιν אA), Jdth. ix. 1 א (ἐδεδ. B), x. 3 Bא, Est. D. 6 Aא.ᶜ·ᵃ (ἐνεδεδ. א*): βεβρώκει, πεπώκει 1 K. xxx. 12: δεδώκειν¹ 2 K. xviii. 11, 3 K. x. 13: πεποιήκεισαν Bel Θ 13: ἐπι-πεπτώκει Est. vii. 8: τεθνήκει Jd. xix. 28 A.

· *Pluperf. pass.* The aug. is always *retained* in ἐγέγραπτο Dt. ix. 10 (ἐπέγραπτο A, with loss of redupl.), 3 K. xx. 9, Ez. ii. 10, 1 M. xv. 15, 3 M. iii. 30: also in ἐπεπλήρωτο 2 M. iii. 30 V (ἐπληρ. A), vi. 5, ix. 7, cf. vi. 4 ἐπεπληροῦτο A (πεπλήρωτο V): so συνεκέχυτο 2 M. xiv. 28, ἐμέμνηντο W. xix. 10.

Omission occurs in ὑπομνημάτιστο 1 Es. vi. 22 B (ὑπεμν. A) and in two instances where the pluperf. has lost its force: τετέλεστο 2 Es. vii. 12 B (-ται A), κεκόλλητο Tob. vi. 18 A (ἐκολλήθη Bא).

Loss of syllabic augment in other tenses receives slight attestation in LXX: it is confined to words in which the syllable which should contain the augment is unaccented (cf. in mod. Greek ἔγραψα but γράψαμε etc.).

Perf. ἀποσπασμένοι Is. xxviii. 9 Bא*. *Aor.* and *impf.*: οὓς ἐξαποστείλατε Jer. xli. 16 B*א* (ἐξαπεστ. cett.), μοιχᾶτο ib. iii. 8 א*, ἀνακάλυψα ib. xxix. 11 א*, ποίησεν Is. xx. 2 א* (read ποίησον), ἐπιτήδευσεν Est. E. 12 A, θαυμάσθησαν 4 M. xviii. 3 A* (cf. παροιμίαζεν ib. 16 א = ἐπαροιμ. AV).

3. **Form of syllabic augment: ἠ- for ἐ-.** In the κοινή the temporal augment of ἐθέλω was retained, although the present was now always written as θέλω. So in LXX (as in papyri, N.T. etc.) we invariably find, beside present θέλω, the past tenses ἤθελον, ἠθέλησα. The ἠ-, of which the true origin was no longer apparent, seems to have been taken for an alternative form of syllabic augment and was commonly

---

¹ So in papyri from ii/B.C.: the dropping of aug. began early in the uncompounded verb.

attached in κοινή Greek to three verbs which had meanings akin to those of θέλω, viz. βούλομαι, δύναμαι, μέλλω[1].

In LXX the aor. ἐβουλήθην is retained (except for an occasional v.l.: ἠβ. Ex. x. 27 B^a, 1 K. xxiv. 11 B, Ψ xxxix. 9 AB^ab, lxxvii. 10 אc.a, 1 M. vii. 30 A): the imperfect is in most books ἐβουλόμην, but ἠβουλ. is strongly supported in Isaiah (i. 29, xxx. 9, 15 B*O, lxv. 12 א, lxvi. 4 אQ: against ἐβ. xxx. 15 B^cאAQ, xlii. 24, lxv. 12 BAQ, lxvi. 4 BA) and in 1 Macc. (iv. 6, v. 48, xi. 45, 49 [ἐβ. אc.aV], xii. 14 [ἐβ. V], xv. 27 [do.]), and occurs as a v.l. in 1 K. viii. 19 B, 1 Ch. xi. 19 א*, Ψ cxiii. 11 א*, Dan. Θ v. 19 *quater* B.

In the case of δύναμαι there is much stronger support for the augment ἠ-. The aor. always appears as ἠδυνήθην (except for two variants with ἐδ. in A: Dan. Θ ii. 47, 2 M. ii. 6) or ἠδυνάσθην (ἐδ. twice only in B, 2 Ch. xx. 37, Jer. v. 4, 6 times in A): in the imperf. there is greater fluctuation, but ἠδυνάμην on the whole is preferred.

The imperf. of μέλλω is used twice only and the two literary writers appear to have differed as to the correct form: ἔμελλεν 4 M. xvii. 1 AאV, but ἤμελλεν W. xviii. 4 BA (ἔμ. א).

The analogy of ἠδυνάμην further produced ὑπερηδυνάμωσαν Ψ lxiv. 4 B*א*T. Ἡδεδοίκειν Job xxxi. 35 A shows how this form of augment, which has survived in some modern Greek dialects (ἤφερα etc.), spread to other verbs.

4. **Loss of temporal augment.** The syllabic augment which took the invariable form ἐ- was always much less liable to omission or alteration than the temporal which affected the different initial vowels of verbs in various ways. The changes in pronunciation which coincided with the spread of the κοινή, particularly the loss of distinction between ε—η (ευ—ην), ο—ω, and the pronunciation of the diphthongs as monophthongs (οι = υ), hastened the extinction of the temporal augment which in modern Greek has all but disappeared (ἄκουσα etc.). In the LXX, however, as in the Ptolemaic papyri, the temporal

---

[1] The augment ἠ- with these verbs does not appear in Attic Inscriptions till after 300 B.C. (Meisterhans 169) : there is however a certain amount of authority for it in earlier literature (Kühner-Blass I. ii. § 197). The old grammarians differed in their verdicts as to the correct forms. The Ptolemaic papyri have ἠ-, Mayser 330.

augment is for the most part regular, except that it is generally dropped in verbs beginning with the diphthong εὐ: there is also some, but less, authority for the loss of augment in verbs with *anlaut* οἰ-. The omission began, it appears, with these two diphthongs: in the case of verbs with a single initial vowel, omission is rare except in compounds[1].

Verbs beginning with *single vowels* are in the main augmented regularly: ἀ- becomes ἠ- etc. The following exceptions may be noted.

In ἀ-: ἀλλοτριοῦτο 1 M. xv. 27 V^vid. The equivalence of ἠ—ἐ appears in the spelling of Cod. A: ἐλλόμην Job vi. 10 (for ἠλλ.). In ἐ-: ἐλαττονώθη (-ήθη) 3 K. xvii. 16 BA. ἐξεγειρόμην Ψ cxviii. 62 AT, ἐξεγέρθησαν Jer. xxviii. 38 Q* (elsewhere always ἐξηγ. and ἠγ.). ἀπελευθερώθη L. xix. 20 F. ἐπιστ(άμην) Job xlii. 3 C, Is. xlviii. 8 א, Jer. ii. 8 A (ἠπ- has overwhelming authority). ἐνυπνιάσθην (-ασάμην) is read by B in Jd. vii. 13, by A (with other uncials) in the remaining (8) passages where the past tenses occur: ἠν. is however attested in all these passages except Gen. xxxvii. 10. Ἐρημοῦν omits the augment in B in ἐρημώθη 1 Es. iv. 45 and elsewhere in about a dozen instances in other MSS, including the compound with ἐξ- (ἠρ- is usual). Ἐρωτᾶν always has the augment: ἐπερωτᾶν omits it in 1 Es. vi. 11 BA, Is. xxx. 2 B*Q, 4 times in A (Jos. ix. 20, 1 K. x. 22, xxviii. 16, 2 K. xi. 7 ἐπαιρώτ.) and once in C (Eccl. vii. 11).

In ἰ-: for ἴδον see 5 below.

In ὀ-: B omits the aug. in the following words (mainly compounds): ὀλιγώθη Na. i. 4 B*Q: ἐξολόθρευεν 1 Ch. xxi. 15 B*, ἐξολεθρεύθησαν Ψ lxxxii. 11 B*אRT: ἀνορθώθησαν Ez. xvi. 7 B*AΓ, κατορτώθη (*sic*) 2 Ch. xxix. 35 B*, κατορθ. ib. xxxv. 10 B*A, 16 B*: ὁμοίωσα Sir. xxvii. 24 B*א, ὁμοιώθη Ez. xxxi. 8 BA: ἐξομολογοῦντο Tob. xii. 22 B: παροξύνθη Hos. viii. 5 B*, Zech. x. 3 B*אAQΓ, παροξύνατε Bar. iv. 7 BΓ: παροργισμένην Sir. iv. 3 BC. Similar instances in the other uncials (א especially), ὀλιγοψύχησεν ὁμοιώθην ὀργίσθην παρόξυνα etc., occur mainly in the Prophetical group. Ὄφελον as a particle introducing a wish never has the augment.

Diphthongs. αἰ-: the augment is sometimes omitted in καταισχύνομαι: καταισχυνθήσῃ καθὼς κατῃσχύνθης Jer. ii. 36 B*אA, cf. καταισχυνθήσεται...ὥσπερ κατῃσχύνθη xxxi. 13 BA, similarly in א κατεσχ(=αισχ)ύνθη(σαν) ib. vi. 15, x. 14, xxvi. 24, and

---

[1] As between ὠι- (ῳ-) and ὠ-, ῃι- (ῃ-) and ἠ-, the evidence of the uncials for and against the writing of the ι adscript has not been tested. We know from the papyri that it was dropped after ω from ii/B.C. and after η as early as iii/B.C.

probably Is. liv. 4. Similarly ἀνταναιρέθην Ψ cviii. 23 A (cf. 5 below, at end).

αὐ-: ηὐλίσθην, ηὐξήθην etc. are regular: Cod. A affords an instance showing equivalence of ηὐ—εὐ, εὐλίζετο Job xxxi. 32 A. The verbs in αὐ- derived from compounds generally take no augment: αὐτάρκησεν Dt. xxxii. 10 BAF, αὐτομόλησα Jos. x. 1 B, 4 B (ηὐτ. A *bis*), 1 M. ix. 24 Aℵ (ηὐτ. V, and so BA in 2 K. iii. 8, x. 19).

εὐ:—εὗρον, εὕρηκα, εὑρέθην etc. are practically universal as in the papyri, Mayser 336 f.: the older Att. ηὐ- is limited in the B text to ηὕρισκον Ex. xv. 22 (with A), ηὑρέθη(σαν) 4 K. xx. 13 (do.), 2 Ch. xix. 3, Dan. Θ vi. 22 and is quite rare in other MSS, ηὑρίσκετο Gen. v. 24 ADE being the only strongly-supported ex. In compounds and words derived from compounds there is fluctuation, but the unaugmented forms εὐδόκησα, εὐλόγησα, (κατ)εύθυνα, εὐφράνθην[1] etc. on the whole preponderate, except in (προσ)εύχεσθαι, in which (προσ)ηυξάμην etc. are usual, -ευξάμην appearing sporadically in B (4 K. vi. 17 etc.), rarely in the other uncials.

οι:—the augment stands as a rule, but there are a considerable number of instances of unaugmented οι which had now come to be pronounced quite otherwise than ωι (in the papyri these begin to appear in ii/B.C., Mayser 337): e.g. ἐν ᾗ κατοικήσατε L. xviii. 3 B, κατοίκισα xxiii. 43 B, κατοικήσαμεν Dt. xxix. 16 B, οἰκοδόμησ(αν) N. xxxii. 34 B*, 37 B*, Jos. ix. 3 B, παροίστρ(η)σεν Hos. iv. 16 BAQ, and always οἰκτείρησα 4 K. xiii. 23 BA, Ψ lix. 3, cii. 13. The insertion of the aug. in these words tended to obscure the etymology (οἶκος etc.).

5. **Form of 'temporal' augment: εἰ- or ἠ-.** The Attic augment εἰ in certain words beginning with a vowel (due to an original ϝ, σ etc. in the *anlaut*: the augment is therefore strictly syllabic, ἐϝε = ἐε = εἰ) is for the most part retained in LXX as in the κοινή generally, but in a few verbs begins to be replaced by ἠ-

    Ἐάω has (Att.) impf. εἴων (3rd plur. Jos. xix. 48 a, 2 M. xii. 2: but with loss of aug. and termin. -σαν ἐῶσαν[2] Jer. xli. 10 BA [ἔασαν Q*, ἔσωσαν ℵ]), aor. εἴασα (1 M. xv. 14, 2 M. x. 20, Job xxxi. 34 [ἴασα A, ἄσα C]), aor. pass. ἰάθησαν (=εἰαθ.) 3 M. v. 18 V (ἰάσθ. A). Εἰθισμένην 2 M. xiv. 30 V is the usual form (ἠθ. A)·

---

[1] The LXX Psalter was at an early time written in two volumes: the scribe of Part I wrote ηὐφρ., the scribe of Part II εὐφρ.: cf. p. 68.

[2] Not from ὠθεῖν under which verb (as well as under ἐᾶν) it appears in Hatch-Redpath. With the phrase in Jer. ἐῶσαν αὐτοὺς εἰς παῖδας cf. Aristeas § 14 εἴασεν εἰς τὴν οἰκετείαν.

εἴωθα N. xxiv. 1 (ἰωθός B*F) etc. Ἕλκω (ἐξ- ἐφ-) has (Att.) εἷλκον -όμην, εἷλκυσα -ύσθην with v.l. ἥλκυσας 2 Es. xix. 30 A, ἥλκυσα Ψ cxviii. 131 ℵ*A. Ἐξῆρψεν Ψ civ. 30 (the only LXX ex. of past tense from ἕρπω) replaces Attic (ἐξ)είρπυσα. The distinction, generally observed in Attic Inscriptions, between augment (ἠ-) and reduplication (ἐι-) in the past tenses of ἐργάζομαι is also the rule in LXX, the imperf. appearing only as ἠργαζόμην Ex. xxxvi. 4, W. xiv. 8 (εἰργ. in correctors of B), and the perf. as εἴργασμαι: in the aorist the books diverge, ἠργασάμην being certainly the right reading in Job (xxiv. 6 B*ℵ, xxxiv. 32 B*ℵ*A) and perhaps in Hos. vii. 1 B* (εἰργ. BᵃᵇAQ), whereas εἰργασάμην is used in Isaiah (xliv. 12 *bis*, 15) and Psalms (vii. 14 ἐξ-, 16, xxx. 20 ἐξ-, xliii. 2, lxxiii. 12). (Εἶχον, ἔσχον as usual.) The aug. is dropped under the influence of the moods (as in N.T.) in ἀνέθη Jd. viii. 3 B, ἀφέθησαν Ψ xxxi. 1 BAR (-ειθ. ℵ), but retained in παρείθησαν 2 K. iv. 1 BA (no perf. act. attested: perf. pass. ἀν-παρ-εῖμαι regular). Ἴδον[1] (Epic for εἶδον=ἔϜιδον) is very frequent in A and ℵ: B usually writes εἶδον but in the Pentateuch also ἴδον e.g. ἐπιδεν Ex. ii. 25, ἴδεν iii. 4 BA, 7 ἰδὼν ἴδον BA, etc. The LXX pluperf. of ἕστηκα usually appears as ἱστήκειν, which is no doubt nothing but another way of spelling the classical εἱστήκειν (the latter is usual in B in 1—4 Kingdoms and appears occasionally elsewhere: the correctors of the uncials usually restore it for ἱστ.): ἐστήκειν (without aug.: Epic) occurs as a variant in Zech. i. 8 ℵ*, 1 M. xi. 38 Aℵ ἀνθ-, 3 M. iii. 5 V* κατ-, 4 M. xvi. 15 A.

There is overwhelming authority in the Ptolemaic papyri for the writing of εἰ- for ἠ- in the perf. act. and pass. of one verb not coming under the foregoing category, viz. αἱρέω. These tenses constantly appear as -εἴρηκα -εἴρημαι, so that, except by the context, they are indistinguishable from the perfect of ἐρῶ[2]. On the other hand ἠ- (ἠι-) is retained in the imperf.[3] This may, as Mayser holds, be a mere case of itacism (cf. for further instances § 6, 20), but the constancy of these forms in the case of this verb and the distinction between the perf. and the imperf. suggest that it is something more than an orthographical

---

[1] Analogy may have played a part in the κοινή use of this form: as εἰπεῖν was inf. of εἶπον, so, perhaps it was thought, ἰδεῖν must be inf. of ἴδον. The Ptolemaic papyri have εἶδον throughout, Mayser 332 note 2.

[2] Mayser 127, 335: he quotes 19 exx. of -ει-, beginning in iii/B.C., one only of ἠρηκέναι. The latest exx. which I have noted are ὑφιειρημένων (*sic*) OP ii. 282. 22 (30—35 A.D.), συνδιειρημένων BU 1037. 10 (47 A.D.).

[3] Mayser 123.

matter : the analogy of εἴργασμαι ἠργαζόμην may very well have produced εἴρημαι beside ἠρούμην. The same forms of the perfect (pluperf.) appear sporadically in LXX in B and א and, in view of the evidence from the papyri, can lay good claim to originality : ἀφείρηται Ex. xxix. 27 B, καθείρητο Jd. vi. 28 B, καθειρημένα 2 Es. xi. 3 Bא, ἀφείρητο Jdth xiv. 15 א, ἀνειρημένοις Jer. iv. 31 B, καθειρημένων ib. xl. 4 א, καθειρημένα 1 M. iv. 38 א.

> The classical forms are however more frequent in the uncials (e.g. 1 K. v. 4, xxi. 6, xxiv. 12, Is. ix. 4, xvi. 2) and are always written in A. The impf. is regular, ἦρουν, ἠρούμην 1 K. xix. 2 etc.: the aor. pass. is -ηρέθην with v.ll. ἀνερέθη Dan. Θ v. 30 B, ἀφερέθη 1 M. ii. 11 V and with loss of aug. ἀντανειρέθην Ψ cviii. 23 A.
>
> Ἡρήνευσα Job iii. 26 A (εἰρ. cett.) is merely itacistic: cf. the reading of the same MS ἀφείλαντο in Ez. xliv. 10 for ἀφῆλαντο of BQ (=the Heb. "went far").

6. **Double augment (temporal + syllabic).** A certain number of verbs beginning with a vowel took in the older language a syllabic augment (accounted for by an original ϝ) in addition to (or in place of) a temporal[1]. In the κοινή these old anomalous forms had ceased to be intelligible and begin to make way for others without the syllabic augment : the latter, where retained, sometimes intrudes into the moods and the future. Four verbs in the LXX fall under this category[2].

(Κατ)άγνυμι keeps the Attic aor. act. κατέαξα Zech. i. 21 (part. κατάξας 2 K. xxii. 35): the corresponding 1st aor. pass. κατεάχθην Jer. xxxi. 25 replaces Att. 2nd aor. κατεάγην: the fut. κατάξω Hb. iii. 12 (and as v.l. elsewhere) is regular (no ex. of κατεάξω as in N.T.).

Ἀνοίγω (original verb ὀϝείγω, then ϝοίγω, K.-Bl. *loc. cit.*) (1) rarely retains the Attic aorist ἀνέῳξα -ῴχθην, but usually still keeps the perf. part. pass. ἀνεῳγμένος, (2) sometimes

---

[1] Kühner-Blass I. ii. § 198, 5. The temporal augment is explained as simply due to the two short syllables εο, εα appearing to the ear as lacking something of the sound of an augment : "man εο, εά nicht als augmentiert empfand."

[2] No ex. of a past tense from ὠνέομαι occurs in LXX. Ἑάλων, ἑάλωκα as in Attic (Is. and Jer. a).

supplements the double classical augment by yet a third
(external) augment, but (3) normally employs for aorist the
new forms ἤνοιξα ἠνοίχθην.

	Class. double augment.	New treble augment.	New single augment.
Aorist	ἀνέῳξα Gen. viii. 6 DE, xxi. 19 AD, xxx. 22 A, xli. 56 : 2 Ch. xxix. 3 : Ψ lxxvii. 23 BᵃᵇℵRT (So προσέῳξα Gen. xix. 6) ἀνεῴχθη Is. xxiv. 18 B	ἠνέῳξα Gen. viii. 6 A, xxx. 22 DE : Ψ lxxvii. 23 B* : 3 M. vi. 18 ἠνεῴχθην Gen. vii. 11 : Sir. xliii. 14 : Is. xxiv. 18 ℵAQΓ : Dan. ΟΘ vii. 10	ἤνοιξα *passim* (including Gen. xxix. 31, xliii. 21, xliv. 11) ἠνοίχθην *passim*
Perf. act.	ἀνέῳγα Tob. ii. 10 B (in late passive sense)		
Perf. pass.	ἀνεῳγμένος N. xix. 15 : Jos. viii. 17 : 3 K. viii. 29 A : 2 Ch. vi. 20, 40, vii. 15 : 2 Es. xi. 6 BA, xvi. 5 : Ψ v. 10, xiii. 3 : Ez. xxix. 21 : Dan. Θ vi. 10 B	ἠνεῳγμένος 3 K. viii. 29 B, viii. 52 : 2 Es. xi. 6 ℵ : Is. xlii. 20 Γ : Dan. Θ vi. 10 A	ἠνοιγμένος Is. xlii. 20 BℵAQ
Pluperf. pass.	ἀνέῳκτο Job xxxi. 32 B	(δι)ηνέῳκτο ib. ℵAC	

The imperfect is only found in the later form ἤνοιγον -όμην 3 Κ. vii. 21, 1 Μ. xi. 2 (not Attic ἀνέῳγον).

Ὁράω keeps the Attic imperf. ἑώρων (ἑόρα 4 Μ. iv. 24 A: the literary essayist no doubt wrote ἑώρα אV), but in the imperf. mid. loses both ε and ω in the compound προορώμην Ψ xv. 8 (προωρ. Bᵃᵇ). Ἑώρακα (which appears to be the older Attic form)[1] is universal in the Pentateuch (excepting ἑόρ. Dt. xxxiii. 9 B*F), is used in literary books (Dan. O, 1 Es., Est., 2 Μ.: once in each) and has preponderant authority in Jeremiah—Baruch: in the majority of the books, however, ἑόρακα is strongly supported. The perf. pass. ἑώραμαι (rare in class. Greek) is so written in L. xiv. 35 (ἑόρ. F) and in the participles παρεωραμένος 3 Κ. x. 3, Eccl. xii. 14, ὑπερεωρ. Na. iii. 11: the late B text of Judges (xix. 30) has ἑόραται. The syllabic augment is dropped in the 1st aor. pass. ὡράθησαν Dan. Θ 1. 15: otherwise this tense, which is not used before Aristotle, occurs only in the moods.

Ὠθέω. The LXX translators, in common with other Hellenistic writers, dropped the Attic syllabic augment (ἔωσα, ἐώσθην, ἐωσάμην, ἔωσμαι), and wrote ὦσα (ἀπ- ἐξ-) Job xiv. 20 etc., (ἀπ- ἐξ)ώσθην, ἀπωσάμην, (ἀπ- ἐξ-)ῶσμαι. The only book which consistently has ἑ- is 4 Kingdoms, where its use is a clear case of unintelligent Atticism, because the translator (or scribe), not content with ἐξέωσεν xvii. 21 and ἀπεώσαντο xvii. 20, has introduced the augment into the inf. ἀπεώσασθαι iv. 27 B and the fut. ἀπεώσομαι xxi. 14 BA, xxiii. 27 B (cf. 9 *inf.*)[2].

For the late double augment in compound verbs see 8 below.

7. Reduplication. Peculiar forms. Initial ρ is reduplicated contrary to Attic rule (Ionic has similar forms) in ῥέριμμαι Jd. iv. 22 B, xv. 15 B (ἐκ-), Tob. i. 17 B, Jdth vi. 13 A,

---

[1] See Veitch s. v. for the claims of ἑώρακα—ἑόρακα. The latter is certain in old Comedy and may have always been the vernacular form.

[2] The aug. appears also in ἐξεωσμένον 2 Κ. xiv. 14 B (this portion of 2 Κ. was the work of the translator of 4 Κ., § 2) beside ἔξωσμ. in the preceding and ἐξῶσαι in the same verse. Ἀπεωσθῆναι Lam. iii. 45 A is a further ex. of augmented inf.

Jer. xliii. 30 A: elsewhere class. ἔρριμμαι (or ἔριμμαι, § 7, 39)[1]. The list of so-called 'Attic' reduplicated forms is enriched in the κοινή by the addition of ἀγήγοχα (for Att. ἦχα), also, through non-pronunciation of intervocalic γ, written ἀγήοχα ἀγείοχα ἀγέοχα[2]: this is the perf. used in LXX, spelt ἀγίοχα in the uncials (later hands correct to ἀγήοχα), Gen. xlvi. 32, L. x. 19 B*F (-αγειόχ. A), 1 K. xxi. 15 -αγειόχ. B* (-αγιάχ. A), Tob. xii. 3 B*אA, Sir. xxv. 3 B* (-αγείοχ. אA), 3 M. v. 19 AV*, 45 AV*: perf. pass. ἦγμαι class. Dt. xxxii. 34 etc. Ὀμώμοκα (Ψ cxviii. 106 א) is becoming obsolete and appears in various degenerate forms: ὀμωμέκαμεν 1 K. xx. 42 B* (ὠμωμόκ. A), ὀμώμεχα Ez. vi. 9 A, ὀμώμοχεν Tob. ix. 3 BA. Μεμνήστευμαι appears thus with re-duplication (on the model of μέμνημαι) Dt. xx. 7, xxii. 23 ff., A once (xxii. 23) writing the more regular ἐμνηστευμένη used by St Luke (no class. instance of the perf.). Βεβλάστηκα (Joel ii. 22) and κέκτημαι are written, not the alternative class. forms without initial consonant. Θέλω has now perf. τεθέληκα Ψ xl. 12 (class. ἐθέλω ἠθέληκα).

Loss of reduplication or substitution of augment. Reduplication, which has disappeared from the modern language, begins to show signs of decay in the κοινή, being either replaced by the augment (on the model set by earlier Greek in the case of initial ῥ or a double letter etc.) or suppressed altogether (cf. the pres. μνήσκομαι § 19, 3). The few LXX examples are practically limited to Codex A and doubtless do not go back to the autographs.

Augment *vice* reduplication: ἐνεδύκει L. xvi. 23 A (ἐνδεδύκει B -δεδοίκει F), ἤλιφα[3] N. iii. 12 A with ἠλιμμένοι ib. 3 BA (F

[1] Other words with initial ῥ take ἐρρ. as in Attic: διέρραγκα (-ανκα B*, -ακα א) Prov. vii. 17 may be mentioned as being apparently the earliest instance of a perf. from ῥαίνω: the earlier language avoided these perfects in -γκα.
[2] Mayser 338.
[3] Εἴληφα of BF (M.T. לִקְחָתִי) is obviously right. The reading of A is a rather clever conjectural emendation, characteristic of this MS, made by a slight transposition of letters, under the influence of οἱ ἠλιμμένοι v. 3, with-

ἤλειμμ.) (class. ἀλήλιφα, ἀλήλιμμαι), ἐπέγραπτο Dt. ix. 10 A, κατέβηκεν 3 K. xx. 18 A, ἀπώλεκας Is. xlix. 20 A, ἐλάληκα Ez. iii. 10 A, Jer. xxviii. 41 ℵ*, ἐνεπυρισμένον 1 M. xi. 4 A (ib. ἐνπεπ. AℵV), ἐπλήρωτο 2 M. iii. 30 A[1]. Suppression of reduplication[2] (as in mod. Greek pass. part. e.g. δεμένος): λογισμένον 3 K. x. 21 A.

Other anomalies of A are μαμακρυνκότων Jd. xviii. 22 (for μεμ.), φεφύλαξαι 1 K. xxii. 23 (πεφ. B). Μεμαρτύρω 2 Es. xix. 34 B* is a strange reduplicated aorist (διεμαρτύρω cett.).

8. Augment and reduplication in composition.

In verbs which are *true compounds* of the *simplex* and a preposition, the augment and reduplication still, as in Attic, occupy the internal position after the preposition (ἀπ-ήντησα, προ-ε-πορευόμην[3] etc.), except—an exception which applies also to Attic—where the simple verb had become obsolete or from the frequent use of the compound the fact of its composition had ceased to be felt, e.g. ἐκάθευδον, ἐκάθισα. There are as yet scarcely any indications of a movement in the direction of giving every augment an external position and, so to speak, stamping upon the forefront the fact that the tense is a past one, as in modern Greek (ἐκατάλαβα, ἐπρόσεξα). Ἤνοιξα already referred to (6 *sup.*) is new, but lacks contemporary support from the papyri.

In verbs *derived from compounds* (παρασύνθετα, *decomposita*) of a preposition the latter was strictly inseparable from the remaining constituent, which did not generally exist as a simple verb, and an external augment was therefore required. Nevertheless, many, indeed the majority of these verbs, were, apparently through mistaken etymology, treated as though

out regard to the Hebrew. A similar instance in this MS of emendation of the Greek occurs close by in *v.* 9, μόνοι for μοί (=ﬡׄﬢ, M.T. ﬡׄﬢ).

[1] Is κ̄εκ̄λη̄κεν 4 K. iii. 10 A intended for a correction to ἔκληκεν?

[2] Examples from the papyri, mainly in compounds, are given by Mayser 341.

[3] The only LXX instance of crasis with προ- is προυφάνησαν 4 M. iv. 10 Aℵ (προεφ. V), see § 9, 11 for crasis in this book: elsewhere προέβαλλον, προεμάχησα etc.

they were true compounds and augmented internally[1]. The κοινή, as illustrated by the LXX, adhered to Attic precedent and the following e.g. have classical support:

'Απεδήμησα (from ἀπόδημος) Ez. xix. 3 A, ἀπελογησάμην 2 M. xiii. 26, ἐνήδρευσα, ἐνεθυμήθην (ἐντεθυμημένης 3 M. i. 25), ἐνεχείρησα, ἐπεθύμησα, ἐπεστάτουν 1 Es. vii. 2, ἐπετήδευσα, ἐπεχείρησα, κατηγόρησα (without syll. aug.), παρενόμουν Ψ cxviii. 51 A (παρηνόμουν RT as from παρ-ανομεῖν), προεθυμήθην, ὑπώπτευσα.

'Ενεγυήσω Prov. vi. 3 (2 sg. aor. mid. from ἐγγυάω) may be illustrated from the papyri, where the augment takes various forms[2]. Other verbs beginning with ἐν- have fluctuating augment as

ἠνεχύρασα (-αζον) Job xxii. 6, xxiv. 3	ἐνεχύρασα Job xxxiv. 31 A, Ez. xviii. 16
ἠνυπνιάσθην (-ασάμην)	ἐνυπνιάσθην (-ασάμην) : 4 *sup.*
ἠνωτισάμην 2 Es. xix. 30 B	ἐνωτισάμην ib. אA, Job xxxii. 11 A, Jer. xxiii. 18.

'Εξεκλησίασα (as if there were a simple verb κλησιάζω) is read by B in 1 Ch. xv. 3, 2 Ch. v. 2 etc. and by A, א, V elsewhere, and in view of the fact that in the unaugmented parts of the verb (imperat. and part.) we find no trace in LXX of a verb ἐξ-εκκλησιάζω with superfluous preposition, it is probable that ἐξεκκλησίασα -άσθην which the uncials read in L. viii. 4 etc. are scribal corruptions of ἐξεκλησίασα -άσθην.

On the other hand with initial augment we have consistently ἐπρονόμευσα (κατεπρο-: correctly as the verb is formed from προνομή, not directly from νομεύω) and πεπρονομευμένος Is. xlii. 22 (AF alone have προενόμευσα twice, N. xxxi. 9, Dt. ii. 35: so א[c.a] in 1 M. i. 61)—ἐπροφήτευσα (B προεφήτευσα only in Sir. xlvi. 20: A 4 times in 1 K.[3], cf. προπεφητεῦσθαι in the citation from Origen in Q[mg] Ez. xxxii. 17)—ἐπαροιμίαζεν 4 M. xviii. 16 (παροιμ. א)—ἐπερίσσευσα (class.). New verbs also tend to external augment: ἡσυνθέτησα (-κα) 2 Es. x. 2 10 etc., ἡκαταστάτησαν Tob. i. 15 B.

---

[1] See the list in Kühner-Blass I. ii. § 204 and Rutherford *NP* p. 79 ff.
[2] Mayser 343.   [3] Also προεφήτευον 3 K. xxii. 12 A.

Verbs derived from compounds in which the first element is not a preposition usually in classical Greek take external augment[1]: so in LXX e.g. ᾠκοδόμησα (or οἰκ., 4 *sup.*), ἐπαρρησιάσατο Ψ xciii. 1 etc.: ἐδυστόκησα, ἐδυσφήμησα, ἐδυσφόρουν are classical, but εὐ- followed by a short vowel has internal aug., εὐηρέστησα always and εὐηγγελισάμην in the only occurrence of the past tense, Ψ xxxix. 10 : between ηὐ- and εὐ- in other *decomposita* (εὐφραίνειν etc.) there is fluctuation as in the direct compounds of εὐ.

Verbs compounded of two prepositions tend to take **two augments** (cf. 6 *sup.*). The older language supplied a few standing examples of this e.g. (παρ)ηνώχλησα (always so written in LXX except in Jd. xiv. 17 B* παρενώχ.) and ἐπηνώρθουν (LXX has only ἐπανωρθώθη 2 M. v. 20 A, ἐπανορθ. V*), in addition to ἠνειχόμην (so 3 M. i. 22 A), ἠνεσχόμην (but LXX ἀνεσχόμην [class. poetry] Is. lxiii. 15, lxiv. 12, 4 M. xiii. 27). The LXX has not carried much further this practice, which became common at a rather later date, and, as it is unrepresented in the Ptolemaic papyri[2], the originality of the commonest LXX instance ἀπεκατέστη(σεν) is open to question.

Further instances are παρεκατέθε(ν)το (-ετιθέμην) Jer. xlvii. 7, xlviii. 10, 2 M. ix. 25 A: παρεσυνεβλήθη Ψ xlviii. 13 AT‫ℵ‬c.a, 21 AT : ἐνεπεριεπατήσαμεν Jd. xviii. 9 A: κατεδιείλαντο Jl. iii. 2 ℵc.a (καταδιειλ. cett.).

Reduplication + augment occurs in κεκατήραμαι[3] N. xxii. 6 (καικατ. or καὶ κατ. F), xxiv. 9 (do. A), Dt. xxi. 23 AF (κεκαταρα-

---

[1] With internal reduplication ἐμπεποδεστάτηκας read by a group of MSS in Jd. xi. 35 (cf. the corruption of it in A) is a curious instance.

[2] Mayser 342. In LXX ἀπεκατέστη(σεν) appears in Gen. xxiii. 16, xl. 21, Ex. iv. 7 B*A, xiv. 27, Jer. xxiii. 8 (Hexaplaric), 1 Es. i. 33 B, Bel Θ 39 : on the other hand with single aug. ἀποκατεστάθη Dan. Ο iv. 33, 34b, ἀντικατέστη(σεν) Jos. v. 7, Mic. ii. 8 A, ἐπισυνέστη(σεν) N. xvi. 19, Sir. xlv. 18, προσκατέστησαν Jd. xiv. 11 A. Similarly with single aug. προκατελάβετο *passim*, etc.

[3] Cf. the external aug. in ἐκαταρασάμην 2 Es. xxiii. 25 B and double aug. ἐπεκατηράσατο Ψ cli. 6 T : the aor. in LXX is elsewhere the class. κατηρασάμην. A curious instance illustrating the insufficiency in v/A.D. of internal reduplication is ἐπροσκέκληται Ex. v. 3 F.

μένος B), Sir. iii. 16 (καικατ. אC): the class. κατήραμαι remains in 4 K. ix. 34, W. xii. 11 (κεκατ. א). Exx. of double aug. in compounds of one preposition only—a half-way house towards the modern Greek elimination of the internal aug.—appear in late books or late texts only: ἐπροσηύξατο 2 Es. x. 1 B*אA (but προσηυξάμην [-ευξ.] xii. 4 and elsewhere in LXX), ἐδιελύσαμεν 2 Es. xi. 7 א*, ἐδιέκρινεν Job xxiii. 10 א*, ἐπαρεκάλουν Job xxix. 25 C, ἐκατέλαβεν 1 M. xii. 30 A, ἐσυνέθετο 1 M. xv. 27 AV.

9. **Misplaced augment.** The augment in vulgar Greek occasionally intruded into the moods[1]. The LXX examples are limited to εἰ for ἰ (which had now become interchangeable sounds) and ὠ for ὀ or οἰ. ῞Ινα μὴ εἴδῃ (for ἴδῃ) Is. xxvi. 10 B*אQΓ, εἰδέτωσαν 4 K. vi. 20 A, Tob. viii. 12 B*A, εἴδετε (imperat.) 4 K. vi. 32 A, εἴδωμεν Cant. vii. 12 א, (ὑπερ)είδῃς Eccl. v. 7 A, Est. C. 9 A, εἰδόντες Est. viii. 15 א, ᾽Ωκοδομήσαντες Jos. xxii. 16 A, (δι)ωκοδομήσωμεν 2 Es. xii. 17 B*, Is. ix. 10 A, ὠκοδομουμένη Ψ cxxi. 3 Τ: ἐξωμολογεῖσθαι Tob. xiii. 3 A (=imperat. ἐξομολογεῖσθε): ὠμόσαντες W. xiv. 29 C.

§ 17. VERBS IN -Ω. TERMINATIONS.

1. The most marked change under this head is the gradual **disappearance of the second aorist forms** and the **intrusion of the first aorist** forms into their place and subsequently into the place of the other past tenses (perfect and imperfect)[2]. This extension of the sphere of the first aorist takes place in various ways. Primarily it affected the *terminations* only, beginning probably with the termination of the 3rd person plural: and here again there was divergence. (i) The α of the 1st aor. replaces the ο (or ε) in the termination of the 2nd aor.: εἶπα -αν -άτω, ἤγαγα. The termination -αν is then extended to the 3rd plur. of perfect and imperfect. (ii) An alternative was to retain the σ of the 1st aorist as well as the α in the 3rd plur. of 2nd aor. and impf.: εἴποσαν,

---

[1] So in the papyri from iii/B.C.: ἀνηλίσκειν with ἀνήλωμα etc. is the commonest instance: Mayser 345 f. Modern Greek has created a new class of verbs in ξ- containing the old syllabic aug., e.g. ξεβράζω from ἐξ-έβρασα. Cf. 6 *supra*, s. v. ὠθέω.

[2] See especially the important article by K. Buresch in *Rhein. Mus. für Philologie*, Bd. 46, 1891, entitled " Γέγοναν und anderes Vulgärgriechisch," and Dieterich *Untersuch.* 234 ff.

ἠγάγοσαν, ἐφέροσαν. This form seems to have been designed to discriminate between the 1st sing. and the 3rd plur. which in classical Greek ended alike in -ον in these two tenses[1] More rarely (iii) a new 1st aorist replaced the old 2nd aorist: ἦξα (ἠγάγησα), § 21, 1. The result was much simplification and greater uniformity. The otiose 2nd aorist, which conveyed precisely the same meaning as the 1st aorist, disappeared, and all past tenses tended to be formed after the same pattern.

2. The beginnings of the first change referred to above— the use of **forms intermediate between 1st and 2nd aor.** without the σ of the former—go back in two instances to Attic Greek: ἤνεγκα (beside ἤνεγκον), εἶπα (beside εἶπον)[2] The κοινή naturally took over the α forms in these words.

In LXX ἤνεγκα has the α forms throughout the indicative and participle (except in 2 M. iii. 35 ἀνενεγκών A [-ας V], vi. 21 ἐνεγκόντα A [-αντα V]) and usually in the imperative (exceptions ἀνενεγκέτω 2 K. xxiv. 22 B*, ἐνέγκετε 2 Es. xviii. 15 B*: B also has exx. of 2nd sing. -ένεγκε, which however may be merely an itacistic spelling of the mid. -ένεγκαι which is often attested by the other MSS, so L. ix. 2 BA [read -και F], N. xvi. 46 [-και AF], Jd. vi. 30, xix. 22, 2 K. xiii. 10, Dan. Οθ Bel 34 [read -και as in ⓦ 33]). The old inf. ἐνεγκεῖν maintained its hold longest, beside ἐνέγκαι[3] which gradually gains ground and in some of the later books nearly succeeds in ousting the former (e.g. ἐνέγκαι in 2 Es. iii. 7, viii. 17, xviii. 1, xx. 34 etc., ἐνεγκεῖν in this book only in viii. 30). The aor. mid. likewise keeps the α forms: but ἀπενέγκοιτο receives some support in Job iii. 6.

Similarly εἶπα -ας -αμεν -ατε -αν, imperat. εἴπατε etc., part. εἴπας are used almost to the exclusion of the ο forms: the inf. is generally εἰπεῖν (εἶπαι B* in Ez. xxxiii. 8, 13, 14, -εῖν BᵃᵇAQ *ter*)[4].

It appears from the papyri that the extension of this type

---

[1] Herodian (ed. Lentz ii. 237) refers to the Boeotian use of this form with certain verbs, and explains it as due to a desire to equate the number of syllables in the plural persons (εἴδομεν, therefore εἴδοσαν).
[2] Attic Inscriptions have ἤνεγκαν, part. ἐνέγκας, from iv/B.C. (but ἐνεγκεῖν, -έτω): εἰπάτω (and εἰπέτω) from 350 B.C., εἶπας from 300 B.C. (but εἰπεῖν): Meisterhans 183 f.
[3] The two forms are used interchangeably in the papyri into i/B.C., Mayser 363.
[4] Ἀνεῖπαι appears already in a papyrus of iii/B.C., Mayser 331.

of aorists to other verbs did not become common till i/A.D. Most second aorists remained unaltered except that, as the LXX shows, in the 3rd plur. the forms in -οσαν were frequently employed in place of -ον. The MSS of the LXX and the N.T. appear to reflect this difference between the Ptolemaic period and the beginning of the Christian era. In LXX the asigmatic aorists in -α, 3rd plur. -αν, apart from a few words, are in the main restricted to a single group of books, while the majority of the books have 1st sing. -ον, 3rd plur. -οσαν (or -ον). In the N.T., on the other hand, 3rd plur. -οσαν is rare and forms in -α -αν are on the increase.

The commonest LXX exx. of the -α type after the two which have classical authority are

εἶλα (εἰλάμην) e.g. act. καθεῖλαν Gen. xliv. 11, 3 K. xix. 14 etc., ἀφεῖλαν 1 M. vii. 47 A, ἀφεῖλας Job xxxviii. 15 (-ες C): mid. (ἀν- ἀφ- ἐξ-)εἴλατο Gen. xxxvii. 21, Ex. ii. 5, xviii. 4, Is. xxxviii. 14 etc.

ἦλθα mainly in imperat. ἐλθάτω -ατε. The ο forms are, however, normal in the ind. (with 3rd plur. ἤλθοσαν), though α forms are attested, even in the Pentateuch, e.g. ἤλθαμεν N. xiii. 28 B, Dt. xxix. 16 B, ἤλθατε Gen. xxvi. 27 etc., ἦλθαν Gen. xlvii. 18 B.

ἔπεσα is much commoner than ἔπεσον, clearly owing to the fact that the old 2nd aorist already contained the σ distinctive of the 1st aorist. The conversion from strong to weak aorist took place without the intervention of a middle stage (as was necessary e.g. in εὗρον—εὗρα—εὕρησα). Later scribes may of course be responsible for the LXX forms: Ex. xxxii. 28, L. ix. 24, N. xvi. 22 *et passim*.

Apart from the 5 exx. quoted, instances of this type are rare and confined to late texts and can in few cases be ascribed to the autographs. They are a distinguishing feature of the group Jd. (B text)—4 Kings. ἔβαλαν (ἐξ-): 3 K. vi. 3, 2 Ch. xxix. 16 A (-ον B). εἶδαν (ἴδαν) Jd. vi. 28 B, xvi. 24 B, xviii. 7 B, 4 K. ii. 15 A, vi. 20 A, Ψ xxxiv. 21 B (contrast εἶδες 22), Jdth vi. 12 BℵA, 1 M. iii. 17 A, iv. 12 A. εὗρα: εὕραμεν Gen. xliv. 8 A, xlvii. 25 A, 2 Es. iv. 19 BA, Ψ cxxxi. 6 AT: εὗρας 2 Es. xix. 8 ℵ (-ες BA): (ἀν)ευράμενοι 4 M. iii. 13 f. A, Aℵ. ἀπέθαναν R. i. 5 A, 2 K. xi. 17 B, 24 B, xiii. 33 B, 4 K. xi. 1 A, Tob. iii. 9 B*A. ἔλαβαν Jd. i. 24 A, 2 K. xxiii. 16 B. ἐγκατέλιπαν 4 K. vii. 7 B, 2 Ch. xxix. 6 B: ἐγκατελίπατε Is. i. 4 B (-ελείπατε Γ -ελείπετε AQ). ἐφάγαμεν 2 K. xix. 42 B. ἔφυγαν Jd. vii. 21 B, 1 K. xvii. 51 A, xxx. 17 A, 2 K. x. 13 B, 14 BA, xiii. 29 B, 1 M. x. 82 A (contrast 83, xvi. 8, 10): κατέφυγα Ψ cxlii. 9 RTℵ^c.a (-ον B*ℵ*A).

ἐπήγαγας Dan. Θ iii. 28 Q. γενάμενος (common in the papyri from 100 A.D.) is written by A in Jeremiah (xiv. 1, xxv. 1, xxxvii. 1, xxxix. 1, xli. 1, 8=γενέμενος א, xlii. 1, li. 1): so ἐγενάμην Jer. ii. 31 A, ἐγενάμεθα Is. lxiii. 19 א, παραγενάμενοι 2 M. xv. 24 V.

3. The first aorist termination -αν begins to replace -ασι in the **perfect** in (iii/) ii/B.C.[1], although -ασι preponderates for some time longer and seems to have survived till the tense became extinct.

Exx. in LXX:—ἑώρακαν Dt. xi. 7 B (ἑώρων AF), ἔγνωκαν 2 K. xix. 6 A (ἔγνωκα B), παρέστηκαν Is. v. 29 Bא*Q, ἑάλωκαν Jer. xxviii. 56 א*, πεποίηκαν Ez. viii. 15 A (passage not in B), πεφύτευκαν xix. 13 BQ, ἠχρείωκαν Dan. O vi. 20, πέποιθαν Jdth vii. 10 Bא A, πέπρακαν 2 M. x. 21 AV, καθέστηκαν 2 M. xiv. 5 V, ἐκπεπόρθηκαν 4 M. xviii. 4 א*V (ἐκπεπολιόρκηκαν אc.a).

4. The extension of 3rd plur. -αν to the **imperfect** is also attested in ii/B.C., but is much rarer than its use with the other past tenses: the alternative termination -οσαν was preferred with this tense. The LXX instances are confined in the B text to one in Jd. and three in the early chapters of 2 K. (K. ββ) besides a few variants in Aא.

Κατέλειπαν Jo. x. 40 A, ἀνέβαιναν Jd. vi. 3 B, ἐλάμβαναν 1 K. viii. 3 A, κατέβαιναν 1 K. xxv. 20 A, διέβαιναν 2 K. ii. 29 B, ἔφεραν iii. 22 B, ἦγαν vi. 3 B, ἀνέψυχαν xvi. 14 A (-ξαν B): א has similar forms in ἤθελαν Is. xxviii. 12, ἐδίωκαν 1 M. xi. 73, ἐλέγαμεν 4 M. xiii. 2.

5. Side by side with the termination -αν in the 3rd plur. of the old 2nd aorists and the imperfect appears the longer termination -οσαν. Though the examples in the papyri are not very numerous[2], the very strong attestation of this form in the LXX leaves no doubt as to its antiquity. It seems to have

---

[1] The earliest exx. cited are from Asia, παρείληφαν (Lydia) 246 B.C., ἀπέσταλκαν (Lydia) 193 B.C., Dieterich *Untersuch.* 235 f. In Egypt the form does not appear before 162 B.C., εἴληφαν, ἐπιδέδωκαν BM i. 17. 23, 49: in iii/B.C. always εἰλήφασι etc.

[2] Mayser 323. The narrative and historical element in the papyri is comparatively small and there is not often occasion in petitions etc. to use the 3rd pers. plural of the past tenses.

preceded the use of -αν in these tenses and to owe its popularity
if not its origin to a desire to discriminate between the 1st
pers. sing. and the 3rd pers. plur.   This was done by retaining
the o and appending the 1st aor. termination -σαν.

> In the earliest papyri exx. a slightly different ending is used,
> viz. -εσαν: ἐλαμβάνεσαν BM i. 18, 31 (161 B.C.), ἀφίλεσαν ib.
> xli. 15 (same date).   The connecting vowel ε in this tentative
> form perhaps comes from the 3rd *sing.*: ἐλάμβανε—ἐλαμβάνε|σαν[1].
> A single ex. of this form occurs in LXX: κατεφάγεσαν Jer. x.
> 25 ℵ*Q (-ον BA).
>
> The form -οσαν was transitional and has not, with one excep-
> tion, survived, like the forms in -αν, in modern Greek.   The
> exception is the imperfect of contract verbs, where the use of
> the -αν termination was out of the question.   In this tense
> modern Greek has not only retained the 3rd plur. in -ούσαν(ε)
> but has modelled the rest of the tense upon it: (ἐ)ρωτούσα
> -σες etc.
>
> Dieterich *Untersuch.* 242 f. traces the origin of -οσαν to
> Boeotia[2].   His statement that its use in Egypt is limited to the
> imperfect is incorrect: besides ἀφίλεσαν referred to above 2 exx.
> of -ήλθοσαν occur at the end of ii/B.C. (Mayser 323), apart from
> later exx.: ἐπήλθοσαν BU 36 (no date), 436 (ii/ or iii/ A.D.).

These forms in -οσαν are exceedingly frequent in LXX,
being distributed over all the translations (excepting one
group) from the Hexateuch to 2 Esdras: the latter book with
Joshua (B text) supplies the greatest number of instances.
The exceptional group is 1—4 K.: the -οσαν forms are entirely
absent from 1, 3 and 4 K. (except ἡμάρτοσαν 3 K. viii. 50 A):
in 2 K. A again supplies one instance of aorist, ἐξήλθοσαν
ii. 13, B has ἐλάβοσαν v. 21, and BA have one ex. of the
imperfect of a contract verb, ἐνοοῦσαν xx. 15.   On the other
hand, as has been seen, it is just in this group that the
termination -αν is specially frequent.

> Exx.[3] (1) *Aorist.* -ήλθοσαν *passim* e.g. Ex. i. 1 BAF, Dt.
> i. 24 BAF (it is observable that in the Pentateuch BAF unite in

---

[1] Both forms had a precedent in the 3rd plur. of the imperf. of verbs in
-μι: ἐδίδοσαν, ἐτίθεσαν.

[2] Cf. note 1 on p. 210.

[3] Cf. with the list in 2 above, p. 211 f.

attesting the -οσαν form only in the opening of these two books
and at the end of Deut. : εὕροσαν Dt. xxxi. 17 BAF, ἡμάρτοσαν
xxxii. 5 BAF) etc. etc. -ηγάγοσαν Jos. vi. 23 B, x. 23, Jer.
xxxiii. 23 *bis* B, 1 Es. i. 17 B, 19, Jdth xii. 5 etc. ἡμάρτοσαν Is.
xxiv. 6, xlii. 24 etc. (παρεν)εβάλοσαν Ex. xvii. 1 B, Jd. xv. 9 A,
xviii. 12 A, Jer. xliv. 21, 2 Es. xxi. 30 etc. (ε)ἴδοσαν Dt. vii.
19 B*, x. 21 B, Is. xxii. 9, Ψ lxxvi. 17, 2 Es. iii. 12, Cant. vi.
8 *passim.* εἴποσαν R. iv. 11 *bis* B, BA, 2 Es. v. 4 B, xi. 3 B etc.
καθείλοσαν Jos. viii. 29 B, Is. xxii. 10. εὕροσαν Ex. xiv. 9 B,
Jos. ii. 22 B, Hos. xii. 4, Jer. ii. 5, xiv. 3, 1 Ch. iv. 41 etc.
-έσχοσαν 1 Es. vi. 5, 2 Es. xiii. 5 Bℵ. ἀπεθάνοσαν Bar. ii. 25.
-ελάβοσαν Dt. i. 25 B, Jos. x. 28 B, Jd. i. 6 B, R. i. 4, Zech. i. 6,
Jer. xxxiii. 8, Ez. xxxii. 24, 2 Es. ix. 2 etc. -ελίποσαν Ex. xvi.
24 B, Dt. xxix. 25 B, Jer. vi. 15. ἐπίοσαν Jer. xxviii. 7, xlii. 14 Bℵ,
1 Es. iii. 3 B. ἐφάγοσαν Gen. xviii. 8, Ex. xvi. 35 B, Jos. v. 11 B,
1 Es. iii. 3 B, vii. 13, 2 Es. xix. 25 etc. -εφύγοσαν Jos. x. 27 B,
2 Es. xxiii. 10.

(2) *Imperfect.* (*a*) Uncontracted verbs. ἤροσαν Jos. iii. 14 B
(ἦραν AF). ἤσθοσαν Ez. xxii. 9 B*Q (imperfects in -ον -ουν and
-οσαν -οῦσαν are used indiscriminately in this chapter). ἀπεθνή-
σκοσαν Tob. vii. 11 ABᵃ (-ον B*). ἐκλαίοσαν Dan. Ο Sus. 33.
ἐκρίνοσαν Ex. xviii. 26 *bis* B, Jer. v. 28. -ελαμβάνοσαν Jer. v. 26,
Ez. xxii. 12 *bis*. ἐλέγοσαν Ν. xxxii. 5 A (-ον BF). κατελύοσαν
Jer. v. 7 Q (-ον, -οντο cett.). ὑπερίπτοσαν 4 M. vi. 25 ℵ. ἐξαπεστέλλοσαν Ez. xxiii. 40 AQ (-ον B). ἐφαίνοσαν 1 M. iv. 50 A.
-εφέροσαν Ex. xviii. 26 B, Jos. xxiv. 33a B, 1 Ch. xxii. 4 B
(ἐφόρασαν A) (contrast ἔφερον 2 Ch. i. 17 etc.). ἐνεχρίοσαν
Tob. ii. 10 ℵ.

(*b*) Contracted verbs: -οῦσαν (-ῶσαν). -ενοουσαν Ex. xxxiii.
8 B, 2 K. xx. 15 BA. ἐπηξονοῦσαν Ν. i. 18 B. ἐπολεμοῦσαν Jd.
xi. 5 A. ἠνομοῦσαν Ez. xxii. 11. ἐθυμιῶσαν Jer. xi. 12 ℵ, xxxix.
29 BℵA, cf. 2 Ch. xxx. 14 (B writes εθυμιωσιν *sic*). εὐθηνοῦσαν
Lam. i. 5 BAQ*. ἐθρηνοῦσαν 1 Es. i. 30 B. ᾠκοδομοῦσαν (οἰκ-)
2 Es. vi. 14 Aᵛⁱᵈ, xiv. 18 BℵA. ἐδολιοῦσαν Ψ v. 10, xiii. 3. εὐλογοῦσαν ib. lxi. 5 B*ℵ*A. ἐποιοῦσαν Job i. 4 B*ℵ*, 1 M. xiv. 36 A.
ἐταπεινοῦσαν Jdth iv. 9 BA. ἐθεωροῦσαν ib. x. 10 A. (παρ)ωκοῦσαν
Dan. Ο Sus. 28, 1 M. xiv. 34 A. ἐζητοῦσαν 1 M. xvi. 22 A.
ὡμιλοῦσαν Dan. Ο Sus. 57. παρετηροῦσαν Dan. Θ Sus. 12.
Ἐῶσαν Jer. xli. 10 is the single ex. from a verb in -άω, see
§ 16, 5.

6. The termination -σαν is further used in LXX, as in
Hellenistic Greek generally[1], for the 3rd plur. of the **imperative**, to the exclusion of the older forms in -ων -όντων etc.

---

[1] From 300 B.C. in Attic Inscriptions : Meisterhans 167.

Exx.: ἔστωσαν Gen. i. 14 etc., γενηθήτωσαν ib., θανατούσθωσαν L. xx. 10 ff.

7. It appears also in the **optative**, where -οισαν -αισαν replace the older -οιεν -αιεν (-ειαν).

Exx.: αἰνέσαισαν Gen. xlix. 8, ποιήσαισαν Dt. i. 44, 3 K. xix. 2 A, xxi. 10 A, ἔλθοισαν Dt. xxxiii. 16 and probably 7, ἐνέγκαισαν Is. lxvi. 20, εὕροισαν Jer. ii. 5 A (read εὕροσαν with BℵQ), εἴπαισαν (εἴποισαν) Ψ xxxiv. 25 *bis*, ἐκλ(ε)ίποισαν ciii. 35, ἐκκόψαισαν (-κολάψαισαν A) and καταφάγοισαν Prov. xxiv. 52, ψηλαφήσαισαν Job v. 14 Bℵ, θηρεύσαισαν xviii. 7 BℵC, ἔλθοισαν 9 and 11 BℵC, ὀλέσαισαν 11 Bᵇℵ (-σαιαν B*, -σιαν A, -σαιεν Bᵃ) and xx. 10 BℵC, πυρσεύσαισαν xx. 10 BC(ℵ), ἴδοισαν xxi. 20 BℵC, φάγοισαν xxxi. 8 BℵC, εὕροισαν Sir. xxxiii. (xxxvi.) 11, εὐλογή-σαισαν Tob. iii. 11 BA. The exceptions to the rule are found in 4 Maccabees which uses the strict Attic forms (e.g. φάνοιεν, θάνοιεν iv. 23, θέλοιεν v. 3, μιεροφαγήσαιεν, ἀντιλέγοιεν viii. 2) and Cod. A in Job, which has ἴδοιεν in xxi. 20 and forms in -(ε)ιαν elsewhere, θηρεύσιαν xviii. 7, ἀπώσιαν xviii. 18, θλάσιαν xx. 10.

The 2nd and 3rd sing. of the 1st aor. optat. similarly end in -αις -αι (for the stricter Attic -ειας -ειε).

The writer of 4 Macc. again shows his Atticizing tendency in using the older forms of the 3rd sing., e.g. νομίσειεν iv. 13, ἐπιτρέψειεν 17, συγγνωμονήσειεν v. 13 etc., and perhaps also of the 2nd sing., ἐκκόψειας v. 30 ℵ, τήξειας ib. ℵᶜ·ᵃ, καταφρονήσειας v. 10 Vʳᵉˢᶜʳ. Job also supplies ἀπώσειεν xviii. 18 BℵC, θηλάσειεν (? Θ) xx. 16 BℵC.

8. **2nd pers. sing. in -ες for -ας** in 1st aor. and perfect. These forms are but slenderly attested in LXX (mainly in the untrustworthy Cod. A) and in the Ptolemaic papyri and clearly did not take root in Egypt. They are interesting however as precursors of modern Greek which in the two past tenses (impf. and aor.) writes -α -ες -ε -αμε -ετε -αν, i.e. in the conflict between the terminations of 1st aor. and 2nd aor. (impf.) the α of the 1st aor. has succeeded in ousting the ο of the 2nd aorist, but the forms in which the 2nd aor. (or impf.) had ε have remained unaltered[1].

[1] See Dieterich op. cit. 239. He speaks of the mod. Greek forms -ες -ε -ετε as the last remnants of the strong aorist active. But they may

In LXX: ἀπέσταλκες Ex. v. 22 A, οἶδες 2 K. ii. 26 A, ἔδωκες Ez. xvi. 21 A, 2 Es. xix. 10 A, ἐφύλαξες Job xiii. 27 A, ἀφῆκες Tob. xi. 2 B. So in the plur. ὑπερβεβήκετε 3 M. vi. 24 V. (Ἔκρινες Job x. 2 A [-νας cett.] and ὑπερῆρες Prov. xxix. 47 א [-ῆρας cett.] may be true imperfects.)

In papyri: παρέσταλκες PP ii. 20, 4, 15 (252 B.C.) is the only early example which I have noted. Παρείληφες occurs in 2 B.C. (OP iv. 742, 4): in ii/ iii/A.D. exx. begin to accumulate, δέδωκες, οἶδες, ἔγραψες, ἐποίησες etc.

9. In the **pluperfect** the (3rd) plural has been assimilated to the singular, i.e. -εισαν etc. are written, not Attic -εσαν etc., even in the literary books[1]: e.g. (καθ)ιστήκεισαν Gen. xviii. 2, 3 M. ii. 33 etc., ἐπεποίθεισαν Prov. xxi. 22 etc., ἐπεπόνθεισαν W. xviii. 1: ᾔδειμεν Gen. xliii. 7 etc., ᾔδειτε Dt. xiii. 13, ᾔδεισαν Gen. xlii. 23 etc.

10. **-εντο for -οντο.** The 3rd plur. of the 2nd aor. act., as we have seen, took over the -αν of the 1st aor. In the 2nd aor. *mid.* in -όμην the o was, in one instance at least, eliminated in another way, the 3rd plur. being modelled on the 3rd sing. in -ετο. Ἐπελάθεντο is the predominant form in LXX: Jd. iii. 7 A, Jer. iii. 21 B*א, xviii. 15 B*אA, xxiii. 27 B*א, xxvii. 6 אA, xxxvii 14 א, Hos. xiii. 6 B*, Ψ lxxvii. 11 B*. So in N.T. Mc. viii. 14 B*.

Ἐπελάθοντο without variant only in 1 K. xii. 9, Ψ cv. 13, 21, cxviii. 139, Job xix. 14 (cf. Job Θ xxxix. 15).

11. The habit of appending an irrational final ν (or ς) has already been referred to (p. 135): further exx. are ἀντελάβοντον 3 K. ix. 9 A, ἐπορεύθηταν Jer. li. 23 א* (for -ται or -τε), ἐπιστράφητες Jer. iii. 14 א*.

12. **2nd person sing. mid. (present and future).** The competition here lay between three rival terminations, -ῃ,

owe their origin rather to the *imperfect*, ἔλυες. The -ε of the third sing. which was alike for all past tenses affected the preceding person, and the 2nd sing. again reacted on the 2nd plur.

[1] In the Ptolemaic exx. (end of ii/B.C.) the 3rd plur. is written with -ησαν, which was probably indistinguishable in pronunciation from -εισαν (§ 6, 20): -εσαν was still used by literary writers like Polybius and Josephus (Mayser 324).

-ει and -σαι. (i) The older Attic -ῃ, used for all verbs in -ω, arose by contraction out of a primitive -σαι (φέρεσαι = φέρεαι = φέρῃ), which was retained in the -μι verbs (ἴστασαι etc.). (ii) Later Attic writers from iv/B.C., when ῃι ει were becoming indistinguishable, wrote -ει or -ῃ indifferently. Some of these -ει forms (βούλει, οἴει, ὄψει) were widely adopted in the κοινή. But (iii) the preference of the κοινή for uniformity led ultimately to the reinstatement of the primitive forms in -σαι (on the model of the perf. pass. in -μαι -σαι -ται) and these are universal in modern Greek.

In the conflict between the -ῃ and the -ει forms the LXX uncials on the whole support the older -ῃ forms for pres. and fut.: Cod. B, however, has a considerable number of -ει forms. It is hardly possible to decide which form is original.

Βούλει is consistently written by B : Ex. iv. 23 (-ῃ A) viii. 2 (-ῃ AF) ix. 2 (-ῃ A) x. 3 BA, 7 BA, 3 K. xx. 6 (-ῃ A), Est. iii. 11 BℵA. Οἴει also is well attested in the few passages where this literary word occurs : Est. ix. 12, Job xxxiv. 17 A, xxxvii. 23 BℵA (-ῃ C), xl. 3 B (-ῃ ℵ), Dan. O ii. 11 (but οἴῃ Job xxxiv. 12 BℵAC). On the other hand ὄψῃ and ἔσῃ largely preponderate over the -ει forms which are limited to a few passages in the B text: ὄψει Ex. vi. 1, 2 K. iii. 13, Ez. viii. 13, 15, Bar. iv. 25 (with Q), ἔσει 2 K. v. 2, 23 (παρέσει), Ez. xxiv. 17, xxxviii. 9: elsewhere they are written by a later hand or hands of B in place of -ῃ of B*

The use of -ει and -ῃ is a distinguishing mark between the two portions of 2 K. which I have called K. ββ and K. βγ (B text).

ἔσει 2 K. v. 2, παρέσει v. 23.	ἔσῃ 2 K. xiii. 13, xiv. 2, xv. 33, xviii. 3, xix. 13, xxii. 27.
ὄψει iii. 13.	
εἰσελεύσει v. 6.	ἐλεύσῃ xiv. 3.

The termination -ῃ also to some extent supplants -ασαι in some deponents of the -μι type.

Ἐπίστῃ (poetical and apparently Ionic) for ἐπίστασαι is well supported in several LXX books: Gen. xlvii. 5 BA, N. xx. 14 BAF, Jos. xiv. 6 BA, Jer. xvii. 16 Bℵ (-ασαι AQ), Ez. xxxvii. 3 BA (-ασαι Q), Tob. v. 5 ℵ and apparently Job xxxviii. 4 εἰ ἐπίστῃ B (-ασαι A): ἐπίστασαι appearing in Dt. (xx. 20, xxviii. 33,

36), Job (xi. 9 A -σε, xxxii. 22 א*, xxxvii. 16 A, xxxviii. 20 BאAC, 33 BאA) and Dan. Θ (Sus. 43).

The only instance where δύνῃ (poetical and late prose) appears to be ind. (and not conj.) is Dan. 0 v. 16: elsewhere δύνασαι: δύνῃ should probably be regarded as from δύνομαι, see § 23, 4.

The reversion to the primitive 2nd sing. termination in -σαι for all middle verbs seems to have begun with certain futures formed from the 2nd aor. (πίομαι, φάγομαι) and with contract verbs. In LXX πίεσαι has entirely superseded πίῃ (Dt. xxviii. 39, R. ii. 9, 3 K. xvii. 4, Jer. xxix. 13 AQ, Ez. iv. 11 etc.) and φάγεσαι is generally written outside the Pentateuch (R. ii. 14, Is. lx. 16, Ez. iv. 9 ff. etc., Mic. vi. 14, Sir. vi. 19, 2 M. vii. 7 V).

Φάγῃ however is constant in the Pentateuch (Gen. iii. 14, 17 ff., Ex. xxxiv. 18, L. vii. 11, Dt. vii. 16, viii. 9 etc. to xxviii. 53) and is found also in 2 K. ix. 7, 4 K. vii. 2 B (φάγῃς A) and perhaps ib. 19 οὐ μὴ φάγῃ (or conj.) and xix. 29 A.

The LXX proper appears to afford only one certain ex. in the case of contract verbs (analogous to ὀδυνᾶσαι, καυχᾶσαι of N.T.) viz. κτᾶσαι Sir. vi. 7; in Gen. xxxii. 10, where A has ἱκανοῦσαί μοι, the impersonal use of the verb elsewhere favours the reading of *D*E ἱκανοῦταί μοι: A again has κοιμᾶσαι in Dt. xxxi. 16, where κοιμᾷ BF is doubtless original: ἀπεξενοῦσαι (no doubt, with Schmiedel, we should read ἀποξενοῦσαι = -ξενοῖ) occurs in 3 K. xiv. 6 A in a passage interpolated from Aquila. The classical termination is kept in Ψ li. 3 ἐνκαυχᾷ.

13. The first hand of B apparently wrote the poetical form of the 1st plur. mid. in Jer. li. 17, ἐγινόμεσθα.

§ 18. VERBS IN -Ω. TENSE FORMATION.

1. **Verbs with pure stem** in the κοινή sometimes retain a **short vowel** in the formation of the tenses. Of contracts in -έω (Att. fut. -ήσω) πονέω in LXX always has the tenses πονέσω (Is. xix. 10, Sir. xiii. 5) ἐπόνεσα (1 K. xxiii. 21 etc.):

φορέω has φορέσω (Prov. xvi. 23) ἐφόρεσα (Sir. xi. 5)¹. Στερέω, on the other hand, keeps the Attic long vowel (e.g. Gen. xxx. 2, xlviii. 11) except in N. xxiv. 11 B*, Sir. xxviii. 15 B*אA, Est. E. 12 א*, 3 M. v. 32 V (ἐστερέθης). Cf. the shortening of the vowel in ὀφειλέσει Tob. vi. 13 B (-ήσει אA, and so elsewhere in LXX) and in ἐρρέθην, which is always so written in LXX (Gen. xv. 13, 2 K. v. 6, Jon. iii. 7, Dan. O vii. 23, Dan. ⊖ Sus. 27)²: the unaugmented parts of the verb, however, keep η, ῥηθείς—ῥηθῆναι—ῥηθήσομαι: the shortening appears therefore in this instance to be due to assimilation of vowels flanking ρ. Ποθέω (ἐπι-) in the aor. has the long vowel only (ἐπ)επόθησα (Att. also -εσα).

In contracts in -άω a similar shortening takes place in πεινάσω, ἐπείνασα³: διψάω however keeps η except in Is. xlix. 10 οὐ πεινάσουσιν οὐδὲ διψάσουσιν B*א*Q : see § 22, 2.

2. **Formation of passive tenses (1 aor., fut., perf.) with or without σ.** Attic practice in this matter was not uniform and shows many exceptions to the general rule⁴: in the κοινή there is a marked tendency to insert σ where it was not used in the older language.

Insertion of σ contrary to Attic practice. Ἐπαινεσθήσομαι has very strong support, Ψ xxxiii. 3 BאA, xliii. 9 BאR, lxii. 12 BאR, lxiii. 11 BאR, Sir. ix. 17 BאA : so ἐπηνέσθησαν Eccl. viii. 10 C (but ἐπηνέθ. BאA as in Attic: this was one of the cases where the Attic forms did not conform to the general rule). The LXX examples of the older Attic ἐδυνήθην (usually written ἠδ. § 16, 3) and the Ionic ἐδυνάσθην (ἠδ.: in Attic not

---

¹ Out of these aorists have come the modern Greek presents πονέξω, φορέξω.
² Later hands of B twice alter to ἐρρήθην.
³ Modern Greek hence forms two new presents πεινάξω, διψάξω.
⁴ Viz. that pure verbs which retain a short vowel in the tense stem strengthen this vowel by σ, while a long vowel in the stem dispenses with it : Kühner-Blass § 242. In some Attic verbs the σ appears in the aorist only, but not in the perfect: Rutherford *NP* 97 ff. has some suggestive remarks on the subject.

before Xen.) are about equal, the proportion being 32 : 29.
Ἰάσθησαν 3 M. v. 18 A = εἰάσθησαν (from ἐάω) stands for Attic
εἰάθησαν (so V ἰάθ.). Attic ἠλάθην (ἐλαύνω) again broke the
general rule as to short vowels : LXX has the later form
συνελασθέντων 2 M. v. 5, with pluperf. συνήλαστο ib. iv. 26
(Att. ἐλήλαμαι, ἠληλάμην). Συνεσχέσθη is read by A in 2 K.
xxiv. 21, 25 (-εσχέθην, -σχεθήσομαι are the usual forms of these
late tenses in LXX and elsewhere). Ἐζωσμένος (ἀν- δι- περι-) is
universal in LXX and is perhaps Ionic : Inscriptions and the
testimony of Photius establish ἔζωμαι as the true Attic form
(cf. ζῶμα)[1]. From κεράννυμι we find both the usual Attic
forms κεκραμένος Dt. xxviii. 66 A (but read κρεμαμένη B), Jer.
xxx. 10 B*A (read κεκαρμένους BᵃᵇℵQ), συγκραθῆναι Dan. Ο
ii. 43, and the later perfect κεκέρασμαι Dan. Ο Bel 33 with
the kindred aorist (συν)εκεράσθην Dan. Ο Bel 11, 2 M. xv. 39,
for which there is some classical authority. Ἐκλαύσθην Ez.
xxiv. 16 AQ*, 23 A and κλαυσθήσομαι Ψ lxxvii. 64 B*ℵT are
κοινή forms (B* keeps the Attic κλαυθῆς in the first passage :
κλαυθήσονται BᶜᵒʳʳR in Ψ is obviously a correction). Κλείω
(ἀπο- κατα- συγ-) now takes σ not only in the aor. ἐκλείσθην
(Att. ἐκλῄσθην) with κλεισθήσομαι, but also in the perf. κέκλεισμαι
(Att. κέκλῃμαι : κέκλειμαι only in Ez. xlvi. 1 B* [contrast xliv.1 f.],
Dan. Θ Sus. 20 and perhaps 1 K. xxiii. 7 A ἀποκέκλιται, unless
the perf. of -κλίνω is intended)[2]. From λούω (Att. λέλουμαι
ἐλούθην) we now have ἐλούσθης Ez. xvi. 4 B*AQΓ and λελου-
σμέναι Cant. v. 12 B (-ουμ. Aℵ). Ὠνάσθην Tob. iii. 8 B*A
(ὠνομάσθης ℵBᶜᵒʳʳ) replaces ὠνήθην Xen. (ὠνάθην Theocr.) : the
older Attic used the 2nd aor. ὠνήμην. The Attic πεπείραμαι
1 K. xvii. 39 and ἐπειράθην 1 M. xii. 10 (cf. i. 15 ℵᶜᵒʳʳ) from
πειράομαι are used with act. meaning "try" : ἐπειράσθην W. xi. 9,

---

[1] Meisterhans 185, Rutherford *NP* 99.
[2] But the Ptolemaic papyri which have only κέκλ(ε)ιμαι cast doubt on
the authenticity of the uncial evidence : Mayser 376. Josephus writes
κέκλεισμαι, Schmidt 470 f.

Dan. O xii. 9 is correctly formed from πειράζω and has pass. meaning "be tried" or "tempted": the act. meaning therefore establishes the readings ἐπειράθη Sir. xxxi. 10 BA (-άσθη א), π(ε)ιραθῖσα 4 M. xv. 16 אV (-ασθ. A). Διαπεπετασμένος 3 K. vi. 33 etc. from -πετάζω "spread" may be paralleled in early poetry (Oracle ap. Hdt. i. 62) for Att. πέπταμαι (πετάννυμι); ἐπετάσθην (ἐξ- κατ-) and πετασθήσομαι are now commonly used as the tenses of πέταμαι (class. aor. ἐπτόμην or ἐπτάμην). Σέσωσμαι, the Hellenistic form of perf., is usual in LXX: the Attic σέσωμαι[1] appears 3 times in B* (1 K. xxiii. 13 δια-, 2 K. i. 3 δια-, Jer. li. 14 ἀνα-), once in A (Jd. xxi. 17); the Attic ἐσώθην, σωθήσομαι are retained.

Κέχρισμαι and χρῖσμα replace Attic κέχριμαι, χρῖμα: ἐχρίσθην is Attic[2], and χρισθήσομαι Ex. xxx. 32 is correctly formed from it. The MSS are divided between συνεψήσθην and συνεψήθην[3], Jer. xxii. 19, xxix. 21, xxxi. 33—both late forms: Attic used perf. ἔψηγμαι from ψήχω, and presumably ἐψήχθην, though found first in Hellenistic Greek, was the older aorist.

Omission of Attic σ is occasionally attested in words with long vowel or diphthong in the stem, in which the Attic σ was therefore contrary to the general rule: ἐγνώθη 2 K. xvii. 19 B, γνωθήσεται Is. lxi. 9 B*: κελευθέντες 4 M. ix. 11 A (-ευσθ. א): θραυθήσεται Is. xlii. 4 B*, cf. θραυμός Na. ii. 11 א* (θραυσμός cett.), θραῦμα Jdth xiii. 5 B (elsewhere θραῦσμα): but usually ἐγνώσθην, γνωσθήσομαι, ἐθραύσθην etc. as in Attic. Ἐξεσπαμένος Zech. iii. 2 B* is probably a slip for the usual -εσπασμένος.

For Attic ἐσβέσθην (usual in LXX) we find the following varieties: ἐσβήθη Job iv. 10 C, σβενθέντος W. ii. 3 א, ib. σβενσθ. A (σβεσθ. B).

[1] Οἱ παλαιοὶ ἄνευ τοῦ σ...οἱ δὲ νεώτεροι σέσωσμαι Photius ap. Rutherford *NP* 99. The later form was constantly written by scribes in MSS of Attic writings, and even the LXX exx. may not be authentic: Ptolemaic papyri keep the Attic form in the few passages where the perf. pass. occurs (Mayser 134).

[2] Ἐχρήθη 2 K. i. 21 A (θυρεὸς Σ. οὐκ ἐχρ. ἐν ἐλαίῳ) is unparalleled, whether intended as from χρίω (=ἐχρίθη) or from χράομαι. Ἐχρίσθη is clearly right.

[3] Cf. περίψημα Tob. v. 19.

3. **Verbs with mute stem.** Attic verbs in -ζω for the most part have a dental stem and therefore have future and 1st aorist in -σω -σα (σ = δσ etc.): others have a guttural stem and form these tenses with -ξω -ξα (ξ = γσ or κσ). In the κοινή confusion was to be expected: there was a tendency to substitute ξ for σ, but only in a rather limited group of verbs, in many of which there is early authority for the guttural in derivative nouns. The majority of the -ζω verbs have retained the old σ in fut. and 1st aorist to the present day[1]. The LXX agrees for the most part with the N.T.[2]

(i) The following have passed over to the guttural class. Νυστάζω (ἐπι-) has νυστάξω Is. v. 27, Ψ cxx. 3 f., ἐνύσταξα 2 K. iv. 6 etc. (ἐνύστασα in Attic Comedy and the Anthology: but cf. the early derivatives νυσταγμός -ακτής). Παίζω (ἐμπαίζω) always has -παίξομαι -ἔπαιξα -πέπαιχα -πέπαιγμαι (cf. Attic παίγνιον: of the Attic forms ἔπαισα πέπαικα -αισμαι the only trace is the v.l. ἔπαισεν Sir. xlvii. 3 C): a change was in this case called for in order to discriminate between παίζω and παίω, the tenses of which in Attic were indistinguishable.

(ii) The converse substitution of σ for ξ occurs in the following 1st aorists (under the influence of the futures which take the "Attic" asigmatic forms σαλπιῶ, συριῶ, § 20, 1 (i): the fut. is unattested in classical Greek): ἐσάλπισα (Att. ἐσάλπιγξα) ἐσύρισα Lam. ii. 15 f., Ez. xxvii. 36 (Att. ἐσύριγξα: cf. σῦριγξ).

(iii) In the following there is fluctuation in LXX.

(*a*) Verbs which in Att. have dental stems, aorist -σα. Ἁρπάζω keeps the Att. forms ἁρπάσω, ἥρπασα, διηρπάσθην 3 M. v. 41, διηρπασμένος, but has the new Hellenistic guttural tenses (δι)ηρπάγην W. iv. 11, Sir. vi. 2, Tob. i. 20 and διαρπαγήσομαι Am. iii. 11 etc. (cf. Attic ἅρπαξ, ἁρπαγή). Βαστάζω keeps Att. βαστάσω in 4 K. xviii. 14 and ἐβάστασα in 2 K. xxiii. 5 A (βλαστήσῃ B), Job xxi. 3 A (ἄρατε cett.), Dan. Θ Bel 36: the later ἐβάσταξα[3] occurs in Jd. xvi. 30 B, R. ii. 16, Sir. vi. 25.

---

[1] Hatzidakis 134 ff. He gives reasons for rejecting the theory of Doric influence, of which there are very few traces in the κοινή (p. 18). Mayser 360 ff. gives no examples of the new ξ forms from the Ptolemaic papyri, but the tenses of the principal verbs affected seem to be unrepresented in any form.

[2] Blass N.T. § 16, 2.

[3] In the papyri of the Imperial age this (with ἐβαστάχθην) is frequent and almost the invariable form from ii/A.D. onwards. Of ἐβάστασα I have

'Αποκνίζω has Att. -κνίσω, -έκνισα in L. i. 15, v. 8, 4 K. vi. 6 B, Ez. xvii. 4: A reads ἀπέκνιξεν in 4 K. l.c.

(*b*) Verbs which in Att. have guttural stems, aor. -ξα. Στηρίζω (ἐπι-: Att. tenses ἐστήριξα -ιξάμην -ίχθην -ιγμαι -ίγμην). The LXX asigmatic fut. στηριῶ (no class. fut. attested) produces the aorists ἐστήρισα *passim* (ἐστήριξα only in Dan. O vii. 28 and as a v.l. in Ψ xxxvii. 3 T, l. 14 RT, Jer. xxi. 10 אc.aQ) and ἐστηρισάμην: the passive tenses are usually guttural ἐστηρίχθην -ιγμαι -ίγμην, but the σ occasionally intrudes here too[1]: ἐστηρίσθην Is. xxxvi. 6 BΓ, Sir. xxxix. 32 א*, 1 M. ii. 49 א, ἐστήρισμαι L. xiii. 55 BA (-ικται F), 1 K. xxvi. 19, Jdth viii. 24 Bא, 1 M. ii. 17 א, xiv. 26 א, 4 M. xvii. 5: the late fut. pass. appears as -στηριχθήσομαι in Jd. xvi. 26 B, Sir. xv. 4 B, as στηρισθήσομαι in Sir. l.c. אAC. Φρυάττειν (class. fut. -άξομαι) has 1st aor. ἐφρύαξα Ψ ii. 1: in the perf. pass. the uncials diverge, πεφρυασμένου 3 M. ii. 2 A -αγμένου V.

The tenses of the majority of -ζω verbs retain their Attic forms e.g. (*a*) ἥρμοσα, ἐσκεύασα, ἐσπούδασα, ἐχώρισα, (*b*) ἔσφαξα.

4. **Verbs with liquid stem** in -αίνω, -αίρω in Attic have 1st aorist in -ᾱνα -ᾱρα where the preceding letter is ι or ρ (e.g. ἐμίανα, ἐξήρανα), otherwise generally[2] -ηνα -ηρα. The κοινή begins to extend the aorists with α to *all* verbs of this type[3], and in modern Greek they are nearly universal[4]. In LXX we have ἐθέρμανα, (ἐξ)εκάθαρα (-ηρα Jos. v. 4 A), ἐλεύκανα Jl. i. 7, ἐσήμανα Jd. vii. 21, Jer. iv. 5, vi. 1, Dan. O ii. 15, 23, 45, Est. ii. 22 (but ἐσήμηνα[5] 1 Es. ii. 4, ἐπεσημήνω Job xiv. 17—literary books), ὕφανα (συν-) Ex. xxxvi. 10 etc., ἔφανα (ἐκφᾶναι, ἐπίφανον etc.) *passim* (but the literary forms ἀποφῆναι Job xxvii. 5, ἀπέφηνεν ib. xxxii. 2, ἀπεφήνατο 2 M. vi. 23, ἀποφηναμένων ib. xv. 4).

---

noted two exx. only: OP iii. 418 (i/-ii/-A.D.), BU 195 (161 A.D.). To judge from Mayser's silence, the verb is not used in the Ptolemaic papyri.

[1] Similarly for the usual form στήριγμα we have στήρισμα 1 M. vi. 18 A, which is also perhaps the true reading in 2 Es. ix. 8 (so Swete · σωτήρισμα B*).

[2] But ἐκέρδανα, ἐκοίλανα etc. are Attic: Kühner-Blass I. ii. § 267, 1, Rutherford *NP* 76 ff.

[3] Thus assimilating the aorist to the future stem. It is the converse process to the employment of gen. -ης dat. -η for all 1st decl. nouns in -ρᾱ (§ 10, 2).

[4] Hatzidakis 286 "heute sind überall nur die Formen mit a bekannt," but see Thumb *Handbuch* 87 f. for surviving examples of -ηνα.

[5] Similar fluctuation between ἐσήμανα -ηνα in the papyri: Mayser 360.

In addition to the literary exceptions noted above we have
ἐρυθῆνας W. xiii. 14 and always the Attic aor. mid. ἐλυμηνάμην
(2 Ch. xvi. 10, Ψ lxxix. 14, Am. i. 11, Is. lxv. 8 etc.)[1].

In the *perfect passive* of liquid verbs in -αίνω -ύνω ν before μ
was usually in Attic altered to σ, probably on the analogy of
the perfect pass. of verbs in -ζω (πέφασμαι like ἐσκεύασμαι)[2]:
the κοινή on the other hand preferred the more regular assimilation of νμ to μμ. In LXX the Pentateuch translators keep the
Att. ὑφασμένος (δι- συν-) Ex. xxviii. 28, xxxvi. 31, L. xix. 19.
In other verbs μμ is preferred: ἤσχυμμαι 1 Es. viii. 71, κατ-
ησχυμμένος Ψ lxxiii. 21 (Epic): μεμακρυμμένος Ψ lv. tit. (-σμ-
Aristot.): μεμιαμμένος (Att. -σμ-) N. v. 13 f., 27, W. vii. 25,
Tob. ii. 9, Hg. ii. 13 BAQ (-σμ- אΓ), 3 M. vii. 14 A (-σμ- V):
μεμολυμμένος (no early form), 1 Es. viii. 80 A (-σμ- B), Is. lix. 3
אAQ* (-σμ- B), lxv. 4 BאAQ, 2 M. xiv. 3 V (-σμ- A): πεπληθυμ-
μένος 1 K. xxv. 10, Lam. i. 1 *bis* (no early pf. pass. attested).

The σ in διεσπαρσμένους Is. lvi. 8 A has no *raison d'être* ·
elsewhere we have the Att. (δι)εσπαρμένος.

§ 19. VERBS IN -Ω. PRESENT TENSE.

1. The present meaning regularly attaching to certain
perfects caused the evolution in the later language[3] of new
present forms out of the perfect forms. In the LXX we have
γρηγορέω (with tenses ἐγρηγόρουν, γρηγορήσω, ἐγρηγόρησα -ήθην)
Jer. v. 6, xxxviii. 28 *bis* (ἐγρηγορήσω א*), Bar. ii. 9, Lam. i. 14,
2 Es. xvii. 3 γρηγορούντων אA (ἐγρηγορούντων B), 1 M. xii. 27,
Dan. Θ ix. 14: the perfect ἐγρήγορα, which it replaces and
which is absent from N.T., is confined in LXX to Jer. i. 12,
li. 27. Similarly as from πεποιθέω we find ἐπεποίθησα in Jd.

[1] Is this another instance, as in the verbs in -μι (§ 23, 1), of the old
forms retaining their place longest in the middle voice? But λοιμανάμενοι
occurs in a papyrus of ii/B.C., Mayser ib.
[2] Kühner-Blass § 264, 7.
[3] But, as Blass points out, the beginnings go back to an earlier age:
γεγωνέω (beside γέγωνα) is as old as Homer.

ix. 26 A, Zeph. iii. 2 AQΓ (ἐπεποίθει Bℵ), Job xxxi. 24 (cf. in the later versions e.g. Ψ ix. 11 πεποιθήσουσιν α΄ σ΄). Στήκω (παραστήκω) is not so well attested as in N.T. (Paul uses the imperat. frequently), occurring as a variant only in the following passages : Ex. xiv. 13 στήκετε A (imperat. = στῆτε BF), Jd. iii. 19 παραστήκοντες A, xvi. 26 στήκει B, 3 K. viii. 11 στήκειν B (στῆναι A), x. 8 παραστήκοντες A (-εστηκότες B), Zech. iv. 14 παραστήκουσιν Γ (cf. N. vii. 2 παρεστήκοντες *sic* A [-κότες BℵF], and in the Hexapla Jos. x. 19 στήκετε α΄θ΄ imperat.). Ἐκέκραγον in Isaiah's vision (Is. vi. 3 f., 3 M. v. 23) should perhaps be regarded as an imperf. of † κεκράγω rather than, as Veitch takes it, a reduplicated 2nd aorist (= Att. ἔκραγον).

2. A few instances occur of the formation of new presents or the recrudescence of old dialectic presents in -(ν)νω. With these may be classed sporadic instances of the doubling of the ν in old forms in -νω. Ἀποκτέννω (for -κτείνω = κτενγω: old dialects, but cf. also ἀποκτ(ε)ίννυμι in Plato etc.) is a fairly frequent variant. Ex. IV. 23 B (-κτενῶ AF), Dt. xxxii. 39 B (do.), Jos. viii. 24 BAF, 2 K. iv. 12 B* (3 K. xi. 24 A from Aquila), 4 K. xvii. 25 BA: Hb. i. 17 BQ, Is. lxvi. 3 BℵAQ: 1 Es. iv. 7 B*, Ψ lxxvii. 34 B*ℵRT· (ἀπέκτενεν B^vid), c. 8 B*RTℵ^{c.a} (-έκτινον ℵ*, -έκτενον A), Prov. xxi. 25 ℵ^{c.a}: Tob. iii. 8 ℵ *bis*, vi. 14 f. ℵ, xiv. 11 ℵ, W. xvi. 14 (ἀποκτενι ℵ), 3 M. vii. 14 A, 4 M. xiii. 14 ℵ (Dan. Θ ii. 13). The Hellenistic and modern form χύ(ν)νω (for χέω), which in N.T. is fairly common (ἐκχύννομαι), in LXX is confined to a single late passage, 3 K. xxii. 35 ἀπεχύννετο (cf. 2 K. xiv. 14 Θ ἐκχυνόμενον). Ἀποτιννύω (Gen. xxxi. 39, Ψ lxviii. 5, Sir. xx. 12) for ἀποτίνω (usual in LXX) seems to be a mixture of -τίννω (= -τίνϝω) and -τινύω: the υ appears in the old poetical ἀποτίννυμαι (-τίνν.).

The form -βέννω (for -βαίνω = -βανγω: assisted by the itacistic interchange of αι and ε, as in -βένω Gen. xli. 3 E, 1 K. ix. 26 A, 1 M. vii. 40 V, ix. 66 A) is practically confined to portions of Cod. A, which has it in Gen. ii. 6, xli. 2, 5, 18 f., N. xxxiii. 51,

xxxv. 10, Dt. i. 41, iii. 21, iv. 26, xi. 8, 29, 1 K. i. 3, v. 5₂ 3 K.
xxii. 6: in the later books only in Na. ii. 8 (with אּ), Jer. xxviii. 14,
xxix. 2 (with אּ), xxxi. 35 (where the form may go back to the
compiler of Jer. a and Jer. β), 1 M. vi. 48: in other MSS, Gen.
xix. 28 E, Sir. ix. 13 C.

φθάννω is read by AC in W. xvi. 28, Eccl. viii. 14 and by BA
in Dan. Θ viii. 7.

3. The following miscellaneous examples occur of the
evolution of a new present out of the aorist, the substitution
of -ω for -μι (for which see further § 23), etc.

Βιβρώσκω, a rare present for which LS quote Babrius, occurs
in the B text of Samson's riddle Jd. xiv. 14 τί βρωτὸν ἐξῆλθεν
ἐκ βιβρώσκοντος...; the repetition of the root makes the
conundrum more pointed.

Βλαστάνω, through the influence of fut. -ήσω and new
1 aor. ἐβλάστησα (§ 21, 1), gives place to βλαστάω, Eccl. ii. 6
δρυμὸν βλαστῶντα + ξύλα אּA, and βλαστέω W. xviii. 2 βλασ-
τοῦσιν אּ* (read βλάπτουσιν BA).

For ἀλήθω (*vice* ἀλέω) see § 24: for δύνομαι § 23, 4: for εἰδήσω,
εἴδησα as from †εἰδέω § 24 s.v. οἶδα.

Ἐνδιδύσκω (2 K. i. 24, xiii. 18, Prov. xxix. 39, Sir. l. 11:
and as v.l. of A ἐνεδιδύσκετο Jdth ix. 1, x. 3) and ἐκδιδύσκω
(1 K. xxxi. 8, 2 K. xxiii. 10, 2 Es. xiv. 23, Hos. vii. 1) supplant
the classical presents -δύω -δύνω. The new forms appear to be
introduced to mark the transitive meaning of the verb: δύνειν
remains with intrans. sense "set" 2 K. ii. 24, 3 K. xxii. 36,
2 Ch. xviii. 34 A, Eccl. i. 5, "escape," Prov. xi. 8 ἐκ θήρας
ἐκδύνει (δύνει A).

Ἔσθω or κατέσθω (class. poetry and late prose) occurs
frequently beside the Attic prose form ἐσθίω in certain portions
of LXX, especially Pentateuch, Prophets and Psalms: on the
other hand ἐσθίω is used exclusively in literary books such as
Job and Dan. O and almost exclusively in the later historical
group (always in 1—4 K. except ἔσθων 1 K. xiv. 30 BA,
ἔσθοντες 3 K. iv. 20 A).

It is noteworthy that the form without ι is preferred in the participle ἔσθων -οντος etc. which is so written in 37 instances, whereas the exx. of this spelling in other parts of the verb amount to 9 only (ἔσθετε -ται 6, ἔσθη -ητε 2, ἤσθοσαν 1 = Ez. xxii. 9 B*Q); on the other hand ἐσθίεις, ἐσθίει, ἐσθίειν are invariable, and the imperf. is always ἤσθιον except in Ez. *loc. cit.* Note e.g. in Prov. ἔσθων xiii. 25 beside ἐσθίει xxiii. 7, -ίειν xxv. 27, in Eccl. ἔσθοντες v. 10 beside ἐσθίουσιν x. 16.

For (ἐπαν)ιστάνω see § 23, 3.

Κρεμάζω ("Byz." LS) for κρεμάννυμι occurs in Job Θ xxvi. 7 κρεμάζων BℵC: κρεμνῶν of A seems to be unparalleled (κρεμάω from Aristotle onwards).

Κρύβω for κρύπτω, formed from the Hellenistic aorist ἐκρύβην, occurs in the simple form (not, as LS, " only found in compounds ἀπο- ἐγ- κρύβω") in 4 K. xi. 3, Jer. xxxix. 27 ℵ (κρυβήσεται cett.) and in what appear to be Hexaplaric interpolations in the A text of 1 K. xxiii. 23, 1 Ch. xxi. 20 (= B μεθαχαβείν). Aquila has ἀποκρύβειν.

Λιμπάνω (Ionic, Hippocrates) is found sporadically in composition: καταλιμπάνω[1] Gen. xxxix. 16 (contrast 13 and 15 λείπω), 2 K. v. 21, 3 K. xviii. 18 B (with assimilation καταλειμμάνειν A, not else attested): ἐκλιμπ. Zech. xi. 16: ἐγκαταλιμπ. Ψ cxviii. 53: διαλιμπ. Tob. x. 7 BᵇA (διελίπανεν B*). Cf. the new form ὀπτάνεσθαι, § 24 s.v. ὁρᾶν.

Reduplication is dropped in μνήσκομαι (cited from Anacreon by Veitch, who compares ὑπομνήσκουσα Orphic Hymns): Is. lxii. 6 B*, 1 M. vi. 12 Aℵ, xii. 11 ℵ. (The present μιμνήσκομαι itself is not used in Attic prose.) For νήθω (*vice* νῶ) see § 24.

Νίπτω (Hellenistic for Attic -νίζω) is the only present form used in LXX. For ὀπτάζομαι, ὀπτάνομαι see § 24 s.v. ὁράω.

Τελίσκω, a rare by-form of τελέω (found in ii/B.C. on the Rosetta stone and in the poet Nicander) occurs in the passive

---

[1] So Thuc. viii. 17 and occasionally in Ptolemaic papyri along with καταλείπω which is much more frequent, especially in wills, Mayser 402. See an interesting note of Dr J. H. Moulton on -λιμπάνω in the *Classical Quarterly*, vol. II. 138 (April, 1908) : further cxx. in Anz *Subsidia* 307 f.

in Dt. xxiii. 17ᵇ apparently = "to be initiated." The latter half
of the *v.* is a doublet but probably the older version: 17ᵃ reads
πόρνη, πορνεύων for the ἅπαξ λεγόμενα (in LXX) τελεσφόρος,
τελισκόμενος of 17ᵇ.

§ 20. Verbs in -Ω. Future Tense.

1. Blass remarks (N.T. § 18, 1): "The so-called **Attic
future** of verbs in -έω, -άζω etc. disappears, almost entirely,
as the name implies, from Hellenistic Greek, and entirely
from the N.T." The tendency was to bring these anomalous
forms into line with the other sigmatic futures and so to
prevent the possibility of confusion between future and present.
The disappearance of the Attic futures was, however, gradual:
the κοινή even employed some 'Attic' futures from verbs in
-ζω which were unknown to Attic writers: the LXX, supported
by the Ptolemaic papyri, presents some contrasts to the N.T.

(i) Futures in -ιῶ from -ίζω verbs were the oldest and
most widespread of these asigmatic forms, being common to
Attic and Ionic[1], and they were likewise the last to disappear.
In LXX the futures in -ιῶ (-ιοῦμαι) are practically used throughout (ἀφανιῶ, ἀφοριῶ, ἐγγιῶ etc.) as in the Ptolemaic papyri[2].

In the N.T. the -ίσω forms preponderate, and a distinction
is observable between the forms used by the writers and those
which they incorporate in O.T. quotations: there is a tendency
to keep 3rd plur. -ιοῦσιν rather than -ίσουσιν with double σ[3]. In
Josephus both forms occur, those in -ίσω again preponderating[4].

Futures in -ίσω in LXX are mainly variants of the (probably
later) A or ℵ text: in B they occur in late books such as Prov.
and Eccl., and sporadically elsewhere. The following exx. have
been noted. Αἱρετίσει Gen. xxx. 20 E: κουφίσουσιν Ex. xviii.
22 A, 1 K. vi. 5 A: σαλπίσεις N. x. 3 B* (-ιεῖς cett., 5 ff. -ιεῖτε,
-ιοῦσιν), Ez. xxxiii. 3 AQ: καθαρίσ(ω) N. xxx. 13 B (-ιεῖ AF, and
so 9 BAF), Ez. xliii. 26 A, Mal. iii. 3 BA: ὀρθρίσεις Jd. ix. 33 A:
πλουτίσει 1 K. xvii. 25 A: (δια)στηρίσω Jer. iii. 12 Q, xvii. 5 Bℵא,

---

[1] K.-Bl. § 227, 4.   [2] Mayser 356.
[3] Blass N.T. ib., WH² App. 170.
[4] W. Schmidt 447 ff.

Sir. xxviii. 1 (where the two forms are combined) διαστηριῶν
διαστηρίσει BAC: διασκορπίσ(εις) Ez. v. 2 B, Job xxxvii. 11 A,
Dan. Θ xi. 24 A: γνωρίσουσιν Ez. xliv. 23 Q: διαμερίσετε Ez.
xlvii. 21 BA: ἀφανίσ(ω) 2 K. xxii. 38 A, Jl. ii. 20 א*, Ψ cxlv. 9 A:
συμποδίσουσιν Zech. xiii. 3 א^{c.b}: θερίσ(ει) Prov. xxii. 8 BאA, Eccl.
xi. 4 BאAC, Job iv. 8 C: ὑπερασπίσει Prov. xxiv. 28 A, W.
v. 16 א*, συνασπίσειν 3 M. iii. 10 V: καταποντίσουσιν Eccl.
x. 12 אA: κομίσεται Sir. xxix. 6 Bא (-ιεῖται A): φωτίσω 2 Es.
xvii. 65 (-ίσων), Bar. i. 12 (-ίσῃ A), Ep. J. 66 B: ψωμίσω Dan. O
iv. 29 and Θ iv. 22 A.

(ii)   Verbs in -άζω in classical Greek take the 'Attic future'
in a few instances as a by-form beside the future in -άσω.   In
LXX the contracted fut. is common in verbs of this type and
is extended to verbs with long stem-syllables, ἁρπάζειν etc., in
which Attic always employed fut. in -σω[1].

The following exx. of fut. in -ῶ receive some support in
earlier (Attic or Ionic) Greek.

ἀναβιβῶ[2] Gen. xlvi. 4 DF.   ἀναβιβάσ(ω) ib. A.
                                           Ex. iii. 17.
                                           Is. lviii. 14-σει(-σῃ א).
          Ez. xxxix. 2 B.   Ez. ib. AQ.
          Am. viii. 10.
ἐπιβιβ(ῶ) Hos. x. 11, Hb.
   iii. 15 -ᾶς B*א*, -ᾷ ib. 19.
καταβιβῶ Ez. xxvi. 20 A.   καταβιβάσω Ez. ib. BQ, Jer.
                                              xxviii. 40 א*.
                                           -άσουσιν Dt. xxi. 4, Ez.
                                              xxviii. 8, xxxii. 18.
συμβιβῶ Ex. iv. 12 F.   συμβιβάσ(ω) ib. BA, iv. 15, L.
                                              x. 11 -σεις.
Ψ xxxi. 8 BאAR.   άσω ib. U.
-βιβάεις sic Dt. iv. 9 A*.   -άσεις ib. BF.
-βιβᾷ Is. xl. 13 B*א*Q*.   -άσει ib. Aא^{c.a}Q^{mg} (with
                                              1 Cor. ii. 16 quot.).
παραβιῶνται[3] Am. vi. 10 BQ.
ἐκδικᾶται[4] L. xix. 18, Dt. xxxii.   δικάσ(ω) 1 K. viii. 20, xii. 7 B.
43 B (-εῖται A), Jdth xi. 10.

---

[1] Kühner-Blass § 228. 3 (b).   [2] Attic -βιβῶ.
[3] Attic βιάσομαι (but see Veitch).
[4] Att. δικάσω -άσομαι: Ionic -δικῶ.

(ἀπο)δοκιμῶ¹ Jd. vii. 4 A, Jer. ix. 7, xxxviii. 35, Zech. xiii. 9, Sir. xxvii. 5 ℵ* -ᾷ, xxxiv. 26 do.　　δοκιμάσ(ω) Jer. ix. 7 ℵ^{c.a}, Sir. xxvii. 5 A.

The following are unclassical (Att. -άσω -άσομαι). ἀγορῶμεν 2 Es. xx. 31. ἁρπᾷ, ἁρπᾶται, (δι)αρπῶνται L. xix. 13 B, Ez. xviii. 7, Hos. v. 14, Zeph. ii. 9: class. ἁρπάσ(ω) L. xix. 13 AF, Jd. xxi. 21 A. (κατ)εργᾷ, -ᾶται, -ῶνται *passim*²: the class. ἐργάσομαι is never used.

(iii)　On the other hand the Attic futures of certain verbs in -άω -έω viz. ἐλῶ (from ἐλάω, ἐλαύνω) καλῶ τελῶ have been replaced³ by (ἀπ)ελάσω (Ex. xxv. 11, Ez. xxxiv. 12) καλέσω and (συν)τελέσω: present and future were thus clearly differentiated.

In Jer. xiv. 12 συντελῶ ℵ (συντελέσω cett.) may be fut.: καλῶ ib. xxxii. 15 (καλέσω A) xli. 17 is probably present.

For class. fut. χέω, χεῖς, χεῖ (indistinguishable from the present) LXX, differentiating the tenses, has (ἀπο- ἐκ- προσσυγ-)χεῶ, χεεῖς, χεεῖ etc.; χεῖ Mal. iii. 3 A is apparently intended for the class. fut.

(iv)　Ὄλλυμι (ἀπ-) in LXX retains the Attic fut. (ἀπ)ολῶ -οῦμαι: ὀλέσω (Epic and late prose) which is normal in N.T.⁴ is confined to Dt. vii. 23 A, Eccl. ix. 18, a gloss in Is. i. 25 (the clause τοὺς δὲ ἀπειθοῦντας ἀπολέσω is absent from MT, and Is. elsewhere uses ἀπολῶ) and Sir. vi. 3 ἀπολέσεις (but ἀπολεῖ vi. 4, x. 3, xx. 22). Ὄμνυμι similarly has fut. ὀμοῦμαι (Ex. xxii. 8, Dt. xxxii. 40, Is. xlv. 23, lxv. 16) not the later ὀμόσω⁵.

2.　To the liquid verbs which retain asigmatic futures ((ἀπ)αγγελῶ, (ἀπο)στελῶ etc.) there is added a new future, formed from the 2nd aor., ἐλῶ ἐλοῦμαι (ἀν- ἀφ- etc.), which

---

¹ Ionic: Att. δοκιμάσω.
² So in papyri and inscriptions from ii/B.C., Mayser 357: κατασκευᾶν appears even earlier, ih.
³ So in the Ptolemaic papyri: Mayser 357 cites one iii/B.C. instance of fut. συντελοῦσιν.
⁴ Ὀλῶ only in an O.T. quotation (1 Cor. i. 19): but ἀπολοῦμαι still remains.
⁵ Ὀμόσω Prov. xxiv. 32 is aor. conj.

has entirely supplanted the old αἱρήσω. A similar new fut., formed from the 2nd aor. on the analogy of ἔπιον πίομαι, is φάγομαι.

The class. ἔδομαι, which is absent from N.T., still remains in the LXX, mainly in the Pentateuch, but φάγομαι is four times as frequent: the proportion for the simple verb is about 56 ἔδ. (40 in Pent.): 225 φαγ.; the only book where ἔδ. has marked preponderance is Exodus (19 ἔδ., 4 φαγ. viz. xii. 8ᵃ, 11ᵃ, 44, xxxiv. 18: contrast Deut. 2 ἔδ., 53 φαγ.).

Διαμαχήσεται Sir. xxxviii. 28 is the only ex. of fut. of μάχομαι (Att. μαχοῦμαι, Ion. -μαχήσομαι -έσομαι).

Ἕξω is used to the exclusion of σχήσω (§ 15, 3).

3. The **future active** begins to supplant the **future middle** which Attic Greek employed with a certain group of active verbs with quasi-deponent meaning, expressing for the most part a physical action or an emotion[1].

ᾄσω Is. v. 1, Ψ (4 times).	ᾄσομαι Jd. v. 3 BA, Is. xxvi. 1, Ψ (6 times).
ἀκούσω 3 times only in B text viz. 2 K. xiv. 16 [but -σομαι xvi. 21 etc.], Is. vi. 9 BℵQ (perhaps under the influence of the N.T. quotations in Mt. xiii. 14, Acts xxviii. 26: elsewhere in Is. -σομαι), Jer. li. 16 Bℵ[2].	ἀκούσομαι (εἰσ- ἐπ- ὑπ-) is the normal LXX form.
ἀλαλάξω Is. xli. 1 ℵ, Jer. xxix. 2, Ez. xxvii. 30.	-άξομαι A in Jer. Ez. locc. citt.
ἁμαρτήσω Sirach (vii. 36, xxiv. 22).	-σομαι elsewhere in LXX.
⎰ ἀπαντήσω and	-σομαι are both equally represented.
⎱ συναντήσω Ex. v. 3 AF, Is. xxxiv. 14.	-σομαι 9 times.
ὑπαντήσω Sir. xv. 2 ℵA.	-σομαι ib. BC, Dan. O x. 14.

---

[1] Kühner-Blass § 323: Rutherford *NP* 377 ff.

[2] Also as a variant or in Hexaplaric interpolations in A and ℵ: 3 K. viii. 42 A (? from Aquila), Jer. xi. 3 ℵ, Mic. iii. 7 AQ, Ψ cxliv. 19 ℵ, Prov. xxviii. 17 a ℵ, Job xxxvii. 23 ℵ: in Ez. viii. 18 AQ οὐ μὴ εἰσακούσω (from Theod.) the verb is no doubt conj.

βαδιῶ Jer. xxx. 3 ℵ*.   else βαδιοῦμαι¹.

βιώσω Prov. vii. 2, Job xxix.
18, 4 M. vi. 20 (ἐπιβ.).

βλέψω rarely: L. xxvi. 9, Is.   -βλέψομαι usually (Dt., 1 and 3 K.,
vi. 9 (as in the N.T. cita-   2 Ch., Is., Min.)
tions: see above on ἀ-
κούσω), lxvi. 2, v. 12 ℵ*,
Ez. xxxvi. 9, Zech. i. 16 B*,
Tob. xi. 8 ℵ, Job Θ x. 4 A.

-βοήσω rarely, usually with   βοήσομαι usually.
v.l.: L. xxv. 10, Jos. vi. 10
B, Is. v. 29 f. Bℵ, xxxiv.
14 ℵ, xlii. 11 BℵΓ (-σομαι
8 times ın Is.), Lam. iii. 8,
1 Ch. xvi. 32 A, 1 M.
iv. 10 ℵ.

γελάσω Job xxi. 3 B, 4 M.   -σομαι elsewhere in LXX.
v. 28.

θαυμάσω (Ionic) L. xix. 15   -σομαι L. xxvi. 32, Job xiii. 10,
(-σης F), Dt. xxviii. 50,   Is. xli. 23, lii. 15, Jer. iv. 9.
Job xxi. 5 B (-σατε ℵA), Is.
xiv. 16 ℵAQΓ (-σονται B).

κύψω Ψ ix. 31.

οἰμώξω 4 M. xii. 15.

ὀλολύξω Is. xvi. 7, lxv. 14,
Am. viii. 3.

ἐμπαίξω Is. xxxiii. 4 Bℵ*Q,   else (ἐμ)παίξομαι.
Job xl. 24 A.

πνεύσω Ψ cxlvii. 7 (perhaps   -σομαι Sir. xliii. 16.
causat. "make to blow"),
Sir. xliii. 20.

σιγήσω Ex. xiv. 14, Sir. xx. 7.   -σομαι Lam. iii. 49.

σιωπήσω Is. lxv. 6 BℵQ   else -σομαι Is. xlii. 14, lxii. 1,
(-σομαι A), Sir. xx. 7 ℵ.   6 etc.

(τρέχω) δραμῶ Cant. i. 4².   else -δραμοῦμαι.

φθάσω (Ionic, Xen.) Eccl.   [Attic φθήσομαι not used.]
xii. 1, προφθάσω 4 K. xix.
32, Sir. xix. 27, Ψ lviii.
11 etc.

With some verbs Attic preferred fut. mid. but also employed
fut. act. So in LXX (κατα)διώξω -ομαι are both used (but only
ἐκδιώξω): similarly ζήσω (causatively Ψ cxxxvii. 7, cxlii. 11 ζήσεις
με) 4 K. xviii. 32, Prov. ix. 11 Bℵ, Am. v. 6 A, Sir. xxxvii. 26 A
and (commonly) ζήσομαι. The fut. act. only is used in the

¹ The later βαδίσομαι -ίσω are not found in LXX.
² And perhaps 2 K. xviii. 19, 22 (δράμω Swete).

following verbs (class. prefers mid.): γηράσω (Job xxix. 18), γρύξω, ἐπαινέσω, cf. ἁρπάσω 1 (ii) above.

Many middle futures remain unaltered e.g. γνώσομαι, δήξομαι, ἀποθανοῦμαι, κλαύσομαι (not -σω as in N.T.), κεκράξομαι (for κεκράξετε Jer. iv. 5 Bℵ read κεκράξατε AQ: the unreduplicated -κράξομαι is a v.l. in Is. xlii. 2 A, Jer. xxix. 2 ℵ*, Jl. iii. 16 ℵ^c.aAQ, Hb. i. 1 B*ℵ': the later κράξω is not found), λή(μ)ψομαι, μαθήσομαι, εἴσομαι, ὄψομαι, πείσομαι, ῥυήσομαι (not the rarer Attic ῥεύσομαι, nor the later ῥεύσω), τέξομαι, τεύξομαι, φεύξομαι.

The converse use of fut. mid. for class. act. occurs in the two new futures of χαίρειν, χαρήσομαι and χαροῦμαι (Att. χαιρήσω: see § 24). Cf. διψήσομαι Is. lxv. 13 ℵ*A.

§ 21. Verbs in -Ω. First and Second Aorist (and Future Passive).

1. **Sigmatic 1st aorist for 2nd aorist.** As has been stated elsewhere (§ 17, 2), the encroachment of the 1st aorist *terminations* in -α (-αν etc.) into the sphere of the old 2nd aorist began in a few instances in Attic Greek: in the κοινή these terminations were rapidly extended to other verbs and in modern Greek they are universal in the past tenses. On the other hand the instances where the old 2nd aorist was replaced in the κοινή by an entirely new 1st aorist in -σα were few, and the later language has not advanced much further in this direction[1]. The few examples supplied by the N.T.[2] may be illustrated from the LXX, some of them, however, only from the later books.

(Ἦξα)[3] for ἤγαγον (the latter *passim* in LXX) occurs in the compound συνῆξα (mod. Gr. ἐσύναξα) in Jd. xi. 20 B (-ήγαγεν A), 2 Es. (vii. 28, viii. 15, xvii. 5), 1 M. i. 4 AℵV (beside συνήγαγον elsewhere in these three books): also in ἐπάξαι Est. ix. 25 (and perhaps ἐὰν δ' ἐπάξω Ez. xxii. 13 B: in ὁρᾶτε μή...ἐπάξω Ex. xxxiii. 5 the verb is probably fut.: cf. Jos. ix. 13 ὅρα μή...κατοικεῖς) ἄναξον 1 M. ix. 58 V.

---

[1] Thumb *Handbuch* 89 "Nur in einigen Fällen hat der sigmatische Aorist sich auf Kosten des asigmatischen bereichert."

[2] Blass N.T. § 19, 1.

[3] The form seems to have been first used in the compounds: Mayser 369 cites one Ptolemaic ex. of 112 B.C. διάξη < σθε >: ἵνα...ἄξωμεν occurs in 2 B.C., OP 742 (= Witkowski 94): exx. accumulate later, Crönert 232 note 2.

Ἡμάρτησα (so mod. Gr. ἁμάρτησα) beside ἥμαρτον, the normal LXX form, occurs only in Lam. iii. 42 ἡμαρτήσαμεν, ἠσεβήσαμεν (contrast the same form of confession with ἡμάρτομεν in Bar. ii. 12, Dan. Oϴ ix. 5), Job xv. 11 C (ἡμάρτηκας cett.), Eccl. v. 5 ἐξαμαρτῆσαι B (in causative sense).

Ἐβίωσα is used (to the exclusion of the usual Attic ἐβίων): W. xii. 23, Sir. xl. 28, Prov. ix. 6 Aℵᶜ ᵃ, διαβιώσῃ Ex. xxi. 21 BF: but far commoner is ἔζησα (Ionic and late: not Attic).

Ἐβλάστησα (usually, if not always, in causative sense) replaces the earlier Attic ἔβλαστον throughout: Gen. i. 11 βλαστησάτω ἡ γῆ βοτάνην, N. xvii. 8, 2 K. xxiii. 5 B, Is. xlv. 8, Sir. xxiv. 17, xxxix. 13: in comp. with ἐκ- Is. lv. 10, Job ϴ xxxviii. 27.

Ἔδυν (intrans.) is still commonly retained: ἔδυ Gen. xxviii. 11, Jon. ii. 6, Tob. ii. 4, 7, x. 7 ℵ, 1 M. x. 50, xii. 27, εἰσέδυ 1 M. vi. 46, ἐπέδυ Jer. xv. 9, δῦναι Jd. xiv. 18 A, conj. δύῃ L. xxii. 7 AF (δῦ B*), 2 K. iii. 35: intrans. sigmatic 1 aor. ἔδυσα in ἐὰν... καταδύσωσιν Am. ix. 3, ὑποδύσαντες Jdth vi. 13, asigmatic 1 aor. δύναντος 2 Ch. xviii. 34 B (δύνοντος A). (Ἐνέδυσα, ἐξέδυσα in causal sense of clothing, unclothing are classical.)

The class. ἀνέκραγον is retained in Jos. vi. 4, 5 (-κραγέντων AFᵛⁱᵈ), Ez. ix. 1, xxi. 12, Zech. i. 14, 17, Sir. l. 16: elsewhere (in the later historical books) ἀνέκραξα Jd. vii. 20, 1 K. iv. 5, 3 K. xii. 24 † B, xxii. 32, 1 M. ii. 27, 3 M. vi. 17, so ἔκραξα Jd. i. 14, 2 K. xix. 4, Jer. xxii. 20 B, Tob. vi. 3 ℵ, but the 1 aor. of the simple verb commonly takes the reduplicated form ἐκέκραξα *passim*.

Ἔλιπον is practically universal in the LXX, as it actually is in the Ptolemaic papyri[1]: ἔλειψα does not seem to have come into general use till the Christian era[2] and in LXX is limited to the B text of Judges (ix. 9, 11, 13, ἀπολείψασα=ἀφεῖσα A) and to 1 Ch. xxviii. 9 B ἐὰν καταλείψῃς (-λίψεις A). The constant substitution in A of the imperf. -έλειπον, -ελειπόμην for -έλιπον, -ελιπόμην of B may be taken as an indication that the 2nd aorist form had ceased to be familiar at the time when Cod. A or a parent MS was written.

Ἀπέδρασα is confined to two passages in Cod. ℵ: Jdth xi. 3 (ἀπέδρας BA), Tob. i. 19 (elsewhere the classical forms ἀπέδρας, ἔδρα, -έδρασαν, ἀπόδραθι, διαδράς).

Ἔφθασα (Attic) is the only aorist of φθάνω used in LXX, not the alternative Attic 2 aor. ἔφθην.

---

[1] Mayser 364.

[2] Papyri exx. of κατέλειψα from i/A.D. onwards are given in Deissmann *BS* 190, Crönert 234 note 6 (earliest date cited 40 A.D.): cf. Dieterich *Untersuch.* 238. Josephus keeps κατέλιπον: Schmidt 458 attributes an occasional -έλειψα in the MSS to copyists. From the same source has probably come παρελείψαμεν in Polyb. xii. 15. 12.

Εὗρον, not εὕρησα, in LXX. For ἔπεσα see § 17, 2: for ἔδωσα, ἔθησα in Cod. A § 23, 10.

2. **Sigmatic for unsigmatic 1st aorist.** New 1st aorists in -σα replace in some instances an older unsigmatic 1st aor. The new ἐγάμησα occurs without variant in Est. F. 3, in conjunction with Att. ἔγημα in 2 M. xiv. 25 (παρεκάλεσεν αὐτὸν γῆμαι...ἐγάμησεν), while in 4 M. xvi. 9 both forms are attested (γαμήσαντες A, γήμαντες אV). Similarly (ἀν)είλησα 4 K. ii. 8, Ez. ii. 10 (Att. εἷλα, as from εἵλω, Epic ἔλσα). Κατενεμησάμην Ψ lxxix. 14 replaces Att. -ενειμάμην (but διένειμα Dt. xxix. 26) as νεμήσομαι Jer. xxvii. 19 etc. replaces νεμοῦμαι. A 1st aor. ὦσα (Ionic, Hdt. I. 157 ἀνοῖσαι) for ἤνεγκα appears in Bar. i. 10 ἀνοίσατε. The desire for uniformity produces the new 1st aor. κατεσκόπησα (class. -εσκεψάμην as elsewhere in LXX): 2 K. x. 3 (with κατασκέψασθαι in same v.) = 1 Ch. xix. 3, 1 M. v. 38 A (-σκοπεῦσαι אV).

Ἀνέθαλον (also in N.T.) Ψ xxvii. 7, W. iv. 4, Sir. xlvi. 12, xlix. 10, Hos. viii. 9 is an example of the reverse rare phenomenon of a new 2nd aorist appearing in the later language (but there is no certain early instance of any aorist from this verb: ἀνέθηλα is late).

3. **2nd aor. pass. for 2nd aor. act.** In ἐρρύην (LXX with class. Greek) we have an early instance of the preference in the case of a υ stem for the *passive* aorist in -ην with active meaning. The κοινή extended this to other υ verbs or perhaps revived old dialectic passive forms. So (for Att. ἔφυν) ἀνεφύη(σαν) 1 K. v. 6, Dan. O vii. 8, viii. 9, προσφυέντος ib. vii. 20. LXX however retains ἔδυν (1 *supra*) and has no instance of ἐδύην (as in N.T. Jude 4, with the early ex. of διεκδυῆναι in Hippocrates).

Cf. class. ἐχάρην and the preference for passive aorists in deponent verbs (6 *infra*).

4. **1st and 2nd aorist (and future) passive.** The

1st aor. pass., like the 1st aor. act., held its own and extended its range in the κοινή, and has survived with altered termination in the modern language (ἐδέθηκα). In a certain number of words, however, the **1st aor. pass. in -θην was replaced by the 2nd aor. pass. in -ην.** The somewhat surprising phenomenon of the introduction of new passive forms of the strong aorist—a tense which in the active was losing some of its ground—is largely due, no doubt, to the increasing preference in the later language for smooth and easy pronunciation, such as was afforded by the single consonant in the termination of the 2nd aor. pass., and the avoidance of the harsh juxtaposition of consonants, especially of two aspirated letters (χθ, φθ), which occurred in most of the discarded passive 1st aorists. In the early vernacular and in poetry there are instances of e.g. ἐκρύφην (for ἐκρύφθην): the κοινή sometimes went further and dropped the remaining aspirated letter, writing ἐκρύβην, and generally preferred a medial to an aspirated letter as the final sound of the stem[1].

-ηγγέλην[2] (for -ηγγέλθην) is universal in LXX: ἀν- ἀπ-ηγγ. *passim*, δι- Ex. ix. 16, 2 M. i. 33 : fut. ἀν- ἀπ- δι- αγγελήσομαι Ψ xxi. 31, lviii. 13, 2 Es. xvi. 7.

ἠνοίγην, fut. ἀνοιγήσομαι, are limited to 2 Esd. (xxiii. 19, xvii. 3): elsewhere in LXX the 1st aor. pass. with χθ is retained either in the classical form ἀνεῴχθην (ἦν. § 16, 6) or more often in the new form ἠνοίχθην with fut. pass. ἀνοιχθήσομαι Is. xxxv. 5, lx. 11, Ez. xliv. 2, xlvi. 1.

ἡρπάγην (δι-) W. iv. 11, Sir. vi. 2, Tob. i. 20, with fut. διαρπαγήσομαι Sir. xxxvi. 30, Am. iii. 11, Zech. xiv. 2, Dan. Θ ii. 5, iii. 96 A : but the class. δι-(συν-)ηρπάσθην is kept by some literary writers, Prov. vi. 25 Bℵ, 3 M. v. 41, 4 M. v. 4.

Fut. ἐλιγήσομαι Is. xxxiv. 4 : the class. aor. is kept in Job xviii. 8 (lit.) ἐλιχθείη (εἰλ. A).

The class. ἐκαύθην, καυθήσομαι, in which there was as yet[3] perhaps no clashing of aspirate sounds, are usual in LXX: ἐκάην (Epic, Ionic and late writers) appears in Jd. xv. 5 B, 2 K.

---

[1] Blass N.T. § 19, 3.
[2] A doubtful ex. occurs in Eur. *I. T.* 932, "the only instance in classic Greek" according to Veitch.
[3] Later they came to be pronounced like ἐκάφθην, καφθήσομαι.

xxiv. 1 (ἐκκαῆναι), Dan. O iii. 19 *bis* (Θ ib. ἐκκαῇ), 94 (κατεκάησαν), and the fut. (ἐκ- κατα-)καήσομαι in (Is. xlvii. 14 AQ*: -κανθ. BℵSir. xxviii. 12, 22 f., xl. 30, Tob. xiv. 4 BA (κανθ. ℵ).

ἐκρύβην, κρυβήσομαι[1] (with compounds) are used throughout, to the exclusion of the classical but ill-sounding ἐκρύφθην, κρυφθήσομαι: cf. the new present κρύβω, § 19, 3.

διαλεγῆναι 1 Es. viii. 45 B has classical authority: A reads διαλεχθῆναι and so in 2 M. xi. 20, Est. i. 18 λεχθέντα Bℵ, διαλεχθήσομαι Sir. xiv. 20 BℵC (-δεχθ. A).

In κατελίπησαν 2 Es. xi. 2 B*vid the reading is supported by the fact that this book has in another instance quoted above (ἠνοίγην) been found the solitary LXX witness to these late 2nd aor. forms : the other MSS have -ελ(ε)ίφθησαν, the classical form of aorist which with -λειφθήσομαι is used elsewhere in LXX.

Fut. pass. νιφήσομαι L. xv. 12 comes under the same head the older aor. pass. of νίζω (νίπτω) was ἐνίφθην (Hippocr.), no class. use of fut. pass. is attested.

The Pentateuch uses the 1 aor. pass. κατενύχθην (a late compound: no passive tenses are attested in class. Greek of the simple verb) Gen. xxvii. 38 E, xxxiv. 7, L. x. 3: the later books employ κατενύγην 3 K. xx. 27, 29, Ψ iv. 5, xxix. 13, xxxiv. 15, Sir. xiv. 1, xlvii. 20, Dan. Θ x. 16 BᵃᵇAQ, κατανυγήσομαι Sir. xii. 12, xx. 21.

(κατ-)ωρύγην[2] Jos. xxiv. 33 a B (class. -ύχθη A), Jer. xxxii. 19 (-ύξωσιν A), Am. ix. 2 AQ (-κρυβῶσιν B), Ψ xciii. 13.

ἐπεσκέπην (συν-) (unclass.) is frequent and fut. ἐπισκεπήσομαι occurs in 1 K. xx. 18 *bis*: the earlier 1st aor. (ἐσκέφθην Hippocr.) is confined to 1 Es. ii. 21 ὅπως...ἐπισκεφθῇ "that search may be made" (contrast vi. 21 ἐπισκεπήτω), the cognate fut. to Jer. iii. 16 BAQ (ἐπισκεφήσ. ℵ*): cf. § 24 s.v. σκοπέω.

ἐτάγην (ἐκ- 2 M. xv. 20, ἐπ- Ez. xxiv. 18, 1 Es. vi. 19 etc., προσ- συν- ὑπ-) is usual, with fut. ὑποταγήσομαι (Ψ lxi. 1, W. viii. 14, Dan. O vii. 27, xi. 37): the class. 1 aor. pass. is confined to the participle in two literary books which also use the 2 aor. : ὅταν ἐπιταγῃ...συντελοῦσι τὸ ταχθέν...τὸ συνταχθέν Ep. J. 61 f., τὰ προσταχθέντα Est. i. 15.

Where in classical Greek a verb possessed both 1 and 2 aor. pass., the former, if it contained two aspirated letters, disappears in LXX : so always ἐρ(ρ)ίφην (some classical authority), ῥιφήσομαι (post-class.), -εστράφην, -στραφήσομαι, to the exclusion of ἐρίφθην[3], ἐστρέφθην etc.

---

[1] An instance in Eur. *Suppl.* 543 : the strong aor. in the form ἐκρύφην is found in classical poetry.

[2] The θ was dropped in the earlier vulgar language : κατορυχησόμεσθα ποῦ γῆς; Aristoph. *Av.* 394.

[3] ριφθις W. xviii. 18 A is clearly a corruption or correction of an original ριφεις.

5. On the other hand the general tendency was to introduce **new first aorists passive**[1] and analogous **futures**. Ἐτέχθην (with τεχθήσομαι) Gen. xxiv. 15, 1. 23 etc. and ἀπεκτάνθην 1 M. ii. 9 were in Attic expressed by different words (ἐγενόμην, ἀπέθανον). Ἐκλίθην (poet.) Ψ ci. 12, Sir. xv. 4 (κλισθῇ ℵ) and κλιθήσομαι Ψ ciii. 5 BT replace the usual Att. 2nd aor. ἐκλίνην and κλινήσομαι. Other new or un-Attic forms are ἐβρώθην (Ionic: not ἠδέσθην)—βρωθήσομαι: ἐσχέθην (Ionic: συν- Gen. viii. 2, 2 K. xxiv. 21 [-έσθη A], 25 [do.] etc., κατ- Tob. x. 2 ℵ, 3 M. v. 12 [κατησχέθη A])—σχεθήσομαι (κατα R. i. 13, συσ- Job Θ xxxvi. 8): in passive sense confined to three books ἐρ(ρ)ύσθην (4 K. xxiii. 18 B, Ψ lix. 7, lxviii. 15 etc., 1 M. ii. 60, xii. 15)—ῥυσθήσομαι (4 K. xix. 11 [in the parallel Is. xxxvii. 11 καὶ σὺ ῥυσθήσῃ; of B is a Hexaplaric addition], Ψ xvii. 30). Other exx. are given in the Table of Verbs (§ 24): a special class of these new forms is dealt with in the following paragraphs.

6. **Aorist (and future) passive for aorist (and future) middle in Deponent Verbs.** Already in classical Greek many deponent verbs, particularly those expressive of emotion, took an aorist passive in -θην in place of the aorist middle which from their reflexive or transitive meaning might be expected[2]: the majority, however, of these verbs retained the future middle. This employment of the passive was a first step in the direction of the elimination of the special forms of the middle voice (as in modern Greek) and the use was quickly extended in the κοινή to other verbs: uniformity was also introduced by the substitution of passive for the old middle futures. Two instances of these new passive aorists stand out from the rest by their great frequency.

Ἐγενήθην (with compounds: Ionic, Doric and Hellenistic)

---

[1] Except ἐτέχθην all the instances quoted have only one aspirated letter.

[2] See the list in Kühner-Blass § 324.

is used interchangeably with the Attic ἐγενόμην throughout the LXX as in the Ptolemaic papyri[1].

The two forms often occur in the same context and it is hazardous to draw distinctions. But, on the whole, there appears to be a tendency to write ἐγενήθην with a predicate and with the more substantive meaning "came," "became," "amounted to," "arose" (e.g. ἐγενήθη ῥῆμα Κυρίου πρὸς ᾿Αβράμ Gen. xv. 1, τὸ πρωὶ ἐγενήθη Ex. x. 13), whereas the introductory formula "and it came to pass" in certain books at least (Pentateuch, 1 and 2 Ch.) is more often καὶ ἐγένετο: in the Kingdom books this distinction disappears.—Ez. a writes ἐγενόμην throughout (except ἐγενήθην xix. 2, xxvi. 1 BQ: also xxvi. 17 AQ, an interpolation from Θ) whereas Ez. β uses ἐγενήθην frequently.—In the moods the old forms preponderate (but conj. γενηθῶσιν Dt. xxiii. 8, inf. γενηθῆναι Ex. ix. 28, Jdth xi. 22, xii. 13, part. rarely γενηθείς e.g. Ex. xix. 16: optat. only γενοίμην etc.) except that in the imperat. γενηθήτω is as frequent as γενέσθω and is preferred in the Pent., e.g. γενηθήτω φῶς· καὶ ἐγένετο φῶς Gen. i. 3.—The perf. γεγένημαι, rare in Attic, is also uncommon in LXX, γέγονα being usual (§ 24).—The Att. fut. γενήσομαι is kept: Gen. xvii. 17 *bis*, Eccl. i. 9, 11 (γενηθησ. A), ii. 18 AC (γινομ. cett.).

᾿Απεκρίθην "answered," the usual Hellenistic form, is employed throughout the LXX[2]: the classical ἀπεκρινάμην in the few passages where it occurs seems to be chosen as suitable for solemn or poetical language: Ex. xix. 19 (God is the Speaker: contrast 8 ἀπεκρίθη δὲ πᾶς ὁ λαός), Jd. v. 29 A ἀνταπεκρίναντο, ἀπεκρίνατο (in Deborah's song), 3 K. ii. 1 (David's solemn last charge to Solomon), 1 Ch. x. 13 (not in M.T.: probably a later gloss), ἀπόκριναι Job xl. 2 B (God speaks: ἀποκρίθητι אА· ἀπεκρίθη Κύριος xxxix. 31 is from Θ), Ez. ix. 11 (the speaker is an emissary from God). The fut. is ἀποκριθήσομαι.

Similarly ὑπεκρίθην "dissemble," "impersonate," -κριθῇς Sir. i. 29, -κριθείς 2 M. v. 25, -κριθῆναι vi. 21 V (ὑποκρίναι A) 24 beside -κρίνασθαι (lit.) 4 M. vi. 17: διεκρίθην and διακριθήσομαι "reason" or "plead" (Ez. a and Joel), and κριθήσομαι in same sense Job xiii. 19, Jer. ii. 9.

[1] Mayser 379, 362.
[2] It is the only form found in the Ptolemaic papyri, but the instances are few (Mayser 379). ᾿Απεκρινάμην continues into iv/B.C. in Attic inscriptions (Meist. 194).

Examples where *verbs expressing emotion* now take on these new forms for the first time are ·

ἠσθήθην: αἰσθηθῇ Job xl. 18
Bℵ (ἔσθηται A).

but class. ἠσθόμην Job xxiii. 5 (αἰσθοίμην), Ep. J 40 (αἰσθέσθαι), 4 M. viii. 4.

αἰσθηθήσομαι Is. xxxiii. 11
Bℵ*Q*, Prov. xxiv. 14 B
(αἰσθήσῃ ℵA).
αἰσθανθήσομαι Is. xlix. 26.

for class. αἰσθήσομαι.

ἐθαμβήθην[1] 1 M. vi. 8, Dan· Ⓗ viii. 17, 18 A.

Causal θαμβεῖν, deponent -εῖσθαι are unclass.

μετεμελήθην (Polyb.) 1 K. xv. 35 etc., fut. -ηθήσομαι Ψ cix. 4 etc.: so perf. -μεμέλημαι 1 M. xi. 10.

Class. Gk uses pres. and impf. only of the personal verb.

Ἠγέρθην (also Attic) is used to the exclusion of ἠγρόμην, together with the new fut. ἐγερθήσομαι.

On the other hand we have only middle aorists in the following cases: ἠγαλλιασάμην (with fut. -άσομαι: N.T. has also ἠγαλλιά(σ)θην), ἀπελογησάμην 2 M. xiii. 26 (-ήσομαι Jer. xii. 1 · N.T. has besides -ήθην), ἠρνησάμην Gen. xviii. 15, 4 M. viii. 7 (Attic preferred ἠρνήθην: fut. as in Att. (ἀπ)αρνήσομαι Is. xxxi. 7, 4 M. x. 15), ἐμαχεσάμην (not ἐμαχέσθην as in Plut.).

In the following both aor. mid. (rare in class. Greek) and aor. pass. are represented in LXX: ἠδέσατο Jdth ix. 3 (else ἠδέσθην 1, 2 and 4 M.), διελέξαντο Jd. viii. 1 B (but διαλεχθῆναι 1 Es. viii. 45 A [-λεγῆναι B], 2 M. xi. 20: fut. -λεχθήσομαι Sir. xiv. 20 is classical beside -λέξομαι).

7. **A new future passive** makes its appearance beside the old classical aorist passive in the following deponent verbs. Αἰσχυνθήσομαι Is. i. 29 etc. (the class. fut. of the simple verb usually -οῦμαι, but ἐπαισχυνθήσομαι): δεηθήσομαι 3 K. viii. 33 etc. (class. δεήσομαι not in LXX): ἐνθυμηθήσομαι W. ix. 13, Sir. xvi. 20 (but class. ἐνθυμήσεται Sir. xvii. 31 B*C: -ηθήσ. ℵ*AB[a]): κοιμηθήσομαι *passim* (no early attestation for fut. pass. or mid.): πλανηθήσομαι Is. xvii. 11 (class. πλανήσομαι): φοβηθήσομαι (doubtful class. authority) is used throughout LXX (except

---

[1] Ἐθαυμάσθην, θαυμασθήσομαι in LXX are used passively only (class.), not as deponents, as in the Apocalypse. Est. C. 21 ἔθηκεν τὰς χεῖρας αὐτῶν, ἐξᾶραι...ἀφανίσαι...καὶ ἀνοῖξαι...καὶ θαυμασθῆναι βασιλέα σάρκινον εἰς αἰῶνα is a possible exception: R.V. translates as passive.

4 M. viii. 19 οὐ φοβησόμεθα A : -ηθησ. א : A is probably right considering the writer's Attic proclivities). Εὐλαβηθήσομαι, εὐφρανθήσομαι, ὀργισθήσομαι, for which there is some classical authority, are used to the exclusion of εὐλαβήσομαι, εὐφρανοῦμαι, ὀργιοῦμαι.

The old middle futures are kept in e.g. δυνήσομαι, πορεύσομαι : Cod. A supplies instances of the later forms, δυνηθήσομαι[1] 1 K. xvii. 33, Jer. v. 22, Ez. vii. 19, πορευθήσομαι 3 K. xiv. 2 (interpolation from Aquila), so R. ii. 9 BA (beside πορεύσῃ in same v.). Further middle futures retained are βουλήσομαι Job xxxix. 9, ἐπιμελήσομαι Sir. xxxiii. 13ᵇ, πειράσομαι 2 M. *bis*.

§ 22. Contract Verbs.

1. **Confusion of forms in -άω -έω.** In modern Greek the three old types of contract verbs have practically[2] been reduced to one, viz. a combination of those in -άω and -έω, in which the forms of the -άω class in ᾷ (ᾶ) have been retained, while the ῶ of the 1st and 3rd plur. has been replaced by οῦ from the -έω class : ῥωτῶ -ᾷς -ᾷ -οῦμε -ᾶτε -οῦν. The merging of -άω -έω into a single class found a starting-point in the forms which were common to the two classes (τιμήσω φιλήσω).

In the LXX the old classes are in the main correctly distinguished, but in the Maccabees portion of Codd. Aא and elsewhere (rarely in B) we see the beginnings of the process[3] in the confusion of ω and ου in the imperf., present and participle.

In the following instances -άω verbs take on forms from those in -έω (ου for ω). Imperf. (3rd plur.) : ἐπηρώτουν 2 M. vii. 7 A (-ων V), ἠρεύνουν 1 M. ix. 26 א (-ων AV), συνήντου̂ 1 M. xi. 2 א (-ων AV) : (1st sing.) προσεδόκουν Ψ cxviii. 166 AR (-ων אT). Pres. τιμοῦσιν Is. xxix. 13 א*, θυμιοῦσιν ib. lxv. 3 א. Part. : καταβοούντων 2 M. viii. 3 A (-ώντων V), σιωπούντων 4 M. x. 18 A (-ώντων א).

---

[1] Cod. A also supplies the only ex. of aor. mid. ἐδυνησάμην (poetical) in 1 M. ix. 9 δυνησώμεθα (δυνώμεθα אV). For the usual aor. ἠδυνήθην -άσθην see §§ 18, 2, 16, 3.

[2] The type πατῶ -εῖς is rare : the -όω class has disappeared and made way for new forms in -ώνω : Thumb *Handbuch* 112 ff.

[3] The instances multiply in Patristic writings : Reinhold 85 f.

T.   16

In the following readings -έω verbs go over to the -άω class (ω for ου). Imperf.: ἐδυσφόρων 2 M. xiii. 25 A (-ουν V), ἐθεώρων Jdth x. 10 ℵ (-ουν B, -ουσαν A), ἐμίσων Mal. ii. 13 ℵ* (-ουν cett.), ἠγνόων W. vii. 12 ℵ^{c.a vid}. Pres.: πτοῶνται Jer. xxvi. 5 B*ℵA (-οῦνται Q), πατῶσιν Is. xxv. 10 A. Part.: (τὸ ἔργον...ἦν) ἀργῶν 2 Es. iv. 24 BA, cf. λαλοντα Zech. i. 19 ℵ* (=λαλῶντα for -οῦντα). Conj.: ἵνα μὴ...ἐκδικᾶ 2 M. vi. 15 A (-ῇ V).

Ἐλεᾶν has almost entirely supplanted the older ἐλεεῖν: the tenses most commonly used (ἠλέησα ἐλεήσω) are of course derivable from either.

So with preponderant authority (B^{ab} and occasionally A reading the -έω form) ἐλεᾷ Tob. xiii. 2 B*ℵA, Ψ xxxvi. 26, cxiv. 5 ℵ (-εῖ AT), Prov. xiv. 31, xxi. 26, Sir. xviii. 14: ἐλεῶσιν Prov. xiii. 9 a Bℵ (-οῦσῖ A): ἐλεῶντι Prov. xxviii. 8 B* (-οῦντι B^{ab}ℵA): ἐλεῶντες 4 M. vi. 12, ἐλέα (impt.) ib. ix. 3. The older -έω forms are retained in two literary books only: ἐλεεῖς W. xi. 23, ἐλεεῖν 2 M. iii. 21.

2. **Verbs in -άω.** Ζάω (ζήω)[1] keeps Attic η and χράομαι has Att. inf. χρῆσθαι (Est. viii. 11 *bis*, E. 19, ix. 13, W. xiii. 18, 2 M. iv. 19, xi. 31), χρᾶσθαι (Ionic and late)[2] only in 2 M. vi. 21 A (χρήσασθαι V). But the remaining "-ήω verbs," as Dr J. H. Moulton terms them[3], are in the κοινή brought into uniformity with other -άω verbs. So in LXX διψᾷ Is. xxix. 8 (ind.), Prov. xxv. 21 (conj.): πεινᾷ Prov. xxv. 21 (conj.), ἐπείνας Dt. xxv. 18.

In the last-named verb the α further encroaches into the fut. and 1st aor. (§ 18, 1), πεινάσω ἐπείνασα always in LXX: similarly διψάσουσιν[4] Is. xlix. 10 Bℵ*Q* (elsewhere always διψήσω Is. lxv. 13 etc., ἐδίψησα). Κατηρήσατο 3 K. ii. 8 A is the Ionic form (-άσατο B is Attic).

3. **Verbs in -έω.** The classical rule that dissyllabic verbs in -έω contract only εε and εει is observed in LXX in the case

---

[1] The only LXX imperf. ἔζην (as from ζῆμι) N. xxi. 9, Jos. iv. 14, 2 K. xix. 6 has some classical authority beside ἔζων: imperat. ζῆθι (similarly formed) Dan. Θθ ii. 4 etc. is post-classical.
[2] Καταχρᾶσθαι appears in Egypt as early as iii/B.C. beside χρῆσθαι: Mayser 347. [3] *Prol.* 54.
[4] The reading is supported by the marginal note in Q, θ'σ' διψήσ. α' ὁμοίως τοῖς ο' διψάσ.

of πλέω, πνέω, ῥέω in the passages, not very many, where these verbs appear. With δέομαι and χέω, the κοινή, as illustrated by the LXX, shows a tendency to extend the use of uncontracted forms still further[1].

Δέομαι in several instances leaves εε uncontracted (δέεται, δέεσθαι are attested in MSS of Xenophon, Veitch s.v.). In LXX:

Uncontracted.	Contracted.
ἐπιδέεται Dt. xv. 8 B, 10 B	δεῖται Sir. xxviii. 4, Dan. O vi. 5.
(-δέηται AF *bis*).	
ἐδέετο Job xix. 16 (ἐδεεῖτο A),	ἐδεῖτο Gen. xxv. 21, Est. C. 14 Bℵ,
Jdth xii. 8 B (ἔδετο A),	Dan. O vi. 10.
Est. C. 14 A.	
δέεσθαι Ψ xxvii. 2, lxiii. 2.	δεῖσθαι Job xxxiv. 20.

A mixture of forms, irregular retention of ε before contracted εῖ, is seen in ἐδεεῖτο A Job *loc. cit.*, cf. ἐπιδεουμένῳ Sir. xli. 2 A (-δεομένῳ cett.). More striking is the juxtaposition twice over of a similar form beside an uncontracted εε in Dt. xv. 8 B, 10 B, ὅσον ἐπιδέεται, καθότι ἐνδεεῖται. Is this intended for a *future* analogous to the LXX fut. χεῶ -εεῖς -εεῖ (§ 20, I (iii))?

In χέω Attic Greek had already relaxed the rule as to contraction in (i) the syllables -εε, which might be contracted or not: but (ii) -εει was always contracted. The LXX keeps the open forms also in (ii) in the new future χεῶ χεεῖς χεεῖ (§ 20, I), which was designed to differentiate the fut. from the present: also occasionally in the present, ἐκχέειν Jer. xxii. 17 (cf. *present* ποιεῖν which follows), προσχέειν Ez. xliii. 18 and (apparently not to be accented as futures) καταχέει Job xli. 14, ἐκχέει Sir. xxviii. 11, χέει ib. xliii. 19. As regards (i) diversity still prevails. Contracted are ἐκχεῖσθαι, διεχεῖτο, ἔγχει 4 K. iv. 41, ἐνέχει ib. iv. 40 B: but uncontracted ἔκχεε Jd. vi. 20 B, ἐκχέετε Ψ lxi. 9 BR [θ' Ez. xxxiii. 25], and *passim* ἐνέχεεν. With διαχεεῖται L. xiii. 55 A cf. ἐνδεεῖται in the preceding paragraph.

Of fluctuation between -ω and -έω (as in earlier Greek) the LXX affords the following examples.

Ἐπιμέλομαι and -μελοῦμαι are both classical: Ptolemaic papyri use the former almost exclusively (Mayser 347 f.). So ἐπιμέλεσθαι 1 M. xi. 37 ℵV* (-μελεῖσθε A), but ἐπιμελοῦμαι Gen. xliv. 21: the frequency of ἐπιμελόμενος in the papyri supports the accent ἐπιμέλου in Prov. xxvii. 25.

Ἐκπιεζοῦντες Ez. xxii. 29 BA (-οντες Q) has Ionic (Hom.

[1] In Patristic writings exx. of ἀποπλέειν, ἐκπνέειν, κατέρρεε etc. occur: Reinhold 84 f.

πιέζευν, Hdt. πιεζεύμενος) and Hellenistic authority (Polybius) : else in LXX πιέζω (-άζω, § 24).

'Ριπτέω in pres. and impf. is classical beside ῥίπτω : so in 2 M. (ἐπιριπτοῦντες iii. 26, ἐξερίπτουν x. 30) and Dan. Θ (ῥιπτοῦμεν -οῦντος ix. 18, 20) : in Ψ lxxxiii. 11 B reads παραριπτεῖσθαι, the other uncials -εσθαι : elsewhere ῥίπτω ἔριπτον Jer. vii. 29, xliii. 23, xlv. 26, W. xvii. 19.

LXX has στερέω (2 M. xiii. 11, 3 M. ii. 33), προσκυροῦσαν (1 M. x. 39), συγκυρούσαις -οῦντα (N. xxi. 25, xxxv. 4 etc.) only : Ptolemaic papyri have στέρομαι only (class. in pres. and impf.) and usually προσ- συγ- κύροντ(α) : Mayser 348.

4. **Verbs in -όω.** These are as a rule regular and unaffected by confusion with the other types, analogous to that which takes place between -άω and -έω verbs. Exceptions[1] are ἐζήλησα Zech. viii. 2 ℵ (-ωσα -ωκα cett.), ἐστραγγαλημένος Tob. ii. 3 AB^{ab} (-ωμένος B*) ἐστραγγάληται ℵ ib. : the converse change is seen in βεβαρωμένος 2 M. xiii. 9 V (-ημένος A).

The inf. is still in -ουν as in the Ptolemaic papyri[2] : the later -οῖν only in ὑψοῖν Tob. xii. 6 B (-ουν A). Cf. the substitution of οι for ου in σφηνοίσθω 2 Es. xvii. 3 ℵ*

Δηλούσουσιν 1 Es. iii. 15 A, ἐπεπληροῦτο (=-ωτο) 2 M. vi. 4 A may be compared with the exx. of replacement of ω by ου referred to above (1).

For 2nd sing. -ᾶσαι -οῦσαι see § 17, 12.

§ 23. VERBS IN -MI.

1. **Transition to the -ω class.** As a consequence of the general tendency of the later language towards uniformity and elimination of real or imagined superfluities, the comparatively small class of verbs in -μι was destined to disappear or rather to be absorbed into the predominant class of verbs in -ω. In modern Greek the absorption is complete. In the LXX the process is only beginning and the -μι forms are still well represented : the transition to the -ω class is less advanced

---

[1] A further instance probably in ἀθῳωμένη οὐ μὴ ἀθῳωθῇς Jer. xxix. 13 BℵQ (ἀθοουμένη A) : the pres. part., not the perfect, is usual in this manner of rendering the Hebrew inf. absolute.

[2] Mayser 349 : the earliest ex. of -οῖν to which Dr J. H. Moulton refers me is dated 18 A.D. (BM iii. p. 136 *bis*). The form owes its origin to analogy (λύει : λύειν :: δηλοῖ : δηλοῖν) as explained in his *Prol.* 53 n. 2.

than in the N.T. In particular the -μι forms in the middle-passive voice are almost universal. The middle -μι forms held out longest, no doubt, because the terminations in that voice differed less widely from the -ω type than in the active· τίθεται, e.g., could be referred to either type; the comparative rarity of the use of the middle of these verbs, mainly in literary writings, also perhaps contributed to the preservation of the classical forms. The new verbs in -ω were not always coined in the same mould. They might be contracts in -άω -έω -όω, or they might be mute (liquid) verbs in -ω. The three forms of -μι verb with infinitives -άναι -έναι -όναι perhaps suggested the formation in the first place of contract verbs in -άω -έω -όω, which ultimately made way for mute verbs. Thus arose ἱστάω —(ἱ)στάνω : τιθέω—τίθω : διδόω—δίδω. In the first of these pairs LXX prefers ἱστάω, N.T. ἱστάνω.

2. The verbs in -νυμι (including ὄλλυμι = ὄλνυμι) may be considered first because they were the first to succumb, active forms as from -ύω appearing already in Attic Inscriptions of v/iv/B.C.[1] In the LXX the -μι forms are universal in the middle voice (the instances occur mainly in the literary books), while in the active the -ω forms are normal, but not quite to the exclusion of the older type. The distinction between active and middle holds good in the Ptolemaic papyri[2].

Active -νμι forms.	Active -νω forms.
ἐπιδείκνυμι 4 M. vi. 35: ὑποδίκνυμεν 1 Es. ii. 20 A: ὑποδείκνυτε Tob. xii. 6 א.	δεικνύω Ex. xxv. 8, Ez. xl. 4, Tob. iv. 20 (ἐπι-), xiii. 6 BA: ὑποδεικνύομεν 1 Es. ii. 20 B: δεικνύουσιν 3 K. xiii. 12.
ἐπιδεικνύναι 4 M. xiv. 18. δεικνύς W. xiv. 4, xviii. 21: -ύντας Ep. J. 3 (δικνύοντας Q*): 2 M. xv. 10 (παρεπι-): 3 M. v. 26 ὑποδεικνύς A (-ύων V), vi. 5 A (δικνύεις V).	ὑπεδείκνυεν 3 M. v. 29. δεικνύων Dt. i. 33, ὑποδεικνύοντος 2 Ch. xv. 3 A, ὑποδεικνύοντες Tob. xii. 6 BA.

[1] Meisterhans 191. In v/B.C. once ὀμνυόντων, iv/B.C. ὤμνυον (but ὀμνύναι), ii/B.C. στρωννύειν and from i/B.C. onwards ὀμνύειν.

[2] Mayser 351 f.

Middle (all in -μι): ἐνδείκνυσαι W. xii. 17 (-νύς אᵃ*): ἐπι-δείκνυσθαι 4 M. i. 1: ἐν-(ἐπι-)δεικνύμενος Prov. xii. 17, Dan. ΟΘ iii. 44, Ep. J. 25, 58, 2 M. ix. 8 A (-ύοντος V).

ἀνεζεύγνυσαν Ex. xl. 30 f.   ἀναζευγνύειν Jdth vii. 1.
                       περιζωννύων Ψ xvii. 33, Job Θ
                           xii. 18 A.
But in the mid. περιζώννυται Ψ cviii. 19.
                       κεράννοντες Is. v. 22 B*א*

This reading is to be preferred to κεραννύντες Bᵃᵇאᶜ·ᵇ Swete (κεραννύντες A). It may be a corruption of an older κεραννύοντες; just as the new-formed contract verbs in -άω etc. subsequently developed into mute or liquid verbs, so the υ in -ύω was afterwards eliminated and ἀπολλύω became ἀπολνῶ, δεικνύω δείχνω etc.[1]

Μείγνυμι does not occur in the act., μίσγω being used instead (Is. i. 22, Hos. iv. 2: so also imperat. mid. συναναμίσγεσθε Ez. xx. 18 B). In the middle the -μι forms are retained:—(προσ)-μίγνυται Prov. xiv. 13, 16, ἀναμίγνυται Dan. Θ ii. 43: συν(αν)ε-μίγνυτο Hos. vii. 8: συναναμίγνυσθαι Ez. xx. 18 AQ*.

ὄλλυμι.   **ὀλλύω.**
ἀπόλλυσι(ν) Prov. xii. 4, xv. 1,   ἀπολλύει Dt. viii. 20, Job ix. 22,
27 (ἐξόλλ.), Eccl. vii. 8 B   Eccl. vii. 8 אAC, 2 M. iii. 39 A,
2 M. iii. 39 V: ἀπόλλυμεν   Sir. xx. 22 A: ἐξόλλύει Prov.
Gen. xix. 13: ἀπόλλυτε   xi. 17 Bא*A (-υσι אᶜ·ᵃ).
1 M. ii. 37.
ὀλλύντα Job xxxiv. 17.   ἀπολλύ(ων) Jer. xxiii. 1 BA (-ύντες
                       אQ), Job (? Θ) xii. 23 אABᵃᵇ
                       (om. B*), Sir. xx. 22.
                       ἀπολλύειν Jer. i. 10=Sir. xlix. 7,
                       Jer. xviii. 7.

In the mid. the -μι forms are universal: ἀπόλλυμαι 1 M. vi. 13, ὄλλυται(-υνται) Prov. ix. 18 etc., ἀπόλλυται Sir. xvii. 28: διώλλυντο W. xvii. 10: ἀπολλύμενος Ez. xxxiv. 29, Prov. xvii. 5 etc. (the reading of A in Eccl. vii. 16 ἀπολλυόμενος is clearly late).

                       ὀμνύω Is. xlv. 23 (-ύων א*), Bel
                       Ο 7: ὀμνύει Am. iv. 2, viii. 7:
                       ὀμνύετε Hos. iv. 15, Jer. vii. 9:
                       ὀμνύουσιν Jer. v. 2.
                       ὤμνυον Jer. v. 7, Ψ ci. 9.
ὀμνύντες Is. xix. 18 B (-ύοντες   ὀμνύ(ων) Is. xlviii. 1, lxv. 16,
א*Γ, -ύουσαι אᶜ·ᵇAQ) is the   Min. Proph. (5 exx.), Ψ xiv. 4,
solitary ex. of an active -μι   lxii. 12, Eccl. ix. 2, Sir. xxiii. 10.
form.
                       ὀμνύειν Jer. xii. 16 *bis*.

---

[1] Dieterich 221 f.

The mid. in -μι: ἐξόμνυμαι 4 M. x. 3: ὀμνυμένων W. xiv. 31 (-νομένων C): ἐξόμνυσθαι 4 M. iv. 26.

'Ρήγνυμι is not used in pres. or imperf., ῥήσσω taking its place : 3 K. xi. 31, διαρρήσσων ib. 11. The mid. keeps the -μι forms: (κατα)ρήγνυται 3 K. xiii. 3, Prov. xxvii. 9, διερρήγνυντο 2 Ch. xxv. 12.

Σβέννυντι W. xvi. 17 is the only ex. of the active: in the mid. σβέννυται Prov. x. 7, xiii. 9, xxix. 36 (ἀπο-), ἐσβέννυτο 4 M. ix. 20. καταστρωννύων Job Θ xii. 23.

New presents in -άζω (-άω), a natural outgrowth from the aor. ἐσκέδασα etc., replace those in -νυμι in Theodotion and late versions: (for κρεμάννυμι) κρεμάζων Job Θ xxvi. 7 BℵC (κρεμνῶν A): (for -πετάννυμι) ἐκπετάζω(ν) Job Θ xxvi. 9, 2 Es. ix. 5: (for -σκεδάννυμι) διασκεδάζει Ψ xxxii. 10 (but mid. διασκεδάννυται Job xxxviii. 24). Cf. ἀμφιάζω (Plutarch etc.) for -έννυμι (in LXX the aorist only is attested, ἠμφίασα -ασάμην or -εσάμην).

There is no attestation for pres. or imperf. of πήγνυμι.

For the new present ἀποτιννύω see § 19, 2.

3. **Transition to the -ω class of verbs in -άναι -έναι -όναι. Ἴστημι.** The -μι forms of the act. are replaced or supplemented by two new presents, the older contract ἱστάω (already used by Herodotus in 3rd sing. pres. and imperf.) and, less often in LXX, the longer ἱστάνω (the termination -νω became increasingly popular in the later language) which makes its appearance once in a papyrus of iii/b.c.[1] and is used by Polybius and later writers, including those of the N.T. The abbreviated στάνω found in MSS of the N.T. is unknown to the LXX. The -μι forms in LXX still hold their own in the pres. sing. act. and, excepting the participle, in the middle.

Present. Ἴστημι (compounds included) is the only form in use for 1 sing.: Gen. ix. 9, xli. 41, 2 K. xviii. 12, Jer. li. 11, Dan. O iv. 28, 1 M. xi. 57 *bis*, xv. 5. No form of 2 sing. occurs. For 3 sing. Attic -ίστησι is used in the literary books (Prov. vi. 14, xvii. 9, xxvi. 26, xxix. 4, Job v. 18, 2 M. vi. 16), elsewhere compounds of ἱστᾷ: ἀνιστᾷ 1 K. ii. 8, ἀφιστᾷ Sir. xxxiv. 1 BℵC= xlii. 9, καθιστᾷ and μεθιστᾷ Dan. Θ ii. 21[2]. 2nd plur. ἵστατε Jdth

---

[1] ἀνθιστάνειν in the Petrie papyri (Mayser 353). καθειστᾳ etc. in papyri of 165, 160 b.c. Aristeas like LXX has both forms: καθιστῶν § 228 but καθιστάνειν § 280.

[2] Probably also ΕΙϹΤΑΜΕ Job xxxi. 6 A should be read as εἱστᾷ με, but it does not represent the original text.

viii. 12 : 3rd plur. from ἱστάω only viz. διιστῶσιν Is. lix. 2, ἱστῶσιν
1 M. viii. 1, μεθιστῶσιν ib. 13.

Imperfect from ἱστάω only : ἀπεκαθίστων Gen. xxix. 3,
συνίστων 2 M. ix. 25.

The *pres. inf.* appears in 3 forms (1) the Attic καθιστάναι
1 M. xiv. 42, 4 M. v. 25 A (-εστάναι ℵ), (2) μεθιστᾶν 3 M. vi. 24,
(3) ἱστάνειν Ez. xvii. 14, ἐξιστάνειν 3 M. i. 25.

The *pres. part.* (1) in its classical form only in 2 M. iii. 26
παριστάντες, 3 M. iii. 19 καθειστάντες A (-τῶντες V), (2) elsewhere
ἱστῶν with compounds is used *passim*, Dt. xvii. 15, xxii. 4, 2 K.
xxii. 34=Ψ xvii. 34, Ψ xv. 5, Job vi. 2, Is. xliv. 26 etc.

A *fut.* -ιστήσω occurs once in A, Dt. xvii. 15 καθιστῶν
καθιστήσεις (καταστήσεις BF): otherwise the new forms are
restricted to pres. and imperf.

In the *middle* the -μι forms are, with the exception noted
below, retained unaltered : the imperat. ἀφίστω Sir. xiii. 10 is
therefore, probably, the old poetical alternative for -ίστασο and
should not be accented, with Swete, ἀφιστῶ (like imperat. τιμῶ),
so ἵστασθε Jer. xxviii. 50 Swete (not -ᾶσθε): παριστάσθω 1 K.
xvi. 22 is ambiguous : the rare optat. ἐξανισταῖτο 4 M. vi. 8.
The part. -ιστάμενος is frequent but the compound **ἐπανιστανόμενος**
is a constant variant: so 2 K. xxii. 40 BA (but -ιστάμενος 4 K.
xvi. 7 BA): elsewhere there is MS authority for both forms,
-ιστανόμενος being apparently the older reading in Ψ (xvii. 40,
49, xliii. 6, lviii. 2 etc.) and Job (xxvii. 7): the true reading
being doubtful in Is. ix. 11, Lam. iii. 62, Jdth xvi. 17 and in
3 M. vi. 12 μεθιστανομένους V (-ισταμένους A).

The paradigm for pres. and impf. in LXX is therefore :

Pres. ind.	1 sing. 3 sing. (2 plur. 3 plur.	ἵστημι -ίστησι ἵστατε	or -ιστᾶ -ιστῶσιν	
Imperf.			-ίστων	
Inf.		-ιστάναι	or -ιστᾶν	or -ιστάνειν
Part.		(-ιστάς 2, 3 M.)	usu. ἱστῶν	
Middle		-μι forms		but ἐπανιστα- νόμενος (μεθιστανόμε- νος)

4. Transition to the -άω class, as in ἰστάω, takes place also in the following verbs. Κιχρῶ 1 K. i. 28 BA (Lucianic text κίχρημι), 3 sing. κιχρᾷ Prov. xiii. 11, κιχρῶν Ψ cxi. 5. Ἐμπι(μ)ράω (no example of *simplex* in LXX) ἐνεπί(μ)πρα 2 M. viii. 6 AV, ἐνεπίμπρων x. 36 A (so from Xenophon onwards). Πίμπλημι keeps the -μι forms twice in Proverbs, but otherwise in the active joins the -άω class.

Pres. ind.	πίμπλησι(ν) Prov. xviii. 20	ἐμπιπλᾷς Ψ cxliv. 16, ἐμ-πιπλᾷ Prov. xiii. 25
Imperf.	ἐνεπίμπλασαν Prov. xxiv. 50 (ἐνεμπίπλ. A)	ἐνεμπί(μ)πλων 3 M. i. 18
Part.		(ἐμ)πι(μ)πλῶν Ψ cii. 5, cxlvii. 3, Sir. xxiv. 25
Middle	-μι forms: pres. ind. Prov. xxiv. 4, xxvii. 20, Job xix. 22 etc.: pres. conj. Prov. iii. 10: part. Hb. ii. 5, Prov. xxiv. 51, Eccl. i. 7, 2 M. iv. 40	imperf. ἐνεπιπλῶντο 3 M. iv. 3 V (A om.)

Φημί so far as used (it is being relegated to the literary vocabulary) is regular, φησίν and ἔφη being the only forms commonly employed as the rendering of אמר: φασίν Ep. J. 19 (in 2 Es. iv. 17 εἰρήνην καὶ φάσιν, subst., should be read): ἔφασαν Est. x. 11: ἔφησα in 2 M. only (3 times): the part. mid. φάμενος Job xxiv. 25 is one indication among several of the translator's acquaintance with Homer: a part. act. is occasionally, as in Attic, supplied from φάσκω.

Of deponents ἐπίσταμαι and (ἐκ- ἐπι-)κρέμαμαι keep the -μι forms except that ἐπίστῃ is used along with ἐπίστασαι (§ 17, 12). So δύναμαι is regular except that δύνομαι[1] occurs as a v.l. in Is. xxviii. 20 B δυνόμεθα, lix. 14 אʘ*vid ἠδύνοντο, 4 M. ii. 20 A ἐδύνετο: 2nd sing. δύνασαι, once δύνῃ (ib.).

5. Τίθημι, δίδωμι. The transition to the class of contract verbs (τιθέω, διδόω) had already begun in Attic Greek in the

---

[1] So in papyri as early as ii/B.C.: Par. 39. 10 [161 B.C.], BM i. 14. 22 [160—159 B.C.]: in papyri dated A.D. the -ω forms, δυνόμενος etc., preponderate.

imperf. sing. (ἐτίθεις -ει for ἐτίθης -η, ἐδίδουν -ους -ου for ων -ως -ω). So in LXX ἐτίθεις Ψ xlix. 18, 20, ἐτίθει Gen. xxx. 42, Prov. viii. 28 (the older ἐτίθη in Est. iv. 4 A : the plur. of the impf. is unattested): ἐδίδουν -ους -ου, but the 3rd plur. is more often the Attic ἐδίδοσαν (Jer. xliv. 21, Ez. xxiii. 42, Jdth vii. 21, 1 M. x. 41 ἀπ-, 3 M. ii. 31) than ἐδίδουν, which was liable to confusion with 1 sing.: the latter occurs in 4 K. xii. 15 B (-ου A), 2 Ch. xxvii. 5 B*A, 3 M. iii. 10 and is usual in N.T.

The extension of the -ω terminations to the *present* of these verbs is slenderly attested in LXX.

> From τιθέω we have only the part. ἐπιτιθοῦσαν 1 Es. iv. 30 BA : elsewhere -μι forms, -τίθημι (no ex. of 2 sg.) -τίθησι, προστίθετε 2 Es. xxiii. 18, παρατιθέασι Ep. J. 29, τιθέναι Prov. viii. 29 א^{c.a}A, τιθείς, and throughout the middle. For present διδόω[1] there is some attestation in the Kethubim and Apocryphal group : διδοῖς W. xii. 19 BA (δίδως א), διδοῖ Ψ xxxvi. 21 Bא*R (δίδωσιν א^{c.a}AT), ἀποδιδοῖ Job xxxiv. 11 B*אC (-δίδωσιν A, ἀποδοῖ B^{ab}), and part. διδοῦντι Prov. xxvi. 8 א (διδόντι BA)[2]. Elsewhere in act. and mid. the -μι forms are retained, except that in the 3rd sing. imperf. and 2 aor. middle forms as from δίδω (by an easy change of ο to ε) appear in late portions or texts of the LXX : imperf. ἐδίδετο Jer. lii. 34 B*א*A (the chap. is a late appendix to the Greek version), Dan. Θ Bel 32 B*AQ, Ex. v. 13 A (ἐδίδοτο AF)· 2 aor. ἐξέδετο 1 M. x. 58 Aא* (-έδοτο א^{c.a}V and so elsewhere· Gen. xxv. 33, Jd. iii. 8 etc.).

6. Ἵημι, never uncompounded in LXX, in composition with ἀπό retains in the active the -μι forms more often than not, whereas with σύν the new forms in -ω preponderate. A doubt arises as to the accentuation of these new forms[3]. We might expect, as we find with other -μι verbs, the first stage in the transformation to be the conversion into a contract verb,

---

[1] Διδοῖ for δίδωσι appears once in an illiterate epistle of ii/B.C. (Par. Pap. 30. 12, 162 B.C., not noted by Mayser) : otherwise the Ptolemaic papyri keep the -μι forms in act. and mid., except that ἀποδιδῶσι once replaces -δίδοασι (Mayser 354). The participle of the -όω type cannot be paralleled till ii/A.D., ἀναδιδοῦντι OP iii. 532. 11.

[2] Mixture of δίδως, διδούς in 3 K. xxii. 6 A, Ψ cxliv. 15 R is merely a matter of phonetic writing : cf. § 6, 34.

[3] Swete (ed. 2) is inconsistent : συνιεῖν 3 K. iii. 9, 11, συνιῶν 2 Ch. xxxiv. 12 : elsewhere συνίειν -ίων etc.

i.e. that the order was ἵημι—ἱέω (like τιθέω)—ἵω. Evidence for the intermediate form is, however, wanting. In the Ptolemaic papyri the verb is rare and only the -μι forms are attested[1]. In the N.T. -ίω is shown to be right by the forms ἀφίομεν, ἤφιεν,

	In -μι		In -ω (?-ῶ)	
Pres. ind.	ἀφίημι 1 M. x. 29 f. 32 f. ἀφίησι(ν) N. xxii. 13, 1 Es. iv. 21, Sir. ii. 11 ἀφίεμεν 1 M. xiii. 39	—	ἀφίω Eccl. ii. 18 ἀφεῖς[2] Ex. xxxii. 32 ἀφίουσι(ν) 1 Es. iv. 7, 50 B* (ἀφιῶσιν A)	συνίεις Job xv. 9, xxxvi. 4, Tob. iii. 8 BA συνίει 1 K. xviii. 15, Prov. xxi. 12, 29, W. ix. 11
Imperf.	ἤφιεις Dan. o Sus. 53	—	—	—
Pres. inf.	ἀφιέναι Gen. xxxv. 18, 1 Es. iv. 7 A (ἀφεῖναι B), 1 M. i. 48 A (-εῖναι אV)	συνιέναι Ex. xxxv. 35, xxxvi. 1, Dt. xxxii. 29, Ψ xxxv. 4 (συνεῖναι א) (lvii. 10 Bab), Is. lix. 15 BQ (συνῖναι א*A), Dan. Θ ix. 13	—	συνίειν 1 K. ii. 10, 3 K. iii. 9 B (συνιέναι A), 11, Jer. ix. 24
Pres. part.	—	συνιείς Ψ xxxii. 15 (-ίων Bab U): συνιέντ(ες) 2 Es. xviii. 3 [contrast 2 συνίων], Dan. Θ i. 4, Θθ xi. 35, xii. 3	ἀφίων Eccl. v. 11 (Sir. xx. 7 A, 2 Es. xix. 17 אc.a)	συνίων (-ίοντος etc.) passim: 1 K. xviii. 14, 1 Ch. xxv. 7, 2 Ch. xxvi. 5, xxx. 22, xxxiv. 12, 2 Es. viii. 16 B etc. etc.

[1] Mayser 354.
[2] Contracted form of ἀφίεις (or ἀφιεῖς): Schmiedel (W.-S. § 14, 16 on the same form in Ap. ii. 20) suggests a present ἀφέω (evolved from -ήσω).

ἀφίονται. In LXX no forms occur but those which are common to -ω and -ῶ verbs[1]. We have seen more than once that N.T. usage represents a later stage than LXX usage: it remains therefore doubtful whether in LXX we should write ἀφίω or ἀφιῶ etc., but, in the absence of attestation for ἀφιοῦμεν etc., the forms in -ίω are on the whole to be preferred.

The following are common to the -ω and -μι forms: imperat. ἀφιέτωσαν 1 M. x. 33, ind. συνίετε Job xx. 2 Bℵ*C: the latter, in view of the table on the preceding page, is no doubt from συνίω and, as it cannot be referred to συνιέω, it favours the N.T. accentuation for LXX.

Ἀνιέναι 1 K. xii. 23 B (no A text): the MSS are divided in 4 M. iv. 10, ἐνίοντες AV ἐνιε͡|τες ℵ.

In the *middle* the -μι forms are, as usual, retained: προίεμαι Prov. viii. 4, ἀφιεμένη 1 M. x. 31 Aℵ^{c.a} (ἀφιμένη ℵ*V*), προιέμεν(ος) 2 M. xv. 12, 4 M. xviii. 3, ἀνίεντο Ez. i. 25 (from Θ) A (ἀνίοντο Q: so προσίοντο 2 M. x. 34 V); to the -μι class should therefore be referred ambiguous forms, προίῃ Job vii. 19, ἀνίεται W. xvi. 24, ἀφίεται 1 M. x. 42 (ἀφῖται ℵ), ἀφιέσθω 1 M. xv. 8 A.

Tenses. Fut. and 1 aor. act. ind. (with 2 aor. in the moods) are regular ἀφ- συν- ήσω etc.: ἀν- ἀφ- καθ- συνῆκα, παρῆκαν 1 K. ii. 5: ἀνῇ ἀνείς ἀνές etc. Perf. act. -εικα is absent from LXX as from N.T.: perf. pass. (ἀνεῖμαι παρεῖμαι: never, as in N.T., -έωμαι) is common in the part. Fut. mid. and pass. προήσομαι, ἀφεθήσομαι. For augment in 1 aor. pass. see § 16, 5.

7. **Remaining moods and tenses of** ἵστημι, τίθημι, δίδωμι. Ἵστημι. **Perfect.** The κοινή gave up the **shorter forms** of the ind. plur. (ἕσταμεν, ἕστατε, ἑστᾶσιν) which already in iv/B.C. had made way for ἑστήκαμεν etc. in Attic Inscriptions[2]. In the inf. however it retained the shorter ἑστάναι: in the participle ἑστηκώς was almost universal in Ptolemaic Egypt[3], but, judging from the N.T.[4] and contemporary and later writings, there appears to have been a reversion to the classical

---

[1] Except the puzzling ϹΥΝΙΕΙΤΕ in Jer. ix. 12 A (συνέτω of BℵQ is probably right).

[2] Meisterhans 189 f.

[3] Mayser 370 f., except that ἐνεστώς was used along with ἐνεστηκώς.

[4] Ἑστώς is about three times as common as ἑστηκώς in N.T. (W.-S. § 14, 5) and in Josephus (W. Schmidt 481 f.) and is usual in Patristic writings (Reinhold 91).

ἑστώς a little before the beginning of the Christian era.   This
(?) Atticistic reversion is apparent in later LXX books.

> In the *ind.* the only ex. of the shorter form is καθεστᾶσιν
> 4 M. i. 18 A V (literary: -ήκασιν ℵ): elsewhere always -εστή-
> κασιν (-έστηκαν Is. v. 29, § 17, 3). *Inf.*: ἑστάναι always, with
> καθεστάναι 4 M. v. 25 ℵ (-ιστ. A), xv. 4: but in comp. with παρά
> we find παρεστηκέναι Dt. xxi. 5, Est. viii. 4 beside παρεστάναι
> Dt. x. 8, xviii. 5.   *Part.*: ἑστηκώς and ἑστώς (compounds
> included) occur in about the proportion of 95/51; the former is
> used throughout the Hexateuch (except ἑστῶτα Ex. xxxiii.
> 10 BAF) as in the contemporary papyri: ἑστώς is practically[1]
> confined to late and literary books, viz. Jd. B text (iii. 19 ἐφ-,
> iv. 21 ἐξ-, xviii. 16, 18: but παρεστηκώς xx. 28 BA), Ruth,
> 2–4 K. (beside ἑστηκώς), 2 Es. (xxii. 44), Ψ (cxxi. 2, cxxxiii. 1,
> cxxxiv. 2), Dan. ΟΘ together with the literary books 1 Es., Est.,
> Jdth, 2 and 3 Macc.
>
> The similar shortened forms from τέθνηκα are confined to
> literary books (elsewhere τεθνήκασιν etc.): τεθνέασιν 4 M. xii. 4 ℵ
> (for correct Attic τεθνᾶσι), τεθνάναι W. iii. 2, 4 M. iv. 22 (1 M.
> iv. 35 V), τεθνεῶτες Job xxxix. 30 (Bar. ii. 17 A).

The new **transitive perfect** ἕστακα[2], in which the α
seems to be taken over from the passive ἕσταμαι, appears in
three LXX books: 1 K. (ἀνέστακεν xv. 12), Jer. α (κατέστακα
i. 10 BℵA, vi. 17 Bℵ*A, ἀφέστακα xvi. 5 BQ with v.l. ἀφέστηκα
ℵA) and 1 Macc. (καθεστάκαμεν x. 20, ἑστάκαμεν xi. 34 -ιμεν ℵ).

> Ἕστηκα is used in present sense "I stand": for the new
> present ·στήκω which is beginning to replace it see § 19, 1.   For
> plpf. (ἐ)ἱστήκειν, ἑστήκειν see § 16, 5.

8.   The 2nd **aorist** active ἔστην (with compounds) and the
1 aor. pass. ἐστάθην (the latter rare outside Gen., Ex. and
literary books) are correctly distinguished, the former intransitive "I stood" and the latter passive "was set up."   The

---

[1] The following sporadic exx. of ἑστώς complete the list: 1 K. ii. 22 A
(elsewhere in this book always ἑστηκώς), 1 Ch. xxi. 15, Jer. xviii. 21 A,
Ez. xxii. 30, Am. ix. 1 (ἐφ-), Zech. i. 11 (ἐφ·), iii. 1, Sir. l. 12 Bℵ
(ἑστηκώς A).

[2] So in papyri, inscriptions and literature from ii/B.C. onwards: Mayser
371, Veitch s. v. ἵστημι, Schweizer *Perg.* 185.   An instance as early as
iv/B.C. is cited from Hyperides *Eux.* 38.

same applies to στήσομαι, σταθήσομαι (with compounds). The only exception[1] in the use of the aorist is Jd. xx. 2 B ἐστάθησαν κατὰ πρόσωπον Κυρίου πᾶσαι αἱ φύλαι (A otherwise with ἔστη): similarly στήσομαι appears to be used for fut. pass. in Is. xxiii. 16 καὶ (Τύρος) πάλιν ἀποκαταστήσεται εἰς τὸ ἀρχαῖον BA (-σταθή-σεται אQΓ).

The two futures occur in juxtaposition or as variants in L. xxvii. 12 οὕτως στήσεται with 14 οὕτως σταθήσεται, Dt. xix. 15 στήσεται πᾶν ῥῆμα B (σταθήσεται AF), but they keep their proper meanings.

In N.T., on the other hand, ἔστην ἐστάθην with στήσομαι σταθήσ. (in the simple verb) are both used intransitively (Blass N.T. § 23, 6).

The 2 aor. imperat. 2 sg. appears both as ἀνάστηθι (45 exx.) and ἀνάστᾱ (poetical: 18 exx.).

The latter mainly in later books viz. Jd. (v. 12 B, viii. 21 BA, xix. 28 B), 1 K. (ix. 26, xvi. 12), 3 K. (xix. 7 B, xx. 15), 2 Es. (x. 4 Bא*), Psalms (iii. 8, xliii. 27, lxxiii. 22, lxxxi. 8), in all of which, except 2 Es., -στηθι is used as well: the remaining exx. of -στα are Jer. ii. 27, Lam. ii. 19 (-στηθι Q), Jon. i. 6, Dan. O vii. 5, Cant. ii. 10, 13, Sir. xxxiv. 21. Ἀπόστηθι (2 K. ii. 22, 1 Es. i. 25, Sir. vii. 2) and ἀπόστα (Gen. xix. 9 ADE, Job *ter*) are equally divided: other compounds have the classical prose form only (ἀποκατάστηθι Jer. xxix. 6, ἐπίστηθι Jer. xxvi. 14, παράστηθι N. xxiii. 3, 15).

The 2 aor. imperat. of βαίνω appears only in the forms ἀνά-(κατά- etc.) -βηθι -βήτω -βητε (not ἀνάβα -βάτω -βάτε which occur in N.T.).

9. **Confusion of ἔστησα and ἔστην** (arising from the 3rd plur. which they have in common) occurs in 2 Es. xviii. 4 καὶ ἔστησεν (א*: ἔστη BA) Ἔσρας ὁ γραμμ. ἐπὶ βήματος ξυλίνου, καὶ ἔστησεν (Bא*A) ἐχόμενα αὐτοῦ Ματταθίας κ.τ.λ. (Lucian ἔστη...καὶ ἔστησαν σὺν αὐτῷ), and apparently in 1 Es. ii. 7 B

---

[1] In Dan. OΘ vii. 4 f. ἐπὶ ποδῶν ἀνθρώπου ἐστάθη κ.τ.λ. the adjacent passive aorists show that the beast is regarded as a mere passive instrument. In Tob. vii. 11 (B text) οὐ γεύομαι οὐδὲν ὧδε ἕως ἂν στήσητε καὶ σταθῆτε πρὸς μέ the meaning seems to be " make covenant with me and have your covenant ratified by me ": the language has a legal preciseness.

καὶ καταστήσαντες οἱ ἀρχίφυλοι...(Α καταστάντες : = 2 Es. i. 5
ἀνέστησαν, וַיָּקִימוּ: in 1 Es. v. 47 correctly καταστὰς Ἰησοῦς).

Cf. further Jd. vii. 21 καὶ ἔστησεν ἀνὴρ ἐφ᾽ ἑαυτῷ Β*vid (MT
has plur. vb and it may be a mere slip for ἔστησαν): Ψ xx. 12
βουλὴν ἣν οὐ μὴ δύνωνται στῆναι אc.aAR (στῆσαι Bא*): Sir. xlv. 23
Φινεὲς...τρίτος εἰς δόξαν ἐν τῷ ζηλῶσαι αὐτὸν...καὶ στῆσαι (στῆναι Α)
αὐτὸν (Swete αὐτὸν) ἐν τροπῇ λαοῦ Bא.

Similar confusion of act. and mid. occurs in Jdth viii. 12
τίνες ἐστὲ ὑμεῖς οἳ...ἵστατε ὑπὲρ τοῦ θεοῦ; Β (ἵσταται) א*Α
(ἵστασθε אc.a), R.V. "stand instead of God."

10. **Τίθημι, δίδωμι.** **Perfect.** Τίθημι has perf. act. τέθεικα
(not τέθηκα as in Attic Inscriptions) and perf. mid. τέθειμαι
(Ex. xxxiv. 27, 2 M. iv. 15), also used in pass. sense (τέθειται
1 K. ix. 24 B [Α τέθεσται like τετέλεσται], προτεθειμένων Ex.
xxix. 23, προσ- Dt. xxiii. 15, 1 Es. ii. 6, Est. ix. 27, 1 M. viii. 1 A)
where classical Greek used κεῖμαι: κεῖμαι has this idiomatic use
in 2 Macc. and occasionally elsewhere.

Aorist. The 1st aorist forms in -κα which were used in
the sing. in Attic (ἔθηκα, ἔδωκα) have in LXX been extended to
the plural (for Attic 2nd aor. ἔθεμεν, ἔδομεν etc.): ἐθήκαμεν
Is. xxviii. 15, 2 Es. xv. 10, 2 M. i. 8 προεθ-, ἔθηκαν and ἔδωκαν
passim; ἔθεσαν (προ- ἐπ-) appears twice in literary language,
2 M. xiv. 21, 4 M. viii. 13, also as a v.l. for -έθηκαν in 1 K. vi.
18 A, 3 K. xxi. 32 B. The 2nd aor. forms are retained in the
moods and in the middle voice.

The introduction of sigmatic aorists ἔθησα, ἔδωσα did not
take place till after the period covered by LXX and N.T.;
Cod. A supplies an early example of each: θῆσαι 1 M. xiv. 48
(στῆσαι אV), ἔδωσεν Sir. xv. 20 (ἔδωκεν BאC): cf. the perf.
δέδωσαν in the clause added after 2 Es. xvii. 71 by the seventh
century hand אc.a.

Moods of the 2nd aorist of δίδωμι. In LXX the *conjunctive* forms are regular (δῶ, δῷς, δῷ etc.) with two exceptions:
(i) the 3rd sing. twice appears in the strange form δῇ (another
case of assimilation to -ω verbs) L. xxiv. 19 BA (δῷ F), xxvii. 9

BA (δῷ F), (ii) -δῷς -δῷ are replaced in a few instances by -δοῖς -δοῖ, viz.:

ὡς ἂν παραδοῖ Jos. ii. 14 BF (παραδῷ A), ἀνταποδοῖ 2 K. iii. 39 A (ἀποδῷ B), μὴ παραδοῖ Ψ xl. 3 B (-δώη אAR, -δῷ T), ἕως ἀνταποδοῖ Sir. xxxii. 24 א* (-δῷ BACא^{c.a}), ἀποδοῖ Ez. xxxiii. 15 BA (ἀποδῷ Q), μὴ δὴ παραδοῖς Dan. Θ iii. 34 B (-δῷς AQ), ὅπως παραδοῖ 1 M. xi. 40 A (-δῷ V).·

The *optative* δοίην -ης etc. is replaced, as in the κοινή generally, by [δῴην, no ex. of 1st sing.] δῴης (Ψ lxxxiv. 8), δῴη *passim.* The classical forms are represented by two v.ll. δοίη in Sir. xlv. 26 א*A, Job vi. 8 א^{c.a}.

Cf. the moods of ἔγνων, § 24. For δῶναι = δοῦναι see § 6, 34.

11. **Εἰμί.** The transformation of this verb, complete in modern Greek, started from the fut. ἔσομαι: to conform to this the remaining tenses have gradually passed over to the deponent class[1]. The change began with the imperfect and with the 1st person sing., for which a new form was required in order to distinguish it from the 3rd person. Hence ἤμην, which is employed throughout the LXX, as in the Ptolemaic papyri[2], to the exclusion of class ἦν (or ἦ).

The transformation in LXX times has hardly proceeded further. The 2nd sing. is generally ἦσθα (17 times); ἦς (which is normal in N.T. and later became ἦσο) is limited to Jd. xi. 35 B, R. iii. 2 (both late translations), Ob. i. 11: it occurs also as a v.l. in Is. xxxvii. 10 א*, Job xxii. 3 A, xxxviii. 4 Bא C (ἦσθα A: possibly the clause is from Θ).

3rd sing. ἦν for which ἦ is a natural slip in 2 Ch. xxi. 20 A*, 2 Es. xvi. 18 B*, Tob. i. 22 א*. (I cannot verify 3 K. xii. 24 quoted in Hatch-Redpath.)

The 1st plur. soon followed the lead of the 1st sing. but in LXX ἤμεθα[3] is limited to Bar. i. 19, 1 K. xxv. 16 BA: in the preceding *v.* in 1 K. BA have the classical ἦμεν, which is also used elsewhere: N. xiii. 34 *bis*, Dt. vi. 21, Is. xx. 6. 2nd and 3rd plur. regular.

[1] See esp. Dieterich *Untersuch.* 223 ff.
[2] Mayser 356.
[3] One ex. of iii/B.C. in the papyri (ib.).

In the *present*, uniformity in the first syllable has been produced in modern Greek by replacing ἐσ- throughout by εἰ-. The only approximation to this in LXX is the vulgar ἤτω (3rd pers. imperat.[1]) in Ψ ciii. 31 (all uncials) and as a v.l. of Cod. A in 1 M. x. 31, xvi. 3: elsewhere ἔστω, including Ψ lxviii. 26, lxxi. 17, lxxxix. 17. 3rd plur. imperat. ἔστωσαν (classical beside ἔστων, ὄντων). 3rd plur. optat. εἴησαν Job xxvii. 7 (class. beside εἶεν: cf. § 17, 7). For ἔσῃ, ἔσει see § 17, 12.

"Ενι (=ἔνεστι), which in mod. Greek in the form εἶνε (εἶναι) has replaced ἐστί and εἰσί, stands for the former, as in N.T., already in Sir. xxxvii. 2 οὐχὶ λύπη ἔνι ἕως θανάτου ἑταῖρος καὶ φίλος τρεπόμενος εἰς ἔχθραν; R.V. "Is there not a grief in it...?" probably lays undue stress on the preposition. (In 4 M. iv. 22 ὡς ἔνι μάλιστα = "as much as possible.")

12. Εἶμι in the LXX period had well-nigh disappeared from popular speech, being replaced by the hitherto unused tenses and moods of ἔρχομαι: the participle and the inf. of a few compounds seem to have been the last to go[2]. Literary writers still made use of it, though not always correctly, missing its future meaning: its revival in Patristic writings is rather remarkable[3].

In LXX εἶμι (always in composition except in Ex. xxxii. 26)[4] is confined to (i) the literary books Wisdom, 2—4 Maccabees, Proverbs, (ii) the latter part of Exodus, with two instances elsewhere of ἐπιών of time.

(i) The Greek books alone use the imperf. viz. περιῄειν W. viii. 18, ἀπῄει 2 M. xii. 1, xiii. 22, 4 M. iv. 8, εἰσῄει 2 M. iii. 14, διεξῄεσαν 4 M. iii. 13: the inf. εἰσιέναι occurs in 3 M. i. 11, ii. 28, the part. ἐξιόντ(ες) ib. v. 5, 48, ἀνιόντος 4 M. iv. 10, προσιόντ(ες) ib. vi. 13, xiv. 16, 19 *bis*, (οἱ) παριόντ(ες) Prov. ix. 15, xv. 10, and (of time) ἡ ἐπιοῦσα (sc. ἡμέρα) Prov. iii. 28 = xxvii. 1 = "the morrow."

(ii) The latter part of Exodus (as distinguished from the earlier part, which uses ἀπ- εἰς- ἐξ- ἔρχεσθαι) has εἰσιόντι xxviii. 23, εἰσιόντι...καὶ ἐξιόντι xxviii. 31, ἴτω xxxii. 26, ἀπιόντος xxxiii. 8, 10 A.

---

[1] It may be due to Phrygian influence, Dr Moulton tells me. Symmachus in ii/A.D. has ἔσο for ἴσθι. Cf. ἔσσο in Sappho: the middle forms of εἰμί occur very early in the dialects, ī. H. Moulton *Prol.* 36 f.

[2] See the scanty papyrus evidence for iii/ii/B.C. in Mayser 355.

[3] Reinhold 87 ff.

[4] Ἴσθι πρὸς τὸν μύρμηκα must be read in Prov. vi. 6 with B*אA[1], not ἴθι A*B[ab].

· Elsewhere (of future time) εἰς τὸν ἐπιόντα χρόνον Dt. xxxii. 29, ἐν τῷ ἐπιόντι ἔτει 1 Ch. xx. 1. A introduces the literary word with correct future meaning in 3 K. xxi. 22 ἄνεισιν (B ἀναβαίνει is no doubt the older reading).

13. Κάθημαι has the regular 2 sing. κάθησαι (not κάθῃ), but the imperat. is usually κάθου (early comedy and late prose: the pres. meaning causing transition to the pres. conjugation), the strict Attic κάθησο appearing only in 2 Ch. xxv. 19: the unclassical fut. καθήσομαι is fairly common (cf. § 24).

Κεῖμαι is regular. For the conjugation of οἶδα (with 1st aor. εἴδησα) see § 24.

§ 24. Table of Noteworthy Verbs.

Ἀγαλλιάομαι(the act. found in N.T., not in LXX), a "Biblical" word, frequent in Is. and Ψ, replacing classical ἀγάλλομαι. Impf. ἠγαλλιώμην Is. xxv. 9, fut. ἀγαλλιάσομαι, aor. ἠγαλλιασάμην (not, as in N.T., -ά(σ)θην), § 21, 6.

Ἀγγέλλω: aor. and fut. pass. ἠγγέλην (ἀν- ἀπ- : for Attic ἠγγέλθην) ἀγγελήσομαι (ἀν- ἀπ- δι-), § 21, 4.

Ἄγνυμι only in composition with κατ-, as usually in Attic (in 4 M. ix. 17 read ἄγξαι with ℵ for ἄξαι A): pres. and impf. un-attested : aor. with Att. augment κατέαξα and pass. κατεάχθην for Att. 2nd aor. κατεάγην, § 16, 6: fut. κατάξω (not with aug. κατεάξω as in N.T.).

Ἀγοράζω: fut. ἀγορῶ (Att. ἀγοράσω), § 20, 1 (ii).

Ἄγω[1]: aor. usually ἤγαγον (with varying terminations ἠγά-γοσαν, § 17, 5, ἐπήγαγα, § 17, 2: cf. impf. ἦγαν, § 17, 4), rarely συν-(ἐπ- ἀν-)ῆξα § 21, 1 : perf. act. ἀγ(ε)ίοχα, ἀγήοχα (for Att. ἦχα), § 16, 7: perf. pass. ἦγμαι regular.

Ἄδω (Att. contraction, not the poetical ἀείδω): fut. ᾄσομαι (Att.) and ᾄσω, § 20, 3.

Αἰδέομαι: aor. ᾐδέσθην and once ᾐδεσάμην, § 21, 6.

Αἰνέω (ἐπαινέω): fut. pass. (in Ψ with middle sense "will boast" or "glory") ἐπαινεσθήσομαι (for Att. ἐπαινεθ.), aor. pass. ἐπῃνέθην with v.l. -έσθην, § 18, 2.

Αἱρετίζω Ionic and late for αἱροῦμαι "choose," the latter being rare in LXX : fut. αἱρετιῶ and as v.l. αἱρετίσω, § 20, 1 (i): aor. ᾑρέτισα and (in Ψ, 1 M.) ᾑρετισάμην.

---

[1] A beginning of the 'Neohellenic' substitution of φέρω for ἄγω (Jannaris § 996, 3) may be traced in some late texts, e.g. Jd. (B text) xviii. 3 Τίς ἤνεγκέν σε ὧδε; (A ἤγαγεν), xxi. 12 (A ἦγον).

Αἱρέω mainly in composition : new fut. ἐλῶ, ἐλοῦμαι (ἀν- ἀφ-
etc.) for Att. αἱρήσω which is dropped, § 20, 2 : new aor. terminations εἷλα εἱλάμην (ἀν- etc.), § 17, 2, καθεῖλοσαν, § 17, 5 :
augment in perf. -είρημαι (for -ῄρημαι) but imperf. -ῄρουν, -ηρούμην
(like εἴργασμαι, ἠργαζόμην), § 16, 5 : augment omitted in ἀνταναιρέθην, § 16, 4.

Αἴρω : new verbal adj. ἀρτός, § 15, 2.

Αἰσθάνομαι : new aor. pass. ᾐσθήθην (beside Att. ᾐσθόμην) and
new fut. pass. αἰσθηθήσομαι and αἰσθανθήσομαι (for Att. αἰσθήσομαι),
§ 21, 6. The late pres. αἴσθομαι occurs in one of the explanatory
notes which Cod. ℵ appends to the Song of Solomon, ἡ νύμφη
ἔσθετε (=αἴσθεται) τὸν νύμφιον v. 2.

Αἰσχύνομαι : fut. αἰσχυνθήσομαι (for usual Attic αἰσχυνοῦμαι),
§ 21, 7 : perf. ᾔσχυμμαι (κατ-), § 18, 4 : aug. omitted in καταισχύνθην,
§ 16, 4.

Ἀκαταστατέω : 1 aor. ἠκαταστάτησα, § 16, 8.

Ἀκούω : fut. ἀκούσομαι (Att.) and rarely ἀκούσω, § 20, 3 ; perf.
pass. (post-classical) ἤκουσμαι Dt. iv. 32 BF, 3 K. vi. 12 A, cf.
§ 18, 2.

Ἀλαλάζω poetical word used in prose from Xen. onwards :
fut. ἀλαλάξομαι and -άξω, § 20, 3 : aor. ἠλάλαξα.

Ἀλείφω : perf. ἤλιφα (Cod. A), ἤλιμμαι, for Att. reduplicated
forms ἀλήλιφα, ἀλήλιμμαι, § 16, 7.

Ἀλήθω Jd. xvi. 21, Eccl. xii. 3 f. with impf. ἤληθον N. xi. 8 in
the κοινή replaces Attic ἀλέω ἤλουν : the old aor. ἤλεσα remains
in Is. xlvii. 2. Cf. similar substitution of mute for Att. contract
verb in νήθω (LXX=Att. νέω), and outside LXX κνήθω, σμήχω,
ψήχω : Rutherford *NP* 240.

Ἁλίσκομαι : perf. 3rd plur. ἑάλωκαν ℵ, § 17, 3 : 1 aor. pass.
(late in *simplex*) ἁλωθῆναι Ez. xl. 1 A (ἁλῶναι cett., and Att. 2nd
aor. ἑάλων is retained elsewhere in LXX).

Ἅλλομαι (ἀφ- ἐν- ἐξ- ἐφ- ὑπερ-: a favourite word in 1 K. and
Minor Proph.) : aor. always ἡλάμην (not the alternative Att.
ἡλόμην), itacism produces the readings ἀφείλαντο Ez. xliv. 10 A
ἐνείλατο 1 M. iii. 23 V : impf. ἡλλόμην (aug. ἑλλόμην once in A,
§ 16, 4) and fut. ἀλοῦμαι are classical.

Ἁμαρτάνω : fut. ἁμαρτήσομαι and (in Sir.) ἁμαρτήσω, § 20, 3 :
aor. usually ἥμαρτον (3rd plur. ἡμάρτοσαν, § 17, 5), rarely ἡμάρτησα,
§ 21, 1. For the trans. (causative) use of ἐξ-(ἐφ-)αμαρτάνειν
"cause to sin" see Syntax.

(Ἀμφιάζω) found only in aor. ἠμφίασα, ἠμφιασάμην and ἠμ-
φιεσάμην, §§ 23, 2 and 6, 6.

Ἀναλίσκω is the usual pres. in LXX as in Att., ἀναλόω (also
Att.) only in καταναλοῦσιν Ep. J. 9 Bᴦ with impf. ἀνήλουν Dan.
Θ Bel 13 (ἀνήλεισκον Q*). As regards augment (Attic writers
seem to have used both ἀνήλωσα and ἀνάλωσα etc., Veitch) the

LXX uncials write ἀνήλωσα (ἐξ-), ἀνηλώθην (ἐξ-), ἀνήλωμαι (ἐξ-παρ-), but with the prefix κατ- the aug. disappears : κατανάλισκον Jer. xxvii. 7 B*Q*A, κατανάλωσα 1 Ch. xxi. 26, Jer. iii. 24 (κατηνάλωσεν ℵ*), καταναλώθην Is. lix. 14 (κατηναλ. Bᵃᵇ) : so ἐξαναλώθη N. xxxii. 13 A. The uncial evidence is, however, shown to be unreliable by the fact that the aug. is not written in the moods and the other tenses and derivative nouns, as it is almost without exception in the Ptolemaic papyri (ἀνηλίσκειν, ἀνηλώσω, (ἐπ)ανήλωμα etc., Mayser 345 f.): cf. § 16, 9.

Ἀνοίγω : see οἴγω.

Ἀνομέω : impf. 3rd plur. ἠνομοῦσαν, § 17, 5 : aug. παρηνόμουν (as from παρ-ανομέω) Ψ cxviii. 51 RT (παρεν. A), § 16, 8.

(Ἀντάω) : fut. ἀπ- συν- ὑπ- αντήσομαι and -αντήσω, § 20, 3.

Ἀπειλοῦμαι deponent as in N.T. etc. (for Att. ἀπειλῶ, which is usual in LXX) is a variant in Gen. xxvii. 42 E, Ez. iii. 17 Q (ἀπειληθῆναι N. xxiii. 19 must have pass. meaning, cf. the citation in Jdth viii. 16) : the dep. διαπειλεῖσθαι Ez. iii. 17 BA, 3 M. vi. 23, vii. 6 is classical.

Ἀπολογοῦμαι : aor. ἀπελογησάμην (not -ήθην), § 21, 6.

Ἅπτω : pf. pass. ἧμμαι is used in mid. sense "touch" (class.), N. xix. 18, Jd. xx. 41 A, 1 K. vi. 9, so ἄνοια ἐξῆπται καρδίας νέου Prov. xxii. 15 B*C (doubtless right, though the Heb. "is bound up in" lends some support to the other reading καρδίᾳ) : fut. pass. ἀφθήσομαι (ἀν-) Jer. xxxi. 9, Sir. iii. 15 ℵ* lacks early authority.

Ἀράομαι : the *simplex* (poet.) in the Balaam story, rarely elsewhere, usually in composition with κατ- (class.) or the stronger (unclass.) ἐπικατ- : fut. and aor. regular -αράσομαι, (κατ)ηρασάμην, the Ionic κατηρησάμην once in A, § 22, 2, the aug. in first syllable in ἐκαταρασάμην 2 Es. xxiii. 25 B, dropped in ἐπικαταράσατο Ψ cli. 6 R, doubled in ἐπεκατηράσατο ib. T : aor. pass. (unclass.) with pass. sense καταραθείη Job iii. 5, xxiv. 18 : perf. pass. with pass. sense "accursed" κατήραμαι and with aug. and redupl. (unclass.) κεκατήραμαι, § 16, 8.

Ἀργέω : neut. part. ἀργῶν = ἀργοῦν, § 22, 1.

Ἀρνέομαι : aor. ἠρνησάμην (for usual Att. -ήθην), § 21, 6.

Ἁρπάζω : unclass. asigmatic fut. (δι)αρπῶμαι, § 20, 1 (ii), beside Att. tenses ἁρπάσω, ἥρπασα, ἡρπάσθην, ἥρπασμαι : new guttural pass. forms ἡρπάγην, διαρπαγήσομαι, §§ 18, 3 (iii), 21, 4.

(Ἀσπίζω) : fut. συν- ὑπερ- ασπιῶ with v.l. -ασπίσω, § 20, 1 (i).

Αὐγέω "shine" is unattested elsewhere : ηὔγει Job xxix. 3.

Αὐλίζομαι : aug. in Cod. A εὐλίζετο, § 16, 4.

Αὐξάνω and αὔξω are both classical, in LXX the latter is limited to Is. lxi. 11, 4 M. xiii. 22 and to compounds in literary books (ἐπαύξω, συναύξω) 2 M. iv. 4, 3 M. ii. 25, 4 M. xiii. 27 Aℵ (-αυξανόντων V) : the verb retains its class. transitive meaning, "grow" "increase" being expressed by αὐξάνομαι, and the intrans.

use, common in N.T., being limited to ηὔξησαν I Ch. xxiii. 17
A* (ηὐξήθησαν cett.): the Attic fut. αὐξήσω in I Ch. xvii. 10,
while the Pentateuch uses the novel αὐξανῶ, Gen. xvii. 6, 20,
xlviii. 4, L. xxvi. 9: the fut. pass. αὐξηθήσομαι is regular, N. xxiv. 7,
Jer. xxiii. 3.

Αὐταρκέω, αὐτομολέω: aug. omitted in αὐτάρκησα, αὐτομόλησα,
§ 16, 4.

'Αφανίζω: fut. ἀφανιῶ and -ίσω, § 20, 1 (i).

'Αχρειόω: 3rd plur. perf. ἠχρείωκαν, § 17, 3.

Βαδίζω: fut. βαδιοῦμαι (Att.) and, once in ℵ, the later βαδιῶ,
§ 20, 3.

Βαίνω rare in the *simplex* (Dt. xxviii. 56 and three times in
literary books in perf. and pluperf.): new present -βέννω (cf.
-βένω), § 19, 2: perf. part. βεβηκώς, not the alternative Att.
βεβώς: aug. omitted in plpf. βεβήκειν, § 16, 2: aug. *vice* reduplication in κατέβηκα Cod. A, § 16, 7: 3rd plur. impf. -έβαιναν,
§ 17, 4: 2nd aor. imperat. ἀνά-(κατά- etc.)βηθι -βήτω -βητε, not
the N.T. forms ἀνάβα-βάτω-βατε, § 23, 8: 2nd aor. opt. καταβοῖ
(for -βαίη) 2 K. i. 21 B (καταβήτω A, καταβῇ Swete).

Βάλλω: aug. omitted in plpf. -βεβλήκειν, § 16, 2, duplicated
in double compound παρεσυνεβλήθην, § 16, 8: aor. terminations
ἐβάλοσαν, § 17, 5 and ἔβαλαν -ας (Hb. iii. 13 Aℵᶜᵒʳʳ), § 17, 2.

Βαρέω only in the old perf. part. pass. βεβαρημένος 2 M.
xiii. 9 A (βεβαρωμένος V, § 22, 4) and once in perf. ind. pass.
βεβάρηται Ex. vii. 14 BA (βεβάρυνται F). Elsewhere in LXX,
as in class. Greek, the verb is always βαρύνω (κατα-), whereas
later the contract verb became universal (mod. Greek βαρειοῦμαι)
and in N.T. βαρεῖν (with compounds ἐπι- κατα-) occurs 10 times
as against one ex. only in WH of -βαρύνειν Mc. xiv. 40. Βεβαρυμ-
μένοι in a papyrus of ii/B.C., no Ptolemaic ex. of βαρεῖν, Mayser 390.

Βαστάζω: βαστάσω and ἐβάστασα as in Attic, also ἐβάσταξα,
§ 18, 3 (iii), with which cf. the late fut. pass. συνβασταχθήσεται
Job Θ xxviii. 16, 19.

Βιάζομαι: fut. παραβιῶμαι (for Att. -βιάσομαι, but see Veitch),
§ 20, 1 (ii).

Βιβάζω: fut. as in Attic -βιβῶ (ἀνα- ἐπι- κατα- συμ-: mainly
in Ez. a and Minor Prophets), elsewhere -βιβάσω (Xenophon),
§ 20, 1 (ii): aor. pass. ἐβιβάσθην (Aristot.): fut. pass. late ἀναβι-
βασθήσομαι L. ii. 12.

Βιβρώσκω: see ἐσθίω.

Βιόω (δια-) rare and except Ex. xxi. 21, Sir. xl. 28, only in
literary books: fut. βιώσω for Att. βιώσομαι, § 20, 3: aor. ἐβίωσα
for the usual Att. ἐβίων, § 21, 1.

Βλαστάνω has alternative present forms βλαστάω, βλαστέω,
§ 19, 3 and new 1 aor. ἐβλάστησα with causative meaning (not
Att. ἔβλαστον), § 21, 1: perf. βεβλάστηκα, § 16, 7.

Βλέπω is used not only in its original sense of the function of the eye "to look," but also, especially in later books, = ὁρᾶν "to see," e.g. Jd. ix. 36 B (=ὁρᾷς A), 4 K. ii. 19, ix. 17: ἀναβλέπειν besides its class. meanings "look up" and "recover sight" (Tob. xi. 8 א) is used causatively in ἀναβλέψατε εἰς ὕψος τοὺς ὀφθαλμοὺς ὑμῶν Is. xl. 26 (for the usual τοῖς ὀφθ.), cf. Tob. iii. 12 א. Fut. βλέψομαι (Att.) and, more rarely, βλέψω (ἐπι-), § 20, 3. Of passive and mid. forms (unclassical except fut. mid.) LXX has impf. pass. (ἐν)εβλέποντο 3 K. viii. 8 = 2 Ch. v. 9 *bis*, and part. pass. βλεπόμενος W. ii. 14, xiii. 7, xvii. 6, Ez. xvii. 5 (ἐπι-): the mid. is constant in περιεβλεψάμην Ex. ii. 12 etc., ὑποβλεπόμενος "suspicious of" 1 K. xviii. 9, Sir. xxxvii. 10.

Βοάω: fut. βοήσομαι (Att.) and βοήσω, § 20, 3: as from βοέω καταβοούντων Cod. A, § 22, 1.

Βοηθέω: unclassical passive forms are introduced, βεβοήθηται Prov. xxviii. 18 has class. authority, but the 1st aor. pass. and fut. pass. are new, the uncials exhibiting a natural confusion with the tenses of βοᾶν: aor. ἐβοηθήθην 2 Ch. xxvi. 15 (the Heb. shows that βοηθῆναι of A is wrong), Ψ xxvii. 7, Is. x. 3, xxx. 2 (βοηθῆναι א*), fut. βοηθηθήσομαι Is. xliv. 2, Dan. Θ xi. 34 (βοηθήσονται Q*).

Βούλομαι: 2 sing. βούλει B and βούλῃ A, § 17, 12: aug. ἐβουλήθην, but impf. ἐβουλόμην and ἠβουλόμην, § 16, 3.

The pres. of βράσσω "shake" appears in ἀναβράσσοντος Na. iii. 2 (Att. βράττω: -βράζω also occurs): the tenses lack classical authority, ἀνέβρασα Ez. xxi. 21, W. x. 19, ἐξέβρασα 2 Es. xxiii. 28, 2 M. i. 12, ἐξεβράσθην 2 M. v. 8.

Βρέχω (class. "wet" or "drench") in LXX usually means "send rain" (hail etc.), being used either absolutely, Gen. ii. 5, or with acc. ὑετόν, χάλαζαν etc., thus supplanting the class. ὕειν which is limited to Ex. ix. 18, xvi. 4 (cf. the new ὑετίζειν Jer. xiv. 22, Job Θ xxxviii. 26): fut. act. and pass. are unclassical, βρέξω Am. iv. 7, Jl. ii. 23, Ez. xxxviii. 22, Ψ vi. 7, βραχήσομαι Am. iv. 7, Is. xxxiv. 3.

Γαμέω is limited to three instances in the Greek books[1] where it is used correctly of the husband: aor. ἔγημα (Att.) and ἐγάμησα (Hell.), § 21, 2. Verbal adj. γαμετή = "wife" 4 M. ii. 11.

Γελάω: fut. γελάσομαι and γελάσω, § 20, 3.

Γηράσκω: fut. γηράσω (not -σομαι), § 20, 3.

Γίνομαι (γείν. § 6, 24) not γίγν. except as a rare v.l., mainly in the A text of the Esdras books, § 7, 32: for aor., ἐγενόμην

---

[1] The translations, partly under the influence of the Heb., use other expressions: of the husband γαμβρεύειν (Gen. xxxviii. 8), λαμβάνειν and in 2 Es. (x. 2 etc.) the Hebraic καθίζειν γυναῖκα (= hiphil of יָשַׁב, "give a dwelling" or "settlement to"): of the wife γίνεσθαι or εἶναί τινι (= הָיָה לְ), ἔχειν ἄνδρα: of both συνοικεῖν, συνοικίζεσθαί τινι.

(ἐγενάμην in Jer. A text, § 17, 2) and ἐγενήθην (dialectic and late) are used interchangeably, § 21, 6: both forms of Att. perf. γέγονα and γεγένημαι (-ένν. Jos. v. 7 B, Ψ lxxxvi. 6 R) are used, the former largely preponderating: aug. retained in ἐγεγόνειν, § 16, 2: Att. fut. γενήσομαι apparently only in Gen. xvii. 17 *bis*, ="shall be born" (cf. τίκτω for Hellenistic τεχθήσομαι and ἐτέχθην): poet. term. ἐγινόμεσθα, § 17, 13.

Γινώσκω (γειν. § 6, 24), not γιγν. except as a rare v.l., § 7, 32, has the classical tenses: the plpf., apparently only in the compound διεγνώκειν N. xxxiii. 56, 2 M. ix. 15, xv. 6, seems to lack early authority: 3rd plur. perf. ἔγνωκαν, § 17, 3: the 2nd aor. ἔγνων (ἀνέγνοι=ἀνέγνω 4 K. xxii. 8 B*) usually has the regular conj. γνῶ, in Jdth xiv. 5 ἐπιγνοῖ B (ἐπιγνῷ אA), while in the rare optat. the MSS are divided between the class. γνοίην and the later γνῴην, which occurs in Job xxiii. 3 A (γνοίη Bא), 5 B*א* (γνοίην A and later hands of Bא: cf. similar fluctuation in the moods of the 2nd aor. of δίδωμι, § 23, 10): 2nd aor. inf. appears once as ἐπιγνοῦναι Est. A 11 א* on the model of δοῦναι, so διαγνοῦναι in a papyrus of iii/B.C., Mayser 366 (for the converse working of analogy in δῶναι see § 6, 34): for ἐγνώθην, γνωθήσομαι in B, *vice* ἐγνώσθην, γνωσθ., § 18, 2: verb. adj. γνωστέον, § 15, ?

Γνωρίζω: fut. γνωριῶ (Att.) and -ίσω, § 20, 1 (i).

Γράφω: aug. always retained in plpf. ἐγέγραπτο, § 16, 2, redupl. dropped in ἐπέγραπτο A (ἐγέγραπτο BF), § 16, 7: tenses regular, perf. γέγραφα 1 M. xi. 31, 2 M. i. 7, ix. 25 (not the late γεγράφηκα), aor. pass. ἐγράφην (ἀπ- etc.: not ἐγράφθην), fut. pass. γραφήσομαι Ψ cxxxviii. 16 (not the more usual Att. γεγράψομαι), aor. mid. ἀπεγραψάμην Jd. viii. 14 A, Prov. xxii. 20, 3 M. vi. 34.

Γρηγορέω (ἐγρηγορέω): new pres., replacing ἐγρήγορα, with tenses ἐγρηγόρουν, (ἐ)γρηγορήσω, ἐγρηγόρησα, ἐγρηγορήθην, found in some, mainly late, books of LXX and frequently in N.T., § 19, 1.

Γρύζω: fut. γρύξω (not γρύξομαι), § 20, 3.

(**Δείδω**): perf. δέδοικα -ας -ασι -ώς (not Att. δέδια etc.) and pluperf. ἐδεδοίκειν (aug. retained, § 16, 2: once in A ἠδεδοίκειν, § 16, 3) are used only by the translator of Job, excepting one ex. of δεδοικότες in Is. lx. 14.

Δείκνυμι and forms from δεικνύω, § 23, 2. The part. ἐπιδεδ(ε)ιγμένος in 2 M. ii. 26 (R.V. "taken upon us the painful labour of the abridgement") and 3 M. vi. 26 (Kautzsch "erduldeten") is used where we should expect ἐπιδεδεγμένος. The confusion of forms from δείκνυμι and δέχομαι (δέκ.) is perhaps due to Ionic influence: cf. the Homeric use of δείκνυσθαι (and δειδίσκεσθαι)=δέχεσθαι "welcome."

Δεῖ "it is necessary": the impers. δεῖ, ἔδει, fut. δεήσει Jos. xviii. 4, is used occasionally, δεῖ being replaced by the paraphrastic δέον ἐστίν in Sir. prol. *bis* and 1 M. xii. 11 (so Polyb., Aristeas and papyri): no ex. of conj. or opt. since με ᾖ of the uncials in Est. iv. 16 is doubtless right (not δέῃ).

Δέομαι "ask": for the extended use of the uncontracted forms and the peculiar forms ἐδεεῖτο, ἐνδεεῖται see § 22, 3: the fut. pass. δεηθήσομαι (ἐν- προσ-) supplants Att. δεήσομαι, § 21, 7: ἐδεήθην (ἐκ- προσ-) and δεδέημαι 3 K. viii. 59 are classical.

Δέχομαι: tenses regular except that the fut. pass. δεχθήσομαι (προσ-) "will be accepted" is new, L. vii. 8, xix. 7, xxii. 23, 25, 27, Sir. xxxii. 20: -εδέχθην with pass. sense is classical: pf. pass. with mid. sense (class.) ἐκδέδεκται Gen. xliv. 32 (in Is. xxii. 3 read δεδεμένοι εἰσίν, A has δεδεγμένοι), for ἐπιδεδειγμένος used like -δεδεγμένος cf. δεικνύναι: verbal adj. ἐκδεκτέον § 15, 2.

Δέω "bind" has the regular tenses δήσω ἔδησα ἐδέθην δεθήσομαι δέδεμαι: ℵ* twice uses forms from δέω "want," δεήσεις Job xxxix. 10, ἐδέησεν ib. Θ xxxvi. 13: the mid. is used only in the 1st aor. (poetical in the *simplex*) ἐδήσατο Jdth xvi. 8, κατεδήσατο τελαμῶνι 3 K. xxi. 38 (the language has a Homeric ring).

Διαλέγομαι: aor. διελέγην, διελεξάμην and (the usual class. form) διελέχθην, fut. διαλεχθήσομαι, § 21, 4 and 6.

Διδάσκω: fut. pass. διδαχθήσομαι Is. lv. 12 is post-classical.

(Διδράσκω) only in composition with ἀπο- δια-: the Att. 2nd aor. ἀπέδραν is used in 2nd and 3rd sing. and 3rd plur. -έδρας -έδρα -έδρασαν, conj. ἀποδρᾷ Sir. xxx. 40, part. διαδράς Sir. xi. 10, imperat. ἀπόδραθι (post-classical) Gen. xxvii. 43, xxviii. 2: the 1st sing. appears as ἀπέδρων in Jdth xi. 16, a form which is explained by an ancient writer cited in Rutherford *NP* 335 as a recognized alternative for ἀπέδραν (τὸ δὲ ἀπέδραν τινὲς τῶν ῥητόρων διὰ τοῦ ω εἶπον, ἀπέδρων, ἀλλ᾽ ἄμεινον διὰ τοῦ a), or it would seem possible to take it as a new *imperfect* as from ἀποδράω (the regular -εδίδρασκον however is used elsewhere in LXX): out of the 3rd plur. of the 2nd aor. arose the new 1st aor. ἀπέδρασα which appears in Cod. ℵ, § 21, 1.

Δίδωμι: beginnings of the transition to the -ω (-όω) class, § 23, 5: ἔδωκαν (for ἔδοσαν), ἔδωσα Cod. A, moods of 2nd aor., § 23, 10: term. ἔδωκες A, § 17, 8: aug. omitted in δεδώκειν, § 16, 2.

Δικάζω has Att. fut. δικάσω 1 K. viii. 20, xii. 7 B (Ionic δικᾶν=δικάσειν Hdt. I. 97), but the rare ἐκδικάζω has fut. 3rd sing. ἐκδικᾶται "shall take vengeance" or "avenge" L. xix. 18, Dt. xxxii. 43 BF (ἐκδικεῖται A: the following καὶ ἐκδικήσει is perhaps a doublet) § 20, 1 (ii): in Jdth xi. 10 ἐκδικᾶται is used passively "be punished", and the present tense used in the next clause suggests that it is intended for pres. pass. as from †ἐκδικάω (cf. for similar exx. Hatzidakis 395): the classical ἐκδικάζω (unrepresented in N.T.) has in LXX almost disappeared to make way for the new ἐκδικέω (tenses regular: in passive -εδικήθην,

-δικηθήσομαι, -δεδίκημαι Gen. iv. 24) which with the subst. ἐκδίκησις (Polyb.) is the ordinary word denoting vengeance or punishment: for a trace of an intermediate ἐκδικᾶν see § 22, 1.

Διψάω: διψᾷ (for Att. -ῇ), § 22, 2: fut. διψάσω, § 18, 1, and διψήσομαι, § 20, 3, as well as Att. διψήσω.

Διώκω: fut. usually διώξομαι (καταδιώξομαι), also διώξω (κατα-) (Attic prefers the middle), but ἐκδιώξω only, § 20, 3: the fut. pass. ἐκδιωχθήσονται Ψ xxxvi. 28 ARTℵ^{c.a} is post-classical: 3rd plur. imperf. ἐδίωκαν in ℵ, § 17, 4.

Δοκιμάζω (ἀπο-): fut. δοκιμῶ and δοκιμάσω (Att.), § 20, 1 (ii), but in Sir. xxvii. 5, xxxiv. 26 δοκιμᾷ of ℵ (= B δοκιμάζει) is probably pres. as from δοκιμάω (cf. δοκιμήσῃς in a papyrus of ii/B.C., Mayser 459, and the subst. δοκιμή in N.T.: the ex. of fut. δοκιμῶ which Veitch and Kühner-Blass cite from Hdt. I. 199 also appears from the context to be present, τῷ δὲ πρώτῳ ἐμβαλόντι ἕπεται οὐδὲ ἀποδοκιμᾷ οὐδένα).

Δολιόω: post-classical N. xxv. 18 and 3 times in Ψ: 3rd plur. imperf. ἐδολιοῦσαν, § 17, 5.

Δύναμαι: traces of transition to the -ω class in 2nd sing. δύνῃ (usually δύνασαι in LXX) and variants δυνόμεθα etc., §§ 17, 12 and 23, 4: aug. ἠ- (usually) or ἐ-, § 16, 3: aor. ἠδυνήθην (ἐδ.) and ἠδυνάσθην (ἐδ.) ib., also ἐδυνησάμην (poet.) Cod. A, § 21, 7: fut. δυνήσομαι and in Cod. A δυνηθήσομαι, § 21, 7.

Δυναμόω (ἐν- ὑπερ-): new verb found in a few late LXX books and in N.T.: aug. ὑπερηδυνάμωσαν (like ἠδυνήθην), § 16, 3.

Δυσφορέω: 3rd plur. impf. ἐδυσφόρων Cod. A (for -ουν), § 22, 1.

Δύω, δύνω, -διδύσκω. Apart from pres. and impf. the classical tenses of δύειν (εἰσ- ἐπι- κατα-) "to sink" (intrans.) are for the most part retained: 2nd aor. ἔδυν (not ἐδύην, § 21, 3) with inf. δῦναι Jd. xiv. 18 A, conj. δύῃ L. xxii. 7 AF (Δγ B*), fut. δύσομαι, pf. δέδυκα: a new intrans. 1st aor. ἔδυσα (evolved out of the 3rd plur. of ἔδυν) appears twice in the compounds καταδύσωσιν, ὑποδύσαντες, § 21, 1: the trans. fut. δύσω "cause to sink" Jl. ii. 10, iii. 15 is late in the *simplex*, cf. καταδύσω Mic. vii. 19. The class. fut. and 1st aor., act. and mid., of ἐκδύειν, ἐνδύειν, "to strip (oneself)," "clothe (oneself)," are also kept, and once the class. impf. ἐνεδυόμην Ψ xxxiv. 13: plpf. without aug. ἐνδεδύκειν or without reduplication ἐνεδύκειν A (cf. ἐν|δύκει Est. D. 6 B*), § 16, 2 and 7: perf. (only in the part.) ἐνδεδυμένος and ἐνδεδυκώς, the latter limited to 1 K. xvii. 5, 2 K. vi. 14 and "Ezekiel a" (ix. 2, 3, 11, x. 2, 6, 7, xxiii. 6 [A mid.], 12 [do.]: contrast in Ez. β ἐνδεδυμένους xxxviii. 4 BAQ).

The *pres. and impf.* of the *intransitive* verb "to set," "sink" are always formed from δύνω (Ionic: in Att. prose not before Xen.), § 19, 3: δύνει Eccl. i. 5, δύνοντος 3 K. xxii. 36, 2 Ch. xviii. 34 A, Jos. viii. 29 (ἐπι-), ἔδυνε 2 K. ii. 24, so ἐκδύνει "escapes" Prov. xi. 8 (δύνει A): the aor. δύναντος 2 Ch. xviii. 34 B is late (Polyb. ix. 15 Schweigh.), § 21, 1. The reading of B*אּ* in Is. lx. 20 οὐ γὰρ δυνήσεται ὁ ἥλιός σοι (δύσεται cett.) is remarkable: a fut. mid. of this form from δύνω is unexampled, and if the fut. of δύναμαι is intended the reading cannot be original: the two roots are elsewhere confused, e.g. 2 K. xvii. 17 and the readings in 1 Ch. xii. 18.

To express the *transitive* meanings "put on," "put off" the new forms ἐν- ἐκ- διδύσκω are used in pres. and impf., apparently first attested in LXX (also in N.T. and Jos.), § 19, 3.

ʼΕάω: tenses regular with aug. εἰ-, except for 3rd plur. impf. ἐῶσαν Jer. xli. 10, beside εἴων elsewhere, § 16, 5: aor. pass. (ε)ἰάθην and in Cod. A (ε)ἰάσθην, § 18, 2: for the itacism cf. ἴασα Job xxxi. 34 A.

ʼΕγγίζω: προσ- (Aristot. and Polyb.: LXX usually intr. "draw near," occasionally trans. "bring near" Gen. xlviii. 10 etc., as also in Polyb.): fut. ἐγγιῶ, § 20, 1 (i): ἤγγικα, ἤγγισα.

ʼΕγγυάω: medial aug. in ἐνεγυησάμην (for ἠγγυησ.), § 16, 8.

ʼΕγείρω "raise up" (no ex. of intrans. use of act.): aug. usually inserted in ἐξηγειρόμην ἐξηγέρθην, § 16, 4: the two perfects are rare, the classical ἐγρήγορα "watch," "be awake" occurring only twice (elsewhere replaced by γρηγορέω q.v.), the later ἐγήγερμαι only in Zech. ii. 13 ἐξ- "is risen," Jdth i. 4 אּ διεγηγερμένας of gates raised to a certain height (διεγειρομένας BA): aor. pass. ἠγέρθην (not ἠγρόμην), § 21, 6: fut. pass. (ἐξ- ἐπ-)εγερθήσομαι N. xxiv. 19, Mic. v. 5, Is. xix. 2 etc. is late (Babrius).

Εἰλέω: 1 aor. (ἀν)είλησα[1] late (Att. εἷλα, Ep. ἔλσα), § 21, 2: perf. pass. (late in *simplex*, ἀπειλημένον Hdt. II. 141, περιειλημένην in iii/B.C., Mayser 337) εἰλημένος Is. xi. 5 BQ (-ημμ. אּA), ἐνειλημένος 1 K. xxi. 9 B (-ημμ. A), κατειλημένος 2 Ch. ix. 20 A (-ημμ. B).

Εἰμί, § 23, 11: 2 sg. fut. ἔσῃ and ἔσει, § 17, 12: ἔστωσαν, § 17, 6.

Εἶμι, § 23, 12.   Εἶπον, εἴρηκα etc.: see λέγω.

ʼΕκκλησιάζω: medial aug. in aor. ἐξεκλησίασα, § 16, 8.

ʼΕλαττονέομαι and more rarely ἐλαττονέω (-ττ- not -σσ-, § 7, 45) with same meaning "fail" etc. appear for the first time in LXX beside the class. ἐλαττόω (-ττ- and -σσ-, § 7, 45): aug. omitted in ἐλαττονώθη, § 16, 4.

ʼΕλαύνω: fut. -ελάσω (not ἐλῶ), § 20, 1 (iii): aor. and plpf. pass. συνελασθέντων, συνήλαστο late (Att. ἠλάθην, ἠληλάμην), § 18, 2.

ʼΕλεάω usually supplants the older ἐλεέω, § 22, 1.

Ἑλίσσω: not the Ionic and late εἰλ., except in A which has εἰλιχθείη Job xviii. 8 and verbal adj. εἰλικτός 3 K. vi. 13: 2nd fut. pass. ἐλιγήσομαι is post-classical, § 21, 4.

---

[1] The corresponding fut. only in Job xl. 21 A ΕΙΛΗϹΕΙϹ, a corruption of ΕΙ ΛΗϹΕΙϹ.

Ἕλκω : fut. ἑλκύσω ἐξ- παρ- (Ionic for Att. ἕλξω): the 1st aor. εἵλκυσα (ἥλκυσα, § 16, 5) and pass. εἱλκύσθην (ἐξ- ἐφ-) have early authority (the late εἷλξα, εἵλχθην do not occur in LXX).

Ἐμποδοστατέω : a new verb "obstruct": the perf. with irregular medial reduplication, ἐμπεποδεστάτηκας, appears in a corrupted form in Jd. xi. 35 A, § 16, 8.

Ἐνεχυράζω : aug. ἠνεχύρασα and ἐνεχ., § 16, 8 : fut. -άσω Dt. xxiv. 6 B and -ῶ -ᾷς ib. AF*, 17 BᵃᵇAF.

Ἐνθυμέομαι : fut. ἐνθυμηθήσομαι (late) and -μήσομαι (Att.), § 21, 7 : -εθυμήθην, -τεθύμημαι classical.

Ἐνυπνιάζομαι : the verb appears to be Ionic (Hippocrates, and then not before Aristot., who uses the active): aor. ἠνυπνιάσθην (or ἐν.) and ἠνυπνιασάμην (or ἐν.), § 16, 4 and 8 : fut. ἐνυπνιασθήσομαι Jl. ii. 28.

Ἐνωτίζεσθαι : verb frequent in LXX, once in N.T., unattested elsewhere, possibly a "Biblical" creation to render the hiphil of אָזַן : aug. ἐνωτισάμην and ἠν., § 16, 8.

Ἐπαξονέω "register," "enroll" (like ἀπογράφειν), a ἅπαξ λεγόμενον in N. i. 18 B ἐπηξονοῦσαν, § 17, 5.

Ἐπίσταμαι : aug. ἠπιστάμην and v.l. ἐπ., § 16, 4 : 2 sing. ἐπίστασαι and ἐπίστῃ, §§ 17, 12 and 23, 4.

Ἐργάζομαι : fut. κατεργᾷ -ᾶται -ῶνται (never Att. ἐργάσομαι), § 20, 1 (ii) : aug. ἠργαζόμην but εἴργασμαι (as in Att.), aor. ἠργασάμην and εἰργασάμην, § 16, 5 : the perf. is used only with pass. meaning¹ (in Attic it has active sense as well): fut. pass. ἐργασθήσομαι (class.) Ez. xxxvi. 34.

Ἐρευνάω and ἐραυνάω, § 6, 12 : 3rd plur. impf. (as from ἐρευνέω) ἠρεύνουν, § 22, 1.

Ἐρημόω : aug., usually ἠ-, sometimes omitted, § 16, 4.

Ἕρπω (ἐξ-) : 1 aor. ἐξῆρψα Ψ civ. 30, with causative meaning "produced," "made to swarm" (cf. ἐξαμαρτάνειν "cause to sin"), is unclassical, Att. using εἷρπυσα from ἑρπύζω for "crept" (Veitch cites εἷρψα from Dio Chrys.).

Ἔρχομαι² : in Att. the pres. stem in the *simplex* is confined to pres. ind., while the moods, imperf. and fut. are supplied from

---

¹ Including Dt. xxi. 3 δάμαλιν...ἥτις οὐκ εἴργασται : witness the Heb. Pual (R.V. "has not been worked with") and the undoubtedly passive use of the tense in the next *v.* Cod. A has an active aor. ἠργάσατε in 2 K. xi. 20, a corruption of ἠγγίσατε.

² A common synonym in LXX and later Greek is παραγίνομαι, this use being possibly of Ionic origin : apart from Hdt. it seems to be rare in classical Greek. The distribution of the word in LXX is noticeable, esp. its absence from Dan. Θ and books akin to Θ, 2 Es. and 1 and 2 Ch. (except 2 Ch. xxiv. 24) : in non-historical portions its absence (Ψ and Prov.) or rarity (Prophetical books) is more easily intelligible. In N.T. it is almost confined to Luke's writings.

εἰμι: LXX employs ἠρχόμην, ἔρχωμαι etc. with fut. ἐλεύσομαι (Epic, Ionic and poet.), εἰμι being now rare and literary (§ 23, 12): aor. ἦλθον with new terminations ἦλθα, ἐλθάτω etc., § 17, 2, ἦλθοσαν, § 17, 5, opt. ἔλθοισαν, § 17, 7

'Ερωτάω: aug. ἠ- but ἐπ-ερώτησα etc., § 16, 4: 3rd plur. impf. ἐπηρώτουν Cod. A, § 22, 1.

'Εσθίω and ἔσθω (esp. in the part. ἔσθων), § 19, 3: fut. ἔδομαι (rare outside Pent.) and Hellenistic φάγομαι, § 20, 2, with 2nd sing. φάγεσαι and occasionally φάγῃ, § 17, 12 (φαγούμεθα Gen. iii. 2 Dsil): terminations of past tenses ἔφαγα, § 17, 2, ἐφάγοσαν, κατεφάγεσαν, ἤσθοσαν, § 17, 5, φάγοισαν, § 17, 7. The rare pres. βιβρώσκω once in Jd. B, § 19, 3: the tenses βέβρωκα (βεβρώκει, § 16, 2), βέβρωμαι, ἐβρώθην (opt. βρωθείησαν Job xviii. 13) are Ionic and late: fut. pass. βρωθήσομαι is new. The Att. ἐδήδοκα, ἐδήδεσμαι, ἠδέσθην have disappeared and the vulgar τρώγω of St John's Gospel is unrepresented.

Εὐαγγελίζομαι "tell good tidings": the act. -ίζω (as in Apoc. x. 7, xiv. 6) occurs in 1 K. xxxi. 9 -ίζοντες (=mid. in the ‖ 1 Ch. x. 9), with fut. εὐαγγελιῶ 2 K. xviii. 19 (mid. -οῦμαι in next v. and elsewhere): otherwise only in the mid.-pass., aor. mid. εὐηγγελισάμην (class.), § 16, 8, and once aor. pass. εὐαγγελισθήτω ὁ κύριός μου 2 K. xviii. 31="receive the good tidings" (cf. Hebr. iv. 6).

Εὐαρεστέω: aug. εὐηρέστησα, § 16, 8.

Εὐδοκέω (Polyb. and papyri of ii/B.C.): aug. omitted in εὐδόκησα, § 16, 4: aor. pass. εὐδοκήθη 1 Ch. xxix. 23="prospered" (perhaps a corruption of εὐοδώθη, cf. Is. liv. 17 A).

Εὐθηνέω Ionic and late for older Attic εὐθενέω: once in pres. mid. Ψ lxxii. 12 Bℵ* (class.): 3rd plur. impf. εὐθηνοῦσαν, § 17, 5.

Εὐθύνειν (κατ-): aug. κατεύθυνα, § 16, 4.

Εὐλαβέομαι: fut. εὐλαβηθήσομαι only (Aristot.: not εὐλαβήσομαι as in Plato), § 21, 7.

Εὐλογέω: aug. εὐλόγησα, § 16, 4: term. εὐλογοῦσαν, § 17, 5, εὐλογήσαισαν Tob. iii. 11: late tenses εὐλόγηκα -ημαι -ηθήσομαι.

Εὑρίσκω: aug. omitted in εὗρον, εὕρηκα, εὑρέθην, § 16, 4: terminations εὗρα, § 17, 2, εὕροσαν, § 17, 5, εὕροισαν, § 17, 7 (1st aor. εὕρησα not used, § 21, 1).

Εὐφραίνω: aug. εὐφράνθην and ηὐφρ., § 16, 4: fut. pass. εὐφρανθήσομαι (not εὐφρανοῦμαι), § 21, 7.

Εὔχομαι (προσ-): aug. usually προσηυξάμην, also -ευξ., § 16, 4, and ἐπροσηυξάμην, § 16, 8.

"Εχω: fut. ἕξω (not σχήσω), § 15, 3: 3rd plur. aor. ἔσχοσαν, § 17, 5: 1 aor. pass. (Ionic and late) κατ- συν- εσχέθην, with v.ll. in A συνεσχέθη, § 18, 2, and κατησχέθη 3 M. v. 12: fut. pass. -σχεθήσομαι (late: 112 B.C. is the earliest ex. in papyri, AP 31, 6), R. i. 13 (κατα-), Job Θ xxxvi. 8: class. perf. ἔσχηκα rare, Sir.

xiii. 6 and in 2, 3 M.: the mid., excepting ἀνέχομαι (aug. ἀνεσχ-όμην § 16, 8), is almost confined to the part. ἐχόμενος -ον -α —"near."

Ζάω or ζήω : fut. ζήσομαι and ζήσω, the latter sometimes with causative sense "quicken"=ζωώσω elsewhere, § 20, 3 : aor. ἔζησα (Attic usually employed ἐβίων): as from ζῆμι 1st sing. impf. ἔζην (not ἔζων) and 2 sing. imperat. ζῆθι (post-class.), § 22, 2.
Ζεύγνυμι, ζευγνύω (ἀνα-): § 23, 2.
Ζηλόω: ἐζήλησα Cod. ℵ as from -έω, § 22, 4.
Ζωννύω (περι- etc.) but mid. περιζώννυται, § 23, 2 : fut. act. ζώσω (post-class.) Ex. xxix. 9 : fut. mid. ζώσομαι (once in a Hexaplaric interpolation in A περιζῶνται Ez. xxvii. 31=περι-ζώσονται Q ib.) with aorists ἔζωσα, ἐζωσάμην are classical : perf. pass. ἀν- περι- ὑπ- εζωσμένος (Ionic : Att. ἔζωμαι), § 18, 2.

Ἡγέομαι: (1) with the meaning "lead" frequent in the part. ἡγούμενος=ἡγεμών : the tenses (class.) are rare, ἡγεῖτο Ex. xiii. 21, ἡγήσεται Mic. ii. 13, Bar. v. 9, ἡγήσατο Gen. xlix. 26 : (2) with the meaning "think," "think good" only in literary books (Job, W., 2—4 M.) with tenses ἡγησάμην and (Job) ἥγημαι with act. meaning.
Ἥκω in virtue of its perfect meaning "am come"[1] in late Greek adopts in the plur. and occasionally in the inf. and part. forms as from a perfect ἧκα : the conjugation in LXX as in the papyri (Mayser 372) is thus ἥκω -εις -ει -αμεν -ατε -ασιν (the last very frequent : ἥκουσιν only in Job xvi. 23 A): the perf. part. appears once as ἥκώς in 4 M. iv. 2 A (ἥκων ℵV and so elsewhere in LXX : the papyri show both forms, Mayser ib.): inf. ἥκειν 4 M. iv. 6 (ἡκέναι papyri): imperat. (rare in class. Gk) ἧκε 2 K. xiv. 32, Jer. xliii. 14, xlvii. 4 ℵAQ, Tob. ix. 3 ℵ, ἐπάνηκε Prov. iii. 28, ἥκετε Gen. xlv. 18, Is. xlv. 20 : fut. ἥξω frequent = "will come" not "will have come" (the late aor. ἧξα is unrepresented).

Θάλλω (ἀνα-): new 2nd aor. ἀνέθαλον (Att. ἔθηλα, Aelian ἀν-έθηλα) used intransitively "revive," § 21, 2 : the pres. ἀναθάλλω (the compound is unclass.) is used transitively "make to flourish" Sir. i. 18 etc., Ez. xvii. 24.
Θαμβέω: in class. Greek "be amazed (at)," so 1 K. xiv. 15 : in LXX also causatively "frighten," ἐθάμβησάν με 2 K. xxii. 5, with pass. θαμβέομαι, aor. ἐθαμβήθην, § 21, 6.
Θαυμάζω: fut. θαυμάσομαι (Att.) and -σω, § 20, 3 : ἐθαυμάσθην, θαυμασθήσομαι keep their class. passive meaning (θαυμασθῆναι

---

[1] Ἥκει in Eccl. v. 14 is used as an aorist "he came," answering to παρεγένετο in the next *v.* The impf. ἧκε in 2 M. 5 times and Jdth xi. 1 ℵ.

Est. C. 21 is perhaps deponent), § 21, 6 : perf. pass. τεθαυμασμένος 4 K. v. 1 (Polyb.).

Θέλω, fut. θελήσω, no longer (Att.) ἐθέλω, ἐθελήσω, consequently has the new perf. τεθέληκα, § 16, 7 : but the old aug. is invariably kept in ἤθελον, ἠθέλησα, § 16, 3 : term. ἤθελαν in א, § 17, 4. The use of εὐδόκησα in Jd. (B text)=ἠθέλησα (A text) is noticeable.

Θερίζω: fut. -ιῶ and -ίσω, § 20, 1 (i).

Θερμαίνω: aor. ἐθέρμᾱνα (since Aristot. for -ηνα), § 18, 4.

Θεωρέω: as in N.T. almost confined to pres. and impf., the aor. ἐθεώρησα -ήθην occurring 4 times in literary books, with Ψ lxvii. 25 -ήθησαν : 3rd pl. impf. in Jdth x. 10 ἐθεώρων א, § 22, 1, ἐθεωροῦσαν A, § 17, 5 (2). The tenses in N.T. are supplied from **θεάομαι**: ἐθεασάμην in LXX is rare, and τεθέαμαι occurs once only.

Θνήσκω ἀπο-: the Att. rule as to the use of *simplex* for perf. and plupf., compound for fut. and aor. is still observed[1]: perf. τέθνηκα -κέναι -κώς, the forms τεθνέασιν (=Att. τεθνᾶσι) -νάναι -νεῶτες in literary books, § 23, 7 : plpf. τεθνήκει A § 16, 2 : fut. perf. τεθνήξομαι (=older Att. τεθνήξω) 3 times in the Atticising 4 M. : terminations ἀπέθαναν, § 17, 2, -εθάνοσαν -εθνήσκοσαν, § 17, 5.

Θραύω: fut. pass. (late) θραυσθήσομαι and once in B θραυθήσομαι, § 18, 2 : aor. pass. ἐθραύσθην is classical.

Θυμιάω θυμιάζω "burn incense": pres. and impf. always from -άω (class.) except θυμιάζουσιν Is. lxv. 3 A : other tenses from -άζω, fut. -άσω, aor. ἐθυμίασα (Hdt. -ίησα) -ιάθην 1 K. ii. 15 f. : 3rd pl. impf. ἐθυμιῶσαν, § 17, 5 : as from -έω θυμιοῦσιν א, § 22, 1.

("Ιημι) only in compounds : ἀφίω συνίω etc., § 23, 6 : aug. omitted in ἀνέθην, ἀφέθην, but παρείθησαν, § 16, 5 : term. ἀφῆκες, § 17, 8.

'Ικανόομαι: unclass., usually impersonal in the phrase ἱκανούσθω (ὑμῖν) : aor. ἱκανώθην : 2 sing. Cod. A ἱκανοῦσαι, § 17, 12.

'Ιλάσκομαι: the *simplex*, in class. Greek "propitiate," "appease," in LXX is used not of the suppliant but of the Divine Pardoner, "be merciful," "forgive" (=ἵλεως γίνομαι elsewhere), in the aor. pass. ἱλάσθην impt. ἱλάσθητι (=Epic ἵληθι in same sense) and fut. *mid.* ἱλάσομαι 4 K. v. 18 *bis*, Ψ xxiv. 11, lxiv. 4, lxxvii. 38 (and probably in 2 Ch. vi. 30 ΙΛΑCΗ should be read for ΙΑCΗ, cf. *v.* 27), once in the fut. pass. ἱλασθήσεται 4 K. v. 18 A. Far commoner is the compound ἐξιλάσκομαι, fut. -άσομαι, aor. -ασάμην, used like the class. *simplex*="propitiate" man (Gen. xxxii. 20, Prov. xvi. 14) or God (Zech. vii. 2, viii. 22, Mal. i. 9), but usually abs. "make propitiation" of the priest περί τινος *passim*, sometimes with acc. of the thing for which

---

[1] E.g. Eccl. iv. 2 τοὺς τεθνηκότας τοὺς ἤδη ἀποθανόντας. The uncompounded fut. θανεῖται in Prov. xiii. 14, possibly for metrical reasons.

atonement is made[1] (ἀμαρτίας etc. Sir. iii. 3+, Ez. xliii. 22+, Dan. Θ ix. 24) and once with acc. of the propitiatory offering, 2 Ch. xxix. 24: fut. pass. ἐξιλασθήσομαι (unclass.)="shall be expiated" or "forgiven" N. xxxv. 33, Dt. xxi. 8, 1 K. iii. 14, vi. 3: A reads ἐξιλᾶτο as from -άομαι in Sir. xvi. 7. The *simplex* has thus become a deponent verb "be propitious," and the causative sense "make propitious" must now be expressed by prefixing ἐξ- (cf. ἐξαμαρτάνειν).

Ἵπτημι : see πέτομαι.

Ἵστημι, ἱστάω (ἱστάνω), fut. once in A ἱστήσω, § 23, 3 : pres. στήκω (παρα-), § 19, 1 : pf. forms with new trans. pf. ἕστακα, § 23, 7, κατ- ἐπ-, § 8, 7 : aor., § 23, 8 and 9 : aug. ἱστήκειν εἱστ. ἑστ., § 16, 5, double aug. ἀπεκατέστησα, § 16, 8 : term. -έστηκαν, § 17, 3.

Καθαίρω (ἐκ- περι-), the class. verb for "cleanse" in literal and met. senses, in LXX is quite rare and restricted to the lit. sense in the *simplex* (="winnow" wheat 2 K. iv. 6, and fennel Is. xxviii. 27) and in comp. with ἐκ- (Dt. xxvi. 13 ="clear out" goods from a house, Jos. xvii. 15 "clear" a forest [but ἐκκαθαριεῖς v. 18 in same sense], Jd. vii. 4 B "thin" an army, "weed out" the inefficient), cf. περι- Dt. xviii. 10, Jos. v. 4, 4 M. i. 29: aor. -εκάθαρα (once -ηρα Jos. v. 4 A), § 18, 4. (Καθαριόω in Lam. iv. 7 is a ἅπ. λεγ.) Far more frequent is the unclass. καθαρίζω (ἐκ- περι-), mainly and apparently originally with metaphorical meaning, but afterwards (see N.T.) used in all senses: Deissmann *BS* 216 f. has shown that the ceremonial use of the word is not wholly "Biblical": fut. καθαριῶ with v. l. -ίσω, § 20, 1 (i): aor. ἐκαθάρισα : pass. καθαρισθήσομαι ἐκαθαρίσθην κεκαθαρισμένος : for ἐκαθέρισα etc., § 6, 3, Moulton *Prol.* ed. 3, 56 note.

Καθίζω, καθέζομαι, κάθημαι. From καθίζω (pres. and impf. have disappeared and the late pf. κεκάθικα is unrepresented) we have aor. ἐκάθισα, used, as in Att., both intransitively "sat," "seated myself," and, less often, transitively "caused to sit": Att. fut. καθιῶ is also both trans. (as always in Attic) Dt. xxv. 2, Jer. xxxix. 37, Ez. xxxii. 4 (ἐπι-), Job Θ xxxvi. 7 and intrans. Jl. iii. 12, Is. xiv. 13, xlvii. 8 : fut. καθίσω (Ion., vulgar and late) only in Sir. xi. 1 B (trans.). The middle is now confined to the fut. (Att. καθιζήσομαι) which appears in three forms: (i) καθίσομαι[2] Dan. O vii. 26 only, (ii) καθιοῦμαι 1 Es. iii. 7, Ψ cxxxi. 12, Hos. xiv. 8, Mal. iii. 3 and in the following passages (except Jd.) as a v.l. for (iii) a form unrecorded in the grammars καθίομαι[3] Jd.

[1] Cf. Deissmann *BS* 224 f.
[2] Swete prints it also in Jd. vi. 18 (καθίομαι B, καθήσομαι A). It may be merely an itacistic form of καθήσομαι.
[3] The form appears to have grown out of the 3rd sing. καθιεῖται which was written as καθίεται from the objection felt to two contiguous *i* sounds:

vi. 18 B, 3rd plur. καθίονται Sir. xxxviii. 33 A, 3rd sing. καθίεται in Cod. B, Dt. xxi. 13, 3 K. i. 13, Jer. xxxix. 5, Dan. Θ xi. 10, and in Bℵ in Zech. vi. 13, Is. xvi. 5, Ψ xxviii. 10.

From καθέζομαι we have the Att. fut. καθεδοῦμαι twice Jer. xxxvii. 18, Ez. xxvi. 16: the late fut. καθεσθήσομαι L. xii. 5 B (4 B^{ab}F), and the late aor. καθεσθείς Job (? Θ) xxxix. 27.

Κάθημαι, ἐκαθήμην are now the only pres. and imperf. for the verb "to sit": 2nd sing. κάθησαι (not κάθη of N.T.), but imperat. usually κάθου (once κάθησο), § 23, 13: the unclassical fut. καθήσομαι is fairly common, ib.

Καθιζάνω (early in poetry with intrans. sense) is used transitively in Job xii. 18 (καθίζων A), Prov. xviii. 16.

Καίω: the old Att. κάω[1] in κάηται Ex. xxvii. 20 B, ἐκκάει Prov. xiv. 5 ℵ, καομένη Mal. iv. 1 Q: tenses regular with 2nd aor. pass. (dialectic) ἐξ-κατ-εκάην, fut. pass. (late) ἐκ-κατα-καήσομαι, § 21, 4.

Καλέω: fut. καλέσω, § 20, 1 (iii): fut. perf. pass. κεκλήσομαι only as a variant for κληθήσομαι in Ex. xii. 16 A, Hos. xi. 12 BQ, cf. § 15, 3: aug. in ἐπαρεκάλουν, ἐπροσκέκληται, § 16, 8: vb. adj. κλητέον, § 15, 2.

Καλύπτω: ἀνακάλυψα ℵ, § 16, 2.

Καυχάομαι: 2 sing. ἐνκαυχᾷ (not the later -ᾶσαι), § 17, 12.

Κεῖμαι: regular § 23, 13, partially replaced by τέθειμαι, ib. 10.

Κελεύω: κελευθέντες Cod. A (for -ευσθ.), § 18, 2.

(Κεράννυμι): pres. part. κεράννοντες, § 23, 2: perf. pass. κεκέρασμαι (late), with doubtful authority for κέκραμαι (Att), aor. pass. ἐκεράσθην συν- (Att. also has ἐκράθην), § 18, 2.

Κιρνάω a collateral form of κίρνημι: impf. ἐκίρνων Ψ ci. 10; as the -μι forms are usually retained in the mid., μετεκιρνᾶτο W. xvi. 21 (Swete) should probably be μετεκίρνατο.

Κιχράω not κίχρημι, § 23, 4.

Κλαίω: not Att. κλάω, but ἔκλαεν 3 K. xviii. 45 B: fut. κλαύσομαι (not the later -σω of N.T.), § 20, 3: aor. and fut. pass. ἐκλαύσθην (-αύθην B), κλαυσθήσομαι (v.l. κλαυθ.) are post-classical, § 18, 2: the perf. pass. is unattested.

Κλείω with tenses κλείσω etc. (not the old Att. κλήω κλήσω etc.): perf. pass. κέκλεισμαι and rarely (class.) -ειμαι, § 18, 2: fut. pass. κλεισθήσομαι (late in *simplex*: Xen. has it in comp.) ib.

Κλίνω: pf. act. κέκλικα (late) Jd. xix. 9 A, 11 A (-ηκ-), 3 K. ii. 28, 4 K. viii. 1 A, Jer. vi. 4: aor. and fut. pass. ἐκλίθην, κλιθήσομαι (not ἐκλίνην, κλινήσ., nor the mid. aor. and fut.), § 21, 5: other tenses classical: the *simplex* is absent from the Hexateuch, the intrans. use of it (of time Jd. and Jer. l.c., and elsewhere in other senses) is late.

---

cf. ταμιεῖον—ταμεῖον etc., § 5 (3). Note that Cod. B keeps 3rd plur. καθιοῦνται Hos. xiv. 8.

[1] Mayser quotes an ex. in ii/B.C., 104 f.

Κνίζω (poetical and in late prose): aor. ἀπέκνισα and (Cod. A) ἀπέκνιξα, § 18, 3 (iii).

Κοιμάομαι: 2nd sing. κοιμᾶσαι Cod. A, § 17, 12: fut. pass. κοιμηθήσομαι, § 21, 7, and perf. κεκοίμημαι N. v. 19, 4 K. iv. 32 A, Is. xiv. 8 are post-classical.

Κολλάω (προσ-) mainly in the passive with new reflexive sense of cleaving to a person, with tenses ἐκολλήθην κολληθήσομαι κεκόλλημαι: aug. omitted in κεκόλλητο, § 16, 2.

Κομίζω: fut. κομιῶ 3 M. i. 8, -ιοῦμαι and -ίσομαι, § 20, 1 (i).

Κόπτω: fut. mid. κόψομαι "will bewail" Jer.-Ez.-Min. Proph., 3 K. xii. 24 m B, xiv. 13 A lacks early authority[1]: fut. pass. κοπήσομαι, late in *simplex*, = (a) "shall be cut down" Jer. xxvi. 5 (so ἐκκοπῆσ. Dan. Θ ix. 26), (b) "shall be bewailed" Jer. viii. 2, xvi. 4: the other act. and mid. tenses are classical, pf. act. wanting: opt. term. ἐκκόψαισαν, § 17, 7.

Κουφίζω: fut. -ιῶ and -ίσω, § 20, 1 (i).

Κράζω: the pres. rare in Att. is equally so in LXX, κράζεις Jd. xviii. 24, else in the part. Ex. xxxii. 17, 2 K. xiii. 19, Ψ lxviii. 4, Jdth xiv. 17 B, and inf. Ψ xxxi. 3, Tob. ii. 13 Bℵ, impf. ἔκραζον Jd. xviii. 22 A: elsewhere the pf. κέκραγα is used with pres. sense as in Attic, Ex. v. 8, 2 K. xix. 28, Jer. xxxi. 3 etc.: fut. κεκράξομαι as in Att. (with v.l. κράξομαι: not κράξω of N.T.), § 20, 3, cf. 15, 3: the aor. takes 3 (or 4) forms, the third only being classical: (i) usually ἐκέκραξα, (ii) ἔκραξα rarely and in books using pres. κράζω, but always ἀνέκραξα, (iii) ἀνέκραγον, (iv) possibly redupl. 2nd aor. ἐκέκραγον, unless this should be regarded as impf. from †κεκράγω, §§ 21, 1: 19, 1. Κραυγάζω is properly used of an animal's bleat in κραυάζειν Tob. ii. 13 A (with loss of γ, § 7, 30: κράζειν Bℵ), of a human cry in ἐκραύγασεν 2 Es. iii. 13.

(Κρεμάννυμι) κρεμάζω κρέμαμαι: the act. goes over to the -ω class, κρεμάζων (κρεμνῶν A) in Job Θ, §§ 19, 3 and 23, 2: in the mid. the Att. κρέμαμαι remains, § 23, 4: fut. κρεμάσω for Att. κρεμῶ: ἐκρέμασα -άσθην as in Att.

Κρίνω: aor. and fut. pass. for mid. in the compounds ἀπεκρίθην (with ἀπεκρινάμην) ἀποκριθήσομαι, διεκρίθην διακριθήσομαι, ὑπεκρίθην (but ὑποκρίνασθαι 4 M.), § 21, 6: the simple fut. pass. κριθήσομαι (class.) has mid. sense "contend," "plead with" in Jer. ii. 9, Job xiii. 19 (-σόμενος), pass. "be judged" Is. lxvi. 16: aug. in ἐδιέκρινεν ℵ, § 16, 8: term. ἐκρίνοσαν, § 17, 5: Cod. C writes κέκρινεν for κέκρικεν Job xxvii. 2.

Κρύπτω and new pres. κρύβω, § 19, 3: aor. and fut. pass.

---

[1] In Jer. xxxi. 37 πᾶσαι χεῖρες κόψονται it appears from the Heb. to keep the meaning "cut" and may even perhaps stand for the passive "shall be cut" (cf. Or. Sib. III. 651 = 731 οὐδὲ μὲν [γὰρ] ἐκ δρυμοῦ ξύλα κόψεται).

(usually with mid. sense) ἐκρύβην, κρυβήσομαι, § 21, 4 (class. ἐκρύφθην, (ἀπ)εκρυψάμην, (ἀπο)κρύψομαι unused).

Κτάομαι: 2 sing. κτᾶσαι, § 17, 12 : class. tenses in use κέκτημαι (not ἔκτ.), § 16, 7, κτήσομαι, ἐκτησάμην : new fut. pass. κτηθήσονται "shall be acquired" Jer. xxxix. 15 (B*א* incorrectly κτισθ.) 43: verb. adj. ἐπίκτητος 2 M. vi. 23.

Κτείνω (ἀπο- κατα-): the *simplex* only[1] in Prov. xxiv. 11 (unclass. passive κτεινομένους), xxv. 5, 3 M. i. 2 : κατακτείνειν (poet.) 4 M. xi. 3, xii. 11 : new pres. (beside -κτείνω) ἀποκτέννω, § 19, 2 : perf. ἀπέκτανκα (late for usual Att. ἀπέκτονα) N. xvi. 41, 1 K. xxiv. 12, 2 K. iv. 11 : -κτενῶ, -έκτεινα, regular : new passive tenses (in Att. expressed by ἀπέθανον etc.) are the aor. ἀπεκτάνθην, § 21, 5, and perf. pass. in the two forms ἀπεκταμμένων[2] 1 M. v. 51 A (-κτανμένων א, -κταμένων V*) and ἀπεκτονῆσθαι 2 M. iv. 36 V (ἀπεκτόνησεν A).

Κυλίω, impf. ἐκύλιον, replaces the older pres. in -ίνδω: the tenses ἐκύλισα ἐνεκυλίσθην (ἐγ)κυλισθήσομαι have early authority.

Κύπτω: fut. κύψω (for -ομαι), § 20, 3 : perf. ἐκκέκυφα Jer. vi. 1.

(**Κύρω, κυρέω**) προσ- συγ-: § 22, 3.

Κύω (κύουσι Is. lix. 4, ἐκύομεν 13) and **κνέω** (ἀποκυήσασα 4 M. xv. 17) are both classical.

Λαλέω: pf. ἐλάληκα in A and א, § 16, 7 : part. λαλοντα א= -ῶντα (for -οῦντα), § 22, 1.

Λαμβάνω: fut. λήμψομαι (λάμψομαι), aor. pass. ἐλήμφθην etc., § 7, 23—25 : perf. pass. regular κατειλημμένος (variously spelt) Est. C. 12, 2 M. xv. 19 : terminations ἔλαβαν, § 17, 2, ἐλάμβαναν Cod. A, § 17, 4, ἐλάβοσαν ἐλαμβάνοσαν, § 17, 5 : double aug. ἐκατέλαβεν Cod. A, § 16, 8 : verb adj. ἀναλημπτέος, § 15, 2.

Λανθάνω: term. ἐπελάθεντο (for -οντο), § 17, 10.

(**Λέγω** "collect") in comp. with ἐκ- (mid. verb only[3]), ἐπισυν- ἀπ- Jdth x. 17 B*א*: perf. pass. (Att. usually -είλεγμαι) in mid. sense ἐκλέλεκται (N. xvi. 7 B^{ab}), 1 K. x. 24, but part. in pass. sense ἐκλελεγμένη 1 M. vi. 35, ἐπιλελεγμ. ib. xii. 41, so plpf. συνελέλεκτο Jdth iv. 3 : -λέξω (-ομαι) -ελεξα (-άμην) and aor. pass. ἐκλεγέντες 1 Ch. xvi. 41 etc., συλλεγέντων 3 M. i. 21 are class.

Λέγω "say" is defective in LXX as in N.T., being used only in pres. and impf. of the act. (terminations ἐλέγαμεν א, § 17, 4, ἐλέγοσαν A, § 17, 5) and, more rarely, of the passive, with two exceptions in literary books: (ἐξ)έλεξεν 3 M. vi. 29, λεχθέντα[4] Est. i. 18 : λέξω λέλεγμαι etc. are not used. The other tenses

---

[1] Also an incorrect reading of A in Sir. xvi. 12.
[2] From perf. act. ἀπέκτακα which occurs in Polyb.
[3] Except ἐκλέξω Ez. xx. 38 AQ (read ἐλέγξω B), ἐξέλεξα 1 M. xi. 23 א (read ἐπ- AV).
[4] ελεχθη L. vi. 5 B stands for ἐλεγχθῇ.

are supplied (as also to some extent in Attic) by aor. εἶπον¹ (or εἶπα, § 17, 2, 3rd plur. εἴποσαν, § 17, 5, opt. εἴπαισαν -οισαν, § 17, 7), fut. ἐρῶ, pf. εἴρηκα (sometimes equivalent to aorist εἶπον, 1 K. xx. 26 B, 4 K. vi. 7 B), and pass. ῥηθήσομαι N. xxiii. 23, Sir. xv. 10, 1 M. xiv. 44 (-σόμενος), εἴρημαι Prov. xxiv. 69, 1 M. xiv. 22, 2 M. vi. 17 (εἰρήσθω), 4 M. i. 33 (ἀπειρημένος) and ἐρρέθην (for Att. -ήθην) ῥηθῆναι ῥηθείς, §§ 18, 1: 6, 16. Cf. διαλέγομαι.

Λείπω (the *simplex* only in literary books) has the alternative pres. form δια- ἐγκατα- ἐκ- κατα- λιμπάνω, once in A καταλειμπάνειν, § 19, 3: aor. act. usually ἔλιπον, rarely the late ἔλειψα, § 21, 1: aor. pass. usually ἐλείφθην, once in 2 Es. B. the late κατελίπησαν, § 21, 4: the increasing disuse of the o aorist shows itself also in the constant reading of A etc. -ἔλειπον ὑπελειπόμην for -ἔλιπον -ελιπόμην of B: other tenses regular: terminations ἐγκατέλιπαν, § 17, 2, ἐλίποσαν, § 17, 5, κατέλειπαν Cod. A, § 17, 4.

Λευκαίνω "make white" and "be white" L. xiii. 19 (Aristot.): aor. ἐλεύκᾱνα, § 18, 4: fut. pass. λευκανθήσομαι Ψ l. 9. A synonym is λευκαθίζω (for λευκανθίζω Hdt. VIII. 27), L. xiii. 38 f. with pf. pass. λελευκαθισμένη Cant. viii. 5 B (-ανθ. אA).

Λογίζομαι: tenses regular λογιοῦμαι (λογίσεται L. vii. 8 A for λογισθήσεται BF) ἐλογισάμην, and with pass. sense ἐλογίσθην λελόγισμαι (A once without redupl. λογισμένον, § 16, 7): new fut. pass. λογισθήσομαι (συλ-) is frequent.

Λούω: ἐλούσθην, λέλουσμαι (Att. tenses without σ), § 18, 2: A writes Attic λουμένην in the only passage where the pres. mid. is used, 2 K. xi. 2, B λουομένην.

Λυμαίνομαι, often written λοιμαίνομαι, § 6, 41: aor. ἐλυμηνάμην (as in Att.: not ἐλυμαν.), § 18, 4.

Λύω: term. κατελύοσαν, § 17, 5: double aug. ἐδιελύσαμεν Cod. א, § 16, 8.

Μακρύνω: used in a few, mainly late, books, esp. Ψ, both transitively=μακρὰν ἀφιστάναι (so pf. pass. in Aristot.) and intr. =μακρὰν ἀπέχειν e.g. Jd. xviii. 22 or="delay" Jdth ii. 13: pf. act. μαμακρυνκότων A, § 16, 7: pf. pass. μεμακρυμμένου, § 18, 4.

Μαρτύρομαι (δια- ἐπι-): fut. (not attested before LXX) διαμαρτυροῦμαι Ex. xviii. 20 etc.: μεμαρτύρω 2 Es. xix. 34 B, § 16, 7.

Μάχομαι: fut. (no ex. of simple fut.) διαμαχήσομαι Sir. xxxviii. 28 (so with -μαχέσομαι in Ionic and late Greek), § 20, 2: aor. regular ἐμαχεσάμην (not the late ἐμαχέσθην), § 21, 6. As from -μαχίζομαι (unrecorded in LS) διαμεμάχισται Sir. li. 19.

Μείγνυμι: for pres. and impf. act. (συμ)μίσγω συνέμισγον are used (συνμίσσει Cod. A, § 9, 5), so συναναμίσγεσθε Ez. xx. 18 Bᶜᵒʳʳ (-μίγγεσθε B* sic, -μίγνυσθαι AQ), whereas the -μι forms are

¹ 1st aor. mid. ἀπειπάμην (Hdt., Aristot. and late prose) Job vi. 14, x. 3, xix. 18 A and Zech. xi. 12.

usual in the middle, § 23, 2: class. tenses used are ἔμ(ε)ιξα, ἐμ(ε)ίχθην in mid. sense "make terms" 4 K. xviii. 23 = Is. xxxvi. 8, (ἐπ)εμίγην Ψ cv. 35, 1 Es. viii. 67, 84, Ez. xvi. 37 (ἀνα)μέμιγμαι (never -μέμειγμαι): 2 fut. pass. συμμιγήσονται Dan. Θ xi. 6 (ἀποσυμ- A: μιγήσεσθαι once in Hom., else late).

Μέλλω: ἔμελλον and ἤμελλον, § 16, 3.

(Μέλω): impers. μέλει rare, impers. μεταμελήσῃ Ex. xiii. 17: ἐπιμελοῦμαι Gen. xliv. 21 (pres. with fut. sense) and -μέλομαι are both Attic, § 22, 3, tenses ἐπιμελήσομαι and ἐπεμελήθην regular: the tenses of μεταμέλομαι (Att. only in pres. and impf.) are new viz. μετεμελήθην, μεταμεληθήσομαι, -μεμέλημαι, § 21, 6.

Μερίζω (δια-): fut. μεριῶ (Att.) with v.l. -ίσω, § 20, 1 (i) and fut. mid. μεριοῦμαι 1 K. xxx. 24, Prov. xiv. 18: fut. pass. μερισθήσομαι N. xxvi. 53 etc. post-classical: else regular.

Μιαίνω: pf. pass. μεμιαμμένος (v.l. -ασμ as in Att.), § 18, 4.

Μιμνήσκομαι (ἐπι- 1 M. x. 46: the act. is only used in composition with ἀνα- ὑπο-): the pres. (rare in early prose) = "make mention" Is. xii. 4, xlviii. 1, lxii. 6, = "remember" Ψ viii. 5, Sir. vii. 36, 1 M. vi. 12, xii. 11, with alternative unredupl. form μνήσκομαι, § 19, 3: class. tenses with the meaning "remember" μέμνημαι, ἐμεμνήμην Tob. i. 12, ἐμνήσθην, μνησθήσομαι (not μεμνήσομαι, § 15, 3): the aor. and fut. occasionally have passive meaning "be mentioned" (unclass.), ἐμνήσθην Sir. xvi. 17 B, Jer. xi. 19, Ez. iii. 20, xviii. 24, xxxiii. 13 A, 16 A, μνησθήσομαι Ez. xviii. 22, Job Θ xxviii. 18.

Μισέω: impf. ἐμίσων (for -ουν) Cod. ℵ, § 22, 1: post-class. pass. tenses μεμίσημαι Is. liv. 6, lx. 15, μισηθήσομαι Sir. ix. 18, xx. 8, xxi. 28, Eccl. viii. 1.

Μνηστεύομαι (act. not used) fut. -σομαι and perf., with pass. and mid. sense, μεμνήστευμαι (ἐμν.), § 16, 7.

Μοιχάομαι an alternative form, probably Doric[1] (first found in Xen. *Hell.* I. 6, 15 in the act. in the mouth of a Lacedaemonian), of the Att. μοιχεύω, confined in LXX to two books, Jer. (iii. 8, v. 7, vii. 9, ix. 2, xxiii. 14, xxxvi. 23—all except the last in "Jer. a") and Ez. a (xvi. 32, xxiii. 37, 43 A), as in N.T. to Mt. and Mc.: it is used only in pres. and impf. (therefore ἐμοίχευσε Jer. iii. 9): aug. dropped in μοιχᾶτο ℵ, § 16, 2. Elsewhere in LXX and N.T. the tenses of **μοιχεύω** are used, including the pres. (L. xx. 10, Hos. iv. 14, vii. 4, Ez. xxiii. 43 BQ), the class. distinction in the use of the act. of the man, the pass. of the woman, not being rigidly observed.

Μολύνω: perf. pass. μεμολυμμένος and -νσμένος, § 18, 4: the fut. pass. μολυνθήσομαι Sir. xiii. 1 etc. appears to be post-classical.

Νέμω has late sigmatic futures and aorist νεμήσω, -ήσομαι,

---

[1] Wackernagel *Hellenistica* 7 ff.

κατενεμησάμην (Att. νεμῶ -οῦμαι ἐνειμάμην), § 21, 2 : class. aor. act. and pass. retained in Dt. xxix. 26 διένειμεν, W. xix. 9 ἐνεμήθησαν.

Νήθω[1] vulgar and late form of νῶ (= νάω or νήω), like ἀλήθω = ἀλέω, Ex. xxxv. 25, with late perf. pass. (δια)νενηνσμένος, Ex. xxvi. 31 etc. and verb. adj. νηστός, Ex. xxxi. 4 (contrast Epic εὔννητος): the old aor. ἔνησα Ex. xxxv. 26 required no alteration.

Νίπτω, the Ionic present from which the tenses are formed, replaces Att. νίζω, § 19, 3 : fut. pass. νιφήσεται L. xv. 12 has no early authority : pf. pass. with mid. sense νένιπται ib. 11 BA (early in comp.): else regular : LXX prefers the simple verb which Attic prose avoided (ἀπο- 3 K. xxii. 38, Prov. xxiv. 35, 55 : περι- Tob vi. 3 ‏א‎).

Νοέω : 3rd plur. impf. (κατ)ενοοῦσαν, § 17, 5 : the deponent fut. of the compounds always takes the pass. form ἐννοηθήσομαι Sir. xiv. 21 ‏א‎A (νοηθ. BC), διανοηθήσομαι Sir. iii. 29 etc., Dan. O ix. 25 etc. (διανοήσομαι is an alternative class. form).

Νομίζω : apart from Sir. xxix. 4 only in literary books : verb. adj. νομιστέον, § 15, 2.

Νύσσομαι (κατα-) : the compound with met. sense "feel compunction" or of lust (Sus. 10) is not found before LXX : for aor. the Pent. uses κατενύχθην, the other books κατενύγην with fut. -νυγήσομαι, § 21, 4 : perf. -νένυγμαι.

• Νυστάζω : νυστάξω ἐνύσταξα, § 18, 3 (i).

(Ξενόω) : term. ἀπεξενοῦσαι Cod. A (from Aquila), § 17, 12.

Ξηραίνω (ἀνα- ἀπο-) has late fut. pass. ξηρανθήσομαι Is. xix. 5 etc. in addition to class. tenses (no pf. pass. attested).

From ξυρέω or the later ξυράω (pres. unattested : no forms from ξύρω in LXX) LXX besides class. ἐξύρησα, ἐξύρημαι, has the following regularly formed tenses which lack early authority · ξυρήσω, ἐξυρήθην, ξυρηθήσομαι, ἐξυρησάμην, ξυρήσομαι.

(Οἴγω only in the compounds) ἀνοίγω, διανοίγω, and once προσοίγω : never -οίγνυμι : for the spelling ἀνύγω, § 6, 41 (i) : the augment (§ 16, 6) is always in the a in διανοίγω διήνοιξα etc. (διηνέῳκτο Job xxxi. 32 C is a solitary ex. of augmented οι) and usually in ἀνοίγω, the compound nature of which is becoming obscured, thus impf. ἤνοιγον -όμην, aor. act. and pass. (i) usually ἤνοιξα ἠνοίχθην, less commonly (ii) Att. ἀνέῳξα ἀνεῴχθην or (iii) with triple aug. ἠνέῳξα ἠνεῴχθην : the perf. pass., on the other hand, appears once only in the later form (i) ἠνοιγμένος Is. xlii. 20 (διήνοικται Job Θ xxix. 19), usually (ii) Att. ἀνεῳγμένος or (iii) ἠνεῳγμένος, plpf. ἀνέῳκτο (ἦν.) Job *l.c.* : the 2nd perf. act. ἀνέῳγα once with intrans. sense Tob. ii. 10 BA : 2 Es. has late 2nd aor. and fut. pass. ἠνοίγην, ἀνοιγήσομαι, the other books 1st aor. in

---

[1] See Rutherford *NP* 134 ff.

-χθην with fut. ἀνοιχθήσομαι, also late (Xen. ἀνεῴξομαι), § 21, 4. Προσέῳξεν Gen. xix. 6 is a new compound, rather strangely used as the opposite of ἀνέῳξεν="*shut* to" (Heb. סגר, rendered ἀπέκλεισαν in *v.* 10: cf. German *zumachen, aufmachen*).

Οἶδα in LXX, as in Hellenistic Greek generally, has the uniform conjugation οἶδας (27 exx.) -ε -αμεν -ατε -ασι(ν). The Attic forms are now an index of literary style: 2 sing. οἶσθα 4 M. vi. 27 and in the degenerate form[1] οἶσθας Dt. ix. 2 B (οἶσθα F, ἦσθα A): plur. ἴστε 3 M. iii. 14 (a letter of Ptolemy), εἴσασιν Job xxxii. 9 א[c.a] (εICIN א*: the translator, notwithstanding his usual classical style, no doubt wrote οἴδασιν here as elsewhere). For 2 sing. οἶδες in A (perhaps influenced by εἶδες: so in later papyri from ii/A.D., Mayser 321) cf. § 17, 8. The plpf. is also uniform, keeping ει throughout: ἤδειν (εἴδην 2 K. i. 10 B* may have arisen out of the 3rd plur. 1st aor. εἴδησαν), ἤδεις (Dt. xiii. 6) -ει -ειμεν -ειτε -εισαν: the classical forms ἤδη ἤδησθα (-ης) ἤδεμεν (ἦσμεν) etc. being unrepresented. Inf. εἰδέναι, part. εἰδώς[2].

The only fut. in LXX (εἴσομαι is not found) is εἰδήσω (Ionic, Aristotle and late writers) in Jer. xxxviii. 34 εἰδήσουσιν[3] אQ (οἰδήσουσιν B, ἰδήσουσιν A). A corresponding 1st aor. εἴδησα strictly="came to know" (Ionic and from Aristotle onwards: εἰδῆσαι in a papyrus of iii/B.C., Mayser 370) occurs in the B text of Deut.: εἴδησαν viii. 3, 16, xxxii. 17[b], AF reading ἤδεισαν in each case (cf. Is. xxvi. 11 Γ), with inf. εἰδῆσαι Dt. iv. 35 B (εἰδέναι AF), Jdth ix. 14 Bא*A.

There is constant confusion in the MSS between the forms of οἶδα and εἶδον, esp. the participles εἰδώς and ἰδών (cf. note 2 below). The existence of a genuine variant form εἰδών as part. of οἶδα can hardly be inferred from the evidence: it occurs in 2 Es. xx. 28 A, Job xix. 14 B*א[c.a], Wis. iv. 14 א, with συνειδ(ών) 1 M. iv. 21 אV*[vid], 2 M. iv. 41 V*. A good illustration of the confusion of forms is Job xx. 7 (Heb. "see"): εἰδότες B, ἰδότες A, ἰδόντες א, εἰδότες ἰδόντες (conflate) C.

Οἰκέω: aug. omitted in κατοίκησα, § 16, 4.

Οἰκίζω: aug. omitted in κατοίκισα, § 16, 4.

Οἰκοδομέω: aug. omitted in οἰκοδόμησα, § 16, 4, retained in part. ᾠκοδομήσαντες, § 16, 9: 3rd pl. impf. ᾠκοδομοῦσαν, § 17, 5.

Οἰκτείρω: so always in B and usually in the other uncials (Inscriptions show that οἰκτίρω was the older form, and so א generally writes, but its testimony is untrustworthy, cf. § 6, 24): fut. and aor. take the late forms (as from -έω, cf. οἰκτείρημα

---

[1] Rutherford *NP* 227 f.
[2] Or ἰδώς: so A writes in Job xix. 19, xx. 7, xxviii. 24, Eccl. ix. 1 and (with א) W. ix. 9: B* has this spelling in Bar. iii. 32 only (Bar. β, p. 13).
[3] The reading is supported by the quotation in Hebrews viii. 11.

Jer. xxxviii. 3) οἰκτειρήσω, οἰκτείρησα (never ᾤκτ., § 16, 4): the class. aor. ᾤκτειρα (οἴκτ.) is now literary 2 M. viii. 2, 3 M. v. 51, and in comp. with κατ- 4 M. viii. 20 אּ, xii. 2 אּV (A twice correcting to the later form), with ἐπ- Job xxiv. 21 A: the writer of 4 M. employs the unclass. mid. οἰκτείρομαι v. 33 (-ήσω A), viii. 10.

Οἶμαι 4 M. i. 33 (rare outside literary books), 2 sg. οἴει and οἴῃ, § 17, 12, has the Attic tenses ᾤμην (not ᾠόμην) Gen. xxxvii. 7 etc., ᾠήθην Est. E. 14 (ηθη אּ*, ωηθει A), 1 M. vi. 43 אּ. The late compound κατοιόμενος "supercilious" occurs in Hb. ii. 5 (Aristeas § 122, Philo).

Οἰμώζω : fut. οἰμώξω (Att. -ξομαι), § 20, 3.

(Οἰστράω) only in the late compound παροιστράω intrans. "rage," Hos. iv. 16 παροιστρῶσα παροίστρησεν (aug., § 16, 4: παροίστρωσεν Q*vid), Ez. ii. 6 -ήσουσι(ν).

Ὄλλυμι ἀπ-δι-ἐξ-προσαπ- : forms as from -ολλύω in the active § 23, 2: the simple vb, confined in early Greek to poetry, in LXX is limited to Job, Prov. (both of which imitate the poets) and Jer. β (also Jer. x. 20 ὤλετο a doublet): tenses regular including fut. ἀπολῶ -οῦμαι, whereas ἀπολέσω (N.T.) hardly belongs to LXX proper, § 20, 1 (iv): ἀπόλωλα is frequent, the trans. pf. ἀπολώλεκα rare and with one exception confined to the part., Dt. xxxii. 28, Is. xlvi. 12, xlix. 20 (ἀπώλεκας A, § 16, 7), Sir. ii. 14, viii. 12, xxix. 14, xli. 2 : term. of aor. opt. ὀλέσαισαν etc., § 17, 7. The Job translator also uses the collateral Epic form ὀλέκω, x. 16, xvii. 1, xxxii. 18.

Ὀλολύζω : fut. ὀλολύξω (Att. -ξομαι), § 20, 3.

Ὄμνυμι (ἐξόμνυμαι in 4 M.) and usually ὀμνύω, but the -μι forms remain in the mid., § 23, 2: fut. ὀμοῦμαι (not the later ὀμόσω), § 20, 1 (iv): perf. ὀμώμοκα appears in degenerate forms, § 16, 7 : aor. regular ὤμοσα, the aug. being retained in part. ὠμόσαντες, § 16, 9, aor. mid. only in 4 M. ix. 23 ἐξομόσησθε.

Ὁμοιόω: aug. omitted in aor. ὁμοίωσα, § 16, 4 : tenses regular.

(Ὀνίνημι): represented only by the class. fut. mid. ὀνήσεται Sir. xxx. 2 and the unclass. 1 aor. pass. ὠνάσθης, § 18, 2.

Ὀξύνω (παρ-): aug. omitted in παροξύνθην, § 16, 4: no perf. act. or pass. attested, other tenses regular, the fut. pass. παροξυνθήσομαι Dan. O xi. 10 occurring already in Hippocrates.

Ὁράω retains most of the class. forms including pres. and imperf., though the latter is rare and both tenses are beginning to be replaced by means of βλέπω and θεωρῶ q.v. : fut. ὄψομαι (ὄψ., § 8, 3 (3)) with 2nd sg. -ῃ and -ει, § 17, 12 : pf. ἑώρακα ἑόρακα, § 16, 6, 3rd pl. ἑώρακαν, § 17, 3: aor. εἶδον or ἴδον, § 16, 5 (ἴδ., § 8, 3 (3)), 3rd pl. εἶδαν (ἴδ.) and (ε)ἴδοσαν, § 17, 2 and 5, aug. retained in moods εἴδῃ etc., § 16, 9. In the passive the class. aor. and fut. ὤφθην, ὀφθήσομαι are frequent: the aor. ἑωράθην (not before Aristot.) occurs in Prov. xxvi. 19 Bאּ* (ὁραθῶσιν), Ez. xii. 12 (ὁραθῇ), xxi. 24 (ὁραθῆναι) and in the form ὡράθησαν in Dan. Θ

i. 15, § 16, 6: fut. ὁραθήσομαι is late and confined to Job Θ xxii. 14 and in compos. with παρ- 3 M. iii. 9 (the comp. occurs in a papyrus of 113 B.C., Mayser 405: Galen, a contemporary of Θ, is the earliest authority for this fut. in the *simplex*): Att. pf. pass. ὦπται occurs in Ex. iii. 16, iv. 1, 5, Jd. xiii. 10 BA, elsewhere the rather later ἑώραμαι (Isocr.) or ἑόρ., § 16, 6. The only examples noted of pres. mid. (pass.) are literary, ὁρώμενος (pass.) W. xiii. 1, ὑφορώμενος (mid.) 2 M. vii. 24, 3 M. iii. 23, of impf. mid. προορώμην Ψ xv. 8. On the other hand two new pres. forms for "I am seen" occur, ὀπτάζομαι N. xiv. 14 and ὀπτάνομαι (ὠπτανόμην) 3 K. viii. 8, Tob. xii. 19 BA (the latter in papyri of ii/B.C., Mayser 404, and in N.T.).

Ὀργίζομαι, παροργίζω: "provoke to anger" is expressed by the late compound παροργίζω -ιῶ -ώργισα, which appears twice only in the pass. (Theophr.), παροργισμένην Sir. iv. 3 (-ωργ.), § 16, 4, παροργισθήσεται Dan. O xi. 36: ὀργίζομαι on the other hand is confined to the passive[1], with tenses ὠργίσθην, ὀργισθήσομαι (never the more frequent Att. ὀργιοῦμαι), § 21, 7.

Ὀρθόω: aug. in ἀν-κατ-ορθώθην, § 16, 4, ἐπανωρθώθην, ib. 8.

Ὀρθρίζω "rise early" (δι- 1 K. xxix. 10 A), often written ὀρθίζω, § 7, 35, replaces the earlier ὀρθρεύω, found only in Tob. ix. 6 B: fut. ὀρθριῶ with v.l. -ίσω, § 20, 1 (i), aor. ὤρθρισα.

Ὀρύσσω (δι- κατ-): 2 aor. pass. (late) κατωρύγην, the earlier 1 aor. -ωρύχθην once in A, § 21, 4.

Ὀφείλω: fut. ὀφειλήσω (Att.) and -έσω, § 18, 1: 2 aor. now only in unaugmented form ὄφελον as particle, § 16, 4.

Παίζω (ἐμ-κατα-προσ-συμ-) has the late guttural tenses -παίξομαι (and -ξω, § 20, 3), ἔπαιξα, -πέπαιχα, -πέπαιγμαι, § 18, 3 (i) (for Att. παίσομαι etc., Rutherford *NP* 91, 313 f.).

Παίω: see τύπτω.

Παροιμιάζω: aug. παροιμίαζεν, ἐπαρ., § 16, 2 and 8.

Πάσσω "sprinkle," used in the *simplex* (poetical) and compounded with κατα-, has the late tenses πεπασμένος Est. i. 6 and aor. mid. κατ-επασάμην.

Πατάσσω: see τύπτω.

Πατέω: πατῶσιν Cod. A for πατοῦσιν, § 22, 1: double aug. ἐνεπεριεπάτησα Cod. A, § 16, 8.

Παύω (ἀνα- ἐπανα- κατα-): the *simplex* is almost confined to the mid., καταπαύω almost to the act. which is used both transitively and intransitively, e.g. τῇ ἡμ. τῇ ἑβδ. κατέπαυσεν καὶ ἐπαύσατο Ex. xxxi. 17: tenses regular, in pass. and mid. παύσομαι (not παυ(σ)θήσομαι nor the late παήσομαι), ἐπαυσάμην with ἀνε-

---

[1] A has the act. twice, but ὀργίζει Prov. xvi. 30 is an error for ὀρίζει and ὅσοι γὰρ ὀργίζουσιν Job xii. 6 for ὅσοι παροργίζουσιν.

παύθημεν Lam. v. 5, πέπαυμαι : under the influence of the Heb. ἀναπαύειν, καταπαύειν τινί="give rest to" 3 K. v. 4, 1 Ch. xxiii. 25, 2 Ch. xiv. 6, xv. 15, xx. 30.

Πείθω (ἀνα-, συμ-) is mainly restricted to the 2nd perf. πέποιθα (rare in Attic prose) with pres. sense "I trust," 3rd plur. πέποιθαν, § 17, 3, and plpf. ἐπεποίθειν (πεπ., § 16, 2) : the paraphrastic construction of πεποιθώς with auxiliary εἶναι (or γίνεσθαι Is. xxx. 12, Sir. ii. 5 א^{c.a}) is frequent, especially in Is., π. εἰ Is. xxxvi. 4, 6, xxxvii. 10 (πέποιθας B), π. ἦς and ὦσιν ib. viii. 14, x. 20, xvii. 8, ἴσθι π. Prov. iii. 5, π. ἦν, fut. π. ἔσομαι 2 K. xxii. 3, Job xi. 18 and 10 times in Is.: so much has πέποιθα come to be regarded as a pres. that a new 1st aor. ἐπεποίθησα is formed from it, § 19, 1, cf. πεποίθησις 4 K. xviii. 19. The remaining tenses of the verb in LXX (πείσω, ἔπεισα, πείθομαι, ἐπειθόμην, πέπεισμαι, ἐπείσθην) are with few exceptions restricted to the literary books.

Πεινάω has a for Att. η in the contracted forms, § 22, 2, and in the tenses πεινάσω ἐπείνασα, § 18, 1.

Πειράομαι (ἀπο-), πειράζω (δια- ἐκ-) : the former is used for "attempt (anything)" with passive tenses ἐπειράθην and πεπείραμαι with mid. sense (class.), the latter for "tempt" or "try (anyone)" with pass. aor. ἐπειράσθην "be tried," § 18, 2.

Περισσεύω has the new meanings "be excessive" or "severe" to anyone (Sir. xxx. 38) and "be superior to" "excel" (Eccl. iii. 19), but is not yet found in causative sense (as in N.T.)="make to abound": aug. regular ἐπερίσσευσα, § 16, 8.

(Πετάζω) ἐκ- replaces πετάννυμι "spread out" in the only two passages where a pres. occurs § 23, 2: aor. ἐπέτασα (ἀνα- δι- ἐξ-) is Attic, and fut. ἐκπετάσω is old (Att. πετῶ): pf. act. διαπεπετακότα 2 Ch. v. 8 is post-class. and pf. pass. διαπεπετασμένος (3 K., 1—2 Ch.) replaces Att. -πέπταμαι, § 18, 2.

Πέτομαι, πέταμαι (πετάομαι), ἵπταμαι "fly": (i) Attic πέτομαι occurs in pres. ind. πέτονται Job v. 7, Is. lx. 8 Bא and part. πετόμενος (9 exx.) with impf. ἐπέτοντο Is. vi. 2 א : (ii) πέταμαι (poetical and late prose) in pres. ind. πέτα(ν)ται Dt. iv. 17, Prov. xxvi. 2, Is. lx. 8 AQ, part. πετάμενος Is. xiv. 29 B (-όμενος cett.), inf. πέτασθαι (?-ᾶσθαι) Ez. xxxii. 10 BQ, impf. ἐπέταντο Is. vi. 2 BAQΓ¹ : (iii) the aor. and fut. in LXX are the late passive forms (as from πετάζω) ἐπετάσθην (ἐξ- κατ-), πετασθή-σομαι² (vice class. ἐπτόμην, πτήσομαι), § 18, 2 : (iv) of the later πετάομαι a possible ex. occurs in Ez. l.c. : πετώμενος Zech. v. 1 Γ* may be a mere itacism for -όμενος : (v) as from ἵπτημι -αμαι

---

¹ Ἐπέτατο W. xvii. 21 BA is doubtless a corruption of ἐπετέτατο (τείνω).
² These forms appear in Hatch-Redpath s.v. πετανύναι, πετάξειν, but with one possible exception the meaning is "fly" (Heb. עוף). See Rutherford *NP* 373 f. for the mixture of forms.

we have the late pres. act. διιπτάντος W. v. 11 B* (διαπτάντος cett.) and late pres. mid. ἀν- καθ- ιπτάμενος Is. xvi. 2, Sir. xliii. 17, ἐξίπτασθαι Prov. vii. 10, as well as aor. ἔπτην (class. poetry) Job xx. 8 (beside ἐκπετασθέν in same *v.*), ἐξέπτησαν Sir. xliii. 14[1]

Πιέζω is used, as in Att., for "press" and ἐκπιέζω for "oppress" with regular tenses πιέσω ἐξεπίεσα ἐκπεπίεσμαι : the later contract form πιεζέω in ἐκπιεζοῦντες Ez. xxii. 29 B, § 22, 3 : πιάζω (Doric and colloquial, mod. Gr. πιάνω) meaning "seize" occurs in aor. πιάσατε Cant. ii. 15 and fut. pass. πιασθήσομαι (else unattested) Sir. xxiii. 21 Bℵ : but the distinction of meaning is not always observed, ἐξεπίασεν Jd. vi. 38 B (ἀπεπίασεν A) being used = "pressed out" and ἐξεπίασα 1 K. xii. 3 A (-ίεσα B) = "oppressed."

Πίμπλημι and πιμπλάω (ἐμ-), § 23, 4.

(Πι(μ)πράω) ἐμ- for ἐμπίπρημι, § 23, 4.

Πίνω : fut. 2nd sing. πίεσαι (not πίῃ), § 17, 12 : 3rd plur. aor. ἐπίοσαν, § 17, 5, imperat. πίε (Att. also πῖθι), inf. πιεῖν and πεῖν (πῖν), § 5 p. 64 : aug. omitted in πεπώκει, § 16, 2.

(Πιπράσκω) has the class. tenses πέπρακα (3rd plur. πέπρακαν, § 17, 3), πέπραμαι 3 K. xx. 20, 2 M. viii. 14, ἐπράθην, with the post-class. fut. pass. πραθήσομαι L. xxv. 23 etc. : the other tenses are still, as in Att., supplied from other verbs, pres. and impf. from πωλέω, aor. and fut. from ἀποδίδομαι·

Πίπτω : aor. usually ἔπεσα, not -ον, § 17, 2 : aug. omitted in plpf. -πεπτώκειν, § 16, 2.

Πλανάομαι : fut. πλανηθήσομαι for Att. πλανήσομαι, § 21, 7.

Πληθύνω (pres. pass. twice in Aeschylus= "receive the support of the πλῆθος") is frequent in LXX as causative of Att. πληθύω "abound" (the latter only in 3 M. v. 41, vi. 4 V) : tenses regularly formed including ἐπληθύνθην, πληθυνθήσομαι, πεπλήθυμμαι, § 18, 4 : the verb is used intransitively in 1 K. i. 12 (ἐπλήθυνεν προσευχομένη), vii. 2, xiv. 19.

Πληρόω : plpf. pass. ἐπεπλήρωτο (πεπλήρωτο V), § 16, 2, also in Cod. A ἐπλήρωτο, § 16, 7, and ἐπεπληροῦτο, § 22, 4.

Πλήσσω : see τύπτω.

Πλουτίζω : fut. πλουτιῶ (Att.) with v.l. -ίσω, § 20, 1 (i).

Πνέω : fut. πνεύσομαι (Att. in compounds) and πνεύσω, the latter once apparently causatively "make to blow," § 20, 3.

(Ποδίζω) : fut. συμποδιῶ with v.l. -ίσω, § 20, 1 (i).

Ποθέω, ἐπι- : aor. ἐπόθησα (Att. also -εσα), § 18, 1.

Ποιέω : spellings in ℵ πιήσατε, ποῆσε, § 6, 36 and 38 : aug. omitted in πεποιήκειν, § 16, 2 : terminations πεποίηκαν, § 17, 3, ἐποιοῦσαν, § 17, 5.

---

[1] The Heb. corroborates ἐκστήσονται in Hos. xi. 11 (cf. 10), ἐξήφθησαν in Lam. iv. 19 : ἐκπτήσονται, ἐξέπτησαν were natural corrections suggested by the context.

Πολεμέω : term. ἐπολεμοῦσαν, § 17, 5 : aor. pass. ἐπολεμήθησαν (class., Thuc. v. 26) Jd. v. 20 A "were fought against," fut. pass. late (Polyh.) πολεμηθήσεται Dan. O ix. 26 : the late fut. and aor. mid. (cited by Veitch from LXX) do not occur in the uncials.

Πονέω : πονέσω, ἐπόνεσα, § 18, 1.

(Ποντίζω) : fut. καταποντιῶ with v.l. -ίσω, § 20, 1 (i).

Πορεύομαι has regular tenses πορεύσομαι ἐπορεύθην πεπόρευμαι (the last, including compounds εἰσ- ἐκ-, not frequent, mainly in Hex.) : the rare πορευθήσομαι in late versions, § 21, 7 : late 1 aor. mid. ἐπιπορευσαμένη 3 M. i. 4 and as v.l. πορευσώμεθα Gen. xxxiii. 12 M curs., πορεύσησθε L. xxvi. 27 A, -σώμεθα 1 M. ii. 20 A.

(Πρίαμαι) : ἐπριάμην, the class. aor. to ὠνέομαι, is still retained in Gen. and Prov. xxix. 34 : the later ὠνησάμην (ἐων.) is not used : the form πριάσασθαι Gen. xlii. 10 A is unparalleled. "To buy" is now usually ἀγοράζειν.

Προνομεύω post-class. : ἐπρονόμευσα (with v.l. προεν.) and πεπρονομευμένος, § 16, 8.

Προφητεύω : aug. ἐπροφήτευσα (with v.l. προεφ.), § 16, 8 : A once has the mid. ἐπροφητεύοντο Jer. ii. 8.

Πτοέω : πτοῶνται = -οῦνται, § 22, 1.

(Πυρίζω) ἐμ- : a late alternative for ἐμπίπρημι or ἐμπυρεύω : pf. pass. ἐμπεπύρισμαι and in Cod. A ἐνεπυρισμένος, § 16, 7.

'Ραίνω "sprinkle" (class. poetry) has fut. ῥανῶ, aor. ἔρανα (ἐπ- προσ-: class. ἔρρανα): pf. διέρραγκα is new, § 16, 7 note. Cod. A once has fut. ῥανιεῖ L. xiv. 16 as from ῥανίζω (Pollux). The aor. pass. ἐραντίσθην (ἐπ- περι-) is formed from the post-class. ῥαντίζω (Athenaeus is the earliest non-Biblical authority cited), which also has fut. act. ῥαντιῶ Ψ l. 9, Ez. xliii. 20 A (περι-).

'Ρέω has classical tenses (except for the occasional omission of the second ρ): impf. κατέρρει 1 K. xxi. 13 (-έρει A), περιέρεον 4 M. ix. 20, impf. pass. κατερρεῖτο ib. vi. 6: fut. ῥυήσομαι (ἀπο- ἐκ-: not the rarer ῥεύσομαι nor the late ῥεύσω), § 20, 3 : aor. pass. as active ἐρρύην (ἀπ- δι-), § 21, 3, but ἐξερύην, § 7, 39 (not ἔρρευσα): pf. κατερρύηκα Jer. viii. 13.

The -μι forms of ῥήγνυμι (δια- κατα-) appear only in the pass., for pres. act. ῥήσσω is used, § 23, 2 : regular tenses ῥήξω, ἔρρηξα, ἐρράγην (for -ρρ- and -ρ-, § 7, 39): post-class. pf. διερρηχώς in "K. βδ" (2 K. xiv. 30, xv. 32, 4 K. xviii. 37), 1 M. v. 14, xiii. 45, Jer. xlviii. 5 AQ: the class. 2nd perf. (intr.) ἔρρωγα (δι- κατ-) in Jos. ix. 4, 13, 2 K. i. 2 B, Ep. J. 30, also in the form ἔρρηγα (δι-κατ-: Doric and late) 1 K. iv. 12, 2 K. i. 2 A, Job xxxii. 19 : with the same sense the rare pf. pass. διερρηγμένος 1 Es. viii. 70, Prov. xxiii. 21 and with mid. sense Jer. xlviii. 5 Bℵ: fut. pass. ῥαγήσομαι (ἀπο- δια-) is late, Is. lviii. 8, Ez. xiii. 11, xxxviii. 20, Hos. xiv. 1, Hb. iii. 10, Eccl. iv. 12.

Ῥίπτω and ῥιπτέω (both Attic) both occur in LXX, § 22, 3: pf. act. (class. ἔρριφα) only in Jos. xxiii. 4 ἐπέριφα A, corrupted in B. to ὅπερ εἶπα: pf. pass. ἔρ(ρ)ιμμαι (-έρριμαι, § 7, 40) and ῥέριμμαι, § 16, 7: aor. and fut. pass. ἐρ(ρ)ίφην, ῥιφήσομαι (not ἐρρίφθην, ῥιφθ.), § 21, 4: term. ὑπερίπτοσαν, § 17, 5: for -ρρ- and -ρ-, § 7, 39.

Ῥύομαι (early in poetry, cf. ἐρύομαι) is common in LXX (esp. in Ψ and Is.) having, besides the class. tenses ῥύσομαι, ἐρ(ρ)υσάμην, in certain books (4 K., Ψ, 1 M.) two late pass. tenses with pass. meaning ἐρ(ρ)ύσθην, ῥυσθήσομαι, § 21, 5: for -ρρ- and -ρ-, § 7, 39.

Σαλπίζω: new fut. σαλπιῶ and -ίσω, § 20, 1 (i): aor. ἐσάλπισα (for older -ιγξα or -ιξα), § 18, 3 (ii).

Σβέννυμι (ἀπο- κατα-) keeps the -μι forms in literary books, which alone use pres. and impf., § 23, 2, and the Att. tenses σβέσω, ἔσβεσα: the passive tenses are (Ionic and) late, ἔσβεσμαι (also Ionic) Is. xliii. 17, Job xxx. 8, 3 M. vi. 34, ἐσβέσθην (Ion.) Job iv. 10 etc. with v.ll. ἐσβήθην σβεν(σ)θέντος, § 18, 2, σβεσθήσομαι L. vi. 9 *et pass.*: the class. -έσβην -έσβηκα -σβήσομαι are unrepresented.

Σημαίνω: aor. ἐσήμανα and (literary books) ἐσήμηνα -ηνάμην, § 18, 4: σεσήμανται (class.) 2 M. ii. 1.

Σιγάω: fut. σιγήσομαι and -σω, § 20, 3.

Σιωπάω: fut. σιωπήσομαι and -σω, § 20, 3: pf. σεσιώπηκα (class.) Job xviii. 3: σιωπούντων for -ώντων Cod. A, § 22, 1.

(Σκεδάννυμι) *simplex* unused, in comp. usually with δια- and, mainly in met. sense, also ἀπο- 4 M. v. 11, κατα- Ex. xxiv. 8: pres. -μι form once in pass. διασκεδάννυνται, for pres. act. -σκεδάζω is used, § 23, 2: class. tenses in use διεσκέδασα -άσθην Eccl. xii. 5, -ασμαι Ex. xxxii. 25, Hb. i. 4, 3 M. v. 30: the futures are post-class., -σκεδάσω (Att. σκεδῶ), -σκεδασθήσομαι Zech. xi. 11, W. ii. 4. Cf. σκορπίζω.

Σκεπάζω (ἐπι- Lam. iii. 43 f. and the later Versions) "cover," "shelter" (later Attic writers) is frequent with regular tenses including 1 aor. and fut. pass. ἐσκεπάσθην, σκεπασθήσομαι: σκέπω (Ionic and late κοινή) is a v.l. of A in Ex. xxvi. 7, Job xxvi. 9.

Σκοπέω, σκέπτομαι in Attic form one verb, the pres. and impf. only of the former being used with tenses σκέψομαι, ἐσκεψάμην. In LXX σκοπέω (ἐπι-) is rare and confined to the pres.[1], but an aor. κατεσκόπησα "spied out" appears in a few passages (the Hexat. to express this sense uses the post-class. κατασκοπεύω), § 21, 2. The stem σκεπτ- in the *simplex* and in comp. with κατα- is, as in Att., restricted to fut. and aor., but ἐπισκέπτομαι συνεπι- (="review," "inspect," or "visit," "punish"): also in pass. apparently "be missed"=פקד niph. e.g. 4 K. x. 19) in addition

[1] Ἐπεσκόπησαν 2 K. ii. 30 B is obviously a slip for ἐπεσκέπησαν.

to (i) the class. fut., aor., and perf. ἐπέσκεμμαι (used both actively e.g. Ex. iii. 16 "visited" and passively e.g. N. ii. 4 "was reviewed"), is used (ii) in the pres. Ex. xxxii. 34 etc. with by-form ἐπισκέπομαι 1 K. xi. 8 B, xv. 4 B (so in a papyrus of iii/B.C., Mayser 351), and (iii) in the late pass. tenses ἐπεσκέπην ἐπισκεπήσομαι, -εσκέφθην (Ion.), -σκεφθήσομαι, § 21, 4.

Σκορπίζω, δια-: "scatter," an Ionic verb according to Phrynichus[1], used by late prose writers from Polybius onwards and in certain portions of LXX, where it has the tenses σκορπιῶ and -ίσω, § 20, 1 (i), ἐσκόρπισα, -ίσθην, -ισμαι, σκορπισθήσομαι. In LXX its distribution[2] and use as a substitute or alternative for διασπείρειν in the literal sense of "scatter" are noticeable, while διασκεδά(ννυμι) is mainly restricted to metaphorical senses.

Σπάω: tenses regular including pf. mid. and pass. ἐσπασμένος (ἀπ- etc.), once in B ἐξεσπαμένος, § 18, 2, aug. omitted in ἀποσπασμένοι, § 16, 2 (no perf. act. used): fut. pass. ἐκσπασθήσομαι Am. iii. 12 (δια- Xen.): the rare fut. opt. ἀποσπάσοι Jd. xvi. 9 B is noteworthy.

Σπείρω (δια- κατα-): post-class. tenses are pf. ἔσπαρκα Is. xxxvii. 30, fut. pass. σπαρήσομαι (with compounds) L. xi. 37, Dt. xxix. 23 etc., Cod. A once using σπερεῖται with the same passive meaning N. xx. 5 (σπείρεται BF): A also has διεσπαρσμένους, § 18, 4: cf. σκορπίζω.

Στάζω (poetical word): the fut. στάξω Jer. xlix. 18, Eccl. x. 18 Bℵ is unrecorded before LXX, ἔσταξα is classical.

Στέλλω: terminations ἐξαπεστέλλοσαν, § 17, 5, ἀπέσταλκες Cod. A, § 17, 8 (not ἀφέσταλκα, § 8, 5): tenses regular except that the fut. mid. δια- ὑπο- στελοῦμαι (2 Ch. xix. 10, Job xiii. 8, W. vi. 7, Hg. i. 10) lacks early authority.

Στερέω (ἀπο-): aor. ἐστέρησα -ήθην and -εσα -έθην, § 18, 1: στερηθήσομαι 4 M. iv. 7 is post-classical: στέρομαι is unrepresented, § 22, 3.

Στηρίζω (poetical and late prose): fut. -ιῶ and -ίσω, § 20, 1 (i): in the other tenses there is fluctuation between ἐστήρισα (-ισάμην) and -ιξα, ἐστηρίχθην -ίσθην, -ιγμαι -ισμαι, -ιχθήσομαι -ισθήσομαι, § 18, 3 (iii).

Στραγγαλάομαι -όομαι v.ll., § 22, 4.

Στρέφω: the *simplex* is trans. only, the compounds of ἀνα- ἐπι- etc. trans. and intr., note διαστρέψεις intr. 2 K. xxii. 27 A =Ψ xvii. 27 "act perversely": pf. act. unclass. ἀπεστρόφασιν

---

[1] Σκορπίζεται· Ἑκαταῖος μὲν τοῦτο λέγει Ἴων ὤν, οἱ δ' Ἀττικοὶ σκεδάννυται φασί: Lobeck p. 218 (cf. Rutherford *NP* 295).

[2] It is absent e.g. from the following portions which use διασπείρειν instead: Pent. (except N. x. 35, Dt. xxx. 1, 3 and Gen. xlix. 7 A where read διασπερῶ), the earlier portions of the Kingdom books, Is., Jer. β and Ez. β (except xxviii. 25, xxix. 13), though frequent in Jer. α and Ez. α.

1 K. vi. 21: pf. pass. regular -ἐστραμμαι, the ε of the present being retained in συνεστρεμμένοι 1 M. xii. 50 A (so in a papyrus of ii/B.C., Mayser 410): aor. pass. ἐστράφην (not the rare ἐστρέφθην) § 21, 4, with imperat. ἀπο- ἐπι- στράφητι (not -ηθι) Gen. xvi. 9, N. xxiii. 16 etc., cf. § 7, 13: fut. pass. στραφήσομαι (post-class. in the *simplex*) 1 K. x. 6, Sir. vi. 28, Tob. ii. 6, Is. xxxiv. 9 and frequent in the compounds, used both passively and to replace the mid. -στρέψομαι (which is not found), e.g. οὐκ ἀποστραφήσομαι αὐτόν Am. i. 3 "reject" "turn away from": aor. mid. ἀπεστρεψάμην "reject" (post-class. with this prep.) Hos. viii. 3, Zech. x. 6, 3 M. iii. 23.

Στρωννύω (κατα- ὑπο-) replaces the older pres. στόρνυμι, § 23, 2: the following are post-classical, the futures of the 3 voices στρώσω (class. in comp.) Is. xiv. 11, Ez. xxviii. 7, στρώσομαι (v. l. ὑπο-) Ez. xxvii. 30, καταστρωθήσομαι Jdth vii. 14, also aor. mid. ὑπεστρωσάμην Is. lviii. 5, aor. pass. κατεστρώθην Jdth vii. 25.

Συρίζω: fut. συριῶ (in Aquila etc. συρίσω: συρίγξομαι Lucian): aor. ἐσύρισα (for Att. -ιγξα), § 18, 3 (ii).

Σύρω: fut. συρῶ 2 K. xvii. 13 and aor. mid. ἀνάσυραι Is. xlvii. 2 (-ρε ℵ) are post-classical.

Σφάλλω has 1 aor. ἔσφᾱλα (for Att. ἔσφηλα) in Job xviii. 7 opt. σφάλαι (σφαλιη A), to which tense should probably also be referred ἔσφᾱλεν ib. xxi. 10, Sir. xiii. 22 (εσφαλη A), Am. v. 2 and not to the dubious 2 aor. ἔσφαλον.

Σφηνόω: σφηνοίσθω ℵ, § 22, 3.

Σώζω: perf. pass. σέσωσμαι, rarely Att. σέσωμαι, but ἐσώθην, σωθήσομαι as in Att., § 18, 2.

Τάσσω and τάττω § 7, 46: the 2nd aor. pass. -εταγην with the fut. ὑποταγήσομαι are post-class., the class. 1st aor. ἐτάχθην (προσ- συν-) being confined to 3 exx. of the neut. part., § 21, 4 the fut. mid. of the *simplex* τάξομαι Ex. xxix. 43 "will make an appointment" or "meet" is also late (Mayser 410 gives an ex. of 200 B.C.): pf. act. τέταχα is rare, Hb. i. 12, Ez. xxiv. 7 and with προσ- συν- in literary books.

Τείνω: the simple pf. act. τέτακα Prov. vii. 16 is post-class., cf. ἐκτέτακα 1 K. i. 16 (ἀπο- is class.): ἐπέτατο W. xvii. 21 appears to stand for ἐπετέτατο (cf. πέτομαι).

Τελέω: fut. τελέσω, § 20, 1 (iii): pf. act. only in the periphrastic ἔσῃ τετελεκώς Sir. vii. 25: pf. pass. has mid. sense in συντετέλεσθε Gen. xliv. 5 and in the *simplex* with the meaning "have oneself initiated" (class.) N. xxv. 5, Hos. iv. 14 (so ἐτελέσθην N. xxv. 3=Ψ cv. 28), elsewhere pass. sense: aug. omitted in τετέλεστο, § 16, 2: fut. pass. τελεσθήσομαι (ἐπι- συν-) is late: aor. mid. (rare in class. Gk) συνετελεσάμην Is. viii. 8 (-σαι A), Jer. vi. 13 Bℵ, 2 M. xiii. 8. For new pres. τελίσκω, § 19. 3.

Τίθημι: § 23, 5 and 10: aug. in παρεκατέθετο, ἐσυνέθετο, § 16, 8.
Τίκτω: fut. τέξομαι (not the rarer τέξω): 1 aor. pass. ἐτέχθην
(frequent in LXX.=Att. ἐγενόμην) and fut. pass. τεχθησόμενος
Ψ xxi. 32, lxxvii. 6 are late forms.
Τιμάω: τιμοῦσιν ℵ § 22, 1 (as from -έω).
Τρέπω -ομαι (ἀνα- ἀπο- ἐν- ἐπι- μετα- προ-): the only tense at
all frequent is the class. 2 aor. pass. -ετράπην (imperat. ἐντράπητι,
§7, 13), to which is now added the post-class. fut. pass. τραπήσομαι
Sir. xxxix. 27, ἐν- L. xxvi. 41 etc.: the compound with ἐν- with
the new meaning "be ashamed of" is the commonest form of the
verb and is limited to these two tenses with ἐντέτραμμαι 1 Es.
viii. 71: other parts of the verb are rare outside literary books.
Τρέχω: fut. δραμοῦμαι and δραμῶ, § 20, 3: no perf. in use:
ἀποτρέχω now replaces ἄπειμι="depart," especially in imperat.
ἀπότρεχε=ἄπιθε, cf. ἀποτρέχοντες ἀπελεύσονται Jer. xliv. 9.
Τυγχάνω (literary: ἀπο- ἐν- [="entreat" "petition" as in the
papyri] ἐπι- συν-): the perf. is τέτευχα Job vii. 2 (τετυχηκώς A),
3 M. v. 35 (so throughout the papyri for Att. τετύχηκα, Mayser
374): ἀντιλήμψεως τεύξασθαι 2 M. xv. 7 = 3 M. ii. 33 A (τεύ-
ξεσθαι V) is an example of the confusion of fut. and aor. forms
which is paralleled by ἔσασθαι, παρέξασθαι etc. in the papyri,
cf. § 6, 6 for another example from 2 M.
Τύπτω, as in Attic, is still defective and supplemented by
other verbs: some of the latter now appear in non-Attic
tenses, but τύπτω itself does not extend its range, and the
κοινή, no less than Attic, affords no excuse to the Byzantine
grammarians for their unfortunate selection of this word as
typical of the verbal system. (1) Τύπτω, ἔτυπτον are the only
tenses used in LXX with one instance (4 M. vi. 10) of pres.
part. pass. (2) The normal fut. and aor. act. are πατάξω,
ἐπάταξα[1], this verb being confined to these tenses, except for the
use of pres. inf. πατάσσειν in the B text of Jd. xx. 31, 39
(A τύπτειν). (3) As aorist, ἔπαισα (also Attic, mainly in Tragedy)
is preferred by the translator of Job (5 times) and occurs
sporadically elsewhere: from this verb we find also pres. conj.
once (Ex. xii. 13), pres. part. four times, and perf. πέπαικα
(post-class. in *simplex*) N. xxii. 28, 1 K. xiii. 4. (4) The passive
tenses are formed from πλήσσειν: aor. ἐπλήγην (ἐξεπλάγην,
κατεπλάγην: καταπλαγείς 3 M. i. 9 A), fut. πληγήσομαι, pf.
πεπληγμένος (κατα-) 3 M. ii. 22 f., but elsewhere πέπληγα (rare
in earlier Greek and with act. sense) is used with passive
meaning, "am struck," N. xxv. 14, 2 K. iv. 4 etc.: the act. of
this verb is rare in LXX, pres. (post-class. in *simplex*) πλήσ-
σουσι 4 M. xiv. 19 (with κατα- in Job), fut. πλήξω 3 K. xiv. 14 f. A

---

[1] See the collocation of pres. and aor. in 1 Es. iv. 8 εἶπε πατάξαι,
τύπτουσιν.

(in an interpolation from Aquila), aor. ἔπληξα I K. xi. 11 A (possibly from same source).

'Υπομνηματίζομαι, a κοινή verb = "record," "enter a minute" · aug. omitted in ὑπομνημάτιστο § 16, 2.

'Υστερέω (ἀφ- καθ-): the new features are the fut. ὑστερήσω Ψ xxii. I, lxxxiii. 12, Job xxxvi. 17 etc., the middle ὑστεροῦμαι Dt. xv. 8 A, Sir. xi. 11, li. 24 B, Cant. vii. 2, and the causative use of the act. = "withhold" 2 Es. xix. 21 B* (ὑστέρησαν cett. "they lacked" with MT), so τὸ μάννα σου οὐκ ἀφυστέρησας ib. xix. 20, ἀπαρχὰς .. οὐ καθυστερήσεις Ex. xxii. 29 (cf. I Ch. xxvi. 27, Sir. xvi. 13 B).

'Υφαίνω: aor. ὕφανα (for Att. -ηνα), pf. pass. (Att.) ὑφασμένος, § 18, 4.

'Υψόω: post-classical verb: inf. ὑψοῖν, § 22, 3.

Φαίνω: I aor. act. ἔφᾱνα and (lit.) ἀπέφηνα -ηνάμην, § 18, 4: I aor. pass. (rare in class. prose) only in ἐξεφάνθη "was shown" Dan. O ii. 19, 30, the Att. 2nd aor. ἐφάνην¹ "appeared" is frequent: fut. φανήσομαι and φανοῦμαι (both Att.), § 15, 3 : term. ἐφαίνοσαν, § 17, 5 : crasis προυφάνησαν, § 16, 8 note : no form of perf. in LXX. The use of ἐὰν (ἂν) φαίνηταί σοι I Es. ii. 18 (cf. 2 Es. vii. 20) = ἐὰν δόξῃ or εἰ δοκεῖ is a standing formula in petitions in the papyri.

(Φαύσκω): an Ionic and κοινή verb found only in composition, in LXX with δια- and (3 times in Job) ἐπι-, "dawn" (of daybreak), "give light": LXX has this form of the pres. with aor. διέφαυσα, fut. ἐπιφαύσω Job xxv. 5 A (also φαῦσις and ὑπόφαυσις): the alternative -φώσκω (Hdt. and N.T.) -έφωσα only as a variant in Jd. xix. 26 B, I K. xiv. 36 A, Job xli. 9 A ἐπιφώσκεται: φαύσκω appears to be the older form, cf. Epic πιφαύσκω.

Φέρω: aor. ἤνεγκα with part. in -ας but inf. -εῖν etc., § 17, 2, once ἀνοίσατε from (Ionic and late) aor. ὦσα § 21, 2 : terminations ἔφεραν, ἐφέροσαν, ἐνέγκαισαν, § 17, 4, 5 and 7 : pf. pass. in LXX rare and literary, ἀπενηνεγμένος Est. B. 3 Bℵ, εἰσ- 2 M. xiv. 38 (pf. act. infrequent): fut. pass. (since Aristot.) εἰσενεχθήσομαι Jos. vi. 19, ἀν- Is. xviii. 7, lx. 7, ἀπ- etc.

Φεύγω: terminations ἔφυγα (κατ-) § 17, 2, ἐφύγοσαν § 17, 5 : ἐκφεύξασθαι (v.l. -εσθαι) § 6, 6.

Φημί: § 23, 4.

Φθάνω (προ-, κατ- Jd. xx. 42 A) also written φθάννω, § 19, 2 : impf. ἔφθανεν (rare) Dan. Θ iv. 17 B : fut. φθάσω (not Att. φθήσομαι) § 20, 3 : aor. ἔφθασα (Att. also had ἔφθην which is absent from LXX) § 21, I : pf. ἔφθακα (post-class.) 2 Ch. xxviii.

¹ φανοιεν 4 M. iv. 23 ℵV is apparently a corruption of φανειεν (φανιε͂ A).

9, Cant. ii. 12 (-σεν א), προ- 1 M. x. 23 A. As regards meaning, the *simplex* retains the original sense of *anticipation* in Wis. (iv. 7, vi. 13, xvi. 28), also in Sir. xxx. 25 (opposed to ἔσχατος), cf. 3 K.· xii. 18 ἔφθ. ἀναβῆναι "made haste": elsewhere (10 times in Dan. Θ, also in the latest group of LXX books, Jd. xx. 34 B etc.)[1] it has its modern meaning "come" or "reach," the sense of priority being lost. "Anticipate" is now expressed by προφθάνω, but the προ- more often has a local than a temporal force "come into the presence of" or "confront" someone: in Ψ lxvii. 32 it is used causatively, προφθάσει χεῖρα αὐτῆς τῷ θεῷ = "eagerly stretch forth."

Φοβέομαι: fut. φοβηθήσομαι (Att. φοβήσομαι only once in 4 M.),, § 21, 7: pf. unused excepting for a wrong reading in W. xvii. 9 A: ἐφοβούμην -ήθην regular. The act. of the *simplex*, apart from ἐφόβει W. xvii. 9, is unrepresented, being replaced in Dan. Θ iv. 2 and 2 Es. (four times) by the new form **φοβερίζω** (cf. φοβερισμός Ψ lxxxvii. 17): but ἐκφοβέω remains (chiefly in the phrase οὐκ ἔσται ὁ ἐκφοβῶν), this prep. tending to confer a transitive force upon some compounds in late Greek (cf. ἐξαμαρτάνω "cause to sin").

Φορέω: φορέσω, ἐφόρεσα, § 18, 1.

Φρυάσσω (-άττομαι): post-class. = "neigh" of horses and met. "be insolent" or "proud": in LXX only in the latter sense, in the act. (unrecorded elsewhere) ἐφρύαξαν ἔθνη Ψ ii. 1, and in mid.-pass. φρυαττόμενος (or **φρυττόμενος** A, cf. § 6, 50), 2 M. vii. 34, perf. part. πεφρυασμένος -αγμένος, § 18, 3 (iii). The subst. φρύαγμα "pride" (in the group Jer. a—Ez. a—Min. Proph. and 3 M.) is classical in the literal sense "snorting."

Φυλάσσω (and -άττω, lit., § 7, 46) δια-, προ- 2 K. xxii. 24: pf. act. πεφύλακα 1 K. xxv. 21 (for Att. -αχα): the pf. pass. is used both in its class. mid. sense (Ez. xviii. 9, cf. 2 Es. iv. 22) and passively, e.g. Gen. xli. 36: the fut. pass. φυλαχθήσομαι Jer. iii. 5, Ψ xxxvi. 28 is post-class.: term. ἐφύλαξες Cod. A, § 17, 8: redupl. φεφύλαξαι Cod. A, § 16, 7.

Φυτεύω: pf. act. (post-class.) πεφύτευκαν, § 17, 3.

Φύω: the pres. act. is used intransitively (late) in Dt. xxix. 18, else trans.: fut. φυήσω (trans.) Is. xxxvii. 31 (for class. φύσω), but ἀναφύσει (intr.) ib. xxxiv. 13 (corrected to -φυήσει by late hands of Bא): the aor. act. is absent (excepting φύσαντες Jer. xxxviii. 5 AQ*, an error for φυτεύσ.) and the pf. act. is

---

[1] Including Tob. v. 19 ἀργύριον τῷ ἀργ. μὴ φθάσαι "let not money (the deposit which Tobias is going to recover) come (or be added) to money." "Be not greedy to add money to money" of A.V. and R.V. is a neat paraphrase, but the marginal note in A.V. (not in R.V.) is needed to explain the construction.

confined to literary portions : the act. 2nd aor. ἔφυν is replaced by the pass. ἀν- προσ- ἐφύην, § 21, 3.

Φωτίζω (not before Aristot.) "give light" and met. "enlighten," "instruct": fut. φωτιῶ and -ίσω, § 20, 1 (i): pass. tenses ἐφωτίσθην φωτισθήσομαι in Ψ.

Χαίρω (ἐπι-, and once each κατα- Prov. i. 26, προσ- ib. viii. 30, συγ- Gen. xxi. 6): the fut. (not the class. χαιρήσω) takes two late forms (i) in the *simplex* χαρήσομαι (12 undisputed exx.), (ii) in compos. -χαροῦμαι, ἐπι- Hos. x. 5, Mic. iv. 11, Sir. xxiii. 3, κατα- Prov. i. 26, συγ- Gen. xxi. 6: the latter occurs also in the *simplex* in Zech. iv. 10 B*ℵ*Q* (with v.l. -ήσονται), ib. x. 7 though χαρήσεται occurs in the same *v*., § 20, 3: aor. ἐχάρην regular except for the loss of the second aspirated letter in the imperat. χάρητι, § 7, 13 : perf. unattested.

Χέω and once -χύν(ν)ω, § 19, 2 : new fut. χεῶ χεεῖς for χέω χεῖς, § 20, 1 (iii): contracted and uncontracted forms, § 22, 3 : pf. act. (post-class.) ἐκκέχυκα Ez. xxiv. 7 : fut. pass. χυθήσομαι (one ex. with συγ- in Demosth.) Jl. ii. 2 and in comp. with δια- ἐκ- συγ-.

Χράομαι : inf. χρῆσθαι (Att.) and once χρᾶσθαι, § 22, 2 : fut. pf. κεχρήσεται "shall have need" Ep. J. 58 can be paralleled only from Theocr. xvi. 73.

Χρίω : pf. pass. κέχρισμαι (with χρῖσμα) replaces Att. κέχριμαι (χρῖμα, ? χρίμα), but aor. pass. ἐχρίσθην (? ἐχρήθη 2 K. i. 21 A — ἐχρίθη) is Attic, § 18, 2 : the fut. pass. χρισθήσομαι Ex. xxx. 32 is post-class., as is also the pf. act. κέχρικα 1 K. x. 1, 2 K. ii. 7, 4 K. ix. 3, 6, 12 : term. ἐνεχρίοσαν Cod. ℵ, § 17, 5.

(Ψάω) only in the aor. pass. συνεψήσθην (v.l. -ηθην) "swept away" in Jer., § 18, 2 : the compound occurs in the act. in Ptolemaic papyri.

Ψύχω is both trans. and intrans., e.g. ὡς ψύχει λάκκος ὕδωρ, οὕτως ψύχει κακία αὐτῆς Jer. vi. 7, cf. καταψύξατε "cool yourselves" Gen. xviii. 4: pf. act. (unattested in class. Gk) ἀνεψυχότα 2 M. xiii. 11 : no pass. forms used.

Ψωμίζω : fut. ψωμιῶ and -ίσω, § 20, 1 (i).

Ὠδίνω, in class. Gk confined to pres., in LXX has impf. ὤδινον Is. xxiii. 4, lxvi. 8, and, as from a contract verb, ὠδινήσω, ὠδίνησα (causative in Sir. xliii. 17 A) : Aquila further has 1 aor. pass. and mid.

Ὠθέω : aug., § 16, 6 : the pf. pass. of the *simplex*, ὠσμένῳ Ψ lxi. 4, is unclassical.

(Ὠνέομαι) unused : see πρίαμαι.

I. INDEX OF SUBJECTS

A, Codex: see Alexandrinus
Accusative sing. 146 f. (-αν for -α), 176 (-ῆν for -ῆ), 150: plur. (-ες for -ας etc.) 73, 145, 147 ff., 150
Adjectives, declension of 172–181: comparison of 181–186
Adjurations, use of ὅτι and εἰ in 54
Adverbs, comparison of 183: replaced by adj. (πρότερος) 183: numeral adverbs 189 f.
"Alexandrian dialect" 19 f.
Alexandrinus, Codex, Egyptian origin of 72, 101, 110: text mainly inferior and secondary 65, 106, 107 bis, 218 bis, 221 n. 2, 258: text probably original 81 (Is.), 93 (Ψ), 152 (Sir.): Hexaplaric interpolations frequent 3 f., cf. Aquila: conjectural emendation of Greek 205 n. 3: orthography and accidence mainly of later date than autographs 55 ff., 67 (Numbers perhaps written in two parts), 72, 74, 98 n. 3 (introduces Attic forms), 110, 115 (1 and 2 Es. a single volume in an ancestor of A), 131, 147 and 176 (3rd decl. acc. in -αν -ῆν), 188 (ἐξ καὶ δέκα), 212 (γενάμενος in Jer.), 234 (ἔλειπον etc.), 241 (δυνηθήσομαι etc.), 255 (ἔθησα, ἔδωσα): foreshadows modern Greek 158, 179, 205 f. (loss of redupl.), 215 f., 241 f.
Analogy plays large part in the κοινή 21, 73, 79 f., 89, 103 n., 120 (δυσεβής), 124 f., 127 bis, 128 (ἐκών), 129 (εὑρίσκω), 174, 178 f., 189, 201 n., 202. Cf. Assimilation
Anaptyxis in ℵ 98
Anthropomorphism avoided 44
Aorist, 1st, extension of, at cost of 2nd aor. 209 ff., 233 f.: sigmatic for unsigmatic 235: in pass. partly replaced by 2nd aor. 236 f.: new

1st aor. pass. 238: 1st aor. pass. replaces 1st aor. mid. 238 ff.: mixture of aor. and fut. inf. mid. 76, 287
Aorist, 2nd, old forms retained longest in inf. 210 (ἐνεγκεῖν, εἰπεῖν): 2nd aor. pass. for 2nd aor. act. 235
Apocalypse, style of 21 n.: δοῦλος 8: ἐνώπιον 43 n.: rel. + demonstr. pron. 46 n.: 240 n.
Apostolic Fathers: see Patristic
Appellative taken for proper name 32 f.
Apposition of verbs 51 f. with n.
Aquila, pedantic literalism of 9: περὶ λαλιᾶς (π. λόγου) 41: ἐπιστρέφειν 53: σύν 55, 133 n.: ἐγώ εἰμι 55: κάθοδος 190: misc. 49, 112 n.: interpolations in A text from Aq., mainly in 3—4 K., 3, 152, 157, 190, 218, 227, 231 n., 241, 287 f.: (?) similar interp. in Joshua 4
Aramaic influence on LXX Greek xx, 28, 34 (γαζαρηνός, γειώρας), 36 (σαμβύκη?)
Archaism in the uncials 60
Archite, Hushai the 37
Aristeas 13, 15 n., 76, 170 n. 3, 200 n., 247 n., 264, 279 (κατολομαι)
Aristophanes 45, 81: Scholiast on 105 n.
Aristotle, a precursor of the κοινή 17, 143 n., 144
Article, omission of 24 f.: sing. art. with plur. Heb. noun 34: loses aspirate 129: crasis with 138: Hebr. art. in transliterations, with Greek art. added 33 f.
Asiatic languages and the κοινή 20: Asiatic orthography 98, 110, 212 n. (term. -αν)
Aspirate, irregular insertion and omission of 124 ff.: throwing back of 126 f. (ἐφιορκεῖν, ὀλίγος, Ἰούδας)
Aspirated consonant, mixture of, with

II. INDEX OF GREEK WORDS AND FORMS

For the Verbs see § 24.

α mixture with ε 73 ff.: with η 76 f.: with ο and αι 77: with αυ 79: for αα in proper names 100: -α pure, nouns in 140 ff.: α for η in ῎Αννας etc. 143: -α, "Doric" gen. sg. of proper names in 162: -α, place-names in 167 f.
ἀβάκ, ἀβαρκηνείν, ταῖς 33 f.
᾽Αβδειού 162
ἀβεδηρείν 33
᾽Αβράμ, ᾽Αβραάμ 100, not ῎Αβραμος 160 f.
ἀγαθωσύνη 90
ἀγαθώτερος 184
ἀγαλιᾶσθαι etc. א 120
᾽Αγγαῖος 161 n.
ἀγιωσύνη 90
ἀγνία 87
ἀγροῦ (ἀγούρ) 37
ἀεί (αἰεί) 77
ἀέναος (not ἀένν.) 120
ἀεργός in Prov. 173
ἀέρινος 37
-άζω: see -ζω
ἀθοωθήσομαι etc. but ἀθῷος 89. fem. -ῴα 172
αι, interchanged with α 77: with ε 68 f., 77 f.: as short vowel 90 with n. 4: αι- loses aug. 199 f.
αιας, proper names in, G. -ου (and -α) 161 f.
αἰγμάλωτος א 103
Αἴγυπτος א 116
-αίνω, verbs in, keep α

in 1 aor. 223 f.: pf. pass. of 224
-αῖος and -ίτης, gentilic names in 171: -αία, names of countries in 170
αἱρετίζειν τὸ πρόσωπον 44
-αίρω, verbs in, keep α in 1 aor. 223
-αις -αι -αισαν, opt. term. 215
αἰσχρότερος 184
ἀκαλλιώμεθα א 102
ἀκάν, τὸν (τὴν) ἄκανα(ν) 157 f.
᾽Ακκαρών indecl. 169
ἀκριβία 87
ἀκροβυστία 27
ἀλάβαστρον, τὸ A 153
ἀλαλάζειν -αγμός 37
ἄλας, τὸ and ὁ ἅλς 152
ἀλεεῖς (but ἀλιέων etc.) 84
ἀλλόφυλοι and Φυλιστιείμ 167
ἀλυκός (not ἁλικός) 96
ἀλώπηκες 151
ἄλως (only in form ἄλω) and ἄλων -ωνος, ὁ and ἡ 144 f.
ἅμα = חם 37
ἀμάξοις א 157
ἁμαρτήσομαι, οὐκ 128
ἀμασενείθ, ἀμαφέθ 33
ἀμβλάκημα, ἀμβλακία 105
᾽Αμμανῖτις 170
ἀμνάς, ἀμνός 152
ἄμπελος, ὁ א 145
ἀμφίταπος (not -τάπης) 156
ἀμφότεροι (not ἄμφω) 192

ἄν replaced by ἐάν with ὅς etc. (not with ἕως, ὅπως, ὡς) 65
ἄν for ἐάν, "if" 99
-αν, 3rd decl. accus. in 146 f.: verbal termination in 209 ff.
ἀνάθεμα -ημα 27 n., 80
ἀνακύμψαι A 110
ἀνὰ μέσον 25: ἀνὰ μ. τῶν ἑσπερινῶν 40
ἀνάπειρος 83
ἀναπηδύει = -πιδ. 85
ἀνάστεμα -ημα 80, -αμα 79 n.
ἀναφάλαντος -θος 104
ἀνδρ(ε)ιώτερος 182
ἀνεξέλεκτος 115
ἀνήρ for ἕκαστος etc., of inanimate things 45 f.
ἄνθρωπος for ἕκαστος etc. 45: ἄνθρωπος ἄνθρωπος 46
ἀνθ᾽ ὧν 25: in late books ἀνθ᾽ ὧν ὅτι, ἀνθ᾽ ὧν ὅσα 10, 25
ἀνοίει א = ἀνοίγει 113: ἀνοίγειν 127
ἀντάμμιψιν A 110
ἄντικρυς = "opposite" 136
᾽Αντιλίβανος beside Λίβανος 166 f. n.
ἀνύγειν 94
ἀνυπνιάζεσθαι א = ἐν. 76
ἀνυπόδετος (for -δητος) 80
ἀνώνητοι = ἀνόν. 90 f.
ἀνώτερον = ἄνω, once ἀνωτέρω 183
ἀπάνωθεν 25, in K. βδ 10
ἀπαρτίζειν in α΄ 3

ἄπας and πᾶς 138 f.
ἀπηλιώτης 128
ἀπό rare as comparative
  particle 23: c. φυλάσ-
  σεσθαι etc. 46 f.
ἀπογρύψω א 101
ἀποκία Β 93
ἀποσκευή of children
  (=טף) in Pent. 14
ἄρα = Heb. inf. abs. 47
ἆρ' οὐ, LXX equivalents
  for 125 f.
Ἀραβά -βώθ 32 f.
ἀράσσω replaced by ῥάσ-
  σω 76
ἀρεταλόγος -λογία 76
ἀριθμῷ = "few" 39
ἄριστος 185
ἄρκος for ἄρκτος 116
Ἀρμαθάιμ in 1 K. =ʹ Ῥαμά
  168
ἁρμονία = המון 37
ἄρνα, ἀρνός 152 with n.
ἄρουρα for γῆ Ionic 142
ἀρραβών 34, 119
ἄρρην rare, usually ἄρ-
  σην 123
ἀρχιεταῖρος 37, 130 n.
ἀρχιευνοῦχος, ἀρχευν.
  130 n.
ἄρχοντες = -ας 149
-αρχος and -άρχης 156
Ἀρωδαῖος -δείτης 171
ἀρωδιός ἐρωδ. 76
Ἀρών 100
-ας (-ᾶς), proper names
  in 163
ἀσεβῆν אΚ 176
Ἀσηδώθ 33
Ἀσκάλων declined 169
ἄσσει Α = ἄλσει 132
ἀσφαλία 87
Ἀταβύριον, Ἰτ. 170 n.
ἀτειχίσταις 172
ἀτός = αὐτός in papyri 79
ἀττέλεβος -λαβος 75
αυ and ευ 78 f.: αυ and
  α. 79: αὔ- loses temp.
  aug. 200
αὐδῷ = αὐτῷ 103
Αὐραν(ε)ῖτις 170

Αὐσ(ε)ῖτις 170
αὐτός, otiose use of oblique cases of 24: αὐτός,
  αὐτοῦ 190: αὐτοῦ, ἑαυ-
  τοῦ 190
ἀφαίρεμα 80
ἄφεμα 80
ἄφεσις 37
ἀφορίσματα, ἀφωρισμένα
  = "suburbs" 4 with n.
ἄχι 32 n.
ἀχούχ, τὸν 34
ἀχρεότης ἀχρεοῦν (but
  ἀχρεῖος) 82
ἄχρι(ς) οὗ 136
ἄχυρος, ὁ (Α) and τὸ -ον
  153
ἄψεσθε, οὐκ 128
-άω, verbs in, short
  vowel in tenses of
  219: "Attic" fut.
  replaced by sigmatic
  230: confusion with
  -έω verbs 241 f.

β, euphonic insertion of
  111: interchange of
  with π 105 f. : with
  μ 106 f.
Βααλείμ (Βεελ-) τῷ 34
Βαβυλών declined 169
Βαδδαργείς 170 n.
βαθέου Α 179
βάθου 159
βακχούρια 34
βάρβαρος 37
βαρ(ε)ία 179: βαρέως
  -έος 179
βάρις (βᾶρις) 34, 150
βαρρα א = βορρᾶ 77
Βασαν(ε)ῖτις 170
βάσανος, ὁ א 145
βασιλεῖς and -έας 148:
  βασιέως 114
βασίλειον, τὸ for ἡ βασι-
  λεία etc. 157
βασιλεύειν "make king"
  24
βάτος, ὁ 145
βάτραχος, ἡ Α 146
Βαχχίδης א 121

βδέλυγμα, βέδεκ 37
βειρά 34
βέλτιστος 185
βέσον, ἀνὰ Α 107
βιβλείδιον 87 n.
βιβλιαφόρος -αγράφος 7
βιβλίον, βίβλος (βύβλος
  βύβλινος, Βύβλιος 95
βῖκος 34
βιωτεύειν 91
βόας 147
βοββήσει = βομβ. 132
βόθρος 37
βόλιβος Α 106
βορρᾶς, rarely βορέ
  (-έης) 123 f., 143
Βόσορρα, G. -ας 167
βράματα א = βρώματα 7
βύσσος, βύσσινος 34

γ, omission of, betwee
  vowels 111 ff., ĵ
  γί(γ)νομαι, γιγ(ν)ώσκ
  etc. 100, 114 f., els
  where 115: insertic
  of, in papyri 111 n
  pronunciation of 11
  difficult to Egyptia
  100 n., 112 n: inte
  changed with κ 100 ff
  γκ for κ 101
γαζαρηνός (Γαζ.) 34, 1ʒ
γαῖαι 143
γαῖσος, ὁ and τὸ -ον ɩ
Γαλααδ(ε)ῖτις 170
γαμβρεύειν 262 n.
γαρπῶν Α = καρπ. 101
γεδδούρ 33
γειώρας ΧΧ, 28, 34
γενεσιάρχης 156
γένημα and γέννημα 1ɩ
γῆ, plural of, and su
  stitutes for 143
γῆρας, G. γήρους and -α
  D. γήρει and -ᾳ 149
γίνομαι and γίγν. 114
  cf. ἐγένετο and § 24
γινώσκω and γίγν. 114
  cf. § 24
γλυκ(ε)ία 179
γναφεύς 101

γνήμην A 101
γνόφος, ὁ (and τὸ A) 159
γόμορ = "omer" and "homer" 32
Γόμορρα, G. -ας (not -ων) 168
γόμος 32
γόνα A = γόνατα 152
γονεῖς and -έας 148
γραμματοεισαγωγεύς 130 n.
γυνηγός D = κυν. 101

δ, omission of 114, 116 : interchange of, with θ 104 f. : with τ 100
δάγνοντες A 101
Δαμάσεκ 167
δασέως -έος 179
δασύπους for λαγώς 145
Δαυείδ (not Δαβίδης) 160 f.
δεβραθά 33
-δειγνύω A 101
δεκάδαρχος LXX, -άρχης Joseph. 156 : δεκάταρχος א 103 f.
δεκάδυο and δώδεκα 187 f.
δένδρον, G. -ου, D. -ει and -ῳ 160
δέομαι = בְּ in Pent. 14
δεσμοί and (lit.) δεσμά 154
διακλέπτεσθαι c. inf. vice adv. 54
διάστεμα -ημα 80
διδόναι = τιθέναι 39 : cf. § 24
δίδραγμον (late MSS) 103
διευτύχει in papyri 57 n.
δικαιωσύνη A 90
διότι and ὅτι 138 f.
δίφορον 99
διχηλεῖν (not δίχαλον) 76
δίψα, δίψος 157
διώρυξ -υγος (and -υχος) 150 f.
δολεία A = δουλ. 91
δόμα and δόσις 79
δόξεως א 158
δουλεύειν and λατρεύειν 8

δουλία 87
δοῦλος and synonyms 7 f.
δραγμή (late MSS) = δραχμή 103
δυνάμεων, Κύριος τῶν 9
δυναστ(ε)ία 69
δύο, G. δύο, D. δύο and usually δυσίν 187, or δυσί 135: lit. δυεῖν (-οῖν) 92, 187 : δύο δύο 54
δυσεβής = δυσσ. 120
δῶναι for δοῦναι 91

ε, mixture with ἄ 75 f. : with αι 68 f., 77 f. : with η 79 ff., aug. 198 f. : with ει 81 f. : with ι 84 f. : with ο 87 ff. : with υ, ευ 97
ἑαλωκυίης א 140
ἐάν, ὃς 65 ff.
ἑαυτοῦ, αὑτοῦ 190 : ἑαυτ. for 1 and 2 sg. illiterate ib. : but ἑαυτῶν for all 3 persons of pl. 190 f.
ἐγ for ἐκ 101
ἐγ γαστρί A 72, 131
ἐγγίζειν (συν-) c. gen. 167 n.
ἔγγονος for ἔκγονος 101
ἐγγὺς ἀπὸ προσώπου in Θ 47
ἐγγύτατοι, ἔγγιστα 182
ἐγένετο ἐγίνετο etc., constructions with 50 ff.
ἔγνοι א = ἔγνω etc. 93
ἐγώ εἰμι with finite verb in late books and Hexapla 10, 30, 55
Ἐδώμ, Ἰδουμαία 167
Ἔζρας A 111
ἐθνάρχης 156
ἔθνου A 160
ει, mixture with ε 81 ff.: with η 83 f., aug. εἰ- and ἠ- 201 f. : with ῑ (ῐ) 85 ff.: with οι 92
εἰ = negat. in adjurations 54 : εἰ (εἶ) μήν, ἦ μήν, εἰ μή 54, 83 f.

-εια and -ία, nouns in 68 f., 87
-είας, proper names in, G. -ου and -α 161 f.
εἰκάς and εἰκοστή 189
εἰκόνα, καθ' 127
εἴκοσι (not -σιν) 135
εἴληφα aoristic 24
εἵλκυσεν, οὐκ 128
εἴν (ἴν) 32
εἵνεκεν, οὗ 82
εἴξουσιν, ἤξουσιν v. ll. 8
εἰρήνη, Hebraic uses o 40 f.
-εις, proper names in 16
εἰς (not ἐς) 82
εἷς as indef. article 54
εἷς (πρῶτος) καὶ εἰ κοστός 189
-εισαν for -εσαν in plpf 216
-είτης -εῖτις : see -ίτης -ι
ἐκ- : see ἐξ-
ἕκαστος for ἑκάτερος 192 substitutes for and distribution of 45, 192
ἑκάτερος 192
ἑκατόνταρχος LXX, -άρ χης N.T. and Joseph 156
ἐκεῖ and ἥκει v. ll. 81
ἐκεῖνος (not κεῖνος) 97
ἐκθές A = ἐχθές 102
ἐκθρός, ἐκχθρός etc. 10
ἑκκαίδεκα B, ἓξ καὶ δέκ A 188
ἐκκλησία first in Dt. 14
ἐκπᾶν = ἐκσπᾶν 117
ἐκφεύξασθαι = -εσθαι 7(
ἑκών, οὐκ 128
ἐλάσσων, ἐλάχιστος 185
ἐλάττων, ἐλαττοῦ ἐλαττονεῖν etc. 121 n. 122
ἔλαφος 37 n.
ἐλαφρώτερος 182
ἔλεος, τὸ and ὁ, an meanings of 158 wit n.
ἔλεον = ἔλαιον 78
ἐλέφανσιν 151

μάχαιρα -ης -ῃ 141 f.
μεγαλοπρέπ(ε)ια 69
μεγαλύνειν, c. inf. 54
μεγάλως = מאד 38
μέγιστος, lit. and elative 185
Μεισώρ 33
Μειχαίας, G. -a and -ου 162
μεριδάρχης 156
Μέρρα, G. -as 168
μες א 190
μεσοπωρῶν = -πορῶν 91
μεταξύ, substitute for 25: written μετοξύ in A 77
μέχρι, Hebraic use of, in Θ 47 : μέχρι(s) οὗ etc. 136
μηθείς and μηδείς 58 ff.
μηθέτερος 61 n.
μιερός, μιεροφαγεῖν etc. 75
μικός א 116
μισει = ἥμισυ 180 n. 9
μνᾶ 35
μογ(γ)ιλάλος 120 f.
μοκλός B 102
μόλιβος, μόλιβδος, μόλυβος 96, 116 : μόλιμος 106
μολλον א = μᾶλλον 77
μονογενῆν A 176
μυελός but μυαλοῦν 75
μύες, μύας and μῦς 147
μυσερός 75
Μωαβ(ε)ῖτις 170
μῶμος = מום 38
Μωυσῆς and Μωσῆς 163 n. : two forms of declension of 163 f.

ν, effect on vowels of 84, 86: omission of 114, 117: νῦ ἐφελκυστικόν 134 f., irrational final ν 135, 143 f. (βορρᾶν א = gen.), 146, 216: doubling of, in verbs in -νω 225 f.
νάβλα 35
Ναγέβ 33
ναός for νεώς 145
νάρδος 35

ναῦς (lit. word) νηός νῆας 152
νέβελ 33
Νεεμίας, G. -a and -ου 162 : Νεέμιος 161 n.
νεκρομαῖον in α´ 3
νέοττος, νεοσσός, νοσσός etc. 98
νεώτερος (=superl.) 181, -ώτατος 182
νῆσσος 117, 120
νῖκος, τὸ and (lit.) ἡ νίκη 157
νίτρον (not λίτρον) 35
νουμηνία and νεομ. 98 : νομηνία A 91
νοῦς, G. νοός 160
νυνί 191
νῶτος, νῶτοι (and νῶτα) 155

ξ for κ + σ 130 : for σ in tenses of verbs in -ζω 222 f.
ξολοθρεύω, mod. Gr. 88

ο, mixture with α 77 : with ε 87 ff. : with υ (ου) 91 : with οι 93 : with ω 89 ff., 194, 198 f. (loss of aug.)
'Οβδειού 162
ὅδε, uses of 191 : οἴδε, αἴδε in Jer. β 14, 37
ὁδηγεῖν -ός (not -αγ.) 76
ὀδύρεσθαι 97
οι, interchanged with ι 92 : with ει 92 : with ο 93 : with ω 93, 256: with υ 93 f. : for ου in א 244 : οἱ- loses aug. 200
οἴγον A 101
οἶδας, οὐχ 125
οἰκέτης 7
οἴμμοι, ὄμμοι 120
-οῖν, inf. in 244
οἰνοφρυγεῖν 107
-οισαν 215
οἰφ(ε)ί 32
ὀκ ὀχ א for οὐκ οὐχ 91
ὀκλα B 93

ὄλεθρος (not -οθ.) 88
ὀλίγος 126 f. : ὀλίο ὀλιοστός, ὀλιοῦν 112 ὀλιγοστός 185
ὀλολύζειν -υγμός 37
ὀλοσφύρητος 141
ὀμείρεσθαι 97
'Ομμόθ 33
ὁμόεθνος A for -εθνής 18
ὄμορα 4 n.
ὄνειροι 155
ὀξ(ε)ῖα for ὀξέα 179
ὀπίσω, ζητεῖν, in Θ 4
ὄρειον 87
ὀρθος (ὀρθίζειν) = ὀρθ 116
ὁρμή, ὅρμος 38
ὄρνεον (ὀρνίθιον) replace ὄρνις 153
ὄρος and ἕλος, mixtui of 107: ὀρέων 151
-ος, masc. and neut interchange of nour in 158 ff.
ὃς ἄν and ὃς ἐάν 65 ff. -οσαν 209 ff.
ὅσπερ, lit. 192
ὅστις 192
ὀστοῦν -ᾶ but ὀστέο etc. 144
ὀσφρασία 76
ὀσφύας (-ῦς) 147
ὅτι in adjurations 54 ὅτι and διότι 138 f.
ου, interchanged with and ω 91 : with υ 9: οὗ εἵνεκεν replaces οὕνεκ 82
οὐαί = אוי etc. 38
οὐθείς and οὐδείς 58 ff. 100, 104 : οὐθὲν ἧττο = Heb. inf. abs. 47
οὐκ and οὐχ 125–129 οὐκ ἰδού and οὐχ ἰδο 70, 125 f.
Οὐλαμμαύς, Οὐλαμαΐς 3 -οῦς, proper names i 164 f. : declension -οι -οῦτος in papyri (nc LXX) 165 n. : con tracted adjectives i 172 f.

pass. tenses 219 ff. :
σσ and ττ 100, 121 ff.
σαβαώθ, Κύριος 9, 33
σάββατον -τα, D. -τοις
and -σιν, σαββατίζειν
35
σαβέκ 33
-σαι, 2 sg. mid. term.
217 f.
σάκκος 36
Σαλωμών, Σαλομών,
Σολομών, orthography
and declension 161,
165 f.
Σαμαρ(ε)ῖτις 170
σαμβύκη 36
Σαμψών 110
Σαναμάσσαρος 106
σάπριγγος ℵ = σάλπ. 132
σάπφειρος 36: σάππειρος
121
σαράκοντα, Cod. E 63 n.
σάραξ ℵ 98
Σαραπιεῖον -πεῖον 64
Σαράπις, Σεράπις 74
σαραφείν ℵ 76
σαυτοῦ, σεαυτοῦ 190
Σαυχαῖος, Σαυχίτης 171
Σαφφάν, Σαφφώθ etc.121
Σεδεκίας, G. ·ου and ·α
162
Σ(ε)ιδών, declined 169
Σειών in Jer. β 38
σευτλίον 123
Σεφηλά 33
Σηδαμείν = Zidonians
167
σήσματι = σεισματι 84
σιβύνη, ζιβ. etc. 108
σιδηρέας ℵ 173
σίελος -ίζειν (not σιαλος)
75 : ὁ σ. and τὰ σίελα
155
σίκερα 33
Σίκιμα 33, beside Συχέμ
167 f.
σίκλος (not σίγλος) 36
σικυήρατον -ήλατον 107
σιμίδαλις Aℵ = σεμ. 84
σινδών 36
σιρώνων 36
-σις and -μα, nouns in 79

σῖτος, σῖτα 155
σκληρύνειν, c. inf. 54
σκνίψ 106
σκόρδον 99
σκότος, τὸ (not ὁ) 159
σμάραγδος 108
σμιρίτης λίθος 96
σμύρνα 108
Σόδομα, G. -ων 168
Σολομών : see Σαλωμών
Σομόηλος = Σαμουήλ 165
n.
Σομορών, Σεμερών =
Σαμαρ(ε)ία 90, 167
Σόρ beside Τύρος 167
Σουσάννα -νης 161
σπεῖρα, G. -ης 141 f.
σπόνδυλος ℵ 106
στάδιον -ους 155
σταθμοί (not -μά) 155
στάμνος, ὁ 146
σταφίς (not ἀστ.) 97
στάχυς (not ἀστ.) 97 :
acc. pl. στάχυας and
-υς 147
στῆρ Θ for στέαρ 153
στίβι, στῖμι etc. 107
στίχος (not στοῖχ.), στι-
χίζειν 92
στόμα, "Hebraic" 44
στρατιῶν, Κύριος τῶν in
α' 9
σύ and σοί, interchange-
able 94
συγγενεῦσι 153
συκάμινος 36
συκοφαντεῖν 38
σύμπας (σύνπας) 133
with n.
σύν, in α' 3 : not ξύν
108 : compounds of,
assimilation in 133 f.
συναγωγή = קהל 14
συνδοιάσω = -δυ. 94
συνέβη, c. inf. 52 with n.
σύνθεμα -ημα 80
συνιέναι ἐπί Θ 47
συνκυροῦντα 4
σύστεμα -ημα 80
σφῦρα -ης -ῃ 141
Σωμωρών 90
σῷοι = σῷαι 172

Σωρείν = Tyrians 167

τ, omission of 114, 116
interchange of, with
100, 103 f. : with
104 : ττ and σσ 121
τάδε λέγει Κύριος i
Jer. α 11
ταλαμών A 76
ταμιεῖον and ταμ(ε)ῖο
63 ff.
ταραχή and τάραχος,
and τὸ 159
τάσσαρας ℵ 76
-τατος, superlatives i
182 f.
ταφνοῦν A = φατνοῦν 10
τάχιον and θᾶττον (nc
ταχύτερον) 184
ταχύνειν, c. inf. 54
τέγος 117
τειχέων and -ῶν 151
τῖχον A 160
τέκτονες = -ας 149
τέλεον, τελέως, τέλεις
-ειοῦν 82
τέλος, εἰς = Heb. inf. ab:
47
τεμένου A 160
τέρμινθος, τερέμ., τερέ
106 f.
τεσσαράκοντα, τεσσερά
κοντα 62 f., 73 f.
τεσσαρισκαιδέκατος 189
τέσσερα etc. 62, 73 f.
τέσσαρες = τέσσαρα
73 f, 148 f.: τέσσερα
= τέσσαρες 74 : dai
τέρσαρσιν A, τεσσό
ροις A, τέτρασιν 16c
187
τετελευτηκυίη 140
τετράπεδος -ποδος -που
88 with n.
τέτρας and τετάρτη 18
with n.
-τι for -θι 104
τιμωρίαν in Jer. β 38
τις, ἀνήρ replaces 45
τίς replaces πότερος 192
τίναν ℵ 147
τοιοῦτος, nt. -οand -ον 19

III. INDEX OF BIBLICAL QUOTATIONS

CAMBRIDGE: PRINTED BY JOHN CLAY, M.A. AT THE UNIVERSITY PRESS.

CPSIA information can be obtained at www.ICGtesting.com
Printed in the USA
BVOW06s2341280116

434696BV00024B/224/P